New Perspectives on

The Internet Using Netscape Navigator™ Software

INTRODUCTORY

The New Perspectives Series

The New Perspectives Series consists of texts and technology that teach computer concepts and microcomputer applications. You can order these New Perspectives texts in many different lengths, software releases, custom-bound combinations, CourseKits™ and Custom Editions®. Contact your Course Technology sales representative or customer service representative for the most up-to-date details.

The New Perspectives Series

Computer Concepts

Borland® dBASE®

Borland® Paradox®

Corel® Presentations™

Corel® Quattro Pro®

Corel® WordPerfect®

DOS

HTML

Lotus® 1-2-3®

Microsoft® Access

Microsoft® Excel

Microsoft® Internet Explorer

Microsoft® Office Professional

Microsoft® PowerPoint®

Microsoft® Windows® 3.1

Microsoft® Windows® 95

Microsoft® Windows NT® Server 4.0

Microsoft® Windows NT® Workstation 4.0

Microsoft® Word

Microsoft® Works

Netscape Navigator™

Netscape Navigator™ Gold

Microsoft® Visual Basic® 4 and 5

New Perspectives on
The Internet Using Netscape Navigator™ Software

INTRODUCTORY

Sharon T. Caswell
CompuTech

COURSE
TECHNOLOGY

ONE MAIN STREET, CAMBRIDGE, MA 02142

an International Thomson Publishing company I(T)P®

Cambridge • Albany • Bonn • Boston • Cincinnati • London • Madrid • Melbourne • Mexico City
New York • Paris • San Francisco • Singapore • Tokyo • Toronto • Washington

New Perspectives on The Internet Using Netscape Navigator Software—Introductory is
published by Course Technology.

Associate Publisher	Mac Mendelsohn
Series Consulting Editor	Susan Solomon
Product Manager	Kim T. M. Crowley
Developmental Editor	Janice Jutras
Senior Production Editor	Catherine G. DiMassa
Text and Cover Designer	Ella Hanna
Cover Illustrator	Nancy Nash

© 1997 by Course Technology – I(T)P®

For more information contact:

Course Technology
One Main Street
Cambridge, MA 02142

International Thomson Publishing Europe
Berkshire House 168-173
High Holborn
London WCIV 7AA
England

Thomas Nelson Australia
102 Dodds Street
South Melbourne, 3205
Victoria, Australia

Nelson Canada
1120 Birchmount Road
Scarborough, Ontario
Canada M1K 5G4

International Thomson Editores
Campos Eliseos 385, Piso 7
Col. Polanco
11560 Mexico D.F. Mexico

International Thomson Publishing GmbH
Königswinterer Strasse 418
53227 Bonn
Germany

International Thomson Publishing Asia
211 Henderson Road
#05-10 Henderson Building
Singapore 0315

International Thomson Publishing Japan
Hirakawacho Kyowa Building, 3F
2-2-1 Hirakawacho
Chiyoda-ku, Tokyo 102
Japan

Trademarks
Course Technology and the open book logo are registered trademarks and CourseKits is a trademark of Course Technology. Custom Editions and the ITP logo are registered trademarks of International Thomson Publishing.
Some of the product names and company names used in this book have been used for identification purposes only and may be trademarks or registered trademarks of their respective manufacturers and sellers.

Disclaimer
Course Technology reserves the right to revise this publication and make changes from time to time in its content without notice.

ISBN 0-7600-4078-8

Printed in the United States of America

10 9 8 7 6 5 4 3 2 1

From the **New Perspectives Series Team**

At **Course Technology** we have one foot in education and the other in technology. We believe that technology is transforming the way people teach and learn, and we are excited about providing instructors and students with materials that use technology to teach about technology.

Our development process is unparalleled in the higher education publishing industry. Every product we create goes through an exacting process of design, development, review, and testing.

Reviewers give us direction and insight that shape our manuscripts and bring them up to the latest standards. Every manuscript is quality tested. Students whose backgrounds match the intended audience work through every keystroke, carefully checking for clarity and pointing out errors in logic and sequence. Together with our own technical reviewers, these testers help us ensure that everything that carries our name is error-free and easy to use.

We show both how and why technology is critical to solving problems in college and in whatever field you choose to teach or pursue. Our time-tested, step-by-step instructions provide unparalleled clarity. Examples and applications are chosen and crafted to motivate students.

As the New Perspectives Series team at Course Technology, our goal is to produce the most timely, accurate, creative, and technologically sound product in the entire college publishing industry. We strive for consistent high quality. This takes a lot of communication, coordination, and hard work. But we love what we do. We are determined to be the best. Write to us and let us know what you think. You can also e-mail us at NewPerspectives@course.com.

The New Perspectives Series Team

Joseph J. Adamski	Jessica Evans	William Newman
Judy Adamski	Marilyn Freedman	Dan Oja
Roy Ageloff	Kathy Finnegan	David Paradice
David Auer	Robin Geller	June Parsons
Dirk Baldwin	Donna Gridley	Harry Phillips
Daphne Barbas	Roger Hayen	Sandra Poindexter
Rachel Bunin	Charles Hommel	Mark Reimold
Joan Carey	Janice Jutras	Ann Shaffer
Patrick Carey	Chris Kelly	Susan Solomon
Sharon T. Caswell	Mary Kemper	Susanne Walker
Barbara Clemens	Terry Ann Kremer	John Zeanchock
Rachel Crapser	John Leschke	Beverly Zimmerman
Kim Crowley	Mac Mendelsohn	Scott Zimmerman
Michael Ekedahl		

What is the New Perspectives Series?

Course Technology's **New Perspectives Series** is an integrated system of instruction that combines text and technology products to teach computer concepts and microcomputer applications. Users consistently praise this series for innovative pedagogy, creativity, supportive and engaging style, accuracy, and use of interactive technology. The first New Perspectives text was published in January of 1993. Since then, the series has grown to more than 100 titles and has become the best-selling series on computer concepts and microcomputer applications. Others have imitated the New Perspectives features, design, and technologies, but none have replicated its quality and its ability to consistently anticipate and meet the needs of instructors and students.

What is the Integrated System of Instruction?

New Perspectives textbooks are part of a truly integrated system of instruction: text, graphics, video, sound, animation, and simulations that are linked and that provide a flexible, unified, and interactive system to help you teach and help your students learn. Specifically, the **New Perspectives Integrated System of Instruction** includes a Course Technology textbook in addition to some or all of the following items: Course Labs, Course Online, Course Presenter, and Course Test Manager. These components—shown in the graphic on the back cover of this book—have been developed to work together to provide a complete, integrative teaching and learning experience.

How is the New Perspectives Series different from other microcomputer concepts and applications series?

The **New Perspectives Series** distinguishes itself from other series in at least four substantial ways: sound instructional design, consistent quality, innovative technology, and proven pedagogy. The applications texts in this series consist of two or more tutorials, which are based on sound instructional design. Each tutorial is motivated by a realistic case that is meaningful to students. Rather than learn a laundry list of features, students learn the features in the context of solving a problem. This process motivates all concepts and skills by demonstrating to students *why* they would want to know them.

Instructors and students have come to rely on the high quality of the **New Perspectives Series** and to consistently praise its accuracy. This accuracy is a result of Course Technology's unique multi-step quality assurance process that incorporates student testing at three stages of development, using hardware and software configurations appropriate to the product. All solutions, test questions, and other supplements are tested using similar procedures. Instructors who adopt this series report that students can work through the tutorials independently, with a minimum of intervention or "damage control" by instructors or staff. This consistent quality has meant that if instructors are pleased with one product from the series, they can rely on the same quality with any other New Perspectives product.

The **New Perspectives Series** also distinguishes itself by its innovative technology. This series innovated Course Labs, truly *interactive* learning applications. Course Labs have set the standard for interactive learning.

How do I know that the New Perspectives Series will work?

Some instructors who use this series report a significant difference between how much their students learn and retain with this series as compared to other series. With other series, instructors often find that students can work through the book and do well on homework and tests, but still not demonstrate competency when asked to perform particular tasks outside the context of the text's sample case or project. With the **New Perspectives Series**, however, instructors report that students have a complete, integrative learning experience that stays with them. They credit this high retention and competency to the fact that this series incorporates critical thinking and problem-solving with computer skills mastery.

How does this book I'm holding fit into the New Perspectives Series?

New Perspectives applications books are available in the following categories:

Brief books are typically about 160 pages long and are intended to teach only the essentials. They contain 2 to 4 tutorials. A Brief book is designed for a short course or for a one-term course, used in combination with other Brief books.

Introductory books are typically about 300 pages long and consist of 6 to 7 tutorials that go beyond the basics. The book you are holding is an Introductory book.

Comprehensive books are typically about 600 pages long and consist of all of the tutorials in the Introductory books, plus 4 or 5 more tutorials covering higher-level topics. Comprehensive books include 2 Windows tutorials, 3 or 4 Additional Cases, and a Reference Section.

Advanced books cover topics similar to those in the Comprehensive books, but in more depth. Advanced books present the most high-level coverage in the series.

Custom Books The New Perspectives Series offers you two ways to customize a New Perspectives text to fit your course exactly: *CourseKits*™, two or more texts packaged together in a box, and *Custom Editions*®, your choice of books bound together. Custom Editions offer you unparalleled flexibility in designing your concepts and applications courses. You can build your own book by ordering a combination of titles bound together to cover only the topics you want. Your students save because they buy only the materials they need. There is no minimum order, and books are spiral bound. Both CourseKits and Custom Editions offer significant price discounts. Contact your Course Technology sales representative for more information.

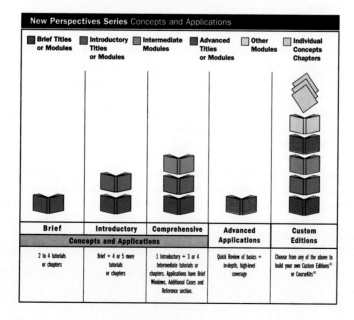

Brief	Introductory	Comprehensive	Advanced Applications	Custom Editions
Concepts and Applications				
2 to 4 tutorials or chapters	Brief + 4 or 5 more tutorials or chapters	1 Introductory + 3 or 4 Intermediate tutorials or chapters. Applications have Brief Windows, Additional Cases and Reference section.	Quick Review of basics + in-depth, high-level coverage	Choose from any of the above to build your own Custom Editions® or CourseKits®

In what kind of course could I use this book?

This book can be used in any course in which you want students to learn all the most important topics of the Internet. *New Perspectives on The Internet Using Netscape Navigator Software—Introductory* is designed for a microcomputer course with a module on the Internet, or a full course on the Internet. The text begins with two conceptual tutorials that introduce students to the Internet, what it is, its exciting history, and how it works. The remaining tutorials teach students how to explore the Internet and the World Wide Web using Netscape Navigator software, as well as how to communicate and share information with the Internet community through the use of e-mail, newsgroups, mailing lists, IRC chat sessions, FTP, Telnet, and Gopher. Finally, the last tutorial of the book covers the same fundamental Internet topics for those users who access the Internet through Unix.

How do the Windows 95 editions differ from the Windows 3.1 editions?

Sessions We've divided the tutorials into sessions. Each session is designed to be completed in about 45 minutes to an hour (depending, of course, upon student needs and the speed of your lab equipment). With sessions, learning is broken up into more easily-assimilated chunks. You can more accurately allocate time in your syllabus. Students can better manage the available lab time. Each session begins with a "session box," which quickly describes the skills students will learn in the session. Furthermore, each session is numbered, which makes it easier for you and your students to navigate and communicate about the tutorial. Look on page NET 53 for the session box that opens Session 3.1.

Quick Checks Each session concludes with meaningful, conceptual Quick Check questions that test students' understanding of what they learned in the session. Answers to all of the Quick Check questions are at the back of the book preceding the Index. You can find examples of Quick Checks on pages NET 44 and NET 82.

New Design We have retained the best of the old design to help students differentiate between what they are to *do* and what they are to *read*. The steps are clearly identified by their shaded background and numbered steps. Furthermore, this new design presents steps and screen shots in a larger, easier to read format. Some good examples of our new design are pages NET 72 and NET 73.

What features are retained in the Windows 95 editions of the New Perspectives Series?

"Read This Before You Begin" Page This page is consistent with Course Technology's unequaled commitment to helping instructors introduce technology into the classroom. Technical considerations and assumptions about software are listed to help instructors save time and eliminate unnecessary aggravation. The "Read This Before You Begin" page for this book is on page NET 2.

Tutorial Case Each tutorial begins with a problem presented in a case that is meaningful to students. The problem turns the task of learning how to use an application into a problem-solving process. The problems increase in complexity with each tutorial. These cases touch on multicultural, international, and ethical issues—so important to today's business curriculum. See page NET 51 for the case that begins Tutorial 3.

Step-by-Step Methodology This unique Course Technology methodology keeps students on track. They enter data, click buttons, or press keys always within the context of solving the problem posed in the tutorial case. The text constantly guides students, letting them know where they are in the course of solving the problem. In addition, the numerous screen shots include labels that direct students' attention to what they should look at on the screen. On almost every page in this book, you can find an example of how steps, screen shots, and labels work together.

TROUBLE?

TROUBLE? Paragraphs These paragraphs anticipate the mistakes or problems that students are likely to have and help them recover and continue with the tutorial. By putting these paragraphs in the book, we facilitate independent learning and free the instructor to focus on substantive conceptual issues rather than on common procedural errors. Two representative examples of TROUBLE? are on pages NET 69 and NET 81.

Reference Windows Reference Windows appear throughout the text. They are succinct summaries of the most important tasks covered in the tutorials. Reference Windows are specially designed and written so students can refer to them when doing the Tutorial Assignments and Case Problems, and after completing the course. Page NET 77 contains the Reference Window for Saving an Image from a Web Page.

Task Reference The Task Reference contains a summary of how to perform common tasks using the most efficient method, as well as references to pages where the task is discussed in more detail. It appears as a table at the end of the book. In this book the Task Reference is on pages NET 265–272.

Review, Projects, Resources, and Glossaries Tutorials 1 and 2 conclude with Review questions that test students' understanding of the concepts covered in the tutorial. These Review questions are followed by a series of Projects designed to give students an opportunity to apply concepts learned to real-life situations. Finally, Tutorials 1 and 2 conclude with a list of additional Resources for students to use to gain deeper insight into the topics covered, and a Glossary summarizing the key terms presented in the tutorial.

Tutorial Assignments, Case Problems, and Lab Assignments Tutorials 3–7 conclude with Tutorial Assignments, which provide students with additional hands-on practice of the skills they learned in the tutorial. The Tutorial Assignments are followed by Case Problems that have approximately the same scope as the tutorial case. Finally, if a Course Lab accompanies the tutorial, Lab Assignments are included. Look on page NET 100 for the Tutorial Assignments for Tutorial 3. See page NET 101 for examples of Case Problems. The Lab Assignment for Tutorial 1 is on page NET 26.

EXPLORE

Exploration Exercises The Windows environment allows students to learn by exploring and discovering what they can do. Exploration Exercises can be Tutorial Assignments or Case Problems that challenge students, encourage them to explore the capabilities of the program they are using, and extend their knowledge using the Help facility and other reference materials. Page NET 101 contains Exploration Exercises for Tutorial 3.

What supplements are available with this textbook?

Course Labs: Now, Concepts Come to Life Computer skills and concepts come to life with the New Perspectives Course Labs—highly-interactive tutorials that combine illustrations, animation, digital images, and simulations. The Labs guide students step-by-step, present them with Quick Check questions, let them explore on their own, test their comprehension, and provide printed feedback. Lab icons at the beginning of the tutorial and in the tutorial margins indicate when a topic has a corresponding Lab. Lab Assignments are included at the end of each relevant tutorial in the textbook.

The Internet
World Wide Web
Tutorial 1
Introductory

E-mail
Tutorial 4
Introductory

Student Files Student Files contain all of the data that students will use to complete the tutorials, Tutorial Assignments, Case Problems and Additional Cases. A Readme file includes technical tips for lab management. See the inside covers of this book and the "Read This Before You Begin" page before Tutorial 1 for more information on Student Files.

Online Companion A special Web site is available specifically for this book at the Course Technology Web site. This Web page can be found at the following URL address: http://www2.coursetools.com/CTI/NewPerspectives/ii/. This Web page is referred to throughout the tutorials as the New Perspectives on the Internet Using Netscape Navigator Software—Introductory Student Online Companion Web page. Having students use this Online Companion ensures that they will access live links, minimizes the possibility of obsolete links, and gives them a more successful Internet learning experience. See the "Read This Before You Begin" page before Tutorial 1 for more information on the New Perspectives on the Internet Using Netscape Navigator Software—Introductory Student Online Companion.

Solution Files Solution Files contain every file students are asked to create or modify in the Tutorials, Tutorial Assignments, and Case Problems. These files are available on the Course Technology Faculty Online Companion page at http://www2.coursetools.com/cti/Faculty.

The following supplements are included in the Review Pak that accompanies this textbook:

- Student Files
- Course Labs

Course Online: A Website Dedicated to Keeping You and Your Students Up-To-Date When you use a New Perspectives product, you can access Course Technology's faculty and student sites on the World Wide Web. You can browse the password-protected faculty online companions to obtain online Instructor's Manuals, Solution Files, Student Files, and more. Please call your Course Technology customer service representative for more information. Student and faculty online companions are accessible through the Course Technology home page at http://www.course.com.

Acknowledgments

Many thanks to the New Perspectives team at Course Technology, particularly Mac Mendelsohn, Managing Editor; Susan Solomon, Series Consulting Editor; Cathie DiMassa, Senior Production Editor; Greg Bigelow, QA Supervisor; Chris Hall and Peter Deacon, Quality Assurance testers; Patty Stephan, Production Manager; Chris Greacen, Webmaster; and especially Janice Jutras, Development Editor, and Kim Crowley, Product Manager.

My sincere gratitude extends to the many people who helped to ensure that this book would be a great success, especially Janice and Kim, who were with me every step of the way. A big thank you goes to Jeff Albrecht of CompuTech, for his assistance on some of the technical aspects of the book and the Online Companion. Most importantly, I would like to recognize my family for their encouragement, support, and patience.

Sharon T. Caswell

Table of **Contents**

New Perspectives on

The Internet Using Netscape Navigator™ Software

INTRODUCTORY

TUTORIALS

Read This **Before You Begin**

STUDENT DISK

To complete the Introductory tutorials, Tutorial Assignments, and Case Problems in this book, you need one Student Disk. Your instructor will either provide you with a Student Disk or ask you to make your own.

If you are supposed to make your own Student Disk, you will need one blank, formatted high-density disk. You will need to copy a set of files from a file server or standalone computer onto your disk. Your instructor will tell you which computer, drive letter, and folders contain the files you need. The following table shows you which files go on your disk:

Student Disk	Write this on the disk label	Put these files on the disk
1	Student Disk 1: Netscape Navigator Introductory Tutorials 1-7	bear.gif, ideas.doc

COURSE LABS

The Introductory tutorials in this book feature two interactive Course Labs to help you understand Internet and E-mail concepts. There are Lab Assignments at the end of Tutorials 1 and 4 that relate to these Labs. To start a Lab, click the Start button on the Windows 95 taskbar, point to Programs, point to Course Labs, point to New Perspectives Applications, and click the name of the lab you want to use.

USING YOUR OWN COMPUTER

If you are going to work through this book using your own computer, you need:

■ **Computer System** Netscape Navigator 3.0 or higher and Windows 95 must be installed on your computer. This book assumes a complete installation of Netscape Navigator software.

■ **Student Disk** Ask your instructor or lab manager for details on how to get the Student Disk. You will not be able to complete the tutorials or exercises in this book using your own computer until you have a Student Disk. The student files may also be obtained electronically over the Internet. See the inside front or inside back cover of this book for more details.

■ **Online Companion** The Introductory tutorials in this book assume your Netscape Navigator browser software is configured such that your home page is the Web page found at the following URL address: http://www2.coursetools.com/CTI/NewPerspectives/ii/. This Web page is referred to as the New Perspectives on the Internet Using Netscape Navigator Software—Introductory Student Online Companion Web page.

■ **Course Labs** See your instructor or technical support person to obtain the Course Lab software.

VISIT OUR WORLD WIDE WEB SITE

Additional materials designed especially for you are available on the World Wide Web. Go to **http://www.course.com**.

To complete the Introductory Tutorials, Tutorial Assignments, and Case Problems in this book, your students must use a set of student files on one Student Disk. These files are included in the Review Pak, and they may also be obtained electronically over the Internet. See the inside front or inside back cover of this book for more details. Follow the instructions in the Readme file to copy the files to your server or standalone computer. You can view the Readme file using WordPad.

Once the files are copied, you can make Student Disks for the students yourself, or you can have them make their own Student Disks. Make sure the files get correctly copied onto the Student Disks by following the instructions in the Student Disks section above.

Online Companion The Introductory tutorials in this book assume your students' Netscape Navigator browser software is configured such that their home page is the Web page found at the following URL address: http://www2.coursetools.com/CTI/NewPerspectives/ii/. This Web page is referred to as the New Perspectives on the Internet Using Netscape Navigator Software—Introductory Student Online Companion Web page.

COURSE LAB SOFTWARE AND STUDENT FILES

Introductory Tutorials 1 and 4 feature two online, interactive Course Labs that introduce basic Internet and E-mail concepts. The Course Lab software is distributed on a CD-ROM included in the Review Pak. To install the Course Lab software, follow the setup instructions in the Readme file on the CD-ROM. Refer also to the Readme file for essential technical notes related to running the Labs in a multi-user environment. Once you have installed the Course Lab software, your students can start the Labs from the Windows 95 desktop by following the instructions in the Course Labs section above. You are granted a license to copy the Student Files and Course Labs to any computer or computer network used by students who have purchased this book.

Introduction to the Internet

OBJECTIVES

When you have completed this tutorial, you should be able to:

- Define what the Internet is, why it was created, and how it grew

- Describe what computer networks are and how they relate to the Internet

- Explain what the World Wide Web is and how it differs from the Internet

- Describe the relationship between how Web sites, Web pages, and home pages relate to one another

- Identify how some communication tools available on the Internet are used

- Discuss how you can use the Internet to achieve professional or personal objectives

- Follow appropriate "netiquette" when using the Internet

LAB

The Internet World Wide Web

Kay Preston is an art major at Rutgers University. She is studying the humanities for her undergraduate thesis. Kay was just selected to attend a summer study abroad program at the Institute of Art History in Paris. Kay never traveled abroad before and has just two weeks to learn as much about France as she can before she leaves. She recently connected to the Internet for the first time and thinks it can help her learn more about France and its culture. Kay soon finds herself viewing precious artworks hanging in the Louvre, entering obscure cafés serving timeless French cuisine, and traveling the countryside to learn more about the country's agriculture and trade.

She even watches a clip from the most popular movie showing in the Paris theaters. By the time she leaves for her summer in France, Kay knows the exhibit hours for the Louvre and plans to meet a high school friend, who is backpacking across Europe, for dinner and a movie.

This tutorial introduces you to the Internet and the many ways it can help you to efficiently find information and communicate with others. You will learn what the Internet is and why it came into existence. You will also learn what the World Wide Web is and discover ways to use the Internet in your professional or personal life. And finally, you will learn what you need to connect to the Internet.

SESSION

1.1

Before exploring all the opportunities and resources the Internet offers, it's important to define exactly what the Internet is and how it originated. This session presents an overview of the Internet and describes its evolution over the last 25 years.

Defining the Internet

What exactly is the Internet?

The **Internet** is a large computer network made of many smaller, interconnected networks. A **computer network** consists of computers connected to other computers for the purposes of communicating and sharing resources. Various local, regional, and national networks join to exchange data and share processing tasks on the Internet. Literally millions of computers are linked together, from the most basic personal computer to the largest mainframe. The Internet is commonly nicknamed the Net, the Information Superhighway, Cyberspace, and the Infobahn.

The Internet is often referred to as a worldwide distributed network, that is, a collective effort of many organizations and individuals who share common goals of encouraging global communications and network services. The Internet is not a single, massive computer, but rather millions of computers connected so that a wide variety of information is readily exchanged and communicated. Although no single governing body establishes rules and regulations for the Internet, several volunteer organizations help regulate the network by contributing technical, engineering, and administrative expertise.

Science fiction writer William Gibson coined the term "cyberspace" in his 1984 novel, Neuromancer.

Founded in 1992, The Internet Society is a non-governmental, international organization that promotes global cooperation and coordination of the Internet. Its members include companies, government agencies, and foundations.

Understanding Computer Networks

How do computer networks work?

Made of many computer networks, the Internet functions as one large worldwide network. Figure 1-2 shows its structure as a large network. Copper or fiber-optic cables and telephone lines most commonly join computer networks together. **Fiber-optic cables** are extremely thin strands of glass capable of transmitting data, sound, and video but occupying very little space. Advanced technologies, which include "wireless" connections such as satellites, link many computers together. A **local area network**, or **LAN**, is a computer network generally located within a limited area such as a single building or a campus. A **wide area network** or **WAN**, operates in a larger geographical area, usually greater than one or two miles. Organizations sometimes connect their entire LANs or WANs to the Internet.

Figure 1-2 ◀
Structure of
the Internet

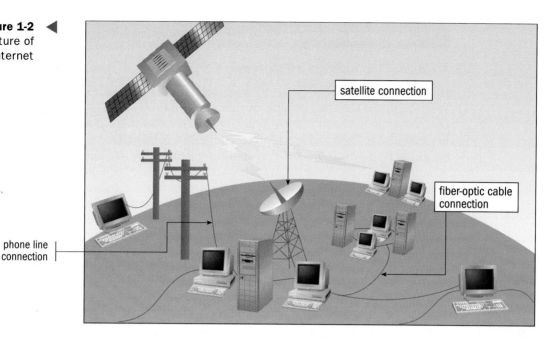

NASA uses the Internet to communicate with its space shuttles via satellite.

Traditionally, computer networks formed so that people could share various resources, such as printers and disk drives. Networks also facilitate sharing computer programs, such as spreadsheets and desktop publishing programs, as well as information in databases. Linking resources in a network together produces time-and-costs savings benefits. Sharing a printer, for example, spreads its purchase and maintenance costs among many employees or departments.

The **host** computer, or **network server**, is a network's central computer: it stores central information and distributes resources across the network to individual workstations. Network servers are computers that receive and manage requests for network resources. Figure 1-3 illustrates how network resources work.

Figure 1-3 ◀
Network
resources

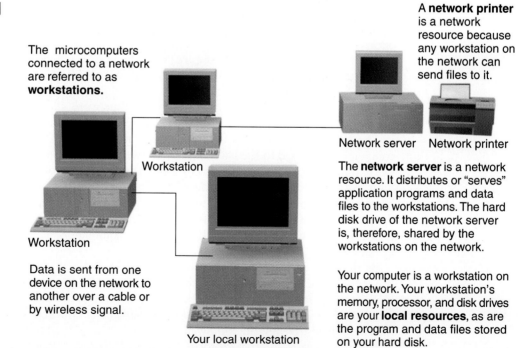

The microcomputers connected to a network are referred to as **workstations.**

Workstation

Workstation

Data is sent from one device on the network to another over a cable or by wireless signal.

Your local workstation

A **network printer** is a network resource because any workstation on the network can send files to it.

Network server   Network printer

The **network server** is a network resource. It distributes or "serves" application programs and data files to the workstations. The hard disk drive of the network server is, therefore, shared by the workstations on the network.

Your computer is a workstation on the network. Your workstation's memory, processor, and disk drives are your **local resources**, as are the program and data files stored on your hard disk.

Creation of the Internet

Where did the Internet come from?

In the 1960s the United States Government first conceived the idea for the Internet. Specifically, the U.S. Department of Defense (DoD) wanted to create a system to ensure constant communication between all its strategic command posts. Relying on research funded by the United States Advanced Research Projects Agency (ARPA), the DoD created a large, decentralized communications network. Its purpose was to ensure the protection and integrity of information passing between critical government entities in the event of a national disaster or war.

This project, called ARPANet, linked various government computer networks together and was structured so that computers from various manufacturers would be compatible. Compatibility was an important factor because many different types of computer systems would need to be connected through the network. The early ARPANet consisted of four experimental university sites. As common standards and technologies developed, the network evolved into what we now call the Internet.

The four institutions originally connected to the ARPANet were the Stanford Research Institute, the University of California at Santa Barbara, the University of California at Los Angeles, and the University of Utah.

The DoD created the Internet with the intention of enabling each network to stand alone or to work together. It intentionally created redundancy throughout the network, so that no one entity depended entirely on another. This ensured that the network would operate effectively, even if one area was inaccessible or destroyed. Twenty-five years later, the Internet still functions this way. For example, if your personal computer breaks down or a university's system fails, the Internet still routes and disseminates the information through different network paths.

Growth of the Internet

How has the Internet evolved over the past 25 years?

The Internet functioned extremely well for DoD's day-to-day needs during the 1970s. A successful public demonstration of ARPANet capabilities encouraged educational and research institutions to try this technology. Soon, many organizations were experimenting with the communication and information-sharing tools the Internet offered. New computer **protocols**, or sets of rules, were developed to ensure reliable connections between many different computer types. Tutorial 2 discusses one protocol set, called Transmission Control Protocol/Internet Protocol (TCP/IP), in more detail. These new protocols fueled interest in and subsequent growth of the ARPANet. In fact, the ARPANet grew so fast that the DoD became concerned about the amount of traffic it was handling. It split the network into two segments: a military network called MILNET and a civilian network that retained the name ARPANet. The split helped reduce traffic—for a short time.

An internet is a connected set of networks using similar protocols; the name "the Internet" originally referred to the connected TCP/IP internets connected to the backbone.

The 1980s was a decade of continued network growth. The DoD mandated that all computers connected to the **backbone**, or major communication lines connecting the network, follow the TCP/IP protocols. By 1983, this was accomplished and the Internet was born. ARPANet became the Internet's backbone and remained the trial base for refining communications structure. About this time, organizations started using the IP protocol on their private networks to connect to the Internet. As users began communicating between their private networks and the public networks, commercial use of the Internet began to increase.

By the late 1980s, the U. S. National Science Foundation (NSF) established the main backbone called NSFNET to accommodate the Internet's growth. The NSF also provided funding that enabled many regional networks to connect to this network. International activity on the Internet grew with the establishment of connections to such countries as the Netherlands, Denmark, and Sweden.

Before the 1980s, Internet Protocol Addresses identified computers on the networks. An **Internet Protocol address**, or **IP address**, is a uniquely assigned address that identifies an individual computer on the network. IP addresses consist of a long string of numbers that follow no discernible numbering scheme. The use of domain names, rather than IP addresses, revolutionized the way computers are presently identified on the network. **Domain Name Services**, or **DNS**, utilize names, rather than numbers, to identify computers on the Net. Domain names are easier to remember and often categorized by activity type or the location of a particular network. For example, instead of using the IP address 128.186.6.103 to access the network at Florida State University, you simply type the address: fsu.edu.

Early in the 1990s, the ARPANet ceased to exist, as the NSFNET backbone began providing the main means of connection. The DoD still maintains its own operational and testing network, known as the Defense Data Network (DDN). It carries on many ARPANet traditions, such as experimental research into high-speed networking. Legislation was also passed to support research into, and implementation of, a nationwide high-speed computing network known as the National Research and Education Network (NREN). The legislation encouraged further research and collaboration between government and private industry and acknowledged the importance of high-speed networks to the future of the national computer networking environment.

Throughout the 1990s, the Internet continues to gain popularity as an efficient and cost-effective business tool, as well as a personal productivity tool. Today, the Internet is the world's largest and most widely used computer network. An estimated 50 million people worldwide use the Internet. Figure 1-4 traces the Internet's phenomenal growth over the past 25 years. For example, during the last six months of 1995 the number of host computers connected to the Internet increased from approximately 6,642,00 to 9,472,000. A dynamic entity, the Internet continues to grow and evolve over time.

At the beginning of the 1980s, the number of hosts on the Internet was barely over 1,000; when the decade ended, the number exceeded 100,000.

In 1990, the Electronic Frontier Foundation was created. A non-profit civil liberties organization, it works in the public interest to protect privacy, free expression, and access to online resources and information.

Figure 1-4 ◀
Internet growth

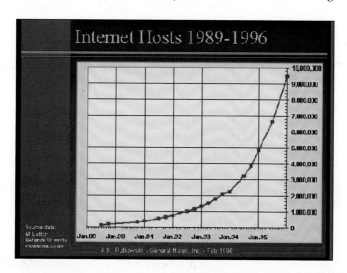

The Internet World Wide Web

One of the biggest breakthroughs in information distribution over the Internet is the World Wide Web. The **World Wide Web**, commonly called the **Web** or **WWW**, connects electronic documents of information on a particular topic. These documents, known as **Web pages**, contain different types of information, ranging from simple text to complex multimedia items. **Multimedia** is an integrated collection of computer-based text, graphics, sound, animation, photo images, or video. Figure 1-5 shows an example of a Web page. In addition to topical information, a Web page might also include one or more links to other Web pages. **Hypertext links**, or **links**, point to other Web pages and make following a thread of related information easy, even if pages are stored on computers elsewhere in the world. Links let you connect to related Web pages by clicking them with your mouse.

Figure 1-5 ◀
Example of a
Web page,
Course
Technology
Online Student
Center

Web pages
typically contain
text and graphics

a graphical
hypertext
link

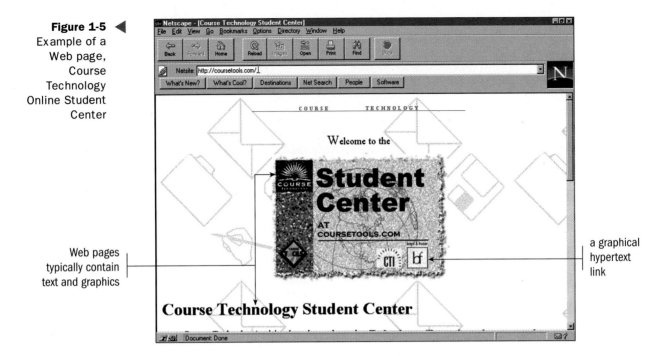

The WWW allows data to be viewed through text-based menuing systems or with graphical user interfaces. A **graphical user interface**, or **GUI**, uses a pointing device, such as a mouse, to select buttons, icons, or other graphics to initiate commands. The Windows operating system is an example of a user-friendly GUI. A GUI features such time-saving and effortless tools as pull-down menus and buttons for performing key tasks. In future tutorials, you will use Netscape Navigator software, a GUI for viewing information and services on both the Internet and WWW. Session 1.2 discusses the WWW in more detail.

Quick Check

1 True or False: The Internet is one large computer that distributes information throughout the world.

2 The Internet grew out of a need for redundancy and reliability for the U.S. Department of _DEFENCE_.

3 Computer _NETWORKS_ were developed that assured reliable connections between the many different types of computers.

4 An internet is a connected set of _NETWORKS_ using similar _PROTOCOLS_

5 Domain Name Services assign _NAMES_ instead of _NUMBERS_ to more clearly identify the computers connected to the Internet.

6 The _WWW_ connects electronic documents of information on a particular topic. _World Wide Web._

SESSION

1.2

The development of the World Wide Web (WWW) has tremendously impacted the Internet's growth. This session provides an overview of the WWW and introduces you to browsers, hypertext, and Web sites.

The World Wide Web

How does the World Wide Web work?

The creation of the WWW has been mainly attributed to Tim Berners-Lee, a former software consultant who collaborated with a colleague on its early design. In November of 1990, they co-authored a design document explaining their vision. It stated: "The texts are linked together in a way that one can go from one concept to another to find the information one wants. The network of links is called a web." They originally called the project the Worldwide Web. Released in May of 1991, the WWW became available for distribution by January of 1992. Another year passed before the WWW took hold. The introduction of GUI browsers increased the popularity of the WWW dramatically. Netscape Corporation estimated in its 1995 annual report that there will be over 125 million users viewing the WWW by the year 1999, as illustrated in Figure 1-6.

Figure 1-6 ◀
Estimated
World Wide
Web growth

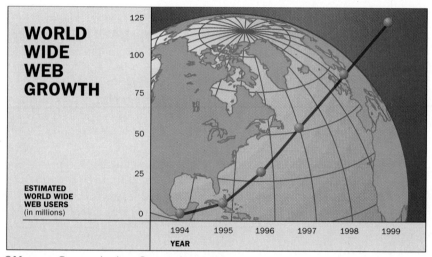

©Netscape Communications Corporation

The structure of the WWW is sometimes compared to a spider's web. For example, no matter which strand a spider follows to get across its web, it always arrives at the other side. To get to the information you want on the Internet, the WWW provides a variety of strands, or ways to get there. Like a spider traveling across an array of webs, you decide where you want to go and which direction you want to travel.

Browsers

What software do I need to access the World Wide Web?

A **browser** is a software program that lets you use the WWW to find, load, and view Web pages. It displays the text, graphics, and links for a Web page. In 1993, a student at the University of Illinois, Marc Andreessen, and a programmer at the National Center for Supercomputing Applications (NCSA), Eric Bina, developed the first graphical WWW browser, Mosaic. Easy to install and use, Mosaic handled protocols for the WWW and other applications. Other browsers soon followed, including Windows Mosaic, Cello, and InternetWorks. Among the more popular browsers today is Netscape Navigator, published by the Netscape Communications Corporation. According to Netscape Communications Corporation sources, this popular browser has captured over 75% of the browser market share. Figure 1-7 shows the Netscape Navigator browser window.

Figure 1-7 ◀
Netscape
Navigator
browser

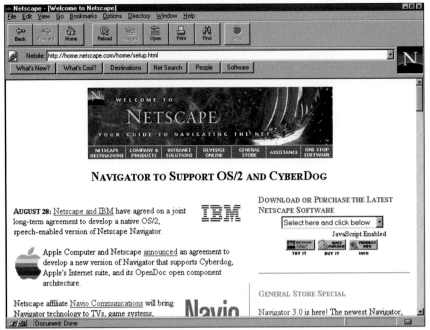

©Netscape Communications Corporation

Hypertext

How does hypertext impact my use of the WWW?

Hypertext has made navigating the Internet much easier. Hypertext increases the average Internet user's ability to manipulate information and locate specific information. You may already have experience with hypertext because Windows Help files use it extensively.

Hypertext links appear as highlighted information on your computer screen. They are underlined and/or in a different color, usually blue. The highlighting indicates that you can select these links, by clicking a mouse, to move to another document. After you select a link, the process of jumping to the requested document or information is called **hypertext linking**. When you start linking to other pieces of information and travel far down a trail, this is called **surfing the Net**. You can always return to your original destination, however, because your browser keeps track of the links you connected to during your "surfing trip."

Figure 1-8 is a conceptual model of how hypertext linking on the WWW works. The example shows the home page for Cable News Network (CNN). From this main page you can link to many other topics such as the weather, sports, and health. If you click the link for the day's health news, you can learn about equestrians with paralysis and the issues they face. From the equestrian page, you can link to a page that has information on possible paralysis cures, and you can click a link with a multimedia movie clip describing the Cure Paralysis organization. As you jump to other Web pages, you arrive at the Medical Breakthroughs page, which has additional detailed information about health-related issues today.

Figure 1-8 ◄
Hypertext
linking on
the WWW

1. Cable News Network (CNN) maintains a Web site that includes images, video clips, narration, and text about the day's headline news stored as a file on the CNN computer.

2. From the home page you can jump to a site with health-related stories.

3. From the Health page, you can read about equestrians with paralysis and jump to a page about curing paralysis.

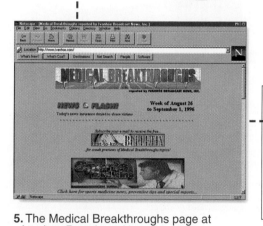

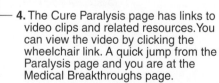

5. The Medical Breakthroughs page at Ivanhoe Broadcast News has links to current sports medicine news, preventive tips, special reports, and much more.

4. The Cure Paralysis page has links to video clips and related resources. You can view the video by clicking the wheelchair link. A quick jump from the Paralysis page and you are at the Medical Breakthroughs page.

Web Sites and Home Pages

What is a Web site?

A **Web site** is a computer or a network of computers that make Web pages available on the WWW. A Web site can also be a group of related Web pages. Think of it as a type of electronic billboard where you can find various information documents, or Web pages. Individuals and organizations use Web sites as business tools for improving sales, conducting market research, providing customer support, and delivering products.

The first Web page that appears when you start a browser like Netscape, or connect to a Web site, is a **home page**. A home page might include information about the host computer, links to other Web sites, or associated graphics and sounds. For example, a company's home page might contain information about the organization; pictures and biographies of its key employees; and links to departments, such as sales or customer service, as well as to Web pages that describe the organization's services or products.

Home pages often incorporate colors, graphics, different fonts and type sizes, backgrounds, icons, buttons, lists, menus, hypertext links to e-mail and other Internet services, and more. Company home pages are often very elaborate and complex, such as Bank of America's home page shown in Figure 1-9, where you can actually complete transactions or apply for a loan online. Other home pages, such as Sony's home page in Figure 1-10, include pictures, sound, and movie samples. Potential customers evaluate a company's home page by the content and quality of its information. This means a small organization, such as a local department store, has potentially the same marketing presence on the Internet as a national department store chain like Kmart.

Figure 1-9 ◄
Bank of America Web site

Figure 1-10
Sony Web site

Inter and Intra Web Uses

How can the WWW be used within a company?

Although most companies create Web sites to share information with the world at large, a new use is developing in the business community. Behind corporate walls, many organizations create Web sites solely for internal use. This is using the Internet as an Intranet. An **Intranet** is a network within an organization that uses the Internet protocol and other Internet technologies to better connect customers and business. Not available to the public, it is usually protected with a password lock. Its existence is known primarily within the organization; it is not accessible like a public Web site.

An organization may have an internal Web site for many reasons. It delivers information immediately without having to wait for printers. It is cost effective and easy to use with a GUI. Finally, it can include many types of information that cannot be presented on paper, such as sounds and video.

An example of intranet usage would be on-line training. For example, trainees need not leave their desks to attend training sessions. Instead they can view the training session according to their schedules, repeat portions that need extra attention, and stop and start the training session whenever they want.

Quick Check

1 Who was the architect of the WWW? *Tim Berners-Lee*

2 *Browsers* are the software programs called that let you access information on the WWW.

3 What does a hypertext link look like on your computer screen?

Highlighted Information.

4 When you jump to another Web page, it is called *HyperText Linking*

5 A *Web Site* is a computer or computer network that makes Web pages available on the WWW.

6 What is a home page? *The 1st Page of the Web.*

7 A Web site designed for internal corporate use is called *Intranet*

SESSION

1.3

There are several communication tools available to users on the Internet. This session discusses several of them, such as electronic mail, newsgroups, and IRC, and their purposes, and introduces you to other tools that let you access and utilize information on remote networks.

Communication Tools

How can I use the Internet to communicate with other users?

By utilizing one of many communication tools available on the Internet, you can communicate with people and access information around the world. The Internet's communication capabilities also let you work with individuals whom you may not otherwise have had an opportunity to even contact. The Internet can bring together teams of people to collaborate efficiently and effectively, regardless of physical limitations and geographical locations. In the future, you will probably work on school and business projects with individuals whom you may have never met in person!

Electronic mail, also known as **e-mail**, lets you exchange messages with individuals or groups. It is the Internet's most basic communication tool for relaying information back and forth electronically among users. After you compose a message and address it, your computer uses specialized software to send it to and deposit it in the recipient's electronic mailbox. You can use e-mail to communicate with people across the street or across the globe. During the 1970s, e-mail was used primarily by researchers to share specific results of laboratory experiments and data. Today, e-mail is used for both business and personal communications. Figure 1-11 shows how e-mail travels across the Internet. Tutorial 4 discusses e-mail in more detail.

You can send e-mail to the President of the United States. His e-mail address is: president@whitehouse.gov.

Figure 1-11 ◀
How e-mail
travels across
the Internet

1. The message originates from a computer in a student's apartment one block from the University of Alaska, Fairbanks, campus. The message travels over the telephone lines to the University of Alaska.

2. From the University of Alaska, the message travels to one of the main Internet hosts in Washington state.

3. Now the message travels to Boston on the Internet backbone—high-speed connections between main Internet hosts.

4. Still on the backbone, the message travels from Boston to North Carolina.

5. The message leaves the backbone and proceeds to Florida, where it is sent to Puerto Rico, then to the Virgin Islands.

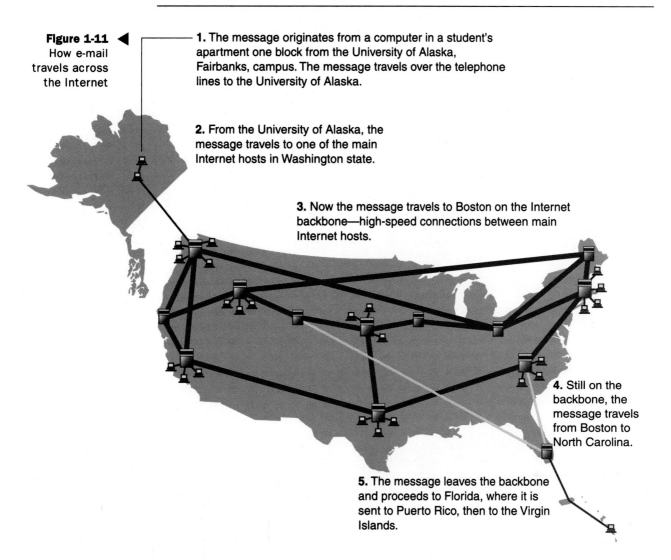

Usenet is a communication tool that enables people to meet and discuss various topics online. Usenet organizes discussions under broad headings called **newsgroups,** specific addresses and sites on the Internet where people leave messages for one another regarding a particular topic of interest. Newsgroups can be considered a type of ongoing group discussion in which participants leave messages, called articles or postings, that express their knowledge or opinions, and answer one another's questions. Usenet newsgroups act much like a large community bulletin board, in that participants can post messages and can view and/or respond to any messages.

Newsgroups are divided into separate topical areas, ranging from astrophysics to zen. The sequence of comments for a particular Usenet session is a **thread.** Newsgroups let users share information with a large group of people without sending individual mail messages. For example, if you place your resume online, thousands of people might see it. This saves you the time and costs involved with sending individual resumes. In addition, newsgroups can help you keep on top of industry trends and help you learn more about prospective employers. Figure 1-12 illustrates how a newsgroup discussion works. Tutorial 5 discusses Usenet newsgroups in more detail.

Figure 1-12 ◀
A Usenet
thread

A. Kate Downey initiates a discussion about scanners on November 8. Her question is added to the newsgroup transcript.

B, C. As other users log into the newsgroup, they read Kate's posting. They can post a reply at any time. Here, participants Smith and Bigelow post replies on November 9 and November 11.

D. On November 12, Kate logs into the newsgroup again and reads the transcripts for November 9, 10, and 11. She sees the replies from Smith and Bigelow, then continues the thread by posting another question.

Mailing lists are another Internet group communication tool. Much like newsgroups, they involve exchanging messages pertaining to a certain topic. However, instead of accessing a newsgroup and reading its postings, mailing list messages are sent automatically through electronic mail to subscribers. For example, if you subscribe to a mailing list for professionals interested in creative marketing approaches, the e-mail messages you receive from the list may range from discussions on tactical marketing communications to suggestions of how to set up an effective trade show booth.

To subscribe to a mailing list, a user sends a specially formatted e-mail message to the list maintainer or administrator. The administrator gathers the messages posted to the mailing list and redistributes them to subscribers via e-mail. For the most part, mailing lists are maintained by software that automates message distribution and retrieval and completes administrative tasks with very little human intervention. Tutorial 4 discusses mailing lists in more detail.

Internet Relay Chat, or **IRC**, allows for real-time, interactive communications on the Internet. Users participating in IRC automatically see the information you are exchanging as you type it. IRC works much like a conference call: people at various locations can actively participate in a live conversation. Common uses for IRC include remote staff meetings for employees scattered across the country, interactive customer forums, and interactive games for casual users. Tutorial 5 discusses IRC in more detail.

Operation Home Front connects soldiers in the field with family and friends back home. One service of Operation Home Front is Party Line. It brings people from around the world together in real time using IRC.

One of the newest and most researched technologies to emerge on the Internet is Voice/Video on the Network. **Voice/Video on the Network**, or **VON**, allows live audio and video conferencing to take place using your Internet connection. Audio conferencing is like live telephone conversations. Special software lets you "call" someone over the Internet and have a live conversation. You can use audio conferencing to talk with a group of people as well or even listen to a live radio broadcast over the Internet. Audio conferencing makes many regular phone system features available such as caller identification, a caller log to track calls, and number recall. In addition, you can transmit data over your Internet connection at the same time. If a business has an audio conferencing link on their Web page, you can call it by clicking its link. Figure 1-13 shows a VON session using CU-SeeMe software.

Figure 1-13 ◀
CU-SeeMe
Voice/Video
session

video image of
person you are calling

camera

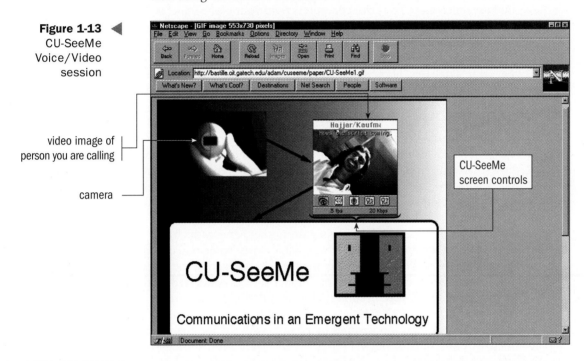

In 1995 the Rolling Stones performed the first online concert using VON technology. A technology called MBONE, or multicast backbone, broadcast the concert using very high-speed network connections.

Video conferencing technology allows real-time person-to-person or group video conferencing to take place over an Internet connection. Video conferencing has the advantages of a live audio connection with live video—meaning you can see the participants you are talking with. For example, you can attend a class halfway around the world right from your computer screen. One such distributed electronic classroom system is currently in use in Norway. For video conferencing to work, both the caller and recipient must have similar software, use a special camera attached to the sending and receiving computers, and be on-line at the same time for the call to connect.

Connecting to Other Computers and Transferring Information

How can I send and receive data across the Internet?

File Transfer Protocol, or **FTP**, is the method for transferring files from one computer to another. FTP lets you access another computer's file systems and transfer, or copy, specific files over the Internet to your computer using special software. After you log on to, or connect to, the FTP host, you can browse through the listing of available files. When you find the file you want, you use FTP software to transmit, or **download**, a copy of the file to your computer's hard disk. You can also transfer text, software, graphics, sound, and video files from your computer to another host on the Net. Many FTP host computers have specific requirements, such as having an account on the remote host, for users. An **anonymous FTP site** is a host on the Internet that lets you access its files without an account. Instead, you identify yourself as an anonymous user. For example, an office manager might be responsible for ensuring that the department's word-processing software is up to date. If an updated version of the software is released, he could use FTP to log on to the software manufacturer's host, download a copy of the updated application to his computer, and then distribute it to the office staff. This process is much quicker than contacting the manufacturer, waiting for updated software to arrive on disks, and then installing it. Tutorial 6 discusses FTP in more detail.

Telephone Network, or **Telnet**, is the capability to access and use a remote computer as if it were in your office with your keyboard attached. This technology lets you connect to and use much more powerful computers than your own. Telnet is useful for accessing data and programs without purchasing a particular application or incurring the expense of more sophisticated hardware and software.

You can use Telnet to research many of the resources available on the Internet, including large databases, library card catalogs, and public-access services. You initiate a Telnet session by logging on to the remote host. Once connected, you can start your Telnet session using special software, with the commands appropriate for the computer you are accessing. For example, if you were concerned about the potential hazard of chemicals in a nearby explosives factory, you could Telnet to the University of Illinois Division of Environmental Health and Safety host and look at its extensive database on chemical properties, hazards, and emergency procedures. Many remote computers let you log on as a guest with open access to many portions of their systems; others require account membership with special access rights to the system. Tutorial 6 discusses Telnet in more detail.

Gopher, a text-based document delivery system, lets you access a wide variety of files throughout the Internet. It also integrates other services such as FTP and Telnet within a sophisticated menuing system. It was widely used to gain access to data before development of the WWW. Because many people find navigating the Internet easier using a GUI rather than Gopher, the number of Gopher servers connected to the Internet has sharply declined. As the WWW becomes more popular and widespread, many Gopher sites are being converted to Web sites.

Gopher was created in 1991 at the University of Minnesota, home of the sports team called the "Golden Gophers." It was also named for the word "go-fer," a slang term for an assistant that finds and delivers items.

Each Gopher site is organized by menus, with the top menu leading to submenus and files. By navigating through a series of text-based menus using your mouse or keyboard, you can find information on any computer that runs Gopher software. Unlike Telnet, Gopher is accessible to all Internet users and requires no special account privileges or passwords. For example, if you are interested in the latest legislation information passing through the U.S. House of Representatives, you could access their Gopher menu, shown in Figure 1-14. In addition to legislative information, you can find information about House members, committees, organizations, and links to other U.S. government information resources and Gophers. Figure 1-14 shows how menus appear in a typical Gopher session. Tutorial 6 discusses Gopher in more detail.

Figure 1-14 ◄
Example of a
Gopher menu

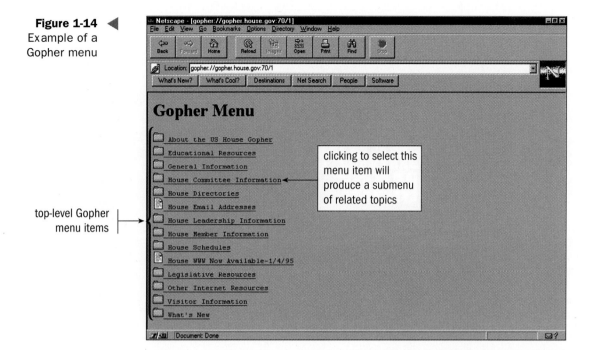

top-level Gopher
menu items

What's Fun on the Internet

What forms of entertainment can I use the Internet for?

Shopping and playing electronic games are two common ways that people use the Internet for entertainment. Online shopping, or cybershopping, lets you buy products or services without leaving your home. You can view competitors' pricing for a product on your screen rather than making several phone calls or visiting various stores. You may find a Web site that is organized much like a catalog, with detailed information about a product you are considering, including pictures, specifications, and pricing information. Most larger Web sites set up for cybershopping have search capabilities that work much like a catalog index; they help you find the product type you are interested in, without looking through many pages. Online order forms make it easy for you to purchase the product you want. Sometimes you can even sample before you buy. For example, you can listen to a song from the recently released compact disk of a new band.

When you find a product that interests you, you select it and it is placed in your virtual shopping cart. It stays there until you are ready to "check out" from that particular Web site. Some Web sites even keep your shopping cart filled with your selections until your next visit, in case you are not ready to purchase. After you indicate your shopping spree is over, a "done," or "finished," link appears, and then you are prompted for payment information. You usually have an opportunity to make sure your order is complete and correct before paying. Figure 1-15 shows an example of The Sharper Image's cybershopping Web site.

Figure 1-15 ◀
Cybershopping
at The Sharper
Image

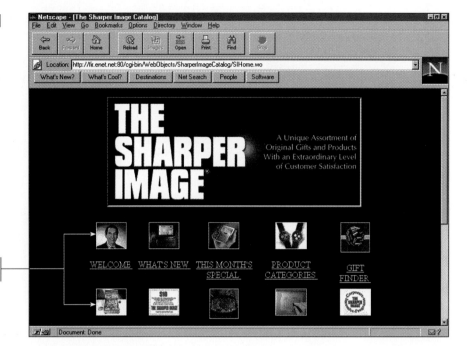

graphical links can be
selected to jump to
other Web pages that
focus on different
aspects of The
Sharper Image's
product line

Playing electronic games with other users over the Internet is increasingly popular. The speed at which games can be played, combined with audio and video conferencing, make interactive game playing just as exciting as if your opponent or team member were playing next to you. Based on game complexity and participants' skill levels and abilities, users agree to meet at a specific game site at a set time. Some games are played in real time; others can be played over a period of time.

Other entertaining Internet activities include reading magazines that you download via FTP or checking the latest standings of your favorite local or national sports team through newsgroups. You can catch a review of a movie you are interested in, or better yet, sample a clip of the movie.

Communication Policies and Regulations

Are there any guidelines or rules that I need to follow to use the Internet?

Most networks attached to the Internet have their own sets of rules and regulations that you must follow to use them. **Acceptable Use Policies**, or **AUPs**, are agreements that outline the terms and conditions of Internet use. Some networks require you to consent to and sign an AUP before you can use their service and then keep your AUP on file. Most networks post AUPs online for all potential users to see. It is the user's responsibility to read and agree to the policies outlined before using that particular network.

AUPs commonly cover the following issues: encouragement of education and communication; support of research; prohibition or allowance of commercial activities; copyright information; facts on transmission of indecent or threatening materials; requirement to comply with local, state, and federal laws; trade secret information; vandalism and harassment data; and procedures for use and warranties. Because most AUPs are similar, you can get a general feel for their contents by reading a few. Penalties for improperly using a network may include loss of network access, disciplinary action, or even criminal prosecution. As more countries struggle to create their own laws governing Internet content and access, more detailed AUPs are likely to be put in place.

The Internet has been likened to a worldwide community bringing together people of all types. Unless you know people you are communicating with over the Internet, you may be unaware of their age, race, or gender. You may not know if a person is disabled, president of a large organization, or a recent graduate. This anonymity makes it important to observe common courtesy rules and basic etiquette codes that apply to Internet communication.

Netiquette is a set of common etiquette rules that outline users' responsibilities and governs how individuals interact over the Internet. Netiquette is the basic code of on-line behavior. Different sets of netiquette are associated with various Internet services, but most share a few specific practices, manners, customs, and expectations. Examples of common netiquette include not typing in all caps (IT LOOKS LIKE YOU ARE SHOUTING!), not using abusive or otherwise objectionable language in either public or private messages, and not sending messages that are likely to result in the loss of a receiver's data. Future tutorials discuss the netiquette associated with each commonly used Internet service.

Quick Check

1. (True) or False: It is possible to send an electronic mail message to a group of people.

2. A(n) _INTERNET RELAY CHAT_ _IRC_ is an online discussion in which participants can post articles for others to read and respond to.

3. You must _SUBSCRIBE_ to a mailing list before you can start receiving e-mail messages automatically from the list.

4. The process of transferring files containing text, graphics, music, or video clips from a remote computer to your computer is called _FILE TRANSFER PROTOCOL_ _FTP_

5. Many text-based _GOPHER_ sites are being converted to Web pages to take advantage of formatting and graphics.

6. _AUPs_ are agreements that users must consent to that outline the terms and conditions of Internet use. _ACCEPTABLE USE POLICIES_

7. The basic code of online behavior when using the Internet is called _NETIQUETTE_

SESSION 1.4

User **Focus:** Connecting to the Internet

Your university configured the software and hardware you need to access the Internet from your classroom or lab facility. What if you want to access the Internet from your computer at home or your office? To access the Internet from another location, you need to obtain specific computer hardware and software as well as fulfill the necessary connection requirements.

Hardware Set-up

What special equipment do I need to access the Internet?

The basic items you need to get on the Net include a computer, modem, and telephone line. The following list gives the minimum configurations required to access the Internet:

- Minimum 386-compatible computer—a 486 computer or better is recommended—running Windows 95, Windows 3.x, or Windows NT; or a computer system running OS2, UNIX, or Macintosh System 7.X
- Minimum memory of 8MB, more recommended
- Minimum 20MB of free disk space for software and disk caching, more recommended
- Multimedia kit (speakers, sound card, and software) if you wish to view multimedia items
- 28.8 bits-per-second (Kbps), or better, modem (14.4 usable, but can be slow)
- Phone line

- Communications software
- Internet account

The Internet is available to any user who has access to a computer, a phone line, and a modem. A **modem** (MOdulator/DEModulator) is a device that attaches to your computer and lets you dial the Internet through your phone line. It translates information between your computer and the phone system. A modem is just one factor that affects the speed at which you can send or receive data. However, a fast modem (28.8K bps or faster) can accelerate the processes of sending and receiving data, as well as viewing information on the Internet. Therefore, you should buy the fastest modem you can afford.

You do not need a special phone line to access the Internet. A typical phone line in your home usually works just fine. You will probably be unable to receive incoming phone calls while connected to the Internet unless your community takes advantage of a technology, Integrated Services Digital Network (ISDN). Tutorial 2 discusses ISDN in more detail.

Locate an Internet Service Provider

How do I obtain an Internet connection, and how much will it cost?

To access the Internet you need an account with an Internet Service Provider (ISP) or a commercial online service. An **Internet Service Provider**, or **ISP**, is an online service that sells telephone access to the Internet. These include such organizations as America Online, CompuServe, Prodigy, Microsoft Network, cable television companies, and many local independent telecommunications firms.

Typical fees for an Internet account run as little as $5 per month for electronic mail access, to approximately $20 per month for 100 hours of access. Most ISPs bill monthly, hourly, or annually, or combine hourly and monthly fees. Some ISPs offer an 800 number for dial up access but charge a higher monthly fee. This 800 number access is expensive but useful if you live in a rural area or if you travel often.

Many people have access to the Internet without knowing it. Universities often provide Internet accounts for students and faculty who wish to use the Internet off campus, so be sure to ask your instructor if this option is available to you. You can also ask your manager if you can access the Internet through your place of employment.

Install Communications Software

How do I get the communications software I need to connect to the Internet?

When you sign up for an Internet account with an ISP or online service, you should receive **communications software** that allows your computer to transmit and receive data using the Internet communication protocols. A **communication protocol** is a set of rules that ensure orderly and accurate data transmission and reception. Following these protocols, different types of computers can communicate and share information with one another on the Internet. All computers connected to the Internet use TCP/IP. Tutorial 2 takes an in-depth look at how TCP/IP works. **SLIP (Serial Line Internet Protocol)** and **PPP (Point to Point Protocol)** are protocols designed to manage communications for a computer that connects to the Internet using a modem. If you connect to the Internet via a modem, you must use the SLIP, PPP, or other similar communications software that you receive from your Internet Service Provider. If your software is self-configuring, the software examines your computer system and automatically selects the appropriate settings to configure your equipment for the Internet. If your software isn't self-configuring, your ISP will instruct you on how to proceed.

Install Browsers and Other Software

What other software do I need to access the Internet?

In addition to the communications software needed to dial in and attach your computer to the Net, you need software to access services such as electronic mail and Telnet. Again, your ISP usually supplies this software; if not, you need to purchase it. Although you can install separate software packages for different Internet services, some applications, such as Netscape, let you access most services through one piece of software.

You may find that some text, graphical, sound, and video information on the Internet is stored in special file formats. Some multimedia files can only be viewed with special software called **viewers**. You can usually download the viewer you need from the site that provides the specially formatted text, graphical, sound, or video file. Many browsers, such as Netscape, have built-in viewers.

Follow the instructions that accompany the software for installation and configuration information. If you obtain software on disk, open a file called "readme" for further instructions. If you download the software directly from the Internet, you should find installation instructions at the online download site.

Connecting to the Internet

After my hardware is set up and my software is installed, how do I connect to the Internet?

The communications protocol software that you installed on your computer should now show up as an icon on your computer's desktop or start screen. Clicking this icon should automatically establish a network connection over your phone line to the Internet via your ISP. You may also be prompted to supply your account name and password. This connection process is referred to as **dialing in**; you may even hear a dialing sound similar to the one a fax machine makes during connection. After you connect to the Internet, you are ready to run your browser or other Internet service applications. Figure 1-16 illustrates the process of dialing in to the Internet.

Figure 1-16 ◀
Dialing in to the Internet

1. Click the Internet icon on your desktop.

2. By clicking the Internet icon, you tell the computer to load your Internet communications software. Your communications software will probably use SLIP or PPP to handle the TCP/IP protocols as your computer transmits and receives data through your modem.

3. Your communications software dials in to your Internet service provider. Usually, your communications software has stored the telephone number, so you do not need to enter it each time you want to connect.

4. If your communications software has stored your user ID and password, it automatically logs you in. Some people prefer to enter their password manually for enhanced security.

End Note

Welcome to the Internet. No one owns it. No one operates it. It provides free information on every type of topic imaginable to anyone who wants it, even if the information is on a computer halfway around the world. Although the Internet grew from the government's need for reliability and redundancy, it quickly became a widely used productivity tool for both professional and personal use. It gives users the opportunity to interact and collaborate with others, including people you may have never even met. In the remaining tutorials, you will use the Netscape Navigator browser to take an in-depth look at several services available on the Internet.

Review

1. Below each heading in this tutorial is a question in italics. Look back through the tutorial, and answer each question using your own words.

2. Using your own words, write three paragraphs briefly describing the Internet and its origins.

3. Describe why protocols are important on the Internet. List five protocols you follow in work-related or personal activities.

4. Two types of WWW browsers are:
   a. serial and parallel
   b. hypertext and hypermedia
   c. text-based and graphical
   d. SLIP and PPP

5. You are the human resources manager of an organization. List four links that you think would be appropriate for its intranet Web page.

6. Describe the differences between domain names and Internet Protocol addresses.

7. Using your own words, briefly describe each of these Internet services:
   a. WWW
   b. e-mail
   c. Usenet
   d. mailing lists
   e. IRC
   f. FTP
   g. Telnet
   h. Gopher
   i. VON

Projects

1. Do you think that regulating content on the Internet violates your freedom of speech rights? Free speech laws protect Americans' rights to express themselves, but should the Internet, which is supported by public taxes, provide an uncensored medium for exchanging information and holding discussions on a variety of topics? Research the Communications Decency Act sponsored by Senator James Exon. Write three paragraphs on the history of this piece of legislation and how it may affect you as an Internet user.

2. Find out what type of Internet connection your school has and if it offers dial-up access to students. Also research local Internet access options, such as commercial online services and independent Internet service providers, to compare costs of connecting to the Internet. Answer the following questions for at least three ISPs in your region:
   a. What is the basic monthly fee?
   b. How many hours of access do you receive per month?
   c. What Internet services are available with the account?
   d. Do you receive communications software and/or a browser with the account?

3. In this first tutorial you read about examples of how you may use some services available on the Internet. As you work through this book, you will have opportunities to explore the Internet with hands-on exercises. Write a list of at least three things you would like to research on the Internet in each of these areas:
   a. professional growth
   b. school studies

4. Research to learn if your school has an AUP and what the consequences are if a student does not follow its rules and regulations. If your school does not have an AUP, list six items that you feel are important for an educational institution's AUP to include.

5. What are the key events in the development of the Internet? Sketch a timeline that shows these major events, and write a sentence or two describing each.

6. Government agencies have a large presence on the Net and an increasing number of government organizations distribute information on the WWW. Almost all federal agencies now have a Web presence. Research your local government entities to find out if they are also on the Web and what types of information they offer. You can include local, regional, or state agencies. List at least two agencies, their Web content, and their URLs. Do they feel their Web presence has been helpful? Why or why not?

7. The Internet changes daily. Its presence is growing and dynamically evolving. In the course of a day, you might hear about it on the radio or television, read about it in a newspaper or magazine, or talk about it with a friend or colleague. Look in your local newspaper, and find at least three items that reference the Internet in some way. These might be simply an e-mail address in an advertisement or a complex article about security issues in the online banking industry. Write one or two sentences about each, briefly describing what Internet service it relates to.

Resources

Fraase, M. *The Windows Internet Tour Guide: Cruising the Internet the Easy Way,* Chapel Hill, NC: Ventana Press, 1994. Good graphics and sample screens.

Gates, B. *The Road Ahead.* New York: Viking, 1995. Microsoft Corporation founder Bill Gates shares his view of what the Internet has to offer and visualizes the future of the network.

Gibson, W. *Neuromancer.* New York: Ace Books, 1984. *Neuromancer* is the science fiction novel that started a new genre of cyberspace science fiction. Gibson paints a world in which Japanese influence has slowly enveloped Western pop culture and in which the search for information or even entertainment involves plugging your brain into a computer.

Hahn, H., and Stout, R. *The Internet Yellow Pages*, second edition. Berkeley, CA: Osborne McGraw-Hill, 1995. This printed Internet directory helps you find information on the Internet, including e-mail addresses, newsgroup names, and thousands of Web pages. An informative listing of Internet sites. You can find it on the Internet at *http://www.mcp.com/nrp/wwwyp/*.

Levine, J. R., and Baroudi, C. *The Internet for Dummies*. San Mateo, CA: IDG Books, 1993. A very useful, well organized, and readable book from the popular *for Dummies* series.

NetGuide. This popular magazine provides a directory of information highway services and destinations. Its Internet Web site address is *http://techweb.cmp.com/net*.

Tolhurst, Pike & Blanton. *Using the Internet*. Indianapolis: Que Books, 1994. *Using the Internet* is a comprehensive guide to understanding the Internet and where it came from. Its highlights include a host resource guide and an in-depth history of the Internet.

Wired. This is the magazine of choice among Internet aficionados. Artsy, glitzy, and off-beat, it has some high-quality articles and unconventional perspectives about the on-line community. *Wired* has an Internet Web site at *http://wired.com*.

Lab Assignment

This Lab Assignment is designed to accompany the interactive Course Lab called Internet World Wide Web. To start the Lab using Windows 95, click the Start button on the Windows 95 taskbar, point to Programs, point to Course Labs, point to New Perspectives Applications, and click Internet World Wide Web. To start the Lab using Windows 3.1, double-click the Course Labs for the Internet group icon to open a window containing the Lab icons, then double-click the Internet World Wide Web icon. If you do not see Course Labs on your Windows 95 Programs menu, or if you do not see the Course Labs for the Internet group icon in your Windows 3.1 Program Manager window, see your instructor or technical support person.

The Internet World Wide Web

The Internet: World Wide Web

One of the most popular services on the Internet is the World Wide Web. This Lab is a Web simulator that teaches you how to use Web browser software to find information. You can use this Lab whether or not your school provides you with Internet access.

1. Click the Steps button to learn how to use Web browser software. As you proceed through the Steps, answer all the Quick Check questions that appear. After you complete the Steps, you will see a Quick Check Summary Report. Follow the instructions on the screen to print this report.
2. Click the Explore button on the Welcome screen. Use the Web browser to locate a weather map of the Caribbean Virgin Islands. What is its URL?
3. Enter the URL http://www.atour.com. A SCUBA diver named Wadson Lachouffe has been searching for the fabled treasure of Greybeard the pirate. A link from the Adventure Travel Web site leads to Wadson's Web page called "Hidden Treasure." Locate the Hidden Treasure page, and answer the questions below.
4. What was the name of Greybeard's ship?
5. What was Greybeard's favorite food?
6. What does Wadson think happened to Greybeard's ship?
7. In the Steps, you found a graphic of Jupiter from the photo archives of the Jet Propulsion Laboratory. In the Explore section of the Lab, you can also find a graphic of Saturn. Suppose one of your friends wants a picture of Saturn for an astronomy report. Make a list of the blue, underlined links your friend must click to find the Saturn graphic. Assume that your friend begins at the Web Trainer home page.

8. Jump back to the Adventure Travel Web site. Write a one-page description of the information at the site, including the number of pages the site contains, and diagram the links it contains.

9. Chris Thomson, a student at UVI, has his own Web page. In Explore, look at the information Chris included on his page. Suppose you could create your own Web page. What would you include? Use word-processing software to design your own Web page. Make sure to indicate the graphics and links you would use.

Glossary

anonymous FTP (anonymous File Transfer Protocol) The feature of FTP software that lets anyone without an account on a host computer log on using the user identification "anonymous."

AUP (Acceptable Use Policy) An agreement that users must consent to that outlines the terms and conditions of Internet use.

backbone A high-speed communications link connecting major Internet hosts.

bandwidth The speed and amount of data that can flow through a communications connection.

browser Software used to view information on the WWW.

commercial online service A for-profit computer network, such as CompuServe, Prodigy, or America Online that provides access to a wide range of financial, informational, and recreational services for an hourly or per-minute charge billed monthly. Also called an online service.

communication protocol A set of rules that ensures the orderly and accurate transmission and reception of data.

communication software Software that allows your computer to transmit and receive data using the Internet communication protocols.

computer network A collection of computers and other devices connected to share data, hardware, and software.

database A group of related information organized so that the information can be easily accessed and manipulated. An example of a database is a list of college students and their addresses, grades, and identification codes.

domain name A name used to identify a computer on the Internet, rather than a numeric Internet Protocol address.

download The process of transferring a file from a host computer to your own.

electronic mail (e-mail) An Internet service that maintains electronic mailboxes and sends messages from one computer to another.

fiber optic Extremely thin strands of glass that are much lighter and more flexible than copper cables. Each strand can transmit data, sound, or video while taking up very little space.

FTP (File Transfer Protocol) A program that moves files from one computer to another on the Internet.

Gopher A menu-driven Internet service that helps you locate the information you need.

graphical user interface (GUI) A type of user interface in which you manipulate on-screen objects to activate commands.

home page The first Web page displayed when you first link to a Website or start a Web browser software program.

hyperlink Elements on a Web page that let you open related Web pages by clicking them with your mouse.

hypermedia The electronic linking of text, graphics, sound, and video that lets you jump from one piece of information to another.

hypertext The electronic linking of documents that lets you jump from a passage in one document to a related passage in another.

Internet The collection of local, regional, and national computer networks linked together to exchange data and distribute processing tasks. The Internet is the world's largest computer network.

intranet A network within an organization that uses Internet technologies to connect its employees and customers to the organization.

IP address (Internet Protocol address) A uniquely assigned numeric address for each computer connected to the Internet.

IRC (Internet Relay Chat) A service on the Internet that allows interactive conversations using your keyboard.

ISP (Internet Service Provider) A service company that provides you with a user account on a host computer that has access to the Internet.

jump The act of moving from one Web page to another.

LAN (local area network) A computer network located within a relatively limited area, such as a building or a campus.

links Elements on a Web page that let you open related Web pages by clicking them with your mouse.

mailing list A group communications tool for posting messages to a group and redistributing them to subscribers through e-mail.

mainframe computer A large, fast, and fairly expensive computer generally used by business and government. It is designed to allow multiple users to access it at one time. Mainframe computers are often host computers on a network.

modem A MOdulater/DEModulator. A device that lets a personal computer communicate with other computers over telephone lines.

multimedia An integrated collection of computer-based text, graphics, sound, animation, photo images, and video.

netiquette A set of common etiquette rules that outlines users, responsibilities and governs the way individuals access the Internet.

network server A computer connected to a network that "serves" or distributes resources to network users.

personal computer A stand-alone computer that allows an individual to work independently of other computers.

PPP (Point to Point Protocol) A version of TCP/IP designed to handle Internet communications for a computer that connects to the Internet using a modem.

protocol A set of rules or regulations.

SLIP (Serial Line Internet Protocol) A version of TCP/IP designed to handle Internet communications for a computer that connects to the Internet using a modem.

TCP/IP (Transmission Control Protocol/Internet Protocol) A widely used network communication protocol on microcomputer, minicomputer, and mainframe networks.

Telnet A computer program that lets you connect to a host computer anywhere on the Internet and use your computer just as if you were using a terminal directly attached to that host computer.

thread A series of messages relating to a particular topic in a newsgroup discussion session.

Usenet An Internet service that maintains thousands of discussion groups involving millions of people.

user Any individual who is served by, and benefits directly or indirectly from, a computer system. Also known as an end-user.

viewer Special software sometimes needed to view certain multimedia items on the WWW.

VON (Video/Voice Over the Net) Interactive audio and video conferencing using your Internet connection.

Web page A set of information on the WWW that may include one or more links to other Web pages.

WAN (wide area network) A computer network that covers a large geographical area.

WWW (World Wide Web) A service on the Internet that presents information in an organized and accessible format and often includes multimedia.

Getting Connected to the Internet

OBJECTIVES

When you have completed this tutorial, you should be able to:

- List each of the components you need to get connected to the Internet

- Explain how a modem functions

- Categorize the various types of Internet accounts available through an Internet Service Provider

- Explain how information travels over the Internet

- Identify the role of protocols in Internet communications

- Compare and contrast the roles of Transmission Control Protocol and Internet Protocol (TCP/IP) in Internet communications

- Describe the function of Internet Protocol (IP) addresses and domain names

Rick Anderson, owner of Cherry Creek Advertising Agency, has seen the nature of his business change dramatically over the last two years due to the emergence of the Internet as a viable medium for presenting marketing information. By incorporating the Internet into his clients' marketing campaigns, he has dramatically increased business and his company has created several award-winning Web sites.

Rick just received a phone call from a long-time customer, Sundance Bookstores. Sundance's six stores located throughout Arizona offer a wide variety of books and stationary supplies. Sundance markets its products through such conventional channels as mail order catalogs and space advertisements. However, their new marketing director, Deborah Yardley, wants to explore the Internet as a strategy to meet the company's marketing and advertising goals.

Rick outlines a general marketing plan that has Sundance using the Internet for such activities as responding to customer e-mail inquiries to generating sales from a comprehensive Web site. For additional exposure, Rick proposes that Sundance consider offering Internet access to customers who don't have Internet access through their home, school, or business.

Although Deborah is excited about Rick's proposal, she needs to understand how the Internet works before she commits Sundance's time and monetary resources to this marketing venture.

In this tutorial you will learn how to access the Internet. First, you will look at the specific tools and procedures required to connect to the Internet. Next, you will learn about protocols and how the Internet relies upon them for seamless connectivity. You will learn about addressing and naming conventions used on the Internet, and finally, you will learn some troubleshooting techniques to use if you have difficulty accessing the Internet.

SESSION 2.1

In this session you will learn what elements you need to connect your computer to the Internet. Session 2.1 presents an overview of the basic elements required and helps you understand some terms used to describe the process of getting online.

Computer System Requirements

What are the computer requirements needed to connect to the Internet?

At a minimum, to access the Internet you will need a 386 or later compatible computer running Windows 95, Windows 3.x, Windows NT, or a system running OS2, UNIX, or Macintosh System 7.x. Although you can use an older system to view text-based information on the Internet, newer systems, such as a 486 computer or one that runs from a Pentium chip, more fully support the memory and speed requirements of a graphical user interface, or GUI, such as Netscape.

A minimum of 8MB of memory and at least 20MB of free disk space is recommended for programs to run and also to allow for disk caching. **Disk caching** is your computer's ability to use available disk space as it would additional memory to store frequently accessed data and program instructions. Disk caching allows your computer to run more quickly and efficiently.

The Modem

What type of modem do I need to connect to the Internet?

A **modem** (MOdulator/DEModulator) is a piece of hardware that translates information between your computer and the telephone system. The computer and telephone system do not use the same communication parameters, or settings. Digital computers communicate with distinct on and off electrical signals. They use 0s and 1s to represent electrical signals as data. The analog phone system communicates with continuously varying data expressed as electromagnetic waves that vary based on such factors as pitch and volume. The modem's job is to make sure that the digital and analog methods of transmitting are compatible.

Modulating is when the modem translates digital computer information into the format the phone line understands. When information is sent from the phone line back to the computer, the modem restructures the signal into digital mode. This is called **demodulating**. Figure 2-2 shows how modems work.

Figure 2-2 ◀
How modems
work

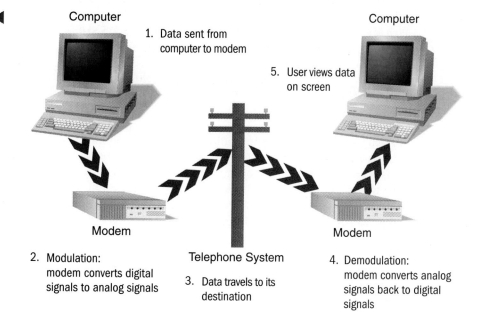

Computer

1. Data sent from computer to modem

5. User views data on screen

Computer

2. Modulation: modem converts digital signals to analog signals

Telephone System

3. Data travels to its destination

4. Demodulation: modem converts analog signals back to digital signals

Modem

Modem

The two basic types of modems are internal and external. **Internal modems** are installed on a card that fits inside the computer. They are slightly less expensive than **external modems**, which attach to your computer from the outside through a serial connection port and cable. Because the features and functions of both types of modems are equivalent, which modem a user chooses is usually a matter of preference. Internal modems do not take extra space on your desktop, and they utilize the computer's power supply. External modems are self-contained, which makes them easier to transfer between different computers. They have a separate power supply, and their display lights let you visually monitor the status of your online connection.

Whether you use an internal modem or an external modem, one of its most important features is speed. As the types of information being transferred over the Internet have evolved from strictly text-based to incorporating a variety of multimedia features, such as graphics and sound, faster modems have become more desirable. The more complex the information, the longer the transfer takes. For example, a page of text can usually be transferred to your computer in about a second, whereas transferring a full-screen black-and-white graphic can take ten seconds or longer. If a full-screen graphic is in color or of photographic quality, it can take a minute or more to appear on your computer screen.

Modem speeds are measured by **baud rate**, which refers to the number of times per second that the transferring signals' state can change. The higher a modem's baud rate, the faster the data transfer. The 14.4 kbps (kilobits per second) modem was the standard used during the early 1990s. As modem prices began dropping in the mid 1990s, the 28.8 kbps modem became more popular due to its increased speed and affordability. Faster 33.6 kbps modems are increasingly common, as many modem manufacturers provide easy upgrade capabilities built in to existing 28.8 models.

Two other important modem features are built-in error correction and data compression capabilities. The newer modems sold on the market today typically include both of these features. Static noise on the phone line is often the source of erroneous data transfer. This line noise can cause data to be garbled or dropped in transit. The error correction function checks information as it passes through the modem. Error correction, if present on both the sending and receiving modems, catches and corrects problems. Although

Baud, named after the 19th century French inventor Baudot, originally referred to the speed at which a telegrapher could send Morse code.

The speed of your modem is only one factor determining the speed at which you can send or receive data online.

The International Telecommunications Union is responsible for setting and developing international data communications standards.

not totally foolproof, error correction ensures almost 100% accuracy as data travels through the connection. High speed modems with data compression compress average text files to about half their original size. Compressing data decreases the modem time needed to transfer the information, and thus increases the speed with which your modem communicates. Data compression algorithms, which are mathematical and logical procedures, find redundancies in data files and then decrease the storage space needed by substituting a few characters for many, wherever repetition occurs. Some data files, such as spreadsheets and databases, can be compressed to a quarter of their original size.

The Phone Line

How is a phone line important to my Internet connection?

Telephone lines carry information from your computer to the Internet and from the Internet back to your computer. To connect to the Internet, your modem must be internally installed or externally attached to your computer, and then your modem must be connected to a telephone line. The telephone line lets you establish an Internet connection via your modem. When sending and receiving, modems translate digital signals to analog signals; they can then send data through the telephone lines. If you use your telephone line for online activities, your phone line will be in use just as if you were making a telephone call. Callers will receive a busy signal or be routed to voice mail if appropriate.

Integrated Services Digital Network (ISDN) is a communications method for telephone systems that use ordinary phone lines and special modems to transmit digital instead of analog signals. Because ISDN eliminates the need to translate signals from digital to analog and back again, its connection speed is much faster. ISDN lines, which cost a bit more than regular phone lines, offer increased speed ranging from 64 kbps to 128 kbps, up to four times faster than a 28.8 kbps modem. The greater bandwidth lets you integrate voice, data, and video transmissions simultaneously over a single phone line. **Bandwidth** is the speed and amount of data that can flow through the online connection. ISDN also allows you to receive incoming phone calls while you're connected to the Internet without losing your online connection.

An Internet Service Provider

What else do I need besides a modem and a phone line to connect to the Internet?

As a student, you'll probably access the Internet using either your own computer or one at your educational institution. You may have even been assigned an Internet account and password when you registered for classes. Many colleges and universities offer Internet access in dorm rooms or dial-up capabilities from your home. For example, the Internet is used increasingly for such activities as class registration and course outline distribution, as well as for general communication among students and faculty.

Business users may find that their companies are already on the Internet through their technical or marketing departments. In addition, many public libraries offer free access to online services. Other places that offer connections to the Internet include local computer user's groups, as well as local and national professional societies.

You can find a comprehensive list of Internet Service Providers at the World Wide Web address http://thelist.com.

If you determine that you don't have access to the Internet through one of these arrangements, you need an account with an Internet Service Provider to access the Internet. An **Internet Service Provider** (ISP) is a company that sells telephone access to the Net. This type of access is also known as dial-up or remote access. There are different types of accounts depending on the level of access a user wants. For example, a salesperson who uses a laptop computer to communicate with company headquarters while traveling may only need access to e-mail, while another user may want access to additional services such as Telnet and IRC.

Most ISPs supply you with communication connectivity software that lets you use their service to access the Internet. This software usually comes on a disk that you install on your computer and then configure to access the Internet. Some ISPs supply self-configuring communications software. The first time you run the software, it examines your computer system and automatically selects the appropriate software settings. Your ISP provides you with an account and password for one of its host computers. You then use your personal computer and modem to access this host computer to gain overall access to the Internet.

ISPs have a limited number of modems to receive incoming requests to access the Internet. When you dial up and connect to the Internet, one of the modems accepts your call and attaches you to the network. The busy signal you may sometimes receive indicates other users are currently using all of the modems. Some ISPs enforce an idle time limitation: if the current user has not actively used the modem connection for a certain amount of time, other users can gain access. ISP equipment checks your Internet connection every set amount of minutes. If it finds idle time or no activity taking place, it may automatically log off your connection. This ensures that other users have a chance to access the Internet. For example, a user online at work may forget to log off from her Internet connection before going to lunch. Because her connection is inactive for a long time period, her session terminates automatically. This lets another user access the modem she was using, but left idle.

Figure 2-3 illustrates a typical Internet dial-up session. First you turn on your computer and modem. Your communications software lets you dial your ISP's host computer. When your modem and that of the ISP connect, the ISP host computer asks for an account name and password. This log-on process formally identifies you to the host computer as an authorized access network user. The host computer verifies your account name and password and welcomes you to the Internet. When you finish using the Internet, you log off from the host computer and exit your communications software. Your connection to the host computer is terminated and your modem is disconnected.

Figure 2-3 ◀
Typical
dial-up
session

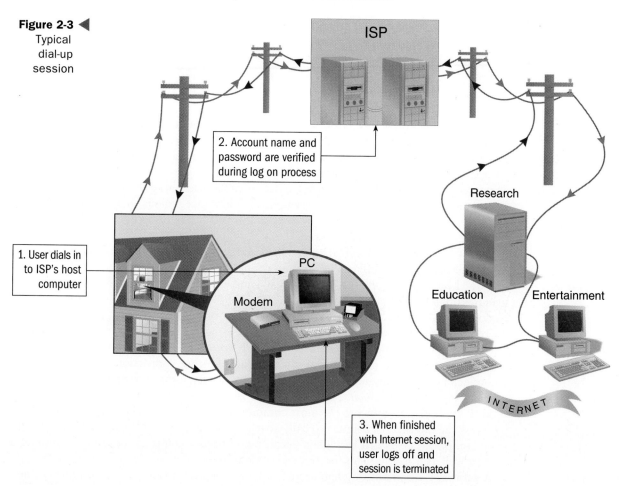

ISP

2. Account name and password are verified during log on process

Research

1. User dials in to ISP's host computer

PC

Modem

Education

Entertainment

INTERNET

3. When finished with Internet session, user logs off and session is terminated

ISP Account Types

What types of ISP accounts are available?

Four different account types are available through an ISP for various levels of Internet access. Hardware and software requirements, as well as costs, differ depending on which account a user chooses. A **shell account** is the most basic entry-level connection account. Using a shell account, your computer emulates a terminal connected to a host computer on the Internet. A **terminal** is a device that has no central processing unit, but rather is restricted to interacting with another computer. The host computer performs all computing and internal processing activities, and a UNIX computer operating system command prompt or menu system completes most navigation. The menu system is actually an application designed to assist users with the UNIX operating system. Instead of typing UNIX commands or learning a new operating system, you move around the Internet using menu options you select by typing a number or letter. Figure 2-4 shows an example of a shell account interface.

Figure 2-4 ◀
Shell account using text-based, menu-driven interface

selections are made by typing menu letter or selecting with arrow keys, then pressing Enter

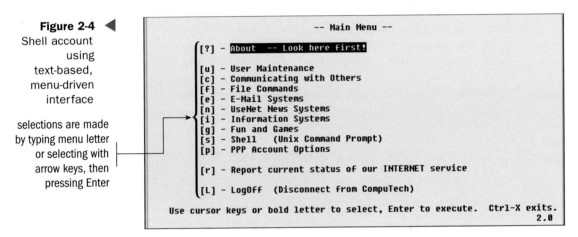

```
                            -- Main Menu --

            [?] - About   -- Look here first!

            [u] - User Maintenance
            [c] - Communicating with Others
            [f] - File Commands
            [e] - E-Mail Systems
            [n] - UseNet News Systems
            [i] - Information Systems
            [g] - Fun and Games
            [s] - Shell   (Unix Command Prompt)
            [p] - PPP Account Options

            [r] - Report current status of our INTERNET service

            [L] - LogOff (Disconnect from CompuTech)

     Use cursor keys or bold letter to select, Enter to execute.  Ctrl-X exits.
                                                                       2.0
```

You can access most Internet services with a shell account; however, its main drawback is that it does not utilize a GUI. For example, instead of using a GUI to view a graphic, such as an organizational chart, you have to download the graphic and view it separately using an appropriate application. **Downloading** is the process of receiving a file that another computer sends via modem. Windows and Macintosh users accustomed to using a mouse to point and click often find working with a shell interface tedious. A shell account's main advantage is its price—about $10 per month for 100 hours of access, significantly lower than its graphical-oriented competitors.

Serial Line Interface Protocol (SLIP) and **Point to Point Protocol (PPP)** accounts are a step up from shell accounts. A SLIP or PPP account connects your computer directly to the Internet. You don't have to navigate the Internet by logging on to a host computer and issuing commands from a UNIX shell prompt. Both SLIP and PPP accounts utilize a GUI for easy navigation of the Internet. In addition, you can use SLIP or PPP to multitask, or perform many operations simultaneously, such as checking your e-mail while downloading a course outline. The main difference between SLIP and PPP accounts is that the latter is designed to check and resend any data erroneously translated during connection. Although a SLIP account can often communicate information slightly faster, it may not be as reliable as a PPP account. Figure 2-5 shows an example of a PPP account.

SLIP and PPP accounts are the most common ways for individuals or small businesses to access the Internet. Accounts typically cost $20 per month for 100 hours of access. Up-front equipment costs can be higher, because you need a computer capable of running a GUI as well as a fast modem for quick downloading.

A **gateway** is a computer system or interface that connects incompatible programs or networks so that data transfer can occur. Commercial online services such as CompuServe, America Online, Microsoft Network, or Prodigy offer gateway access to the Internet. These large online services generally have central systems that store data in huge mainframe computers as opposed to thousands of computers networked worldwide. Figure 2-6 lists some more popular commercial online services.

Figure 2-5 ◀
PPP account

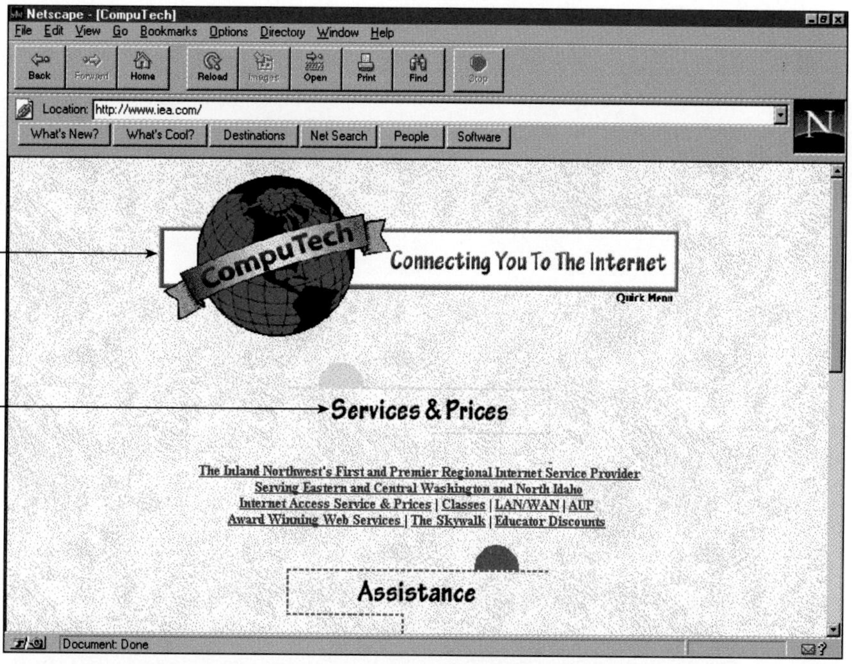

selections are made
by clicking graphics
or text

Figure 2-6 ◀
Popular ISPs

Service Provider	For Information Call	Internet URL	Date Established
America Online	1-800-827-6364	http://www.aol.com	1985
CompuServe	1-800-848-8990	http://www.compuserve.com	1979
Delphi	1-800-695-4005	http://www.delphi.com	1992
Earthlink	1-800-395-8425	http://www.earthlink.net	1994
IBM Global Network	1-800-775-5808	http://www.ibm.com	1995
Microsoft Network	1-800-386-5550	http://www.msn.com	1995
Prodigy	1-800-776-3449	http://www.prodigy.com	1990
The WELL	1-415-332-9200	http://www.well.com	1985

Online services require users to open an account with them, or subscribe to their service. Most offer a free startup kit, which contains disks with the communication software, a user manual, a temporary user account identification and password, and some initial free online time. After installing the communications software and specifying a local telephone access number, you log on to the remote system and give the service your subscription and billing information. After subscribing to a service, you are generally charged a monthly fee of about $15 for 20 hours of access and an extra $2 per hour charge for additional use. Drawbacks to a gateway connection include limited access to some Internet services. For example, standard packages do not always include costs for accessing the Internet and may limit, or not offer, access to Telnet or FTP services. Commercial gateways' advantages include using a GUI to find and view information, as well as national service so that you can access your account from many different locations. Gateways are a very popular method for accessing the Internet; their free startup kits are readily available in computer stores and frequently packaged in magazines. Figure 2-7 shows an example of a gateway account.

Figure 2-7 ◀
Gateway
account with
America Online

most gateway
services, such as
America Online, offer
use of a GUI

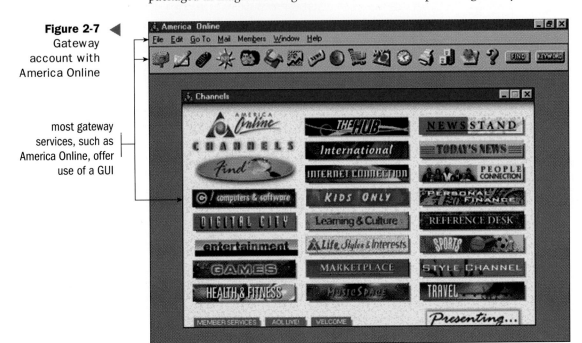

With a full-time **dedicated connection** account, your computer or your local area network (LAN) can be hooked up to the Internet twenty-four hours a day. This type of connection offers faster Internet connectivity than the standard modem and phone line, with common access speeds of 56 kbps to 1.544 mbps (mega bits per second). The 1.544 mbps connection, commonly called a **T1 connection,** is approximately forty-eight times faster than a 28.8 kbps modem. Users with a full-time connection simply launch the Internet program they want to use, such as Netscape, to immediately access the Internet, rather than using a modem to dial up to the Internet. This type of connection benefits organizations with multiple users who depend on the Internet for routine day-to-day business, such as e-mail communications with remote offices and clients, research, or transferring information and files between distant locations. For instance, a law firm with several lawyers and legal assistants may require fast and easy access to the Internet to research current laws or past litigation. Other organizations that require multiple-user Internet access from a single location, such as colleges and universities, benefit from full-time connections as well.

Full-time dedicated connections offer the most flexibility, because the user determines how fast he wants his connection to be. However, complicated hardware and software used to connect to the Internet sometimes costs several hundred to several thousands of dollars. Depending on the bandwidth an organization uses, Internet connection access rates vary but can easily costs hundreds of dollars per month. A 56 kbps full-time connection to the Internet typically costs from $200 to $300 per month.

If a user's entire LAN is placed on the Internet, it should be secured by some type of firewall. A **firewall** combines software and/or hardware to filter the types of activities and services that are allowed on a network. Employers sometimes use firewalls to prevent employees from using the Internet for personal use by locking access to certain Internet sites. The firewall also protects the LAN from incoming traffic. For instance, a company may allow Internet users to browse their Web site but not employee personnel records.

In 1969, an insurance company in Columbus, Ohio, purchased a larger and faster mainframe computer than it needed. It leased the computer's excess capacity to other companies. In 1979, this venture evolved into the online service CompuServe, the first commercial online service. CompuServe currently has over five million subscribers worldwide.

America Online (AOL) is the fastest growing commercial online service, with over six million subscribers worldwide. Prodigy was established as a joint venture between IBM and Sears Roebuck & Co. Microsoft Network (MSN) is the newest giant in the commercial information service industry. Windows 95 includes software to access MSN.

Additional Components

Are there any other components I can use to access the Internet?

Although not necessary for connection, some hardware and software can enhance the quality, level, and enjoyment of information that you view on the Internet. **Multimedia** presents information using animation, sound, graphics, and text. To view this type of information over the Internet, your computer needs special hardware and software. One common enhancement is an **audio/sound card**, a piece of hardware installed in your computer that allows audio capability. A sound card takes information, such as a file containing music, processes it, and then outputs it to a set of speakers either attached or built in to your computer. A sound card usually has additional capability to use external devices such as a microphone or a musical keyboard for recording audio or music. A **multimedia kit** includes a wide range of enhancements such as a sound card and speakers, along with the specialized software you need to run them. A standard multimedia kit ranges from $100 to $200.

Quick Check

1. A _____ computer or better is recommended for viewing multimedia items on the Internet.

2. The modem translates computer _____ signals into telephone _____ signals and vice versa.

3. ISDN allows telephone systems to use ordinary phone lines and special modems to transmit _____ instead of _____ signals.

4. A shell account on the Internet is text-based; a SLIP or PPP account is _____.

5. What type of access to the Internet do commercial online services provide?

6. An organization that needs its LAN on the Internet twenty-four hours a day may want to consider a _____ connection to the Internet.

7. A _____ screens a LAN from certain Internet activities.

SESSION 2.2

Information travels through many networks and uses various telecommunication methods to reach its final destination on the Internet. In this session we will take a look at how data is routed over the Internet.

Internet Communication

How is information distributed via the Internet?

You may want to think of information sent over the Internet as similar to a letter placed in an envelope ready to be mailed. Each piece of information sent over the Internet requires an address, just as an envelope containing a letter being sent to a friend requires his or her address. The Internet uses addresses to track the origin and destination of every piece of information that travels across the network.

The information within one datagram is usually between approximately one and 1,500 characters long.

An "envelope" full of information sent via the Internet may be split into several smaller envelopes, or datagrams. A **datagram** is the basic unit of information that passes across the Internet. Each envelope, or datagram, contains both data and header information. The datagram's **header** portion provides each network or computer it passes through with several important pieces of information, including origin and destination addresses, size of the datagram, and a sequential number. The **sequence number** is used to reassemble the datagrams in correct order at their final destination, because each datagram may travel a different path or take a different amount of time to reach its destination. Figure 2-8 shows a datagram's structure.

Figure 2-8 ◀
Structure of a datagram

IP addresses indicate origin and destination of sender and recipient, respectively

datagram size information

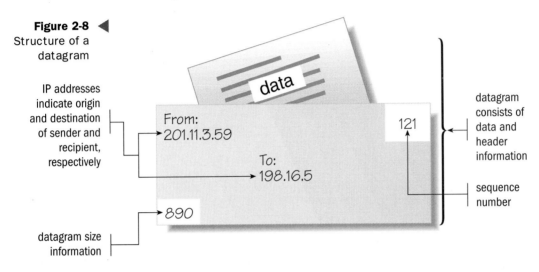

datagram consists of data and header information

sequence number

Cables, telephone lines, and other transmission medias link computers together on the Internet. Special pieces of hardware called **routers** also interconnect the networks. Routers are responsible for physically moving datagrams of information from one Internet location to another. In determining how to route envelopes containing e-mail, they function much like postal substations. When letters are sent to a location, the local post office sends the envelope to a substation; the substation then sends it to the next substation, and so forth, until it reaches its final destination. Similarly, with the assistance of protocols, a router receives a datagram, checks its address information, determines the best subsequent path for the datagram to take, and then sends the information to a new router along with new header information that corresponds to its new destination. (Protocols are discussed in more detail in the next section.) This process continues until the datagram reaches its intended address. The process of passing datagrams from one computer to another is called **routing**.

If the router encounters a problem with forwarding the datagram, it works with Internet Protocol (IP) to select and send the datagram to a different router. Problems may include a network overloaded with too many datagrams, or hardware or software problems putting the receiving network out of service. At their final destination, the datagrams come together and are reassembled in the original envelope for the recipient. Transmission of datagrams over the Internet is incredibly fast. For example, sending an e-mail message from Seattle to New York City can take seconds. Figure 2-9 illustrates how datagrams travel over the Internet.

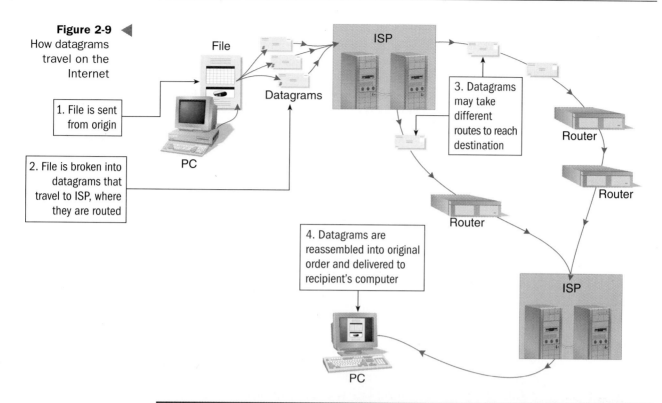

Figure 2-9
How datagrams travel on the Internet

1. File is sent from origin

2. File is broken into datagrams that travel to ISP, where they are routed

3. Datagrams may take different routes to reach destination

4. Datagrams are reassembled into original order and delivered to recipient's computer

Protocols

What is the significance of protocols?

As you recall from Tutorial 1, ARPANet researchers began experimenting with new communication protocols to provide more stable and reliable network communications. **Protocols** are a formal set of rules and standards that enable systems connected to the Internet to communicate with one another. The most prominent protocols, Transmission Control Protocol (TCP) and Internet Protocol (IP), work together as the foundation for sending datagrams across networks and ensuring reliable transmission of information. Other protocols have very specific functions and work closely with TCP/IP to provide diverse services on the Net. Later tutorials discuss additional protocols, including e-mail, Telnet, and FTP, in more detail. Together, all the prototcols are called the **TCP/IP protocol suite**. All computers that communicate with other hosts on the Internet must support TCP/IP.

Transmission Control Protocol (TCP)

Why is Transmission Control Protocol important to the Internet?

Transmission Control Protocol (TCP) is responsible for the end-to-end reliable communications for transmitting datagrams across Internet networks. TCP breaks up, and subsequently numbers, information sent over the Internet into datagrams. TCPs at both ends of a network determine a datagram's size parameters, depending on the capabilities of the network, or networks, it intends to travel through. Some networks can receive larger datagrams than others. TCP also places detailed information in the datagram's header. This information helps TCP track the number of datagrams being sent, determine their reassembly at their destinations, and decide if a datagram needs to be re-sent due to a transmission error. Datagrams may take different routes and arrive at their final destinations at different times. For example, if you sent two letters to a friend on subsequent days, you have no guarantee that the letters will travel the same route to arrive at their destination or that they will arrive in the order that you sent them. This is true for Internet information as well. When data arrives at its final destination, TCP re-sequences out-of-order datagrams and also discards duplicate datagrams that may have been transmitted.

A major TCP function is to error-check datagrams. If a datagram is missing or is damaged, the complete set of datagrams is resubmitted. TCP's recovery capability ensures that the information we receive over the Internet is complete. TCP recognizes even one sentence or punctuation mark inadvertently omitted during transmission.

To complete its error-checking responsibilities, TCP uses a technique called checksum. A **checksum** is a number calculated by summing up all bytes in a datagram. A **byte**, the basic unit of measurement for computer storage, usually consists of one data character, such as a single letter or number. For instance, when a datagram arrives at its destination, the receiving TCP calculates its checksum by comparing it to the one the sending TCP calculated. If the numbers don't match, an error has most likely occurred in transmission. The receiving TCP then discards the datagram and asks the sending TCP for another. In addition, the sending and receiving TCPs always acknowledge receipt of information to ensure datagrams were received and processed correctly. If the sending TCP doesn't receive an acknowledgment within a certain time period, it resends the datagram.

The Internet Protocol (IP)

How is the Internet Protocol important to the Internet?

The **Internet Protocol** (IP) provides addressing information needed to move datagrams across Internet networks. IP works in conjunction with TCP to perform a critical routing task; it ensures that all information traveling over the Internet reaches its final destination using the fastest and most productive route. IP is responsible for addressing a datagram and ensuring that routers know what to do with the datagram when it arrives. When sending datagrams to the next router, IP determines the datagram's destination address, how to get it to its next router destination, and then sends it along. As opposed to TCP, IP is not responsible for the accuracy of the information it transmits. IP may also break a datagram into smaller datagrams if needed, depending on the structure of the networks along the transmission route.

The most important piece of information that IP uses is the receiving and sending address for each datagram. One of the most common ways IP tracks this information is to add a header to the datagram. You might think of it as putting the TCP envelope into another envelope. IP places three main pieces of information in this header. First, it lists the origin and destination addresses. Second, it lists protocol information that tells the receiving system to recognize that TCP is the communication protocol. IP makes sure that all of the computers the datagram passes through use a standard set of protocols. Third, it adds its own checksum to help ensure accurate transmission. This checksum makes sure that the IP header is intact, so that the datagram goes to the right destination.

At first, it may seem that TCP does most of the work by actually taking information, separating it into manageable parts, assigning sequence numbers, and ensuring the packet's quality and completeness. However, IP's assigned routing task plays just as important a role in data transmission. Often IP has to overcome a number of obstacles to send datagrams of information across multiple networks. For example, datagrams often travel through many different types of computers and networks, in addition to utilizing various transmission methods. Datagrams commonly pass through at least a dozen different networks before reaching their final destination. A datagram's typical journey may begin on your computer, transfer to a phone line, travel through a fiber-optic cable to a satellite and then back before reaching the intended recipient's computer. IP provides the basis for almost all Internet communication. It lets information travel between multiple networks to its final destination and allows computers to communicate with one another.

Various other protocols that make up the TCP/IP protocol suite enable a wide range of computers containing many hardware and software programs to participate on the Internet. Some protocols handle the simplest task, such as seeing if a particular user is logged on to his or her computer; others, like the Internet Control Message Protocol, handle intricate functions, such as providing feedback about problems in the communication environment to the IP. All these protocols work together to make the Internet more user friendly and able to offer users a wide variety of services.

Understanding Internet Addresses

How is each computer uniquely identified on the Internet?

When you send a letter to someone through the postal system, you must know more than just that person's name. The Internet also uses an addressing system to identify computers and to route information across hosts' computers. An **Internet Protocol address**, or **IP address**, is an assigned set of hierarchical numbers used to identify Internet hosts. The protocols that govern Internet information exchange, such as TCP and IP, use these numbers to ensure that information reaches the correct destination.

Each IP address commonly has four sets of numbers, each lower than 256. These number sets each represent a byte and are separated by a period, which is pronounced 'dot'. The IP address 198.17.231.11 would be pronounced, "1 9 8 dot 1 7 dot 2 3 1 dot 1 1." The unique number consists of a network identification number, which is always the same for every network host, and a host number, which is always unique for each network host. IP addresses are assigned to each computer by appending a unique host number to the network number. If you sign up for an Internet account with an ISP, you may be given an IP address to enter into your communications software settings. Some services automatically assign the IP address each time you log on to the service.

The Internet Network Information Center consortium, known as the **Internic**, assigns and tracks IP addresses. The Internic generally assigns only a portion of the IP address, the network identification number. The network administrator assigns the remaining portions of the IP address for whatever hosts or network interfaces they need to identify on the Internet. The first number set of an IP address, which represents a byte, determines the network's class. Common IP addresses are divided into Class A, Class B, and Class C network numbers. Class A networks reflect the network identification number set from 1 to 127. These IP addresses are reserved for major service providers and Internet participants such as AT&T. Class B networks are in the network identification number set from 128 to 191. Large network organizations such as campus-wide systems for universities and larger businesses are assigned these addresses. Class C addresses are in the network identification number set from 192 to 223. These IP addresses are typical for small networks. Class D and Class E IP addresses above 223 are used for specific applications such as broadcast messaging and are reserved for future use. Figure 2-10 shows the structure of a typical IP address.

The four-byte IP addressing scheme is quickly running out of addresses. One solution—a sixteen-byte addressing scheme that would create adequate address space to accommodate Internet growth—would require significant software and hardware changes on networks throughout the Internet.

Figure 2-10 ◀
Structure of an
IP address

IP addresses consist of up to four sets of numbers, each representing a byte

each byte is separated by a period, pronounced as a "dot"

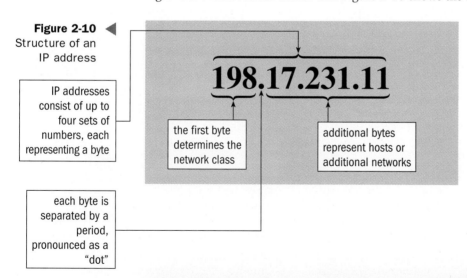

198.17.231.11

the first byte determines the network class

additional bytes represent hosts or additional networks

Domain Name Services

How can I possibly remember all those IP address numbers when using the Internet?

Many of us more easily remember a name, rather than a series of numbers. The Domain Name System was developed to correlate numeric IP addresses to unique names, known as **domain names**. The **Domain Name System** (DNS) is a method of concisely and consistently administering domain names. A domain name consists of logical sections, much like a mailing address, except that a period separates each section of the address. Each separate section is known as a **domain**. Domain names reflect a hierarchy of groups that are responsible for the computers or networks underneath them, as Figure 2-11 shows. There can be any number of domains within a domain name, but you rarely see more than four or five.

Figure 2-11 ◀
Domain
hierarchy

the edu domain
contains all Internet
hosts in U.S.
educational
institutions

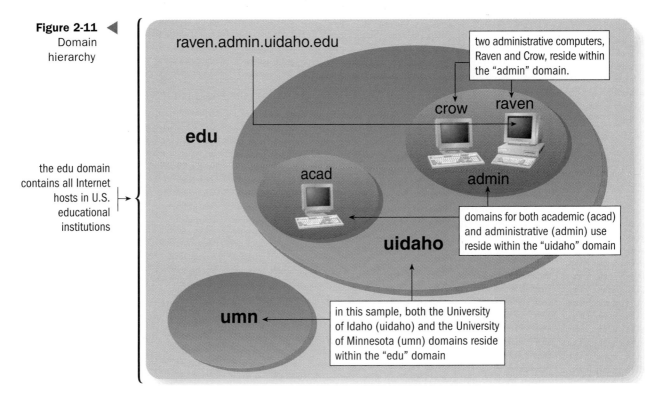

Domain names often indicate a lot about the network a user is attaching to. Among other things, they tell you a system's name, its location, and the type of organization it belongs to. In Figure 2-11, the domain name "raven.admin.uidaho.edu" represents a host named "raven," which is in the "admin" domain used for computers doing administrative tasks at the University of Idaho, which uses the "uidaho" domain. The University of Idaho is part of the larger "edu" domain, which contains Internet hosts in U.S. educational institutions. As you read the domain name from left to right, each domain is larger than the previous one. The final domain is the top-level or trailing domain. It tells you what category or kind of organization you are accessing. The top-level domains group computers on the Internet into the broad categories shown in Figure 2-12. Each country also has its own domain level. Figure 2-13 lists some domains for specific countries.

Figure 2-12 ◀
Top-level
domains

Domain	Category	Domain Name Sample	Description
com	Commercial and industrial organizations	novell.com	Novell, Incorporated
edu	Educational institutions	uidaho.edu	University of Idaho
gov	Governmental organizations	sba.gov	Small Business Administration
mil	Military organizations	navy.mil	U.S. Navy
org	Not for profit organizations	greenpeace.org	Greenpeace International
net	Network services and resources	internic.net	Network Solutions, Inc.

Figure 2-13 ◀
Country
domains

Country	Top-level domain
Australia	AU
Brazil	BR
Denmark	DK
Germany	DE
Israel	IL
Japan	JP
Mexico	MX
Saudi Arabia	SA
South Africa	ZA
United Kingdom	UK
United States	US

The DNS is a hierarchical, distributed method of organizing addresses on the Internet with the individual domains responsible for tracking host names within its domain. In the example shown in Figure 2-11, an "admin" server is responsible for assigning and tracking host IP addresses in the "admin" domain. Special DNS software runs on an Internet server and converts the multi-part domain names to IP addresses that the rest of the Internet can use. This server provides the tracking information necessary to get from the domain name to the actual IP address. This process is called **resolving** the name and address. A DNS advantage is that it is decentralized: it eliminates dependence on a centrally maintained file to track correlating host names to IP addresses. In the Internet's early days, all this information was kept in one main information file, which was routinely distributed to every computer on the network. As the Internet grew, keeping track of all hosts being added to the network was impossible; thus DNS grew from a need to manage IP addresses and names more efficiently.

Many organizations try to procure domain names that include some aspect of their organization. Using a company's name within its domain name is the most popular method of supplying name recognition. For example, the domain names "toyota.com" and "mcdonalds.com" identify the Toyota and McDonald's corporations. Other naming conventions include the type of industry associated with an organization or the product or service it provides, such as "movies.com," "stock-quotes.com," or "girlscouts.org." Figure 2-14 shows how dramatically the number of organizations registering domain names has grown.

Figure 2-14 ◀
DNS growth

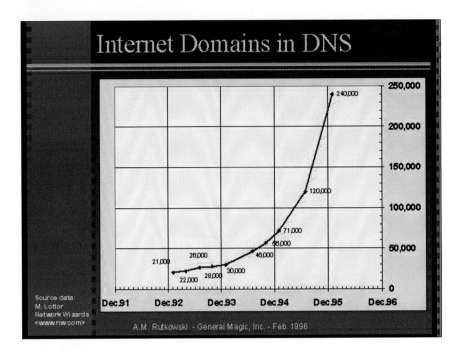

The domain system is not limited to designating IP and domain name addresses. It also stores different types of information about the domain including such items as the actual computer type, a list of services available, information about users, or mailing lists. The domain system is particularly important for handling e-mail. For example, entries in the DNS tell what computer handles mail for a given name or specifies where an individual is to receive mail.

Quick Check

1. Name three important pieces of information contained in the datagram header.

2. True or False: Information can take different routes while traveling to its Internet destination.

3. What is the function of a router in transferring information on the Internet?

4. What are the three main functions of TCP?

5. What are the main functions of IP?

6. True or False: The TCP/IP protocol suite is made up of two protocols.

7. True or False: Each host computer on the Internet must have a unique IP address.

8. What system correlates IP addresses to names?

SESSION	User **Focus:** Troubleshooting Hints and Tips
2.3	*There are many different methods of connecting to the Internet, depending on the type of hardware and software that you have, as well as the account that you choose. The information in this section assists you in solving common challenges and problems you may experience using an online service.*

Difficulty Connecting to Your Internet Account

Why am I having problems accessing the Internet?

If you just set up your account, it may not be activated yet. It often takes a day or two for a new account to get into the system. Administrative tasks need to be taken care of before your account can be created and activated. You may want to try again in a few hours or on the next day.

You may be incorrectly typing your account name and password in all caps or all low-ercase letters, or adding improper spaces. Capital and lowercase letters often indicate different commands to different types of computers and computer operating systems. Your ISP host may be case sensitive, or responsive to the difference between uppercase and lowercase letters. Check with your ISP to see if it requires all caps or lowercase, and confirm the exact spelling of your account name and password.

Most local ISPs schedule maintenance for their systems. This gives them the opportunity to perform such tasks as upgrading their hardware or software. The system may be unavailable during this time frame, which can range from half an hour to half a day. Check with your ISP to see if they have set aside a standard time for maintenance.

A phone line that won't dial usually indicates a problem between your communications software and your computer or modem. Your software may try to communicate with your modem at incompatible speeds or through a port on your computer other than where your modem is attached. Your software may "think" that your modem is at a different location than it actually is. Most modems attach to one of two communication ports on a personal computer. If one doesn't seem to work, try attaching the modem to the other port. You may also want to plug a regular phone into your phone jack to make sure that you get a dial tone. If you don't hear a dial tone, you may need to call your phone company, as your wiring may be faulty, or your phone line may be out of service.

If your modem is working but you receive no answer on the other end, check to make sure you dialed the correct phone number or try an alternative number. If the remote system does not answer your call, it may be temporarily out of service, or "down," or the modem at your provider's end may be faulty. If you continue to have trouble, contact your ISP so that the problem can be fixed.

Sometimes seemingly large problems have simple causes, such as the modem not being turned on or the cable not being plugged in securely. If you recently made adjustments to your software or hardware or are working at another person's site, the problems may be related to these factors.

Disconnection from the Internet

Why is my Internet connection occasionally terminated?

Another person may pick up the phone line you are using to access the Internet and disconnect you. You can avoid this by making other people aware that you are using the phone line for online purposes. If you have call-waiting service on your phone line, call your phone company to find out how to disable it temporarily when you are on the Internet.

Sometimes the problem may be with your modem. Different modems handle Internet connectivity better than others. You may need to send a series of special initialization codes to your modem to improve its performance while it's connected to the Internet. If you are unfamiliar with initialization codes, contact your ISP for assistance or reference the Internet address http://www.shiva.com.

When talking with a technical support person at your ISP, have this account information at your fingertips: account name, account type, the hardware and software you are using, and specific error messages you have encountered. If possible, sit at the computer during your call so that you can try different solutions the technician may propose. If you must leave a message, try to give as much detail as possible. Don't forget that e-mail is another source for communicating with your ISP.

End Note

How we communicate with others over the Internet will continue to change as technology evolves. As connection costs decline and the transmission quality increases, new protocols will be adopted to facilitate the transparent and smooth flow of information to Internet users. The trend toward convergence will continue as commercial online services and telephone companies as well as cable companies and electrical utilities join forces to help build an interactive future. Watch as the technology develops to provide new ways of communicating, completing research, and gathering information as well as making phone calls, shopping, and watching television—all over the Internet.

Review

1. Below each heading in this tutorial is a question in italics. Look back through the tutorial and answer each question using your own words.

2. Define the following terms:
   a. online
   b. ISDN
   c. multimedia
   d. bandwidth
   e. ISP
   f. datagram
   g. routing

3. What are three differences between a shell, a SLIP, and a PPP account? Explain what type of account best suits your Internet needs.

4. List factors to consider when buying a modem. Explain briefly why each factor is important.

5. Find out if your educational institution has a firewall in place. If so, write approximately two paragraphs describing the firewall's structure and goals. If not, write one page explaining why your institution needs one.

6. Describe, in your own words, protocols' importance to the Internet.

7. Draw a figure depicting how information travels across the Internet from your computer to another computer elsewhere in the world.

8. What do these IP addresses and domain names tell about their organizations?
   a. 198.93.3.1   sony.com
   b. 18.72.0.3   bitsy.mit.edu
   c. 15.255.152.4   hp.com

Projects

1. **Pricing the Elements to Connect to the Internet** There are many options to consider when connecting to the Internet, such as the type of hardware you have or the type of telephone service available in your area. To complete this project, write a one-page report based on information obtained from answering these questions:
   a. Check your local newspaper or a recent computer magazine to locate a current price for both a 28.8 Kbps and a 33.6 Kbps modem. List prices for both internal and external models. What features do the modems have? Does it matter if you use the modem on a Windows system versus a Macintosh? How much does it cost for a modem that will serve an ISDN connection?
   b. Contact your local telephone company. What is the monthly cost for a single phone line? Is there a calling plan for using a phone line to make only outgoing phone calls? Is ISDN service offered in your calling area? If so, how much does it cost to set up the service and what is the monthly fee?

2. **Domain Names** Many organizations are scurrying to register domain names. Domain names provide a logical way for people to find companies and institutions on the Internet. Find out what domain name your educational institution uses. If it uses more than one, explain why. Try to find at least three other domain names that are used in your community. List at least three organizations in your community that qualify for each of the following top-level domains:
   a. edu
   b. com
   c. gov
   d. org
   e. net
   f. mil

3. **Protocols** Many protocols work together to form the TCP/IP protocol suite. Each protocol has a specific job. Using library resources, locate information on the following protocols and briefly describe the role they play on the Internet.
   a. SMTP
   b. NNTP
   c. FTP

4. **OSI Protocol Standards** Over the last several years, the Organization for International Standardization has been working on a new set of protocol standards known as the Open System Interconnect protocol suite (OSI). The U.S. Government mandated that all its computers should be able to communicate with these new protocols. Using library resources, locate information on the new protocol suite. How does it differ from the TCP/IP suite? Is there an advantage to using the new protocols? Do you think there will be problems implementing the new protocols? Write a report of your findings and your general views on implementing the new OSI suite.

5. **BBS** Many users are first introduced to online services through local Bulletin Board Systems (BBS). Generally run by individuals as a hobby, these services are not for profit. They often provide local community information as well as a message center. Using local resources, find out if there are any local BBS in your area. Do they charge an access fee? What type of information is available? What are the minimum hardware and software requirements to access the service? Does the BBS offer access to any Internet services? Write a report summarizing your research. If there are more than one BBS, create a table comparing at least two of the services.

6. **Cable Companies** Cable television companies use wires to carry digital signals into homes. In addition to television, these companies are looking for ways to provide Internet and other services by creating their own networks. They hope to provide services for interactive home shopping, video games, interactive television, and full Internet access. Using library resources and information from your local cable company, determine if special equipment will be needed to access these services. What will the approximate costs be? List two other types of services that may be available through the bandwidth the cable companies provide. Write a brief report of your findings that summarizes your research.

7. **Internet Appliances** Some computer companies are creating low-cost computers made specifically for accessing the Internet. Some attach to your television, whereas others include built-in monitors and modems. Using local resources, locate information regarding at least two of these Internet "appliances." Create a table comparing features and prices of two products. What effect do you think low-cost equipment will have on the Internet? What types of additional features would you like included with the products? Do you think prices are reasonable compared to a computer? Write a summary report on your research findings.

Resources

Albitz & Liu. *DNS and Bind*. Sebastopol, O'Reilly & Associates, Inc. 1992. This book discusses a fundamental building block of the Internet, the distributed host information database responsible for translating names into addresses.

Fraase, M. *The Windows Internet Tour Guide: Cruising the Internet the Easy Way*. Chapel Hill, NC, Ventana Press, 1994. A beginner's guide to the Internet, this book includes a disk for Internet access and some step-by-step instructions on Internet service usage.

Hedrick, C. *Introduction to the Internet Protocols*. Rutgers, NJ: State University of New Jersey, 1987. This introduction to TCP/IP also summarizes major protocols in the TCP/IP protocol suite *(http://www.cis.ohio-state.edu/htbin/rfc/hedrick-intro.html)*.

Hunt, C. *TCP/IP: Network Administration*. Sebastopol, O'Reilly & Associates, Inc., 1992. An excellent book for administrators who are running systems that utilize the TCP/IP protocol suite. It takes a practical approach on how to put your systems on the Internet.

Internet Protocol: DARPA Internet Program Protocol Specification. Arlington, VA: Defense Advanced Research Projects Agency, 1981. The Request for Comment document that specifies the Department of Defense's standard Internet Protocol *(ftp://nic.merit.edu/documents/rfc/rfc0791.txt)*.

The Internet Society Web site. This Web site *(http://info.isoc.org/)* offers detailed information about the society and charts showing usage and growth of the Internet at large.

Introduction to Modems. University of Chicago Campus Stores Technical Note Web site. This Web site *(http://www-ccs.uchicago.edu/technotes/Modems.html#compress)* provides detailed information about how modems work, a comprehensive glossary, explanation of modem features, and a troubleshooting section.

Welcome to the ITU. The International Telecommunications Union Web site *(http://www.itu.ch/index.html)*. Headquartered in Geneva, Switzerland, this international organization is responsible for coordinating, developing, and regulating global telecommunications networks and services.

Glossary

audio/sound card Hardware that allows computers to play and record sound.

bandwidth The speed and amount of data that can flow through an online connection.

baud rate The number of times per second that transferring signals over a communication line change state.

byte The basic unit of measurement for computer storage.

checksum An error-checking technique used in data communications to ensure reliable transmissions.

datagram The basic unit of information passed along the Internet.

dedicated connection A type of Internet connection that offers continuous Internet access to a specific computer or Local Area Network (LAN). Offers faster Internet connectivity than the standard modem and phone line method.

demodulating The process of receiving and transferring analog signals into digital signals.

disk caching The ability of your computer to use RAM to store frequently used data.

domain A category used within the Domain Name System.

domain names Unique names that correlate to IP addresses.

Domain Name System (DNS) A method of administering domain names to correlate to IP addresses, and vice versa, in a consistent and concise manner.

downloading The process of retrieving a file that is sent from another computer via an online communication method.

external modem A modem attached to a computer through an outside serial connection.

firewall Software and/or hardware that filters activity and protects data on a network.

gateway A computer system or interface that connects incompatible programs or networks so that data transfer can occur. Gateway access to the Internet is often achieved through use of a commercial online service.

header A section of the datagram that tells the datagram's size, its sequence number, and the origin and destination IP address.

Integrated Services Digital Network (ISDN) A communications method for telephone systems that uses ordinary phone lines and special modems to transmit digital instead of analog signals.

internal modem A modem that fits inside the computer in an expansion slot.

Internet Protocol (IP) Standard used for providing addressing information needed to move datagrams across Internet networks.

Internet Protocol address (IP address) An assigned set of hierarchical numbers used to identify hosts on the Internet.

Internet Service Provider (ISP) A company that sells access to the Internet.

Internic (Internet Network Information Center) The governing body that assigns and tracks IP addresses.

modem A piece of hardware used to translate information between computers and phone lines.

modulating The process of receiving and transferring digital signals into analog signals.

multimedia The presentation of information using animation, sound, graphics, and text.

multimedia kit Hardware and software that accommodate viewing of multimedia items.

Point to Point Protocol (PPP) A communication standard that allows a computer to be directly connected to the Internet using a GUI.

protocols Formal sets of communication rules and standards.

resolving The process of providing the necessary tracking information to get from the domain name to an actual IP address.

router Equipment responsible for moving datagrams from one Internet location to another.

routing The process of passing datagrams from one computer to another.

sequence number Used to reassemble datagrams at their final destination in correct order.

Serial Line Internet Protocol (SLIP) A communication standard that allows a computer to be directly connected to the Internet using a GUI.

shell account An entry level dial-up Internet account, usually text-based.

terminal A device that is restricted to interacting with another computer, often used with multi-user systems.

Transmission Control Protocol (TCP) The standard that is responsible for reliable end-to-end communications for transmitting datagrams across Internet networks.

TCP/IP Protocol Suite All protocols that operate together to connect systems to the Internet so they communicate with one another.

Using Netscape Navigator to Explore the Internet

The Birdland Bay Clothing Company Learns to Use Netscape

OBJECTIVES

In this tutorial you will learn to:

- Start and exit Netscape Navigator

- Identify the components of both the Netscape window and a Web page

- Navigate the Netscape window

- Use a URL to open a Web site and move among visited Web pages

- Save Web page text and images

- Preview and print a Web page

- Search the Web using various methods

CASE

Birdland Bay Clothing Co.

The Birdland Bay Company (BBC) has enjoyed great success over the last five years. The company sells unique clothing and gift items imported from around the world in its chain of stores throughout the East Coast. Last year, the company expanded its business by creating a mail-order catalog offering some of its most popular items. The catalog helped increase the company's sales by 15%. This year, BBC chose the World Wide Web (WWW) as a sales and marketing tool and is planning to place the catalog online. Shannon Parker, catalog sales manager, will attend a strategic planning session next month and has been asked to provide insight on how the company can leverage the technology to serve a global market. Shannon is responsible for providing information on how BBC can use the WWW to enhance its marketing strategies to attract and keep new customers, and on how successfully BBC's competitors have used the WWW in these areas.

As Shannon's marketing assistant, you research information on the WWW so that Shannon can prepare her report for next month's meeting. She needs some examples of competing Web sites as well as demographic information on the typical Internet user. She also wants an estimate of the number of online catalogs currently on the WWW and is especially interested in knowing if any of the competitor's sites are secure ones. Finally, she wants you to keep your eyes open for particularly innovative and interesting features on other Web sites that you feel would be appropriate for BBC. You use Netscape Navigator to search for the information you need. Because you are unfamiliar with the program, Shannon asks Shantu Bartlett, from the Computer Services Department, to teach you how to use it. Shantu teaches you the software program's functions, explains how to view information on the WWW using Netscape, and shows you how to navigate the WWW.

Using the Tutorials Effectively

These tutorials will help you learn about the Internet. Designed to be used at a computer, each tutorial is divided into sessions. Watch for session headings, such as "Session 3.1" and "Session 3.2." Each session is designed to be completed in about 45 minutes, but take as much time as you need. We recommend taking a break between sessions.

Before you begin, read the following questions and answers. They will help you use the tutorials effectively.

Where do I start?

Each tutorial begins with a case, which sets the scene for the tutorial and gives background information to help you understand what you will do in the tutorial. Read the case before you go to the lab. In the lab, begin with the first session of the tutorial.

How do I know what to do on the computer?

Each session contains steps that you perform on the computer to learn to use the Internet. Read the text that introduces each series of steps. The steps are numbered and set against a colored background. Read each step carefully and completely before you try it.

How do I know if I did the step correctly?

As you work, compare your computer window with the corresponding figure in the tutorial. Don't worry if your window looks somewhat different from the figure. The important parts of the window are labeled in each figure. Check to make sure you see these parts on your window.

What if I make a mistake?

Don't worry about making mistakes—they are part of learning. Paragraphs labeled "**TROUBLE?**" identify common problems and explain how to get back on track. Follow the steps in a "**TROUBLE?**" paragraph *only* if you encounter the problem described. If you run into other problems:

- Carefully consider the current state of your system, the position of the pointer, and any messages in the window.

- Complete the sentence, "Now I want to...." Be specific: you are identifying your goal.

- Develop a plan for accomplishing your goal, and put your plan into action.

How do I use the Reference Windows?

Reference Windows summarize the procedures you learn in tutorial steps. Do not complete the actions the Reference Windows describe when you are working through the tutorial. Instead, refer to the Reference Windows when you work on the assignments at the end of the tutorial.

How can I test my understanding of the material I learned in the tutorial?

At the end of each session, you can answer the Quick Check questions. The answers for the Quick Checks are at the end of the book.

After you complete the entire tutorial, you should complete the Tutorial Assignments. They are carefully structured to help you review what you learned and then apply your knowledge to new situations.

What if I can't remember how to do something?

Refer to the Reference Windows in the tutorials and the Task Reference at the end of the book. The Task Reference summarizes how to accomplish commonly performed tasks.

What are the Interactive Labs, and how should I use them?

Interactive Labs help you review concepts and practice skills that you learn in the tutorial. Lab icons at the beginning of each tutorial and in the margins of the tutorials indicate topics that have corresponding Labs. The Lab Assignments section includes instructions on using each Lab.

Now that you know how to use the tutorials effectively, you are ready to begin.

> **SESSION**
>
> **3.1**
>
> *In this session you will learn what Netscape Navigator is and how to start using it. You will identify the components of the Netscape window and a Web page, navigate the Netscape window, and learn to set Netscape options. Finally, you will learn how to access online Help from the Netscape Handbook.*

What Is Netscape Navigator?

As you learned in Tutorial 1, computer networks that contain information and the physical connections between them comprise the Internet. The World Wide Web (WWW), a hypermedia information system, provides easy access to a multitude of documents. Netscape Navigator, or simply **Netscape**, is a browser program used to navigate and view information on the Internet and the WWW. Figure 3-1 shows how the Internet, WWW, and Netscape work together.

Figure 3-1 ◀
Relationship
between the
Internet, the
WWW, and
Netscape

Netscape Navigator is
the single viewer to
retrieve information
from any Internet
service

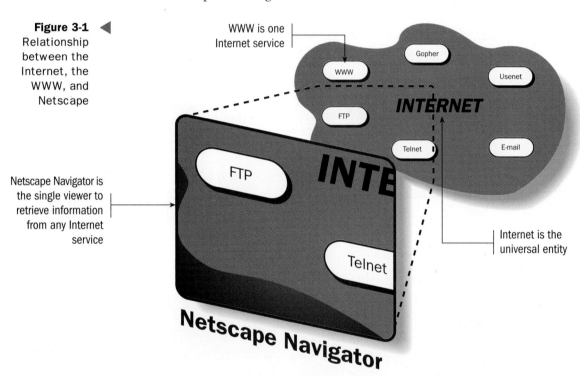

You use Netscape to view **Web pages**, electronic documents that are specifically formatted and designed for viewing information on the WWW. A typical Web page may include text, graphics, animation, multimedia items, and even programs that run directly from the page. Many Web pages also have links to other Web pages. Later in this session, you will learn about the specific elements of a Web page. Subsequent tutorials teach you to use Netscape to perform other tasks, such as sending and receiving electronic mail (e-mail) and downloading a file to your computer using FTP.

Starting Netscape

To start exploring Netscape's features and to view information on the WWW, you need to launch Netscape from your computer. Unlike many other software programs, Netscape does not always open with a standard start-up window. The first page that loads when you start Netscape is called a **home page**. Different computers may show different home pages when Netscape is launched, depending on the configuration of the Netscape software. Your computer may show the home page for your educational institution, the Netscape Corporation, or may even be blank. When you launch Netscape, your default home page, located in the content area, should be the New Perspectives on the Internet

Using Netscape Navigator Software—Introductory Student Online Companion. If it is not, ask for your instructor or technical support person for assistance. If you are using a computer at your educational institution, it is most likely already connected to the Internet. If you are not sure, ask your instructor.

Launching Netscape

You launch Netscape in Windows 95 just as you launch any other program. Within Netscape, you find many window elements and menu options that you find in other Windows programs, as well as others that are unique to the Netscape program.

Shantu installed the Netscape program on your office computer. Before you can research information on the WWW for Shannon, you need to launch Netscape and learn about the elements of the Netscape window.

To start Netscape:

1. Turn on your computer, if necessary, and go to the Windows 95 desktop.

2. Click the **Start** button [Start] on the Windows 95 taskbar. See Figure 3-2.

Figure 3-2 ◀
Launching
Netscape
Navigator

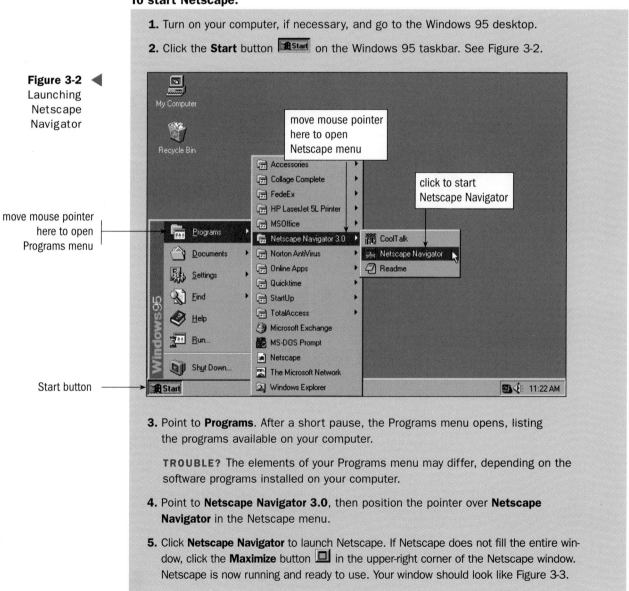

move mouse pointer
here to open
Programs menu

Start button

3. Point to **Programs**. After a short pause, the Programs menu opens, listing the programs available on your computer.

   TROUBLE? The elements of your Programs menu may differ, depending on the software programs installed on your computer.

4. Point to **Netscape Navigator 3.0**, then position the pointer over **Netscape Navigator** in the Netscape menu.

5. Click **Netscape Navigator** to launch Netscape. If Netscape does not fill the entire window, click the **Maximize** button ☐ in the upper-right corner of the Netscape window. Netscape is now running and ready to use. Your window should look like Figure 3-3.

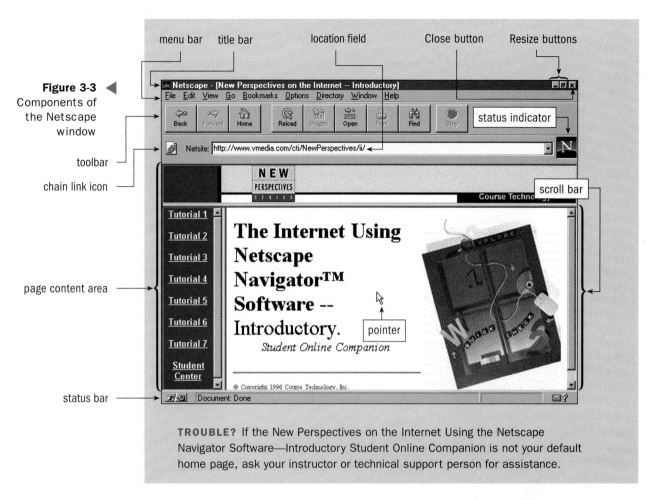

Figure 3-3 ◀
Components of
the Netscape
window

TROUBLE? If the New Perspectives on the Internet Using the Netscape Navigator Software—Introductory Student Online Companion is not your default home page, ask your instructor or technical support person for assistance.

Components of the Netscape Window

Netscape features a standard Windows interface and some additional features. Like Windows, the Netscape Graphical User Interface (GUI) uses a mouse pointer to click menus, buttons, icons, and other graphical symbols to select items and perform tasks. Figure 3-3 shows the Netscape window displaying the New Perspectives on the Internet Using Netscape Navigator Software—Introductory Student Online Companion, your home page. Refer to this figure as you learn about each component of the Netscape window.

Title Bar and Menu Bar

The **title bar** is located at the top of your active window. It identifies the program that is currently active, and within brackets, the Web page that you are currently viewing. For example, the title bar on your window should read "Netscape–[New Perspectives on the Internet—Introductory]," as shown in Figure 3-3.

The **menu bar** directly beneath the title bar contains lists or menus of all Netscape commands. If you click one of the menu bar selections, a drop-down menu appears listing commands that are available for tasks such as printing a home page or accessing online Help.

You can select commands in various ways. For example, you can click an item with your mouse or use one of the keystroke combinations listed to the right of the menu item. Alternatively, instead of selecting the Open Location option from the File menu to open a specific Web page, hold down the Ctrl key and press the L key at the same time. In the steps, keystroke combinations appear as Ctrl+L. As you become more familiar with Netscape, you may want to use some keystroke combinations to move around more quickly.

Scroll Bars

You use the **scroll bars**, located on the right and near the bottom of the viewing area, to move around the content area of a Web page. Scroll bars let you quickly and easily navigate a Web site. For example, clicking the vertical scroll bar arrow lets you move the Web page up or down; the horizontal scroll bar arrow lets you move from side to side. Clicking either the Back [⬜] or Forward [⬜] buttons on the toolbar takes you back or forward one Web page at a time. Finally, the Page Up and Page Down keys move the information up or down one window at a time.

Because the entire content of a Web page does not always fit in one window, you use scroll bars to move to another part of the Web page. If no scroll bars appear on the side or bottom of a Web page, it means that you are viewing the entire page. Figure 3-4 lists some common commands that you use to move around a Web page.

Figure 3-4 ◀
Methods for
moving around
a Web page

To Move	Click or Press
Down one inch	Down arrow [▼] in the vertical scroll bar or press ↓
Up one inch	Up arrow [▲] in the vertical scroll bar or press ↑
Down one window	Below the scroll box in the vertical scroll bar or press Pg Dn key
Up one window	Above the scroll box in the vertical scroll bar or press Pg Up key
To the top of the Web page	Press Ctrl + Home
To the end of the Web page	Press Ctrl + End

Some Web pages' content areas are divided into smaller rectangular viewing areas called frames. Each **frame** is a separate Web page containing its own information. A Web page with frames is called a top-level page, or **frameset**. Frames are like the picture-in-picture feature that some television sets offer. Figure 3-5 shows a sample Web page with frames.

Figure 3-5 ◀
Sample Web
site using
frames

each rectangular
frame is a separate
Web page

Toolbar

The **toolbar** is the band of graphical icons beneath the menu bar. The toolbar offers yet another way to select Netscape commands. For example, to go to a specific Web page, you could click the Open button ⊡ on the toolbar and type the appropriate Universal Resource Locator (**URL**) address. (You will learn more about URLs in the next session.) By selecting the Home button ⊡ on the toolbar, you arrive at the default Web page, or home page, that has been configured on your version of Netscape—this should be the New Perspectives on the Internet Using Netscape Navigator Software—Introductory Student Online Companion. All options available on the toolbar are also available on the menu bar. In this tutorial, you use the quickest and easiest method to perform an action. Figure 3-6 shows various toolbar buttons and lists their uses.

Figure 3-6 ◄
Toolbar buttons

Toolbar Button Name	Button	Description
Back	 ⇦ Back	Displays previous page
Forward	 ⇨ Forward	Displays the next page in the series of pages already viewed
Home	 ⌂ Home	Displays your home (opening) page
Reload	 ↻ Reload	Forces Netscape to completely reload page
Images	 Images	Loads images for the current page, if images are not loaded automatically
Open	 Open	Displays text box to enter a Web page address
Print	 Print	Prints the current Web page
Find	 Find	Locates text in a page based on the keyword(s) specified
Stop	 ● Stop	Halts the page-loading process

Location Field

The **location field** is directly below the toolbar. It displays the address of the Web page you are currently viewing. You can also use this area to input the URL of the next Web page you want to view. A drop-down menu at the right end of the location field also lets you choose a Web site to visit from the 10 most recent URL addresses you have typed in the location field.

Status Bar and Status Indicator

The **status bar** at the bottom of the Netscape window contains the status message area and the progress bar, and indicates the progress of the current operation. The **status message area** indicates how much data has been transferred to your computer when you request a connection to a particular Web site. A **Web site** is a computer or a network of computers that makes Web pages available on the WWW, or is a group of related Web pages. When the transfer is complete, the status message area displays the message "Document: Done." In addition, it shows the URL of a particular Web page when you position your mouse pointer over a highlighted word or image that links to another Web page. The color band of the **progress bar** signifies how much of the Web page has been transferred. It gradually fills in until it becomes a solid color block; this indicates that Netscape has completely loaded the Web page.

The **status indicator** near the top-right portion of the Netscape window also shows how quickly the Web page is loading. Unlike the status bar, it doesn't show the percentage of the Web page that has loaded. Instead, the icon is animated as the transfer progresses. When Netscape loads the entire Web page into your computer's memory, the icon becomes still. Clicking the status indicator loads the Netscape Corporation home page.

Directory Buttons

The **directory buttons** positioned below the location field are divided into categories so that you can easily link to predetermined Web sites. Netscape Corporation uses categories such as What's New What's New? and What's Cool What's Cool? to group specific Internet Web sites that may appeal to a broad range of users. The company updates the links on these buttons quite frequently, usually at least once a month.

Other directory buttons include People People , which links to Web sites that help locate names and e-mail addresses of other Internet users. The Net Search Net Search and Destinations Destinations buttons help you locate information on the Internet using search tools and directories. **Search tools** let you type a word or phrase that corresponds with the category you are seeking while **directories** list information by category and location. Session 3.3 discusses search tools in more detail. Figure 3-7 lists and describes the various Netscape directory buttons.

Figure 3-7 ◀
Directory buttons

Directory Button Name	Button	Description
What's New?	What's New?	Information describing what's new on the Internet
What's Cool?	What's Cool?	Information describing what's unique and innovative on the Internet
Destinations	Destinations	Information leading to Internet directories
Net Search	Net Search	A directory of Internet search tools
People	People	Links to sites that help you locate people on the Internet
Software	Software	Information on Netscape Navigator software

Chain Link Icon

The **chain link icon** to the left of the location field creates a shortcut between the Windows desktop and a Web site. When you drag the chain link icon to the desktop, an icon on the desktop represents the Web page you are currently viewing and directly links you to the site.

Page Content Area

The main Netscape window where you view a Web page is the **page content area**. The **page title** in the title bar at the top of the Netscape window briefly describes the page's content.

Now that you have learned about the elements of the Netscape window, you are ready to learn the different components of a Web page and use them to move around a Web page.

Anatomy of a Web Page

A **link**, or **hyperlink**, is a connection point for jumping to another Web page, to another section of the current Web page, or to a multimedia item. Hyperlinks can point to graphics, text, videos, sound clips, or other multimedia items. Colors or underlining highlight text hyperlinks that link to other Web pages. **Hyperlinking** is the process of jumping from one Web page to another. Once you use a link to another Web page, the hyperlink text changes color to show you where you've been.

Moving Around a Web Page

Now that you know the elements of a Web page and are familiar with the components of the Netscape window, you're ready to apply your knowledge and begin using Netscape. Begin by moving around the New Perspectives on the Internet Using Netscape Navigator Software—Introductory Student Online Companion home page.

To navigate a Web page:

1. Click the **scroll down arrow** ▼ at the bottom of the vertical scroll bar. The document window scrolls down one inch at a time to reveal new information.

2. Continue scrolling until you reach the bottom of the Web page. At the bottom of the Web page, you see the text © Copyright 1996 Course Technology, Inc. The scroll box should now be at the bottom of the vertical scroll bar, indicating that you are at the end of the Web page.

3. Press **Ctrl + Home**. This keystroke combination quickly brings you back to the top of the Web page you are viewing.

4. Press **Ctrl + End**. This keystroke combination quickly brings you to the bottom of the Web page.

5. Position your mouse pointer on the **Tutorial 3** link. Note that the pointer changes from an arrow ⇖ to a pointing hand ☝ whenever you place it over a hyperlink. The status message area also changes to show the link's address. See Figure 3-8. The address listed in your status message area may differ from the one shown in Figure 3-8. This is normal: Web site names often change due to Web site modifications or simple name changes.

Figure 3-8 ◀
Status
message area

pointer changes
shape

URL link

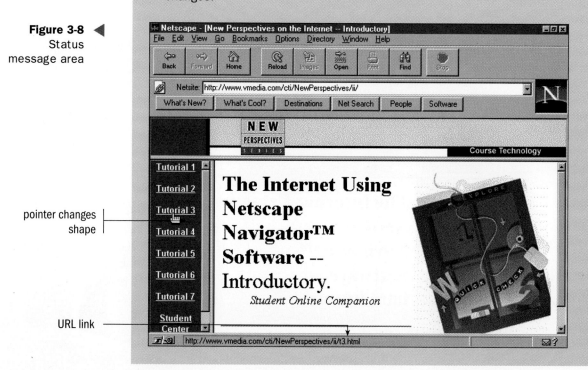

6. Press the **Page Up** key on your keyboard. The document window scrolls up one window at a time. Continue scrolling until you reach the top of the New Perspectives on the Internet Using Netscape Navigator Software Introductory—Student Online Companion home page.

Setting Options for Netscape

Just as your word-processing program has default margin settings and preset tab stops, your copy of Netscape has predetermined and pre-configured settings for font size, style, and color that your instructor or technical support person has set for you. You can also set various other configurations, such as e-mail settings, so that Netscape performs such tasks as remembering your account password or checking your e-mailbox for new messages every 10 minutes.

Default option settings can sometimes change, especially when you share your computer with another person. These tutorials assume that your Netscape window matches those shown in the figures. For example, some options either display or hide the directory buttons, the toolbar, and the location field. These options are handy, as hiding these elements increases the amount of window space available for viewing Web pages in the content area. Commands used to hide or display the elements are located on the Options menu. These commands are called toggle switches. **Toggle switches** are any key or command that turn features on and off, much like a light switch. You turn on the option by selecting the command and turn it off by selecting it again.

You want to confirm that the Show Toolbar, Show Location, Show Directory Buttons, and Auto Load Images commands on the Option menu are toggled on. You can normally tell by looking at your Netscape window; however, this time you also use the Options menus so you can toggle on any command that isn't on.

To show or hide commands:

1. Click **Options** on the menu bar to open the Options menu. A command is toggled on if a check mark precedes it. You should see a check mark before Show Toolbar. It indicates that the toolbar is toggled on and will appear in the Netscape window. See Figure 3-9.

Figure 3-9 ◄
Options menu

check mark indicates
option is toggled on

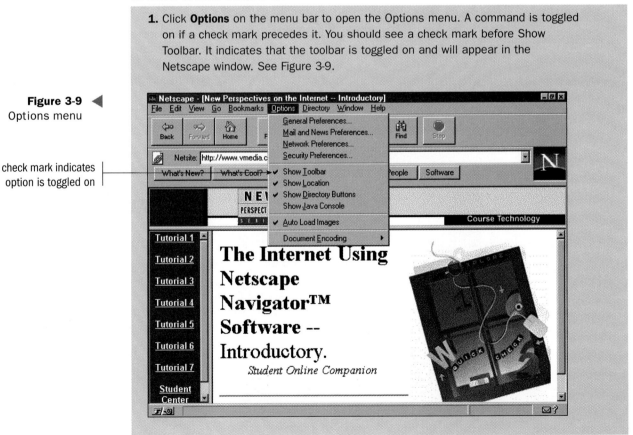

TROUBLE? If no check mark precedes the Show Toolbar command, then the toolbar is already hidden. Continue to Step 3.

2. Click **Show Toolbar** to remove the check mark and toggle the command off. The toolbar disappears from the Netscape window.

For these tutorials, make sure the toolbar shows in the Netscape window. Select the same command again to toggle the command back on.

3. Click **Options**, then click **Show Toolbar**. The toolbar appears in the window.

4. Repeat Steps 1 through 3 to ensure that the Show Location, Show Directory Buttons, and Auto Load Images commands are toggled on. When you finish, your window should match Figure 3-10.

Figure 3-10 ◄
Show commands toggled on

toolbar, location, and directory buttons are all toggled on and appear in your Netscape window

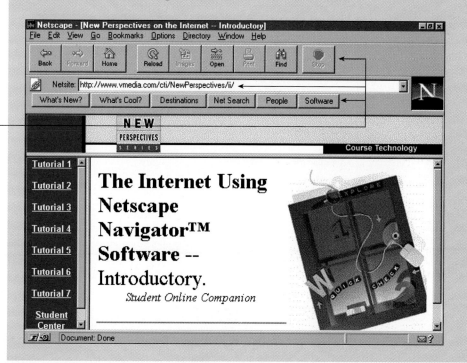

Getting Online Help

Although you will learn a lot about Netscape throughout these tutorials, you may have questions about particular features or need additional assistance with certain commands. Like most Windows programs, Netscape offers various Help menus that link you to further information on a topic or command. Most topics have an index for cross-referencing subjects so that you can find a specific entry under various headings. Netscape's Help menu aids in utilizing all the program's features. The Handbook command on the Help menu offers several useful options, including basic information on program concepts and the Internet in general as well as lessons on using Netscape's features.

Shannon requested that you gauge how many of your competitors' sites use a secure server for online transactions. While you view the Netscape window, the security indicator in the bottom-left corner of your window catches your eye. Because you are unfamiliar with the indicator, you use the Netscape Help features to learn about its function. As you view competitors' Web sites, you track how many use secure servers.

To get online Help:

1. Click **Help** on the menu bar to open the Help menu.

2. Click **Handbook** to open the Netscape Navigator Handbook Web page. See Figure 3-11. The Netscape Navigator Handbook Web page has several hyperlinks to information on various help subjects, including a Frequently Asked Questions (FAQ) area.

Figure 3-11 ◄
Netscape
Navigator
Handbook

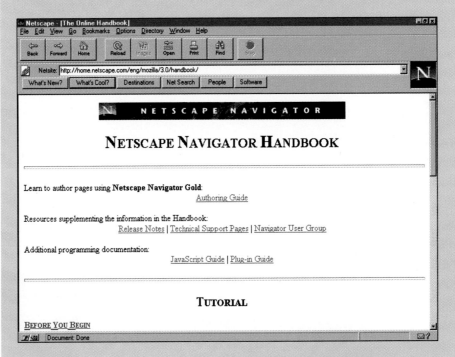

3. Scroll down the page until you see the **Onscreen Fundamentals** link, then click this link. This hyperlink jumps you to a Web page with information about the elements of the Netscape window. See Figure 3-12.

Figure 3-12 ◄
Online help

tutorials to learn
Netscape

search index

Help topics listed
by category

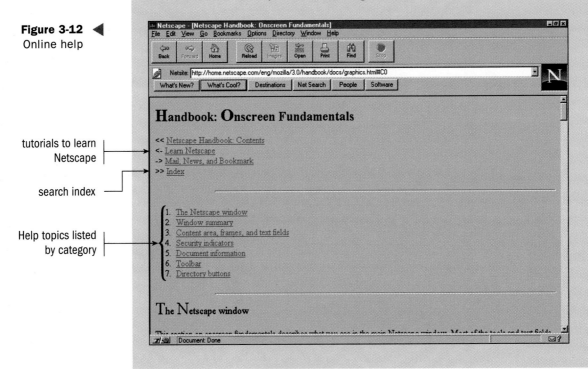

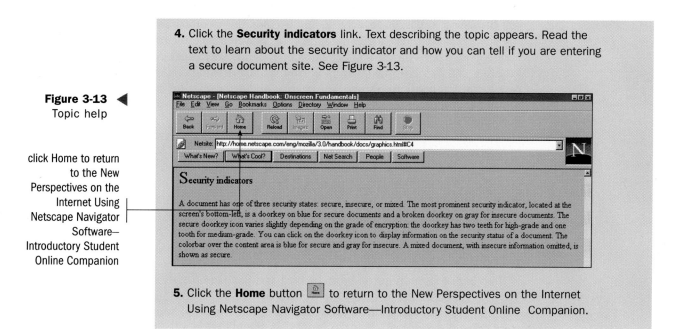

4. Click the **Security indicators** link. Text describing the topic appears. Read the text to learn about the security indicator and how you can tell if you are entering a secure document site. See Figure 3-13.

Figure 3-13 ◀
Topic help

click Home to return to the New Perspectives on the Internet Using Netscape Navigator Software— Introductory Student Online Companion

5. Click the **Home** button to return to the New Perspectives on the Internet Using Netscape Navigator Software—Introductory Student Online Companion.

Shantu is impressed with how quickly you learned to use Netscape's basic features. In the next session you will build upon what you learned to locate the information Shannon needs.

Quick Check

1 True or False: Netscape is a browser program used only to view information on the WWW.

2 Is every home page a Web page? Why or why not?

3 You may use the _____ to view a Web page that does not fit entirely in the window.

4 A Web page may be broken down into smaller rectangular viewing areas called _____.

5 The location field displays the _____ of a Web page.

6 The _____ and _____ display information about the progress of a Web page loading into your computer's memory.

7 _____ is the process of jumping from one Web page to another.

8 The _____ command in the Help menu is very useful for learning about the features Netscape offers.

SESSION 3.2

In this session, you will learn to view the source file used to create a Web page, to initiate and abort a link, to use URLs, and to move among Web pages. You will also learn to save Web page text and images, to preview and print a Web page, and to exit Netscape.

Viewing a Web Page Source File

Because Web pages often market products and services and are designed to be visually appealing, their function is often compared to an electronic billboard. Like billboards, a Web page uses various typefaces in different sizes and styles such as bold, italic, or underlined text and headings. A Web page may feature a color theme or unique backdrop and usually contains graphics. Unlike a billboard, however, a Web page can contain hyperlinks that connect users to related pieces of information on separate Web pages. Modifying Web pages is a lot easier and less expensive than modifying standard billboards. This feature is important because the information on some Web pages is updated daily—for example, those Web pages providing weather forecasts.

A Web page is usually evaluated by three different criteria: quality of information, creative and interesting design and appearance, and the quality and effectiveness of its hyperlinks. When Netscape links to a Web page, it determines how to display the information on the page with the assistance of a special programming language called Hypertext Markup Language. **Hypertext Markup Language**, or **HTML**, is a programming language designed specifically to create Web page contents simply. Special HTML codes indicate how text within a document should look. For instance, if a heading is to be centered, HTML uses a special "center" code as an instruction. Netscape then interprets these special codes to determine how to display the Web page in your window. When a Web page is created, Netscape saves all its HTML information in a file called a **source file**.

To compile suggestions on how the Birdland Bay Company should best create its own Web page, you decide to view source codes of Web pages for the company's competitors that you are researching. To understand more fully how the Web pages you are viewing were created, Shantu suggests that you view the HTML source file for the current Web page loaded on your computer. All source files for Web pages look like the one you will view. In addition to the elements that comprise the page layout such as headings, font sizes, and text, the source file also shows what hyperlinks are available from that page.

To view the HTML source file of a Web page:

1. The New Perspectives on the Internet Using Netscape Navigator Software—Introductory Student Online Companion Web page should still be displayed on your screen. Click **View** on the menu bar, then click **Document Source**. The Source File for this Web page opens. See Figure 3-14. Netscape uses the HTML codes that you see listed within the brackets (< >) to designate how information looks in your window.

Figure 3-14 ◀
Source file

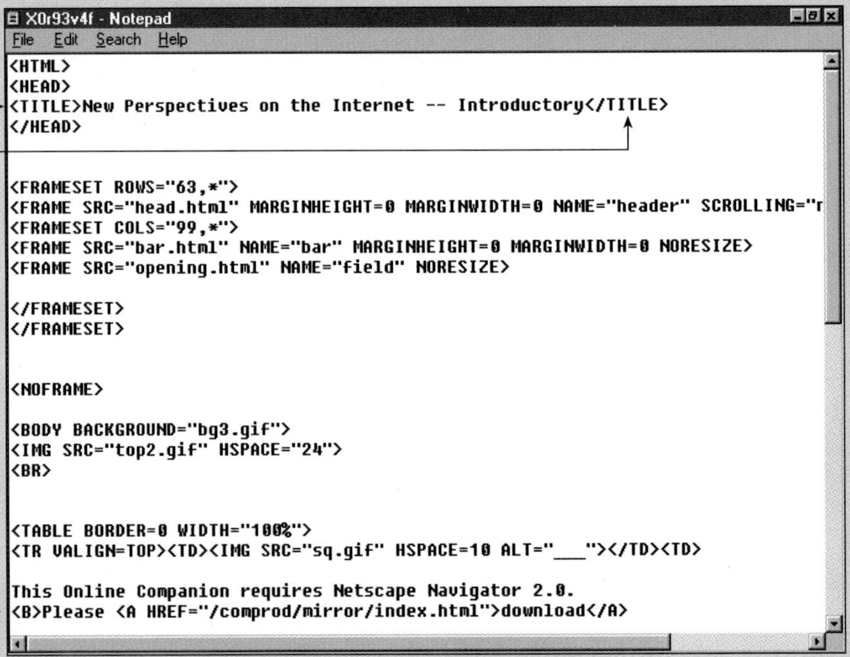

page title codes ───▶

graphic image code ───▶

boldface code ───▶

```
X0r93v4f - Notepad                                               _ □ ✕
File  Edit  Search  Help
<HTML>
<HEAD>
<TITLE>New Perspectives on the Internet -- Introductory</TITLE>
</HEAD>


<FRAMESET ROWS="63,*">
<FRAME SRC="head.html" MARGINHEIGHT=0 MARGINWIDTH=0 NAME="header" SCROLLING="r
<FRAMESET COLS="99,*">
<FRAME SRC="bar.html" NAME="bar" MARGINHEIGHT=0 MARGINWIDTH=0 NORESIZE>
<FRAME SRC="opening.html" NAME="field" NORESIZE>

</FRAMESET>
</FRAMESET>


<NOFRAME>

<BODY BACKGROUND="bg3.gif">
<IMG SRC="top2.gif" HSPACE="24">
<BR>


<TABLE BORDER=0 WIDTH="100%">
<TR VALIGN=TOP><TD><IMG SRC="sq.gif" HSPACE=10 ALT="___"></TD><TD>

This Online Companion requires Netscape Navigator 2.0.
<B>Please <A HREF="/comprod/mirror/index.html">download</A>
```

2. Click the **Close** button ☒ in the upper-right corner of the document window displaying the source file. The window closes and you return to your home page.

Using Netscape, you can view the source file for any Web page you come across. People often view the source code to better understand how a particular feature has been incorporated, such as frames.

Linking to a Site

When you link to another Web page, you may experience several different outcomes. Usually you have no trouble reaching a Web site and a Web page automatically transfers to your computer. During a successful link, Netscape contacts the server where the Web page is stored, transfers the requested information to your computer, and displays the data in your window. Sometimes, however, a site may be busy or hard to reach. If many people try to access a site at once, the server may become congested and the site inaccessible. You may also run across some Web pages that have changed their addresses or are no longer available.

Sometimes when you link to a Web page, the transfer occurs so rapidly that you don't have a chance to observe the status message area, progress bar, and status indicator. At other times, the transfer may take many seconds or even minutes. The amount of time needed to access a Web page varies depending on the number of people trying to access the site, the number of people on the Internet at that time, and even the design and layout of the Web page. For instance, a long Web page or one with sound, graphics, or movies may take longer to load.

Initiating a Link

When you initiate a link using Netscape, a multi-step process begins. Although Netscape takes care of this process in the background, you need to understand the sequence of events so that you can troubleshoot any problems that may occur as you access various Web sites on the Internet.

Figure 3-15 illustrates what happens when you link to a site. First the Stop button changes to red, indicating its active state, and the status indicator becomes animated. Also during this time, the status message area displays a series of messages indicating that Netscape has contacted the site you requested, that it is waiting for a reply, that it is transferring the requested data, and finally, that the transfer process is complete.

As a Web page begins to appear in your window, all of its information does not always appear at once. Graphics may first look blurry or hazy and then become more clear as Netscape transfers additional data to your computer. Netscape transfers this information in multiple passes, with each pass adding more detail to complete the page. The progress bar widens showing the progress of the page loading. The vertical scroll box scrolls as Netscape adds more detail to the page. You don't need to wait for the Web page to load completely before you start to navigate the window or jump to another Web page.

As you may have observed, some Web pages load faster than others. By estimating how long a typical Web page takes to load, you can relay information to Shannon on the role of the linking process in developing a Web site. You now link to the Tutorial 3 Web page to observe the hyperlinking process.

Figure 3-15
Hyperlinking
process

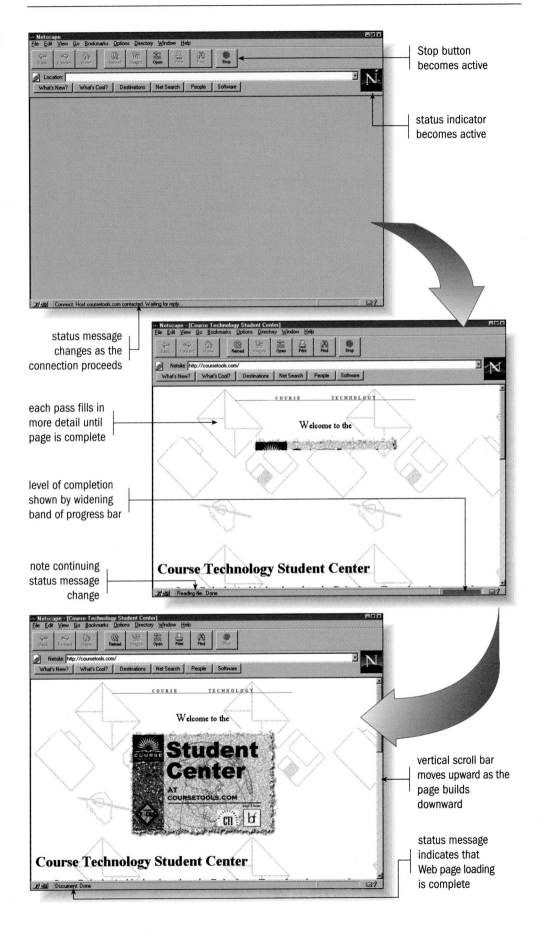

Stop button
becomes active

status indicator
becomes active

status message
changes as the
connection proceeds

each pass fills in
more detail until
page is complete

level of completion
shown by widening
band of progress bar

note continuing
status message
change

vertical scroll bar
moves upward as the
page builds
downward

status message
indicates that
Web page loading
is complete

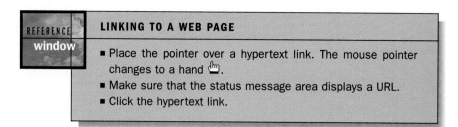

REFERENCE
window

LINKING TO A WEB PAGE

- Place the pointer over a hypertext link. The mouse pointer changes to a hand 🖑.
- Make sure that the status message area displays a URL.
- Click the hypertext link.

To link to a Web page:

1. If necessary, scroll the New Perspectives on the Internet Using Netscape Navigator Software—Introductory Student Online Companion Web page until you see the link Tutorial 3.

2. Position your mouse pointer on the **Tutorial 3** link. The message status area shows the URL for the link.

   TROUBLE? If your status message area is blank, or the pointer shape doesn't change, try again to position your pointer over the link by slowly moving the pointer over Tutorial 3. When the Web page address appears in the status message area, you have correctly positioned the pointer.

3. Click the **Tutorial 3** link. Watch closely as the status message area and the progress bar change to show how much data has been loaded. As Netscape transfers the Web page, the status indicator becomes animated. When the "Document: Done" message appears in the status message area, the Web page you linked to has loaded successfully. See Figure 3-16.

Figure 3-16 ◄
Linking to a
Web page

Web page URL
address

graphical link

text link

status message area

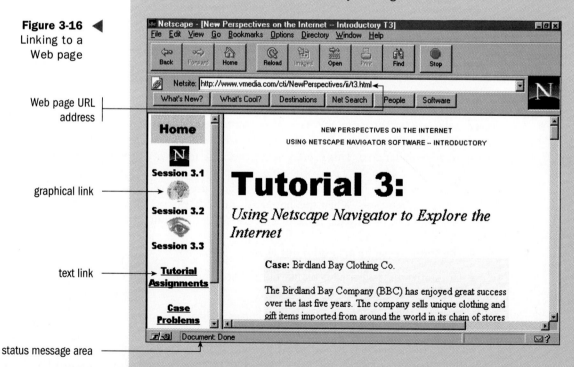

TROUBLE? If you see an error message, the hyperlink was not successful. Click the OK button to close the dialog box, and repeat Steps 2 and 3. After you click the link, make sure not to click elsewhere on the Web page.

4. Click the **Session 3.2** link to view the Session 3.2 section of the Web page. See Figure 3-17.

Figure 3-17 ◀
Online
companion
Session 3.2
Web page

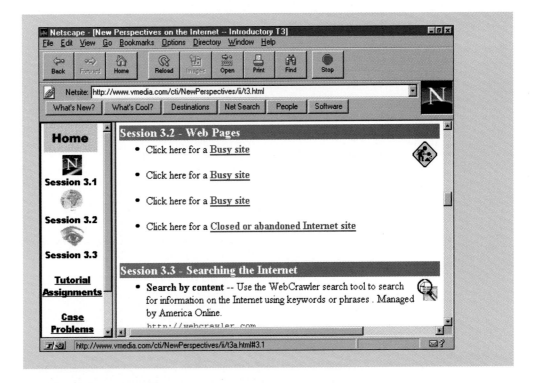

You used the hyperlink to move simply from one Web page to another and observed the linking process in action. As you can see, navigating through a Web page using links is quite simple. You observed that graphics for the online catalog often load a bit slower than text, but you also tell Shannon that hyperlinking will work well for navigating the different clothing and gift categories.

Aborting a Link

Sometimes the Internet becomes so congested that its paths cannot support the many users who are accessing its services. This commonly occurs during peak times, such as early morning or evening, when Internet use is most heavy. Sometimes Web sites become temporarily unavailable. This usually occurs because too many people are trying to access the site at once, as is the case with some very popular sites such as Netscape's software download site. It may happen simply because there are just too many people are using the Internet at a given time. When this happens, traffic backs up, slows to a halt, and closes the road. You can usually tell if a site is overloaded when one of these situations occur:

- The status message area does not change.
- The status message area is blank, but the Stop button ![Stop] on the toolbar indicates that the site is active.
- The status message is blank, but the status indicator is animated.

Shantu recommends that you abort the link if the wait for a site is too long for your schedule. **Aborting,** or interrupting a link, is like taking the next available exit ramp from a highway rather than slowly traveling in heavy traffic to your intended exit. Because Shantu wants your Internet time to be as productive as possible, he wants to show you how to abort a delayed link. By doing so, you do not need to wait for an overloaded site or one with a long delay; instead, you're free to navigate to other Web pages. From the Session 3.2 section of the New Perspectives on the Internet Using Netscape Navigator Software—Introductory Student Online Companion Web page, use the links listed there to practice aborting a delayed link.

To abort a delayed link:

1. If necessary, scroll the Web page until you see the Busy site links in the Session 3.2 section of the Tutorial 3 Web page.

2. Click a **Busy site** link to initiate the link. Watch the status message area closely. The message display halts, yet the status indicator is continually animated and the Stop button shows an active status. The link is stalled. See Figure 3-18.

Figure 3-18 ◄
Delayed link

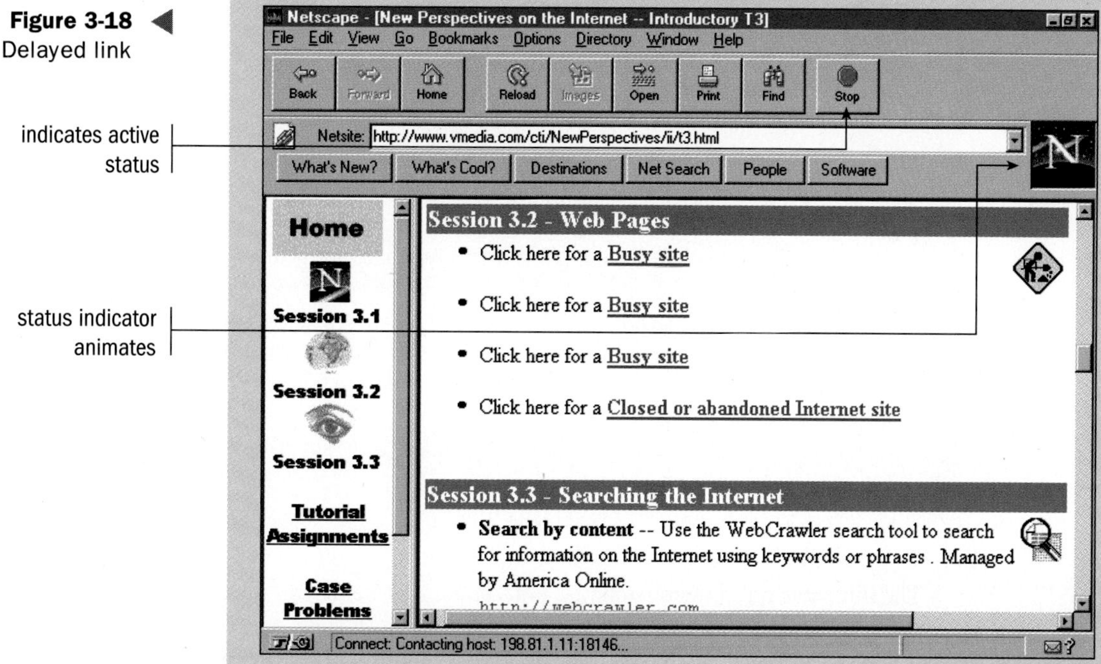

indicates active status

status indicator animates

TROUBLE? If the status message area reads "Document: Done" and a new Web site opens, you connected to this site without delay. Click the Back button to try connecting again until you experience a delay in page loading, or try linking another Busy site link.

The waiting time means that the line to this site may be very long. Instead of waiting for the site to become available, you want to abort the link and try again later.

3. Click the **Stop** button on the toolbar to abort the link. The status indicator is no longer animated, and the Stop button dims or deactivates.

4. If necessary, click the **Back** button to return to the Session 3.2 section of the Tutorial 3 Web page.

At times you may try to access a Web site that no longer exists or is temporarily out of service for maintenance. If this occurs, Netscape terminates the connection and displays an error message to alert you to the problem. Seeing the error dialog box is similar to receiving a busy signal on a telephone line or seeing a closed sign on a business door. Common reasons for being unable to reach a site include:

■ The URL address of the Web page may have changed, or the page may no longer exist.

■ You may have typed the URL address incorrectly.

■ Netscape may not have been able to reach the Web site in the amount of time allotted by the server's programmed wait time (for example, 90 seconds).

As you use Netscape to locate information for Shannon, you may encounter a link that Netscape has terminated. In such a case, you end the terminated link so that the Netscape window becomes active again.

To end a terminated link:

1. If necessary, scroll the **Session 3.2** page, and then click the **Closed or abandoned Internet site** link. This initiates the link to a site that no longer exists. A message dialog box opens. See Figure 3-19.

Figure 3-19 ◀
Closed or abandoned site message dialog box

terminated link; click OK to proceed

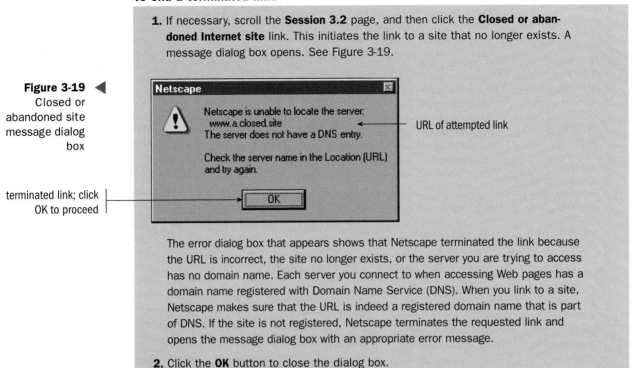

URL of attempted link

The error dialog box that appears shows that Netscape terminated the link because the URL is incorrect, the site no longer exists, or the server you are trying to access has no domain name. Each server you connect to when accessing Web pages has a domain name registered with Domain Name Service (DNS). When you link to a site, Netscape makes sure that the URL is indeed a registered domain name that is part of DNS. If the site is not registered, Netscape terminates the requested link and opens the message dialog box with an appropriate error message.

2. Click the **OK** button to close the dialog box.

The information in the terminated link dialog box helps you determine why you may not successfully reach a site. If you see an error message such as "Server not available" or "Server not located," you know that the site you requested is not currently available. Shantu is impressed with how quickly you learned to use the Netscape program. He told Shannon of your progress and offered his assistance in the future if you need it. Shannon is anxious for you to begin checking out information on the company's competitors. The sooner she has the information, the more prepared she can be for her upcoming meeting.

Using URLs

Clicking a hypertext link is an effective way to navigate the WWW if you have no specific destination in mind or are seeking information simply by following related links. However, you often want to access a specific Web site. Entering a Web's site URL is the most direct way to get there. Recall that URLs identify files on the WWW are so that computers can find and retrieve them. Like domain names, URLs employ a simple addressing scheme that helps unify the many Internet services available through the WWW. Figure 3-20 shows the anatomy of the URL for one Birdland Bay Company competitor, JCPenney.

server or computer portion, located at the jcpenney.com domain

path portion, locates the index.html file in the shopping subdirectory

Figure 3-20 ◀
Anatomy of a URL

protocol portion, using HTTP protocol for Web pages

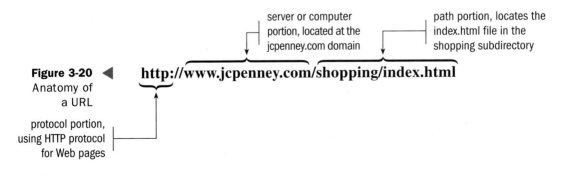

http://www.jcpenney.com/shopping/index.html

The first portion, called the **protocol portion**, tells Netscape what protocol is being used. In the example http://www.jcpenney.com/shopping/index.htm, the protocol would be HTTP, or the hypertext transfer protocol. **HTTP** is the standard that lets computers transfer hypertext and multimedia files to one another. This tells you that the Web page is a hypertext document created using HTML. Whenever you see a URL address starting with the http:// protocol, you can be certain it refers to a Web page.

The protocol portion of the URL can also list other network services available on the Internet, such as FTP services and Gopher. You can even access a file on your local hard drive with a URL such as file:///c:/data/report.may, where Netscape will find a document named report.may located in the data subdirectory on your local (c:) hard drive. The (c:) usually follows the protocol portion characters **://** to separate the service from the server.

The **computer** or **server portion** of the URL tells Netscape the computer, or server, that is being used. It can also refer to the site by its domain name or IP address. In the URL http://www.jcpenney.com/shopping/index.htm, the /www portion tells us that this Web page information is stored on a WWW server located at the jcpenney.com domain. Many Web server addresses begin with the www characters. This indicates that the server's main purpose is administering Web pages.

The third portion of the URL, the **path portion**, tells Netscape where to find the document you are looking for on the WWW. For example, the URL http://www.jcpenney.com/shopping/index.htm leads you to a document named index.html in the /shopping subdirectory on the Web server.

Path and filenames on most servers are case sensitive. For example, if a file's name is USA and you type usa, Netscape cannot access the file. If a URL does not list a path and filename, Netscape assumes that you are requesting a file named index.html in the home directory of the server you are requesting. Under the HTTP protocol, the index.html file transfers by default. In the URL sample, http://www.jcpenney.com/shopping would also automatically load the HTML source file, index.html, that is located in the /shopping subdirectory.

At times, you may try to access a Web page and receive an error message like the one shown in Figure 3-21, indicating that the URL you have requested cannot be found. This often happens because the filename was typed incorrectly. If you receive this type of error message, make sure that you typed the URL correctly, and try again.

Figure 3-21
URL error
message

incorrectly typed URL —

file not found
error message

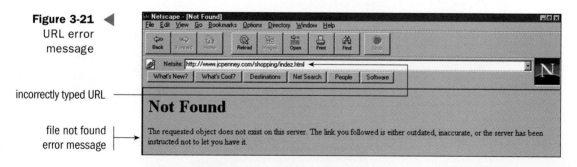

Opening a Location with a URL

When you want to go directly to a particular Web page, you can simply type its URL in the location field. You can also connect to a Web page by clicking the Open button on the toolbar and entering the Web page's URL in the location text box in the Open location dialog box. Netscape connects to the server the URL specifies, sends a request for information based on the address, and accepts the information. Netscape then displays this information in your window and automatically terminates the connection to the site.

One competitor that Shannon wants you to investigate is JCPenney, which sells both clothing and gifts on its Web site through an online catalog. She gave you the site's URL, http://www.jcpenney.com. You can open the location directly using its URL.

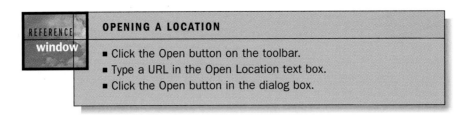

OPENING A LOCATION

- Click the Open button on the toolbar.
- Type a URL in the Open Location text box.
- Click the Open button in the dialog box.

To open a location:

1. Click the **Open** button 🔲 on the toolbar to open the Open Location dialog box. Type the URL of the location you want to open in the Open Location text box.

2. Type **http://www.jcpenney.com** in the Open Location text box. Make sure that you type the URL exactly as it is shown, with no spaces and with a colon and two slashes after the protocol portion. A colon and two slashes always follow the protocol portion. See Figure 3-22.

Figure 3-22 ◀
Open Location
dialog box

type URL here ──────

click here to
initiate link

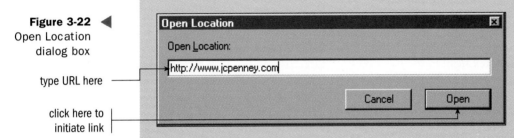

3. Click the **Open** button in the Open Location dialog box to open the JCPenney site. When opening a site directly with a URL, Netscape follows the same steps it uses when hyperlinking to a site. It makes the connection, requests information, and then displays it in your window. See Figure 3-23.

TROUBLE? If the JCPenney home page displayed in your window differs from Figure 3-23, the Web page was recently updated. If the text and images vary, use the links most similar to the ones described in this tutorial.

Figure 3-23 ◀
JCPenney home
page

URL of current page ──────

Shopping link ──────

your JCPenney home
page screen may look
different because
most Web pages are
continually updated
and modified

status bar indicates
that page successfully
loaded

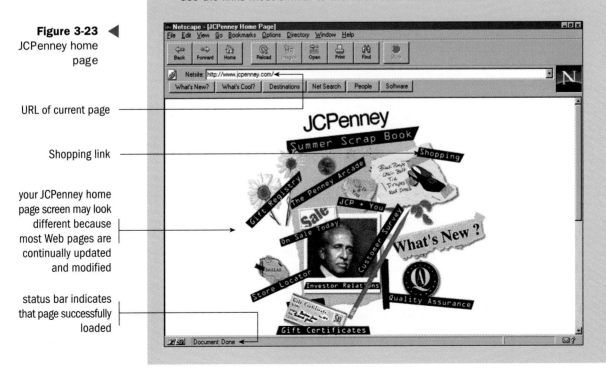

TROUBLE? If you receive a "Not Found" error message or a message saying the server has no DNS entry, you may have typed the URL incorrectly. Try Steps 1 through 3 again, making sure that the URL you type in the text box matches the URL that Figure 3-22 shows. If the URL matches the one shown in Figure 3-22, or if you see a different error message, press the Enter key to try to re-open the location. If you receive the same error message, ask your instructor or technical support person for help.

4. Scroll the JCPenney Web page until you see a link called Shopping, or one similar to it. Click the **Shopping** link. This Web page contains links to different shopping services JCPenney offers at its site. You are interested in the categories and types of products it offers.

5. Click one of the **shopping services** links to view the variety of services offered by JCPenney.

JCPenney offers an impressive variety of products and services online. Its site is attractive, with a variety of colors and graphics, as well as an easy-to-navigate menu system for moving throughout the site. You decide to explore the site more thoroughly.

Moving Among Web Pages

When you open multiple Web pages, Netscape creates a temporary history list. This **history list**, which is a log of pages that you recently viewed in your current session, is available from the Go menu. You can quickly move between recently accessed Web pages by selecting a Web page from the history list. For instance, if you access a Web page that gives office products information, you can link to the office furniture Web page, and from there, link to the Web page that displays information on filing cabinets. The history list would include an entry for each page. You can move quickly among Web pages by selecting the page you want from this list.

You can also move quickly among the Web pages in the history list using special buttons on the toolbar. With the toolbar buttons you can move back or forward page by page or quickly return to your home page. This method is often easier than trying to remember URLs of the sites you visited.

You use the history list and the toolbar buttons to move among the JCPenney Web pages. Shannon asked for electronic files and printouts for this site. She plans to use these to provide supporting information for her report. After you locate a page that you think is representative of JCPenney's Web site, you will save and print the information for Shannon.

To move among recently visited Web pages:

1. Click the **Home** button ⬛ on the toolbar. The Home button returns you to your home page. It generally contains familiar information and resources, so you frequently may want to return to it. The Home button provides a quick way to do this. Your home page is your starting point for navigating Web pages and, for this text, is the New Perspectives on the Internet Using Netscape Navigator Software–Introductory Student Online Companion.

2. Click **Go** to open the Go menu and see the history log. See Figure 3-24. The history list shows titles of Web pages you viewed recently. Your history list may differ from the one shown.

Figure 3-24 ◀
History log

current Web page —

visited sites (your list
may differ)

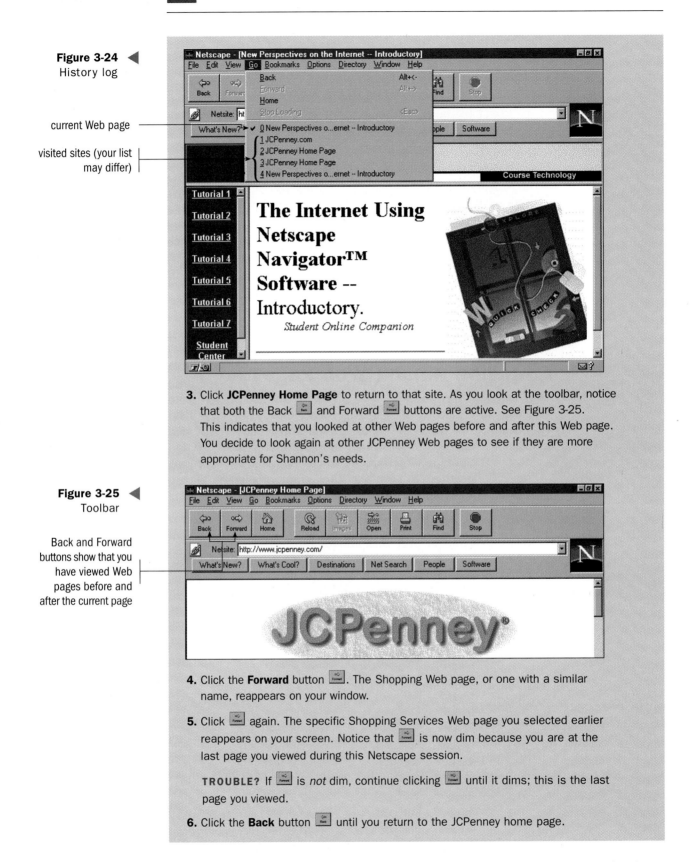

3. Click **JCPenney Home Page** to return to that site. As you look at the toolbar, notice that both the Back 🔙 and Forward 🔜 buttons are active. See Figure 3-25. This indicates that you looked at other Web pages before and after this Web page. You decide to look again at other JCPenney Web pages to see if they are more appropriate for Shannon's needs.

Figure 3-25 ◀
Toolbar

Back and Forward
buttons show that you
have viewed Web
pages before and
after the current page

4. Click the **Forward** button 🔜. The Shopping Web page, or one with a similar name, reappears on your window.

5. Click 🔜 again. The specific Shopping Services Web page you selected earlier reappears on your screen. Notice that 🔜 is now dim because you are at the last page you viewed during this Netscape session.

TROUBLE? If 🔜 is *not* dim, continue clicking 🔜 until it dims; this is the last page you viewed.

6. Click the **Back** button 🔙 until you return to the JCPenney home page.

You decide that the JCPenney home page most closely represents the type of Web site that the Birdland Bay Company wants to create. Information from this competitor's Web page will help your company prepare its site.

Saving Text and Images

Sometimes you may want to save information you find on a Web page either to read or print later. Saving a Web page can be particularly useful if you don't have much time to read information while logged on to the Internet or if you pay for access by the minute. After you save a Web page, you can view its information later without incurring online charges.

You can use Netscape to save a Web page with or without its text formatting. Graphical images must be saved in separate files. There are two ways to save a Web page. The first is to save it simply as a text file. When Netscape saves a Web page formatted in HTML as an ordinary text file, it won't include features such as graphic images, colors, fonts, and links. Before using this method, you must determine if the information you want to save will still be valuable without accompanying graphics. You can view the text file with a word-processing program, modify if necessary, and subsequently print it. The next section discusses printing with Netscape.

The second method of saving a Web page retains features such as fonts and colors. Saving a Web page as an .HTM file with its HTML coding intact lets you view the file complete with its text formatting and page layout features. This method embeds all of the HTML programming code within the document so that hypertext links also function as you use Netscape to read each one. You can also retrieve the .HTM file with a word-processing program.

Saving a Web Page as a Text File

Shannon requested that you save the competitor's Web page information in two separate files—a text file and a separate graphics file containing the main image. The manager of the Graphic Design Department will participate in the upcoming meeting. Shannon wants to forward the graphics file to the manager before the meeting for his comments and suggestions. She will use portions of the saved text file in her report. You first save the Web page as a text file without the images.

REFERENCE window

SAVING A WEB PAGE AS TEXT

- Place your Student Disk in drive A.
- Click File, then click Save As.
- Select Plain Text in the Save as type list box.
- Type the filename in the File name text box, then press Enter.

To save a Web page as a text file:

1. Make sure the JCPenney home page appears in your content area.

2. Insert your Student Disk in drive A or the appropriate drive on your computer.

3. Click **File** on the menu bar, then click **Save As** to open the Save As dialog box.

    TROUBLE? If the Save As command is dimmed, you might not have finished loading the entire Web document. Click the Reload button 🔲 on the toolbar to reload the Web page.

4. Click the **Save in** list arrow to see a list of available drives and folders. Click **3½ floppy (A:)**.

    TROUBLE? This book assumes your Student Disk is in drive A. If you are using a drive other than A, substitute the appropriate drive letter wherever you see drive A.

5. Click the **Save as type** list arrow to see the file type options.

6. Click **Plain text (*.txt)** in the Save as type list to save the Web page as a readable text file without HTML programming codes.

7. Double-click the **File name** text box, then type **jcp.txt** to name the file you're saving. See Figure 3-26. Your window may look slightly different.

Figure 3-26 ◀
Save As
dialog box

type filename here ──

click to change
file type ──

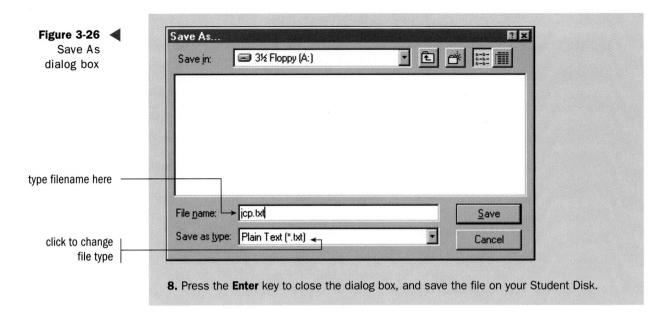

8. Press the **Enter** key to close the dialog box, and save the file on your Student Disk.

You have made it a habit to double-check any work you are presenting to another person. Before saving additional Web page information, you want to make sure that you saved the Web page properly by using Netscape to open it.

Opening a Text File in Netscape

Because you saved the document as a text file, you can open and edit it with any word-processing program. That's how Shannon will use the file after you give it to her on disk. Now open the file with Netscape to make sure you copied it successfully.

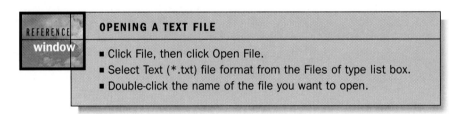

REFERENCE
window

OPENING A TEXT FILE

- Click File, then click Open File.
- Select Text (*.txt) file format from the Files of type list box.
- Double-click the name of the file you want to open.

To open a text file:

1. Click **File** and then click **Open File**. The Open dialog box displays.

2. Click the **Files of type** list arrow, and then in the file list click **Text (*.txt)** to display the jcp file you just saved. See Figure 3-27.

Figure 3-27 ◀
Open dialog
box

double-click to ──
open file

select to show ──
.txt files

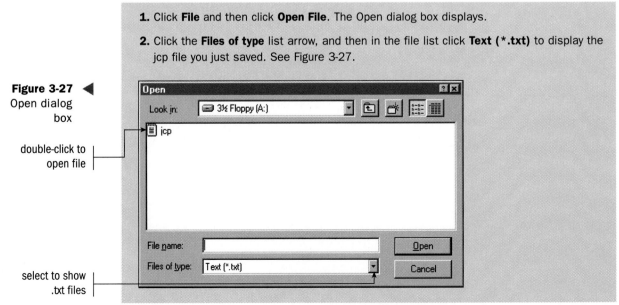

TROUBLE? If jcp.txt is not in your file list, you may be looking in the wrong drive or at the wrong file type. Make sure the Look in text box displays "3½ Floppy (A)" or the drive you are using. Also, make sure that the Files of type text box shows "Text (*.txt)." If you still can't find the file, repeat the steps under "To save a Web page as a text file."

3. Double-click **jcp** to open the file in the Netscape window. Notice that only the text of the page appears. See Figure 3-28.

file location

Figure 3-28 ◀
Viewing a
text file

indicates replaced
image

text of your JCPenney
Web page may
be different

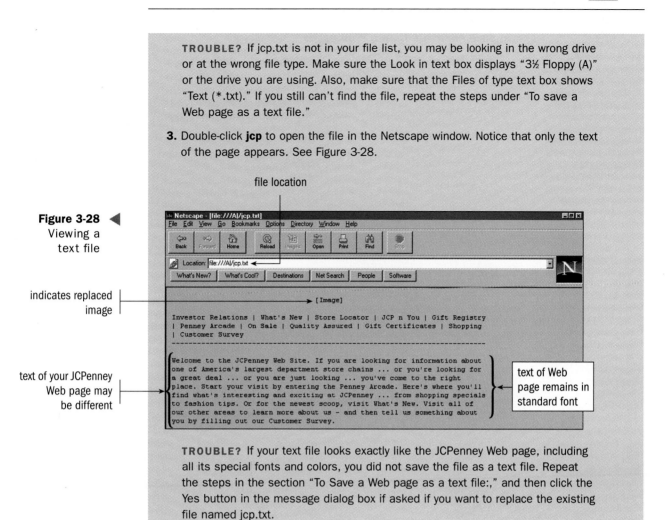

text of Web
page remains in
standard font

TROUBLE? If your text file looks exactly like the JCPenney Web page, including all its special fonts and colors, you did not save the file as a text file. Repeat the steps in the section "To Save a Web page as a text file:," and then click the Yes button in the message dialog box if asked if you want to replace the existing file named jcp.txt.

You saved and verified the Web page as a text file for Shannon. Next you save an image from the JCPenney home page on disk.

Saving an Image from a Web page

Although Web page images cannot be saved in a file along with text, you can use Netscape to save images as separate files to view or print later. You can save images in a variety of file formats; the most popular on the WWW are .GIF and .JPG formats. You will save an image on the JCPenney home page on disk as a .GIF file. Shannon will forward this file to the Graphic Design Department, which is familiar with this graphic file format.

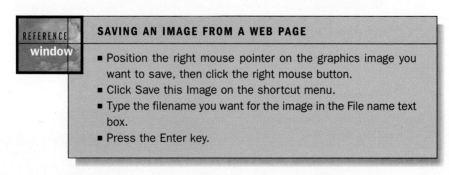

REFERENCE
window

SAVING AN IMAGE FROM A WEB PAGE

- Position the right mouse pointer on the graphics image you want to save, then click the right mouse button.
- Click Save this Image on the shortcut menu.
- Type the filename you want for the image in the File name text box.
- Press the Enter key.

To save an image from a Web page:

1. Click **Go** on the menu bar, then click **JCPenney Home Page** in the history list to return to the company's home page.

2. After the home page completely loads, click an **image** with the **right** mouse button to open a shortcut menu. See Figure 3-29. The image you see may be differ slightly as many Web sites are regularly modified.

Figure 3-29 ◀
Shortcut
menu

click to open Save As
dialog box

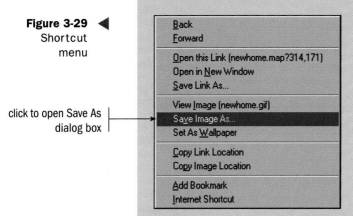

3. Click **Save Image As** to open the **Save As** dialog box.

4. Type **jcpimage.gif** in the File name text box to name the file.

5. Click the **Save As type** text box list arrow, then click **GIF File (*.GIF),** then press the **Enter** key. The **Save As** dialog box closes, and the image is saved on your disk.

Once again, to verify that you copied the file correctly, next open the image file in Netscape.

Opening an Image File in Netscape

Because you saved the graphics image in the .GIF file format, you can open the file in most graphics programs. Netscape lets you view the .GIF file only; you cannot modify the graphic with Netscape. Now you open the image file to make sure you saved the image properly.

REFERENCE
window

OPENING AN IMAGE FILE

■ Click File, then click Open File.
■ In the Open dialog box, click the Files of type list arrow, then click All Files to display the contents of your disk.
■ Double-click the name of the image file you want to open.

To open an image file:

1. Click **File** on the menu bar and then click **Open File**. The Open dialog box opens.

2. Click the **Files of type** list arrow, and then click **All Files (*)** to display the contents of your Student Disk.

3. Double-click **jcpimage.gif** to open the image of the home page you saved. See Figure 3-30.

Figure 3-30 ◀
Viewing an
image file

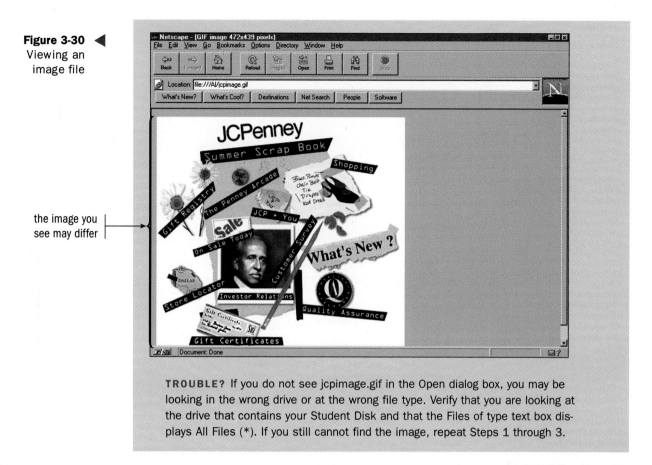

the image you
see may differ

TROUBLE? If you do not see jcpimage.gif in the Open dialog box, you may be looking in the wrong drive or at the wrong file type. Verify that you are looking at the drive that contains your Student Disk and that the Files of type text box displays All Files (*). If you still cannot find the image, repeat Steps 1 through 3.

You copied and verified both text and image files from the Web site Shannon was interested in. You will eventually give her the files on disk along with a printout of the home page.

Previewing and Printing a Web Page

Like most other Windows programs, Netscape provides printing capabilities. The Print dialog box lets you select such printing options as how many copies you wish to print. In addition, Netscape lets you print only the pages you want, even if a Web site has multiple pages. You can also select and print just an area of a Web page by simply selecting it with your mouse pointer before you print. Figure 3-31 gives additional information on all Netscape printing options.

Figure 3-31 ◀
Printing options

Options	Description
Name	Displays the name of the active printer
Status	Displays active or inactive status of printer
Type	Displays the type of the active printer
Where	Displays connection interface used for printer
Comment	Additional comments about printer
Properties	Displays menu to set additional printing characteristics such as paper size, orientation, and source tray
Print to file	Prints current document to an electronic file instead of hard copy output
Print range	Indicates the pages to print All prints the entire document Pages prints pages you specify Selection prints the portion of the document you select
Copies	Indicates the number of copies to print
Collate	Prints all the pages of the document in sequence

The **Print Preview** feature lets you see how a Web page will look before you print it. Previewing a document before you print it is important because a printed page sometimes looks different from how a page displays on screen. Netscape uses the size of the printed page, rather than the amount of information displayed in your window, to determine a printed page's layout. It automatically rearranges text and graphics for word wrap and other page layout definitions, depending on your printer settings and page setup selections. If you choose to print a Web page in landscape orientation (horizontally on a page) rather than portrait (vertically on a page), for example, the printed version differs from the one that appeared in your window. You can change these type of settings from the Page Setup option on the File menu.

You want to make sure the printout you give Shannon with the text and image files is perfect. You decide to preview the printout of the home page.

To preview a Web page printout:

1. Click **Go** on the menu bar, then click the **JCPenney Home Page** link in the history list to return to the company's home page.

2. Click **File** on the menu bar, then click **Print Preview**. The Print Preview window opens displaying the first page of the home page. See Figure 3-32. Your window may look different because most Web pages are modified regularly.

Figure 3-32 ◀
Print preview of
JCPenney home
page

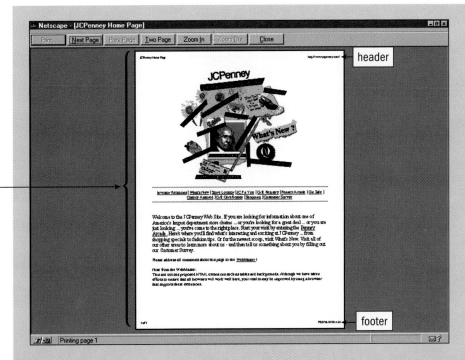

header

your home page
may differ

footer

TROUBLE? If you see two pages in your window, click the One Page button on the Print Preview toolbar.

The pointer shape changes to a magnifying glass 🔍. You can click this pointer anywhere on the document to enlarge its size.

3. Click the vertical scroll bar **up arrow** to move to the top of the page. Notice that the Web page's name appears in the window's upper-left corner and the Web page's URL appears in the upper-right corner. Text printed at the top of the page is called a **header**. Netscape prints a header on every page so you always know where to find that Web page on the Internet. Click 🔍 to enlarge the image at the top of the page.

4. Click the vertical scroll bar **down arrow** to move to the bottom of the page and look at the page number in the lower-left corner of the page and the date and time in the lower-right corner. Text printed at the bottom of the page is called a **footer**. Netscape prints a footer on every page so you can tell how many pages are in your document and when you printed it.

5. Click 🔍 twice to return the page to its original size.

You can use the Print command to print only those pages you need. The Next Page and Prev Page buttons let you browse through a print job that includes more than one page of information.

The preview of your printed page looks good. Next, you print two copies of the page: one copy for Shannon, and the other for your files.

REFERENCE
window

PRINTING A WEB PAGE

- Click File, then click Print.
- Specify the number of copies you want to print in the Number of copies text box.
- Make sure the printer is turned on and contains paper.
- Click OK.

To print a Web page:

1. Click the **Print** button on the Print Preview toolbar to open the Print dialog box.

2. Click the **Number of copies** spin box up arrow until the number of copies value is **2**. See Figure 3-33.

Figure 3-33 ◀
Print dialog box

this information differs depending on the type of computer you are using

set number of copies to 2

click OK to print document

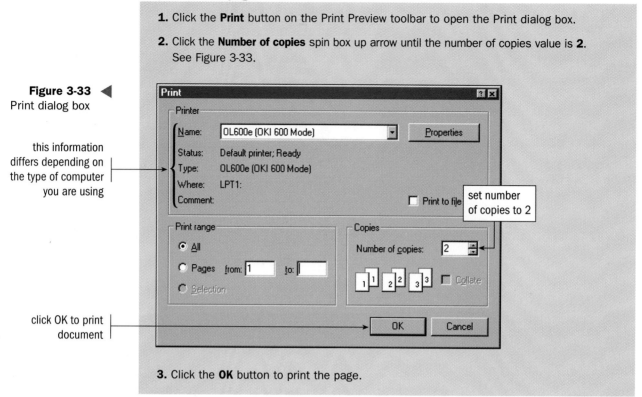

3. Click the **OK** button to print the page.

The printed document well represents the online site your company's competitor uses. While you view the Web page, you notice the status of the security indicator in the lower-left of the page. On Shannon's copy of the printed document you will make a handwritten notation highlighting the home page's security status.

Exiting Netscape

Before you leave for your lunch break, you need to exit the Netscape program. After lunch, you want to begin searching the Internet for some information on demographics and on the presence of online catalogs. Because you are using Netscape to simply view or browse specific Web sites rather than to create or edit Web pages, no work needs to be saved or closed before exiting. You can simply exit the program.

To exit Netscape:

1. Click **File** on the menu bar.

2. Click **Exit**. The Netscape window closes and you return to the Windows desktop.

Quick Check

1. Web pages are electronic documents created with the special programming language called _____.

2. True or False: When linking to a Web page, Netscape contacts the server that stores the Web page, transfers the requested information to your computer, and displays the data in your window.

[3] Which of the following indicates an overloaded Web site?
a. The status message area displays the "site busy" message.
b. The status indicator is not animated.
c. The status message area is blank, but the Stop button on the toolbar indicates that the site is active.

[4] _____ identify files on the WWW so that computers can find and retrieve them.

[5] True or False: Netscape keeps track of Web pages you recently visited in your current session so that you can quickly return to them.

[6] True or False: You do not save HTML coding with the Web page when you save the page as a text file.

[7] The two most common file formats for saving a graphical image from a Web page are_____ and _____.

[8] True or False: You must save the Web page you are viewing before you exit Netscape.

You have completed Session 3.2. When you start Session 3.3 and start Netscape, make sure the Show Toolbar, Show Location, Show Directory Buttons, and Auto Load Images options are toggled on.

SESSION

3.3

In this session you will learn to search the Internet using search tools, guides, and Boolean operators; determine the value of the search results you obtain; use bookmarks; listen to an audio clip; and follow copyright guidelines on the Internet.

Searching the Internet

Search tools are programs that help you navigate the Internet. Search tools available on the WWW can help you find Web pages, files, and multimedia items, as well as help you search through information in some of the other network services, such as Newsgroups. Search tools use different techniques, depending on their particular capabilities as well as the user's request. Search tools use information that has been collected and saved in a database to locate what you want. A **database** is a collection of related information. When you search the WWW, you follow three primary steps. First, you choose and load a search tool. Second, you enter your search criteria in the form of a query. A **query** is a written request structured as a question that indicates what specific documents or information you want the search tool to search for. The search tool uses the **keywords**, or specified words or phrases you are looking for, that are contained in the query to perform the search. Most search tools provide "fill-in-the-blank" search forms to enter your query. After you submit the query, the search tool uses a search engine to return a list of Web sites or other network services that contain or relate to the keyword(s) that most closely match the criteria. The **search engine** retrieves information from the search tool's information database based upon your query. In the final step, you look through the information returned to determine its value and usefulness. You can select a Web site or service you would like to link to based on the returned list. One of the more popular search tools is **WebCrawler**. It began as a small single-user program for finding information on the Web. Eventually purchased by America Online, Inc., it became the first successful commercially operated and supported search tool on the WWW. Figure 3-34 lists some other popular search tools and identifies the types of searches they are best suited for.

Figure 3-34 ◀
Popular search
tools

	Original Creator(s)	Year Established	Description
WebCrawler	Brian Pinkerton	1994, bought by America Online in 1995	First commercial search tool. Searches all Internet services.
DejaNews	DejaNews staff	1995	Searches Usenet Newsgroup listings.
Yahoo!	David Filo and Jerry Yang, Ph.D.	1994	Grew from a hobby. Searches all Internet services. Presents information in a categorical format.

Spiders

Search tools use spiders to index information on the Internet. A **spider** is a type of software that combs through Web documents, identifying text that is the basis for keyword searching. The term "spider" originated because it lends well to the "web" analogy. These automated programs, also sometimes called **wanderers** or **robots**, constantly search the Net for new and useful information. The search engines query the indexed information that the spider collects. Figure 3-35 shows how a typical spider works.

After a spider receives a document, it may put the information in its index database, depending on its indexing capabilities. A spider doesn't necessarily move from one site to another, but rather just requests a particular site to pass along any pertinent documents it comes across. Most spiders are preset to view and index documents in one of two ways. A **depth-first** approach is more inclusive. The spider starts with a particular Web page and then investigates every link available, keeping track of what it finds. Although usually the more accurate method, it can slow down a server with its repeated requests, especially requests involving graphics or large files. Also, a spider can get stuck in a loop while searching a hyperlink that refers back to its original connection. The second approach, the **breadth-first** approach, primarily searches a document's top level, such as its title and headings, rather than referencing each individual link within that document. Some spiders simply store the URL and the document title in its index, while others may store the entire HTML document. Because spiders gather information differently, each most likely yields different query results. Therefore, trying more than one search tool is wise when performing a Web search.

A spider periodically (daily or weekly) connects to servers across the Internet to update its databases. A spider usually starts its indexing search from a list it has searched in the past, a list under a "what's new" heading, or a list that the server maintains. Some searches begin from a scanned list or a mailing list. Many search tools let you submit your own URLs for the spider to search. Although a spider may eventually find and index a site, organizations favor this method if their Web site's intent is to help the general public find them quickly and easily by conducting a search.

Figure 3-35 ◀
How a spider
works

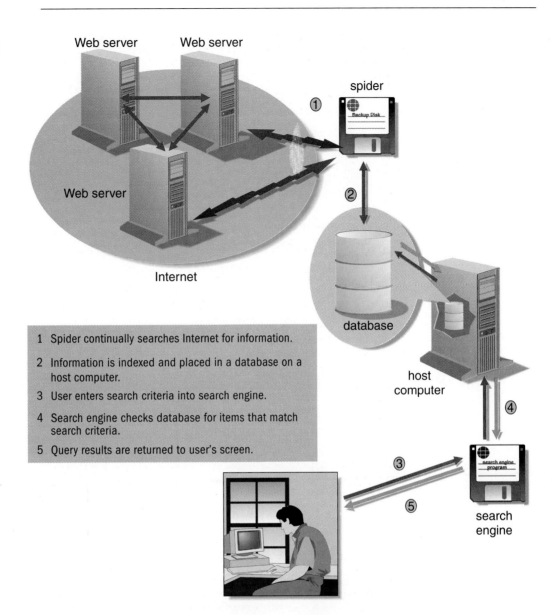

Web server   Web server

spider

① Backup Disk

②

database

Internet

host
computer

1 Spider continually searches Internet for information.

2 Information is indexed and placed in a database on a host computer.

3 User enters search criteria into search engine.

4 Search engine checks database for items that match search criteria.

5 Query results are returned to user's screen.

③

④

⑤

search engine
program

search
engine

Searching by Content

As the number of users who join the Internet increases, the amount of data increases as well. Many organizations and individuals find the Internet useful for distributing information as well as for converting their text-based files to Web pages. The debut of the WWW prompted increased Internet use, and the creation of search tools produced an easy-to-use technique for locating information.

While "surfing" the Internet is a more leisurely browsing of available resources, more focused use of the Internet involves research and fact gathering. When you need information for a school report or are looking for a good deal on productivity software, you have a specific goal. For these activities you do searches that have a topic or theme. Most search tools let you search by the topic or content. The next section discusses other search tools that let you search by categories.

After lunch, you are ready to continue your research. Shannon requested that you locate information about Internet demographics. She wants facts on the median age, male/female ratio, and educational background of Internet users. She will use this information to help determine the audience for the online catalog. You use the WebCrawler search tool to perform a content search and locate this information.

REFERENCE
window

SEARCHING WITH WEBCRAWLER

- Click the Open button.
- Type the WebCrawler URL http://webcrawler.com in the Open text box, then click the Open button.
- Type your search criteria in the Query text box, then click the Search button.
- Browse through the content search results list to find the document you want.

To conduct a search using WebCrawler:

1. If necessary, click the **Home** button [icon] to return to the New Perspectives on the Internet Using Netscape Navigator Software—Introductory Student Online Companion Web page.

2. Click the **Tutorial 3** link, and then scroll to the **Session 3.3** section. See Figure 3-36.

Figure 3-36 ◀
Search by
content

click to access Web
Crawler search tool

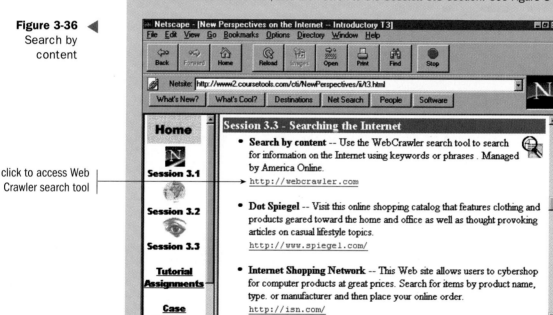

3. Click the **Search by Content** link. After Netscape loads the WebCrawler Web page, briefly look at the window of this popular search tool and note some of the button and menu options available. See Figure 3-37.

Figure 3-37 ◄
WebCrawler
search tool

query text box for
search criteria

search categories

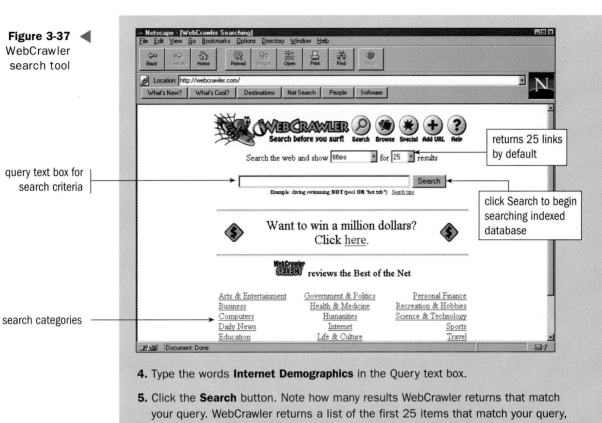

returns 25 links
by default

click Search to begin
searching indexed
database

4. Type the words **Internet Demographics** in the Query text box.

5. Click the **Search** button. Note how many results WebCrawler returns that match your query. WebCrawler returns a list of the first 25 items that match your query, but you can access additional matches in sets of 25. See Figure 3-38.

Figure 3-38 ◄
WebCrawler
search results

number of search
results; first 25
appear

relevancy represented
by graphical element

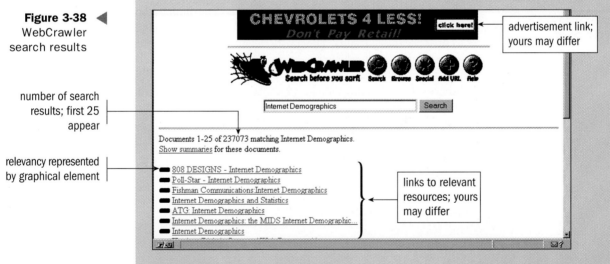

advertisement link;
yours may differ

links to relevant
resources; yours
may differ

TROUBLE? If a Security Information dialog box opens, click the Continue button.

Notice the advertisement link on the page. Many search tools use these small advertisements to earn revenue by selling advertising links on their page to organizations. The advertisements change regularly.

6. Scroll until you see the **Internet Marketing Report by Internet Services Group** link(s). (There may be more than one.) Click this link.

TROUBLE? If you do not see the Internet Marketing Report by Internet Services Group link in your window, you may need to click the Get the next 25 results link on the WebCrawler Web page.

TROUBLE? If you still do not see the Internet Marketing Report by Internet Services Group link in your window, open the URL http://www.thehost.com/info.htm.

7. Browse the Web site until you find the most recent demographic information on Internet usage.

While searching for you, WebCrawler returned several thousand search results of links that matched your query. WebCrawler rates the search results so that you can tell which more closely matches the information you are looking for.

Determining Relevancy

Although the list of items a search tool returns contains the keyword(s) in your query, the sites might not be exactly what you are looking for. Keyword search results primarily indicate the word's presence within a document, not necessarily its context. For instance, a search for the keywords "laser" and "printer" may return results that include information about laser use in the medical field, newspaper printing presses, and office equipment that prints electronic documents. Some basic information can help you determine those sites relevant to your topic and those to ignore. A search tool orders the query results by their level of relevance, according to methods the tool's developer chose. One such method is proximity of keywords within a document. When a user submits a query containing two or more keywords, the closer the keywords are to each other in the document, the more relevant the document is considered. In our example, a document having "laser" and "printer" next to each other would rank higher and appear earlier on the search results list than one with "laser" in the first paragraph and "printer" in the third paragraph.

Another common method for rating relevancy is determining how many times the word(s) appear in the document. Some methods are more complex and accurate than others but take longer to produce query results. The most relevant references in your query appear at the top of the list, while the least relevant is at the bottom. In some search results, a numerical rating precedes each reference, typically with ranges from 100 (most relevant) to 0 (least relevant). Others show relevancy with graphics. See Figure 3-39 for two samples of search results with relevancy ratings.

Figure 3-39
Relevancy
ratings

Lycos search tool ⟶

search criteria ⟶

relevancy to query ⟶

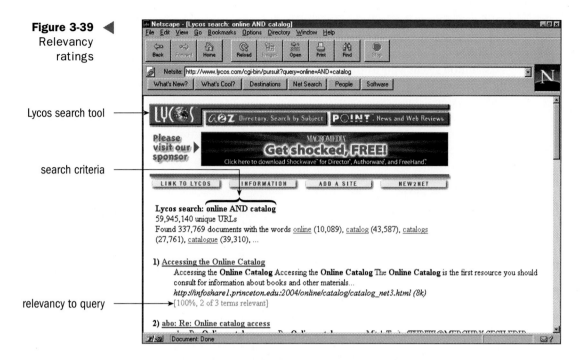

DejaNews
search tool ⟶

search
criteria

relevancy to
query

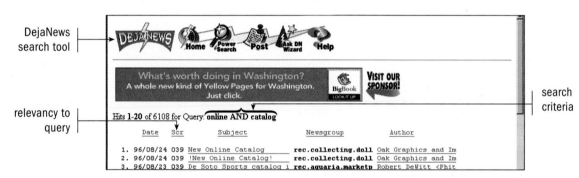

Searching Using Boolean Operators

When your query has more than one keyword, most search tools offer the option of using a Boolean operator. **Boolean operators** are words and symbols that let you narrow your search by setting specific search criteria conditions.

The Boolean OR operator specifies that either keyword can be contained in the retrieved documents listed among the search results. Most search tools automatically use the OR Boolean operator when you enter more than one keyword in a query. The search tool assumes that you are most interested in retrieving documents that contain all of the words within it. Because of this, these documents are at the beginning of the returned search list. The Boolean operator **AND** in the search query specifically tells the search tool that you want only documents containing both words to be listed in the search results. The Boolean operator **NOT** tells the search tool to find documents that contain the first word listed, but not the second.

Shannon needs you to find an estimate of how many online catalogs are currently on the Internet. Using the WebCrawler search tool, you will query with the words "online" and "catalog." First, you search for the words using the default OR Boolean operator. You note the number of search results returned and then search again, this time using the AND Boolean operator to see if the difference between the results is notable.

To search using the AND Boolean operator:

1. Click the **Back** button 🔲 until you return to the WebCrawler Query text box.

2. Highlight the previous search query in the text box, and type the new query **online catalog**. The new search query replaces the previous one.

3. Click the **Search** button. Write down the number of results WebCrawler returns. WebCrawler uses the OR Boolean operator by default when you include two or more words in a query.

   TROUBLE? If a Security Information dialog box opens, click the Continue button.

4. Click the **Back** button 🔲 to return to the **WebCrawler Query** text box.

5. Highlight the previous search query, and type the new query **online AND catalog**. The new search query replaces the previous one. See Figure 3-40.

Figure 3-40 ◀
Using Boolean operators

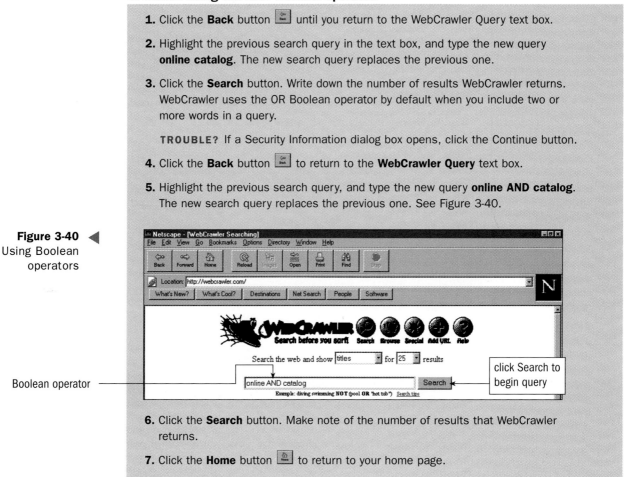

Boolean operator ———

6. Click the **Search** button. Make note of the number of results that WebCrawler returns.

7. Click the **Home** button 🔲 to return to your home page.

You are surprised to see how much difference the Boolean operator makes. You decide to just surf the Internet for the next half hour to see if you come across interesting sites selling products online. You wonder where to start looking.

Searching by Guide

Some search tools reportedly index over 500 new Web pages each day; thus, browsing each new Web page is nearly impossible. Netscape guides help keep you abreast of new and interesting sites. **Guides** are Web pages that provide a good starting point with links for browsing the WWW. Two Netscape guides are useful for surfing the Web: the What's Cool site and the What's New site. You decide to use these two guides to surf the WWW.

Finding What's Cool

Netscape Communications Corporation maintains the What's Cool site. This site contains links to interesting and unusual Web sites. Often, these sites contain multimedia items or unusual layouts. Some sites are purely entertaining, whereas others are useful business tools. Netscape routinely scours the Internet for these unusual sites and then hyperlinks them to their What's Cool Web page. Netscape updates the page routinely, usually at least monthly. Because the site is constantly kept current with new information, it's a good place to start surfing and routinely return to. Similar types of cool link lists exist all over the WWW. You decide to check out Netscape's What's Cool site first.

To look at the What's Cool list:

1. Click the **What's Cool?** directory button `What's Cool?` to link to a list of unusual Web sites. See Figure 3-41. Netscape Communications Corporation frequently updates the hyperlinks on the Web page, so your window may look different from Figure 3-41.

Figure 3-41
Netscape's
What's Cool?
Web page

click to open
Netscape's list of
"cool" sites

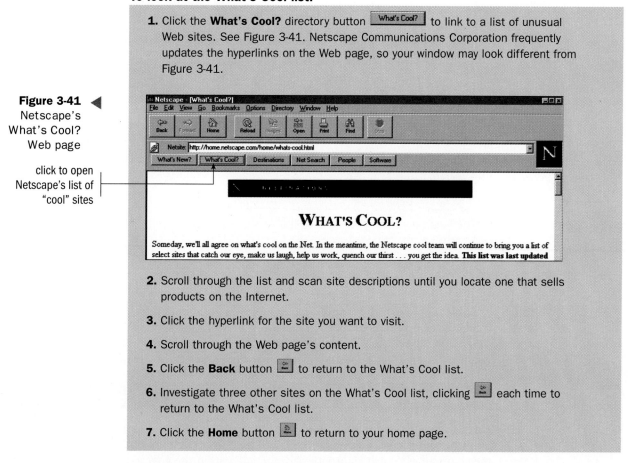

2. Scroll through the list and scan site descriptions until you locate one that sells products on the Internet.

3. Click the hyperlink for the site you want to visit.

4. Scroll through the Web page's content.

5. Click the **Back** button to return to the What's Cool list.

6. Investigate three other sites on the What's Cool list, clicking each time to return to the What's Cool list.

7. Click the **Home** button to return to your home page.

After you look at some unusual sites on the What's Cool page, you decide to use the What's New page and compare the two guides.

Finding What's New

Netscape's What's New site contains hyperlinks to new Web sites. Anyone can recommend a Web site for this list. Netscape Communications Corporation doesn't necessarily endorse any of the sites listed. It does, however, reserve the right to accept or reject any URL submitted. Overall, Netscape tries to list new sites that are innovative or that use a new technique or technology. Netscape also updates this list frequently so it is a good place to start learning about new and exciting Web sites. Other individuals or groups also maintain lists of new Web sites. Each list maintains its own set of rules and regulations for collecting and listing new Web sites. You will now use the What's New site to look for sites that present products or information in clever or imaginative ways.

To look at the What's New list:

1. Click the **What's New** directory button [What's New?] to connect to a list of new Web sites that Netscape compiled. See Figure 3-42. Your window may look different because Netscape routinely updates the list.

Figure 3-42 ◀
Netscape's
What's New?
Web page

click to open
Netscape's list of new
sites on the WWW

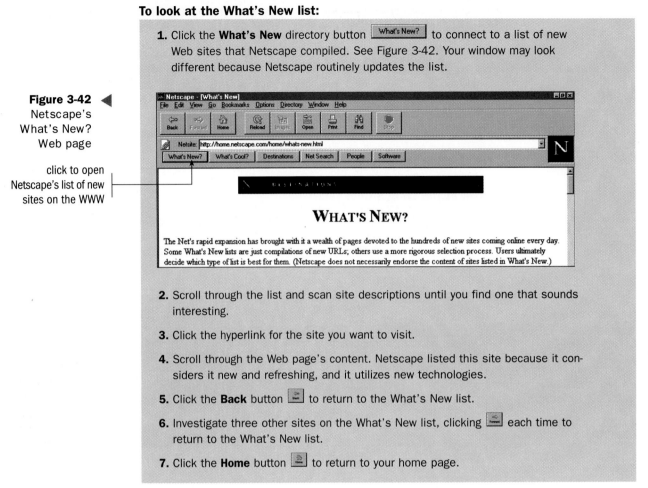

2. Scroll through the list and scan site descriptions until you find one that sounds interesting.

3. Click the hyperlink for the site you want to visit.

4. Scroll through the Web page's content. Netscape listed this site because it considers it new and refreshing, and it utilizes new technologies.

5. Click the **Back** button to return to the What's New list.

6. Investigate three other sites on the What's New list, clicking each time to return to the What's New list.

7. Click the **Home** button to return to your home page.

Netscape's What's New and What's Cool sites are very popular. So popular, in fact, that reaching them is sometimes hard. As a result, you may sometimes be unable to link to these pages or even to other pages that the same server hosts. If these sites are busy when you want to use them, consider using one of the other guides available.

Using a Navigational Guide

Navigational guides are a means of navigating the Internet or a Web site with the click of a mouse. A **navigational guide** lists or indexes Web pages that are organized around a central theme or subject, such as lists of departments within the government's executive branch. Each navigational guide follows its own format, style, and timetable for updates. Most navigational guides use graphical icons or other graphical elements to link to the listed pages. Figure 3-43 shows a navigational guide the Hewlett-Packard organization uses. The navigational guide's easy-to-use buttons link to the organization's products, services, business solutions, and support pages. Clicking the buttons jumps the user to a corresponding Web page. The navigational guide acts as a starting point for locating information on the Hewlett-Packard Web site.

Figure 3-43 ◀
Navigational
guide

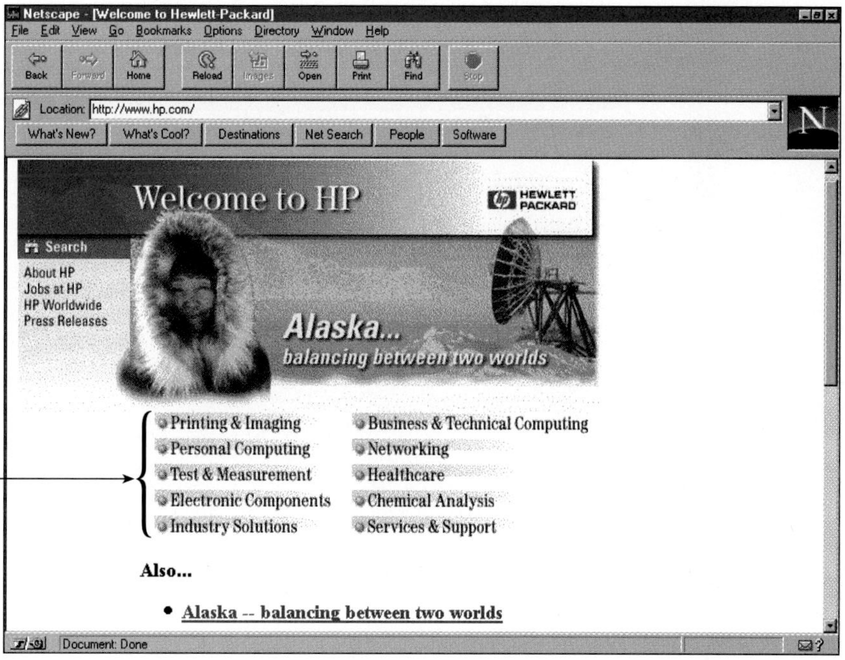

links →

Your project file continues to grow with useful information for Shannon to use to prepare for the online marketing effort. Although you enjoyed using the What's New and What's Cool sites, you need to know how to easily return to the sites you chose without having to remember their URLs or referring to your handwritten notes each time. Earlier, Shantu mentioned a feature called Bookmarks that lets users quickly return to a Web site at a later date. You found some especially good Web sites. You use the Bookmark feature to mark the sites that you would like Shannon to view later.

Using Bookmarks

If you find a Web page that you think you may want to revisit, you can easily mark the page for future reference. The Netscape feature **bookmarks** lets you save the URLs of these Web pages so you don't need to use a search tool, guide, or handwritten reminder. You can collect several bookmarks together in a master list called a **bookmark list**.

When you add the link of a favorite Web site to your bookmark list, Netscape adds the Web page title and a hypertext link to the bottom of the list and updates the file bookmark.htm on your computer's hard disk. After you add a bookmark to your list, the title remains on the list until you remove it or change lists. To access a page on the list, you simply select it. Netscape bookmarks are good tools for personalizing your access to the Internet. As your bookmark list grows, you can manage it by creating bookmark categories. For instance, you could have a bookmark category called "research" for Web sites that deal with research for an upcoming report or one called "graduate_schools" that contains links to Web sites of graduate schools you are considering attending next year. The categorization is much like the file and folder hierarchy of your hard drive.

If you browse the WWW from several different computers, you can actually save the bookmark file on disk and take it with you to each location. Because you store bookmarks in files, sharing a bookmark file with another user is easy. You decide to create a bookmark list on disk for Shannon that includes three impressive Web sites you found while using the What's New and What's Cool guides.

To create a bookmark file on disk:

1. Click **Window** on the menu bar, then click **Bookmarks**. The Netscape Bookmarks window opens. See Figure 3-44. If you already created bookmarks, the window displays a directory of all your bookmarks. If not, the window is empty.

Figure 3-44 ◀
Bookmarks list

if you have created
bookmarks already,
they will be listed here

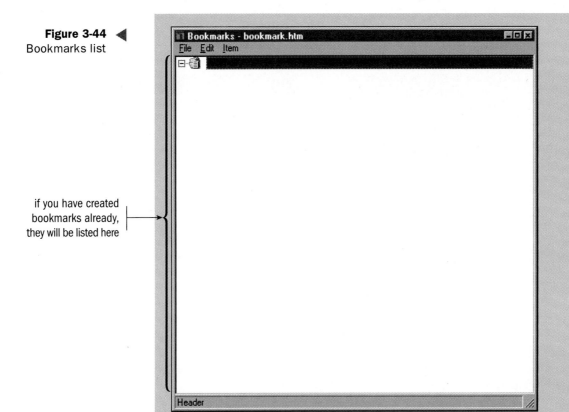

2. If necessary, insert your Student Disk into drive A or the appropriate drive on your computer.

3. Click **File** on the Bookmarks menu bar, then click **Save As**.

4. Type **a:\bookmark.htm** in the File name text box, and then press the **Enter** key. A copy of the bookmarks list is saved on your disk. You will add Web site information to this bookmark file and present it to Shannon.

5. Click **File** on the Bookmarks menu bar, then click **Open**. The Open bookmarks file dialog box opens.

6. Click **bookmark.htm** in the file list, and then press the **Enter** key to open the bookmark file from your disk. Any bookmarks you add will be added only to the bookmark.htm file on your disk, not the copy on your computer's hard drive.

7. Click **File** on the Bookmarks menu bar, then click **Close** to exit the Bookmarks window.

With your disk ready to save bookmarks, you will add a bookmark for the first site that you want Shannon to view.

Adding a Bookmark

The Bookmark list gives you fast and easy access to your favorite or most frequently visited Web pages. You can add a bookmark for any page using the Bookmarks menu. You want to add a bookmark for the Spiegel Company's online catalog, the Internet Shopping Network Web site, and your home page.

ADDING A BOOKMARK

- Load the Web page that you want to create a bookmark for.
- Click Bookmarks, then click Add Bookmark.

To add a bookmark:

1. Click the **Home** button to return to the New Perspectives on the Internet Using Netscape Navigator–Introductory Student Online Companion Web page.

2. Click the **Tutorial 3** link, and then scroll to the **Session 3.3** section.

3. Click the **Dot Spiegel** link to jump to the Spiegel Web site. The Web site loads. The Spiegel site offers online shopping, an online magazine, a bulletin board site, and more.

4. Click **Bookmarks** to open the Bookmarks menu.

5. Click the **Add Bookmark** to create a bookmark for the current Web page and add the bookmark to the bookmark.htm file on your disk.

6. Click the **Back** button to return to the Session 3.3 section.

7. Click the **Internet Shopping Network** link to jump to the Internet Shopping Network Web site. The Web site loads. Among other features, this site offers online shopping, a comprehensive search engine, and contests.

8. Click **Bookmarks** to open the Bookmarks menu.

9. Click **Add Bookmark** to add the current Web page's bookmark to the bookmark.htm file on your disk.

10. Click the **Back** button to return to the Session 3.3 section.

11. Click the **Home** button to return to your home page. Create a bookmark for your home page.

12. Click **Bookmarks** on the menu bar, then click **Go to Bookmarks**. The Bookmarks window opens. The bookmarks you just added to your bookmark. htm file are displayed in this window. See Figure 3-45.

Figure 3-45 ◀
Modified
bookmarks list

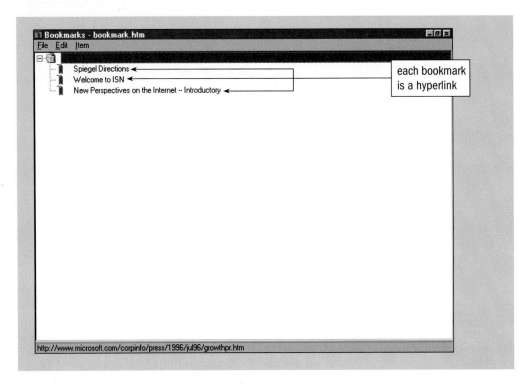

Now that you added bookmarks for each site, you want to make sure you added them correctly before giving the file to Shannon.

Accessing a Bookmark

You can easily access bookmarks from the Bookmarks menu on the menu bar. When you add a bookmark to your bookmark.htm file, it remains on the Bookmarks menu until you delete it or alter the bookmark file. Now you use the Bookmark feature to return to the Spiegel Web site.

To access a bookmark:

1. Click **Bookmarks** on the menu bar. The bookmarks you added are now listed at the bottom of the Bookmarks menu.

   TROUBLE? If the bookmarks do not appear on your Bookmarks menu, you may need to click the More Bookmarks option at the bottom of the Bookmarks menu.

2. Click **SpiegelHomepage**, the bookmark you added, to quickly return to that Web page.

3. Click the **Home** button.

Because the bookmark file you copied to your disk may have bookmarks of no interest to Shannon, you remove them from your bookmarks list.

Deleting a Bookmark

Deleting or removing bookmarks from your bookmarks list is as easy as adding them. Just as occasionally cleaning out and organizing your files is a good idea, so is keeping your bookmark file up to date. You may have a bookmark for a site that no longer interests you, or one for an abandoned site. Deleting unnecessary bookmarks keeps your list of bookmarks manageable.

You delete the home page bookmark file entry because Shannon doesn't need it.

DELETING A BOOKMARK

- Click Window, then click Bookmarks.
- Click the bookmark you want to delete, then press the Delete key.
- Click File, then click Close.

To delete a bookmark:

1. Click **Window** on the menu bar.

2. Click **Bookmarks**. The Bookmarks window opens, showing all bookmarks in the bookmark.htm file on your disk.

3. Click **New Perspectives on the Internet—Introductory**. You want to remove this bookmark.

4. Press the **Delete** key to remove this bookmark from the list.

5. Click **File** on the Bookmarks main menu, then click **Close** to close the Netscape Bookmarks window.

Pleased with the content of the bookmark.htm file you created for Shannon, you place the disk with the file in your project folder. Shannon can open the bookmark file on her own computer using Netscape and view the bookmarks you placed in it. Now you work on the final task Shannon assigned: evaluating elements that will make a Web site more appealing and inviting. You research audio-visual capabilities through multimedia items.

Displaying Multimedia Using Netscape

Many Web sites have multimedia links: audio, video, and graphical elements whose purpose is to make the pages more visually exciting and interesting. These elements range from a simple recorded greeting to an animated 3-D graphical representation of a corporate headquarters. Some Web sites consist primarily of multimedia items. For instance, the Web site of a music group that wants you to buy their latest CD may be entirely devoted to a particular song.

Most sound and video clips you view on the WWW are actually files, instead of live shots, that can be arranged in a variety of formats. Some offer better quality, while others provide just the basics; some require large amounts of disk space, others do not. Sound and video take more disk space than simple text.

Multimedia items on a Web site require special software that interprets how to present the information. These software programs are called **viewers** or **helpers**. If you click a link to view a video clip, for example, Netscape decides how to handle the file and whether it is capable of showing the video clip on your computer. If not, it may prompt you to save the video clip file for later viewing or instruct you to configure the software you need to view that particular file type.

Netscape has many built-in viewers and helpers. However, the type of computer you are using and its multimedia capabilities, such as a built-in sound card and speakers, determines what you can view.

Listening to an Audio Clip

The LiveAudio feature of Netscape lets you hear music and voices directly from Web pages without downloading a separate helper program or waiting for an independent program to load. The player console looks much like a home stereo console. It lets you select, play, stop, or pause the audio clip. As soon as you select the audio link, the console appears. You have the option of saving the clip as well so you can listen to it later.

If the audio file being transferred to your computer is not in a recognizable format, Netscape opens the Unknown File Type dialog box so you can:

- Save the file on disk so that you can listen to the audio clip on another computer that recognizes the file format.

- Cancel the transfer.

- Select another program that can interpret the sound file. Then you have the opportunity to add the program to Netscape's list of Helper programs.

Shannon asked you to search for ways to ensure that the online catalog the Birdland Bay Company is creating is as innovative and interactive as possible without being over-engineered. As you surfed the WWW, you noticed links for audio clips. You want to listen to an audio clip on a Web page to see how Netscape plays the sound. You are anxious to hear the type of sound quality that can be obtained from a Web site.

To listen to an audio clip:

1. Click the **Home** button to return to the New Perspectives on the Internet Using Netscape Navigator—Introductory Student Online Companion Web page.

2. Click the **Tutorial 3** link, then scroll to **Session 3.3**.

3. Position your pointer over one of the **Audio** buttons. See Figure 3-46.

Figure 3-46 ◄
Audio clip

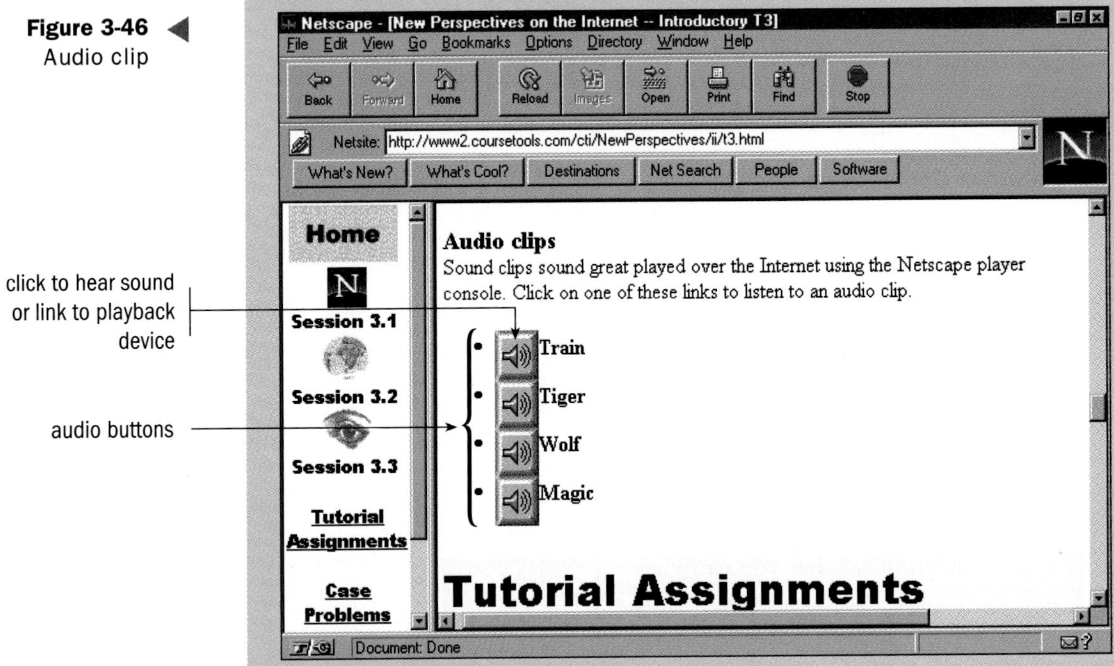

click to hear sound
or link to playback
device

audio buttons

4. Click  to open the LiveAudio playback device, similar to the one shown in Figure 3-47.

Figure 3-47 ◀
Playback
device

Play button ─────

Some sounds automatically play after the file loads; others require you to click the Play button.

5. If the status message area indicates that the sound has loaded, but you hear nothing, click the **Play** button to hear the audio clip.

TROUBLE? If you do not hear any sound after you click the Play button on the playback device, your computer may not have audio or multimedia capabilities, or the sound on your speakers may be turned down. If you continue to have trouble, check with your instructor or technical support person.

TROUBLE? If the Unknown File Type dialog box opens, your Netscape installation does not recognize this type of audio file, and you cannot hear the audio clip. Click the Cancel button to close the dialog box and continue with the tutorial.

6. Click the **Close** button ☒ in the upper-right corner of the playback device to close it, if necessary.

Reproducing Material from the Internet

Reproducing text and images from Internet sites is easy, perhaps even easier than photocopying. The copied material's quality is the same as the original; colors, shading, and graphics do not darken or distort, as they may in a photocopied version. However, restrictions apply to the use of these files.

Copyright law protects all printed material, such as books and magazines, and all audio material, such as music CDs or books on tape, from unlimited reproduction. A **copyright** is a federal law that lets an author (or the copyright holder) control the use of his or her work, including how it's reproduced, sold, distributed, adapted, performed, or displayed. As soon as an author's original material exists in a tangible form, such as on paper, electronic file or a compact disk, the work is copyrighted whether it carries a copyright notice or not.

Depending on the quantity and purpose of reproducing material from the Internet, permission from the Web page owner (the copyright holder) may be needed. In some cases, a fee may be required. Figure 3-48 outlines some guidelines for determining if you need to request permission before reusing material from the Internet.

After going over some copyright guidelines associated with Web pages, you decide to jot a quick note to Shannon to let her know that you will forward some copy-protected material. You attach the note to the project folder. If Shannon decides to include any copyrighted information in her report, she needs to write the page owner a letter requesting permission to use it. Usually this is a very simple task because most Web pages have a hyperlink to automatically send an electronic message to the page's creator.

You provided Shannon with all materials she needs for her strategic planning meeting. She is pleased with the amount of work you have done and its quality.

Figure 3-48 ◄
Guidelines for
reusing material
from the Internet

Copyright Notice	Academic Use (Term Paper, Research Paper, Class Materials)	Commercial Use (Advertisement, Will Be Copyrighted, Will Be Sold)
Copyrighted	Can reuse certain amount without permission. Include proper citation. Request permission to reuse large amounts.	Request permission from page owner.
No copyright or mention of use	Assume copyrighted.	Assume copyrighted.
Source states "use freely no restrictions"	Can reuse without permission.	Can reuse without permission.

Quick Check

1 _____ let you search for information on the Internet using keyword(s) queries.

2 Two common methods that search tools use to determine search document relevancy are _____ and _____.

3 _____ lets you narrow your search criteria.

4 Two good guides that provide starting points for surfing the Internet are Netscape's _____ and _____ sites.

5 A professional association's Web site may have a _____ that lets users easily link to related Web pages from the site.

6 _____ provide an easy way to save URLs of the Web pages you visit most.

7 Netscape has built-in _____ that assist in displaying multimedia items.

8 True or False: Web pages on the Internet are copyright protected.

Tutorial Assignments

The Birdland Bay Company (BBC) has moved ahead with its plans for expansion via a new online catalog. A counter on its Web site gauges how much activity the site is experiencing. Currently, about 1200 users per day are accessing the site. BBC hopes that number increases dramatically over the next six months.

Since the Web site is not stored on a secure server, Shannon is concerned about a possible break-in to the corporate LAN. Although a physical break-in is nearly impossible, users who access the server that hosts the Web site pose a potential threat. Shannon wants the Web site to be housed on a secure server and is interested in how a firewall might protect data on the server and keep users from accessing the corporate LAN. BBC needs to develop and implement a security strategy. Once again, Shannon recruits you to help. She wants you to research some information about firewalls before her next management meeting.

If necessary, start Netscape and then follow these steps:

1. On your home page, click Tutorial Assignments and the Case Problems link.
2. Scroll down until you see the Tutorial 3 Tutorial Assignments.
3. Click the WebCrawler link.
4. Type "firewall solutions" in the Query text box, and press the Enter key.
5. Link to the first five documents listed on the returned search list.
6. Print the first page of each Web site.
7. Evaluate each site, write a brief description of the information each covers, and rate the sites from one to five on their relevancy to your search criteria.

E EXPLORE

8. Return to the WebCrawler Web page, and enter the search criteria again, this time using the AND Boolean operator, for example, firewall AND solutions.
9. Write a brief paragraph comparing the first five listings with the previous searches' top five finds.
10. Exit Netscape.

Case Problems

1. Researching University Admissions Policies on the Web Andrew Vic, a sophomore at Lakeland Community College, plans to attend a four-year university and needs admissions information from two schools he is considering. He wants admissions information on Trent University, in Peterborough, Ontario, Canada, and Arizona State University. His mother attended Trent University and hopes he will also attend this school. However, Arizona State University has a great baseball team, and some of its scouts have expressed interest in Andrew. Andrew has also heard good things about its Honors program. He asks you to help him locate information on the Web for these two schools. For each university, locate program deadlines for next semester.

If necessary, start Netscape. The New Perspectives on the Internet Using Netscape Navigator Software—Introductory Student Online Companion Web page displays in your window. Do the following:

1. Click the Tutorial 3 link, then click the Case Problems link.
2. Click the Yahoo Search link in the Case Problem 1 section.
3. Type the search criteria "Trent University Ontario Canada" in the Criteria text box, then click the Search button.
4. Scroll through the search results list to find the Trent University Web page, then link to the site.
5. Search for the admissions policy for full-time students.
6. Print the admissions policy and the admissions deadline information for next semester.
7. Return to Yahoo! and enter the search criteria "Arizona State University" in the Criteria text box.
8. Search for the admissions policy for transfer students into the Honors program.
9. Print the admissions policy and the admissions deadline information for next semester.
10. Exit Netscape.

2. Travel Arrangements Using the Alaska Airlines Web Site Several managers at the Techmat Corporation are preparing for a trip to Las Vegas. They will attend an information technology show at the LV Convention Center between November 2 and 7. They asked you to check into flight reservations and prices for two different departure dates. They are also interested in the price differences between coach and first-class seating.

If necessary, start Netscape. The New Perspectives on the Internet Using Netscape Navigator Software—Introductory Student Online Companion Web page displays in your window. Do the following:

1. Click the Tutorial 3 link, then click the Case Problems link.
2. Click the Alaska Airlines link in the Case Problem 2 section.
3. Select the Reservations link.
4. Using the online form, fill in reservation information to find a round trip flight from Seattle to Las Vegas for four people in the coach section. The departure date is the morning of November 2 and the return date is the afternoon of November 7.
5. Search for the available flight information, and then print the search results.
6. Return to the online form, and use the same information, but this time request first-class seating.
7. Search for the available flight information, and then print the search results.
8. Return to the online form once again, and search for the same flight information, except with an evening departure on November 1 and an afternoon return on November 7.

9. Search for available flight information for both coach and first-class seating.
10. Print the results of each search.
11. Exit Netscape.

3. Send a Virtual Flower Bouquet to Your Administrative Assistant Dana Henskamp has been your administrative assistant for two years. Next Thursday, she turns 30 years old. You decide to surprise her with an electronic bouquet of flowers ordered over the WWW.

If necessary, start Netscape. The New Perspectives on the Internet Using Netscape Navigator Software—Introductory Student Online Companion Web page displays in your window. Do the following:

1. Click the Tutorial 3 link, then click the Case Problems link.
2. Click the CyberPark Virtual Flower Shop link in the Case Problem 3 section.
3. Fill in the online order form. For learning purposes, place your e-mail address in the Recipient's E-mail address text box. If you do not know your e-mail address, ask your instructor or technical support person for assistance.
4. Scroll through the Web site, and select the type of flowers you want to send to Dana.
5. From the Occasion list, select Happy Birthday.
6. In the message text input field, type "Happy 30th Birthday Dana!"
7. Preview the card.
8. Print the current Web page showing the completed card and greeting.
9. Send the card and bouquet.
10. Exit Netscape.

4. Creating Bookmarks for Interesting Web Sites Now that you have some experience using search tools on the WWW, you should be able to locate almost any type of information on the Internet. Using WebCrawler or any search tool listed under the Net Search button, investigate Web pages to answer the following questions. When you find the answers, write down the URLs where you found the information. Save the Web page locations on your bookmark list on your disk so that you can share the bookmark list with others.

If necessary, launch Netscape, then search for answers to the following questions:

1. What is the weather report for today in or near your home town?
2. When is the next scheduled NASA space shuttle flight, and what will be its mission?
3. Find five reasons why fans believed Paul McCartney of the Beatles was dead.
4. What is the U.S. President's e-mail address?
5. What is the address, phone number, and e-mail address of your Congressional representative in the U.S. House of Representatives?
6. Can you view images sent back to earth from the Hubbell Telescope via the Internet?
7. Who was the voice of the character Woody in the movie *Toy Story*?
8. What is the URL for the Discovery Channel Online?
9. Finally, open and print your bookmark list.
10. Exit Netscape.

Using E-mail and Mailing Lists to Communicate

Copper King Outdoor Adventures Reaches Customers with Electronic Communication Tools

CASE

Copper King Outdoor Adventures

Copper King Outdoor Adventures (CKOA) is a family-owned business on the beautiful Thompson River in northwestern Montana. The mid-sized company specializes in guided trout fishing tours, hiking, and mountain backpacking trips. Even though CKOA is in a rural area, its managers find that marketing their business on the Internet provides worldwide exposure and brings them many customers. Richard and Rose Hensyel, proprietors of CKOA, currently use electronic mail to communicate with employees, business associates, and clients. They are considering creating a mailing list to publicize details of upcoming activities as well as offer general outdoor adventure information.

A recent college graduate, you have been hired by Richard and Rose to fill the newly created position of special projects coordinator. Your first project is to work on a new CKOA event: the upcoming fall wildlife photography excursion. To complete your responsibilities and meet your deadlines, you will communicate with your colleagues via e-mail during various stages of the project. In addition, you will research how a mailing list may be useful for distributing information about this excursion and future CKOA offerings.

LAB

E-mail

SESSION

4.1

In this session you will learn what e-mail is and how it works. You will learn about the elements that comprise an e-mail address and e-mail message. You will become familiar with the Netscape Mail window in order to compose and send e-mail messages, as well as create an address book to store commonly used e-mail addresses. Finally, you will learn how to attach files to an e-mail message and create a distribution list to send e-mail messages to a group of people.

E-mail

What Is E-mail?

E-mail, short for **electronic mail**, transfers electronic correspondence between one or more network users. This correspondence consists of **e-mail messages**, which are essentially letters, memos, or pieces of information sent electronically from one user to another. E-mail messages can be just text or can include multimedia items, such as sound clips or graphics. E-mail is a low-cost and fast way to communicate both domestically and internationally without incurring large phone bills or relying on postal delivery. It has become the most reliable and popular way for people to communicate over the Internet, with millions of messages sent every day.

How E-mail Works

In Tutorial 1 you learned how information travels over the Internet. E-mail travels over the Internet in much the same way. Figure 4-1 shows how the e-mail system works. After you compose your e-mail message, you identify its intended recipient and specify the message's destination by typing the user's unique e-mail address. The next section discusses the e-mail addressing system in more detail.

Figure 4-1 ◀
How e-mail
works

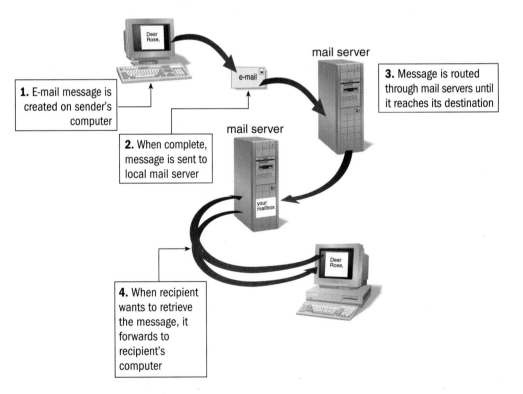

1. E-mail message is created on sender's computer

2. When complete, message is sent to local mail server

mail server

3. Message is routed through mail servers until it reaches its destination

mail server

4. When recipient wants to retrieve the message, it forwards to recipient's computer

By means of networked hosts connected to the Internet, e-mail messages can travel electronically between computers that aren't connected directly to one another. After you "send" your message, it starts an electronic journey to its destination. First it arrives at a **mail server**, a system that determines the best route for a message to take to reach its intended recipient. The mail server uses the destination domain address and the recipient's identification information included with the message to determine the location of the next mail server stop. The mail server specifically uses Mail Exchange (MX) records located in the DNS database to route e-mail from one host to another. A message for a person outside the original domain simply passes along to other mail servers that sort and route it. An e-mail message may pass through any number of mail servers before finally reaching its destination. The network standard Simple Mail Transfer Protocol, or **SMTP**, governs the way e-mail is sent and routed across mail servers. SMTP, a part of the TCP/IP protocol suite, is a common set of rules that mail servers follow so that e-mail is routed correctly and efficiently. While SMTP primarily handles outgoing messages, Post Office Protocol generally manages incoming messages. Post Office Protocol, or **POP**, is a network standard used for accessing e-mail messages remotely on TCP/IP networks.

After the e-mail message arrives at its destination, it is delivered to the recipient's computer mailbox by special Internet software called mail server software. **Mail server software** controls the flow of the e-mail between the server and the user's computer. **Mail client software** helps each user retrieve, compose, send, save, and delete messages. Later in this tutorial, you will use Netscape's built-in mail client software to create and send your own e-mail messages.

The mail server stores e-mail messages. When you want to retrieve e-mail messages you have received, the server forwards them to your computer. Thus e-mail is a **store-and-forward** technology. Because the server stores your messages, you will continue to receive messages when your computer is turned off.

Anatomy of an E-mail Address

An e-mail address consists of two distinct parts: the user ID and the host address. These two pieces of information tell the mail server the name and address of the recipient. An entire e-mail address may vary in length from a minimum of two parts to as many as six, depending on the length of the host address. An e-mail address with more than six parts is rare. Figure 4-2 shows the e-mail address that Rose uses at the Copper King company.

Figure 4-2 ◄
Anatomy of an
e-mail address

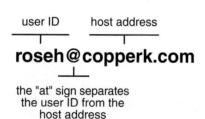

The first part of an e-mail address is the user identification, more commonly known as the **user ID**. It generally consists of the login or account name that a person uses to identify his or her online account. The organization that manages your account usually assigns user IDs, although sometimes you may be able to pick your own. E-mail user IDs commonly consist of some combination of a person's first and last name and/or initials, but typically do not exceed eight characters. Another method of assigning user IDs is using computer-generated random numbers. Notice in Figure 4-2 that Rose's user ID is roseh.

The second part of an e-mail address is the **host address**, the physical location where an e-mail message should be delivered. This portion of the e-mail address identifies the domain, or host, where the user has an account. Periods separate the host address, indicating a specific host's or sub-domain's location. In Figure 4-2 the host address portion of Rose's e-mail address is copperk.com. To limit length, e-mail addresses are often abbreviated. For example, the wording "copperk" stands for the Copper King company. The .com portion of the host address indicates CKOA is part of the commercial domain, a domain used by commercial entities ranging from large corporations to small businesses. The e-mail @ symbol separating the user ID and host address stands for and is pronounced as the word "at," while the period is pronounced "dot."

Becoming Familiar with the Netscape Mail Window

The Mail window in Netscape acts as your personal assistant in retrieving, sending, replying to, forwarding, deleting, and saving e-mail messages. The Mail window looks and operates much like the main Netscape window, with its toolbar, pull-down menus, and buttons for accomplishing specific messaging tasks. Netscape's built-in mail client lets you manage e-mail messages with ease.

Opening the Netscape Mail Window

As coordinator for the upcoming wildlife photography excursion, you work with a few key people to bring the project to realization. Rose wants to call a staff meeting of these team members to discuss the excursion. She asks you to start e-mailing people about the upcoming staff meeting first thing tomorrow morning so that they have at least a week's notice. Before you need to start using e-mail, you've set aside some time this afternoon to become familiar with the elements of the Netscape Mail window so that you're comfortable in the environment. First you start Netscape and open the Mail window.

To open the Mail window:

1. Start Netscape.

2. Click **Window** on the menu bar, then click **Netscape Mail** to open the Mail window. See Figure 4-3.

Figure 4-3
Elements of the Mail window

mail folder pane showing mail folders

message content pane

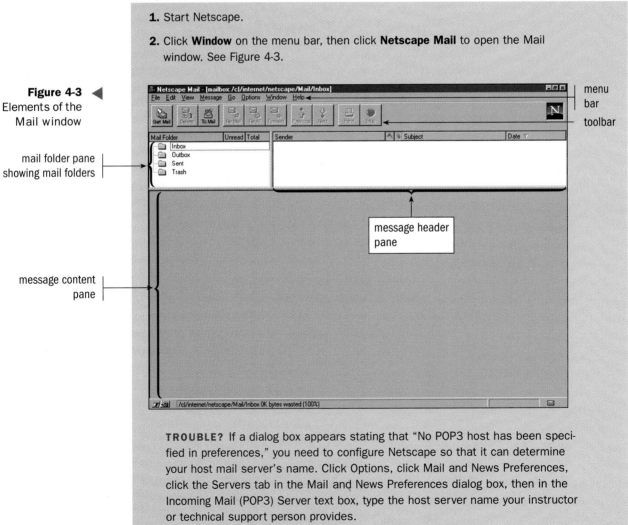

menu bar

toolbar

message header pane

TROUBLE? If a dialog box appears stating that "No POP3 host has been specified in preferences," you need to configure Netscape so that it can determine your host mail server's name. Click Options, click Mail and News Preferences, click the Servers tab in the Mail and News Preferences dialog box, then in the Incoming Mail (POP3) Server text box, type the host server name your instructor or technical support person provides.

TROUBLE? If a dialog box appears stating that "Netscape is unable to use the POP3 server because you have not provided a username. Please provide one in the Preferences and try again," you need to configure Netscape with your user ID and e-mail address information. Click Options, click Mail and News Preferences, click the Identity tab in the Mail and News Preferences dialog box, then enter your full e-mail address in the Your Email text box. If you don't know your e-mail address, ask your instructor or technical support person for assistance.

TROUBLE? If you are prompted to enter a password to use the mail client, Netscape may be configured to automatically check for incoming e-mail messages every time you open the Mail window. Type your POP password in the Password Entry dialog text box, and then press the Enter key. If you don't know your POP password, ask your instructor or technical support person for assistance.

Elements of the Mail Window

The various menu options of Netscape Mail let you retrieve and manage e-mail with settings customized for your particular needs. Figure 4-3 shows the Mail window's three panes: a mail folder pane, a message header pane, and a message content pane. The **mail folder pane** in the upper-left corner displays the folders used to organize both incoming and outgoing messages. Some key folders in the mail folder pane include the **Inbox folder**, which contains all e-mail messages you have received, and the **Sent folder**, which contains copies of all e-mail messages you have sent. The **Outbox folder** contains messages that you have created but not yet sent, while the **Trash folder** holds all your discarded e-mail messages until you empty the Trash folder.

The **message header pane** in the upper-right corner displays titles of messages in the current mail folder selected in the mail folder pane. If you click a specific message in the message header pane, Netscape displays the message's entire contents in the **message content pane** along with header information items such as Subject, Date, From, and To. Folders used to store incoming and outgoing correspondence remain closed until you want to view their contents. To make sure that an outgoing message has been sent, you select the Sent mail folder. Subjects of outgoing messages appear in the message header pane. By clicking a particular message title in the message header pane, you can view the entire message in the message content pane, as well as the date you sent it, its subject, and the recipient's e-mail address. This information helps to verify that an e-mail message has been sent.

Both the mail folder pane and message header pane are organized in columns. Columns in the mail folder pane list individual mail folder names, such as Inbox or Trash, the total number of messages each folder contains, and the number of unread messages. Columns in the message header pane list the sender's name for each message, indicators that note if a message has been read or marked noteworthy, the subject the message's author assigned to the e-mail message, and the date and time the message arrived or was sent. This information quickly tells you if you have any unread mail. You can then browse for messages pertaining to a general topic according to the subject titles. The details listed in these columns make tracking the status of your electronic correspondence easy.

Anatomy of an E-mail Message

Rose provided you with the list of people who need to be contacted for your upcoming meeting, along with their e-mail addresses. This destination information, as well as your memo text, form the content of an e-mail message. An e-mail message has two main parts: the header lines and the message body. Figure 4-4 shows **header lines** that contain specific information about the origin and destination of an e-mail message. For example, the Mail To text box contains the message recipient's e-mail address. Figure 4-5 lists other text boxes that the header lines may contain and their specific functions.

Figure 4-4
E-mail
displayed in
Message
Composition
window

header lines

message body

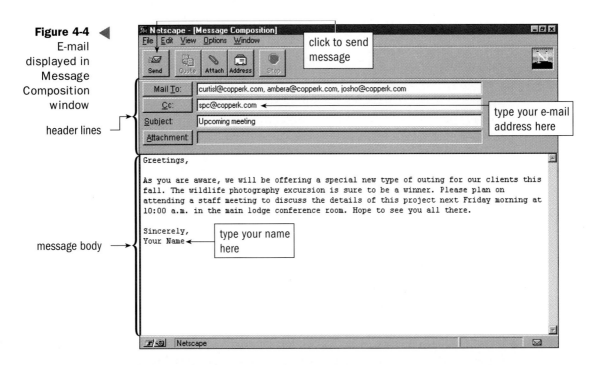

Figure 4-5
Header fields

Field Name	Description
BCC	List of other users to receive a copy of the message without the original recipient or CC recipients knowing. Stands for "blind carbon copy."
CC	List of other users to receive a copy of the message. Stands for "carbon copy."
File CC	Location on your local hard drive where copies of outgoing messages are kept.
Follow-up To	Lists the newsgroup where subsequent news postings will be sent.
Message ID	An internal number that identifies the message to the hosts transferring the message.
Newsgroups	Identifies the newsgroup a message will be posted to.
Received	Identifies the host or hosts through which the message is routed.
Reply To	E-mail address where message replies should be sent in case they are to go to an e-mail address other than the original sender's.
Return Path	The route the message has taken to get to the recipient.
Subject	Indicates subject or topic of message.

The **message body** contains the message itself. Its size can range from a few words to a few pages. Some Internet Service Providers prohibit e-mail messages over 100 kilobytes, which is about 25 text pages. E-mail is not usually the fastest and most efficient means to transfer large amounts of data, such as 50-page documents or entire accounting databases. Tutorial 6 discusses more appropriate methods of transferring this type of information, such as FTP.

The end of an e-mail message often includes a short signature file. Using **signature files**, or .SIGS, the sender can quickly and easily include additional contact information without retyping the information for every message. The signature file often includes the kind of information you find on a company letterhead or a business card—such as the company name, its slogan, a simple graphic, and the sender's name, job title, address, phone and fax numbers, and e-mail address. Some .SIGS include a quote or a brief statement of personal philosophy to add a personal touch. Attaching a signature file to the end of messages is a good way to ensure others have your contact information on file if they need to get in touch with you. You can create signature files with any word processor, and then configure the mail client software to append the file to the end of each outgoing e-mail message. You use the Identity tab of the Mail and News Preferences dialog box to configure the Netscape Mail program to attach your signature file to the end of each e-mail you send. Figure 4-6 shows Rose's signature file.

Figure 4-6 ◄
Standard
signature file

Copper King Outdoor Adventures
Box 3476 - Snyder, MT 59987
roseh@copperk.com
==============================
"Come join us in the Great Outdoors"

Composing an E-mail Message

When composing an e-mail message, you should follow some common guidelines. Keeping messages brief helps you get your point across efficiently and also cuts online access costs. Although e-mail messages should be short, they should include standard memo or letter components, such as a greeting and a salutation, as well as proper grammar and punctuation. Generally, e-mail lacks the personal touch of verbal communication. Always review your message to make sure that its contents convey your intent. Sarcasm can be easily misinterpreted; what may seem funny to you may seem inappropriate or rude to others. In addition, try not to relay negative information or bad news—it can be exaggerated in a written message.

Using written text to communicate emotions and body language can be difficult. One way to convey them is to use **emoticons**, which are icons and abbreviations representing specific emotions or body language. You can create emoticons from keyboard characters. For example, the emoticon :-) consists of the colon, dash, and right parenthesis symbols. To interpret the emoticon, tilt your head to the left and look at the characters. They represent a smiling face, an emoticon you can use to add warmth or humor to your e-mail message. The asterisk, dash, and the underline characters can also add emphasis to parts of your message. Abbreviations are also used as shorthand in e-mail communications. For example, BTW stands for "by the way" and IMHO stands for "in my humble opinion." Figure 4-7 shows some commonly used emoticons and abbreviations.

Figure 4-7 ◀
Emoticons

Emoticon	Meaning
;-)	Winking
:-(	Frowning
:-&	Tongue-tied
:-D	Laughing
8-)	Smiling with Glasses
ROTFL	Rolling on the floor laughing
TTFN	Ta Ta for now
Pry	Probably
<G>	Grinning

You are now ready to compose your e-mail message. You decide to route a copy to yourself for your records and to help you track the project's progress.

To compose an e-mail message:

1. If necessary, click **Window** on the menu bar, then click **Netscape Mail** to open the Mail window.

2. Click the **To Mail** button [icon] on the Mail toolbar to open the Message Composition window. Click the **Maximize** button [icon] on the Mail Composition window title bar to maximize the window.

   TROUBLE? If a message dialog box opens indicating "Your e-mail address has not been specified. Before sending mail or news messages, you must specify a return address in Mail and News Preferences," you need to enter your e-mail account information. Click Options, click Mail and News Preferences, click Identity, then enter your full e-mail address in the Your Email text box.

3. Click the **Mail To** text box in the Message Composition window, and type the following three e-mail addresses for staff members invited to the meeting: **curtisl@copperk.com, ambera@copperk.com, josho@copperk.com.** Separate each e-mail address with a comma and a space.

4. Click the **Cc:** text box, and type your e-mail address. This routes a copy of the message to your e-mailbox.

5. Click the **Subject** text box, and type **Upcoming meeting**.

6. Click the message body area, and type **Greetings,**. (Do not type the period.) Press the **Enter** key twice to move down two lines.

7. Type the message **As you are aware, we will be offering a special new type of outing for our clients this fall. The wildlife photography excursion is sure to be a winner. Please plan on attending a staff meeting to discuss the details of this project next Friday morning at 10:00 a.m. in the main lodge conference room. Hope to see you all there.**

8. Press the **Enter** key twice to move down two lines, then type **Sincerely,**. (Do not type the period.)

9. Press the **Enter** key again, then type your name. Your e-mail message should look like the one shown in Figure 4-4.

Sending an E-mail Message

After you compose your e-mail message and complete the header information, you click the Send button to send the message to your mail server for distribution. The From text box automatically contains the sender's e-mail address when the software is configured, or set up in the Mail and News Preferences dialog box. If you use the Netscape Mail program on a computer other than your own, it is very important to remove your e-mail address information from the Mail and News Preferences dialog boxes before exiting Netscape. If you don't, another person could use your e-mail address information to send e-mail messages that appear to be your own.

Although sophisticated encryption software tools do exist to help ensure message security and privacy, they do not provide complete protection. Therefore, it is not a good idea to send memos containing sensitive or high-security information via e-mail. Also, there is no guarantee that the recipient of your e-mail message will receive or retrieve it within a set amount of time. Some mail servers only receive mail messages once every few hours or every few days. Some users check their e-mail routinely, others only infrequently.

Now your e-mail message is ready to be sent.

REFERENCE window	**SENDING AN E-MAIL MESSAGE**
	■ Click Window, then click Netscape Mail.
	■ Click the To: Mail button.
	■ Type the destination e-mail address.
	■ Type the message you want to send.
	■ Click the Send button.

To send an e-mail message:

1. Make sure the Mail Composition window is open and the message regarding the upcoming meeting is still displayed.

2. Click the **Send** button on the Mail Composition toolbar to send the e-mail message to the staff members and yourself.

The Stop button activates and the status message area indicates the progress of the sent message. When transmission is complete, the Message Composition window closes, and you return to the main Mail window.

TROUBLE? If a message dialog box opens which indicates "A network error occurred: unable to connect to server," the server might be too busy to send your message. Click the Send button again. If you receive the same message, you need to check your host mail server's configuration. Click Options, click Mail and News Preferences, click the Servers tab in the Mail and News Preferences dialog box, and then in the Outgoing mail server (SMTP) text box, type the server name your instructor or technical support person provides.

An e-mail message may possibly reach a destination other than that intended. A simple mistake in typing an e-mail address, such as an incorrect letter or number, can send your message to someone other than the intended recipient. A message may be returned because the host or user is unknown, the hardware or software is faulty, or the transmission lines are malfunctioning. Mail servers interpret information precisely and depend on adherence to specific protocols in order to transmit successfully. If you misplace or omit a character in an e-mail address, or a portion of an e-mail address, the server will not deliver your message and will **bounce** it, or return it to your e-mailbox. A message in your Inbox with the subject worded similarly to "Returned mail: Undeliverable" or "Returned mail: Unknown Host" indicates that your message didn't transmit properly. Make sure that you typed the recipient's address correctly and resend it, or confirm with the recipient that you have his or her correct address.

Now that you've sent your message, you can create an address book so that you can automatically select e-mail addresses of users you contact regularly, for example, your colleagues on the CKOA excursion project.

Creating an Address Book

If you communicate with certain colleagues, vendors, and clients routinely, you may find yourself typing their e-mail addresses over and over. Rather than looking up or memorizing e-mail addresses, you can record them in an address book. The **address book** feature lets you create an electronic address book on your computer that contains user names and e-mail addresses.

For each entry in your address book, Netscape provides fields for first and last name, nickname, e-mail address, and description. In the description field, you can provide information that further identifies a person, such as a company mailing address or professional organization membership. After you add an e-mail address to your address book, it appears as an icon in your address book.

Adding Entries to an Address Book

After you create your address book, you can access an address by using an easy-to-remember nickname or by browsing through your entries. You can update your address book as often as you want. If you receive e-mail from a person whose name you would like to add to your address book, you can do this while you read his or her e-mail message. Choosing the Message menu and then Add automatically inserts the sender's address in your address book.

You decide to create an address book listing some of your in-house colleagues. Because you sometimes use Rose's computer to complete various tasks, you also need to access your address book from her computer. That way, you can send e-mail messages from her computer without having to remember specific addresses. To access your address book from another computer, you need to save the address book on a disk.

To save an address book file on a disk:

1. Insert your Student Disk in drive A or the appropriate disk drive.

TROUBLE? If your 3½" disk drive is B, place your Student Disk in that drive instead. For the rest of the tutorials, substitute drive B wherever you see drive A.

2. Click **Window** on the menu bar, then click **Address Book** to open the Address Book window. See Figure 4-8.

Figure 4-8 ◄
Address Book
window

indicates empty
address book

name of address
book file

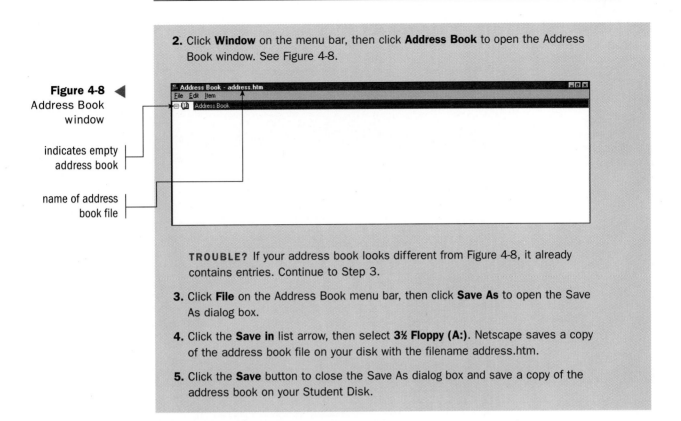

TROUBLE? If your address book looks different from Figure 4-8, it already contains entries. Continue to Step 3.

3. Click **File** on the Address Book menu bar, then click **Save As** to open the Save As dialog box.

4. Click the **Save in** list arrow, then select **3½ Floppy (A:)**. Netscape saves a copy of the address book file on your disk with the filename address.htm.

5. Click the **Save** button to close the Save As dialog box and save a copy of the address book on your Student Disk.

You are now ready to begin entering addresses. The first address you want to appear in your address book is Rose's address.

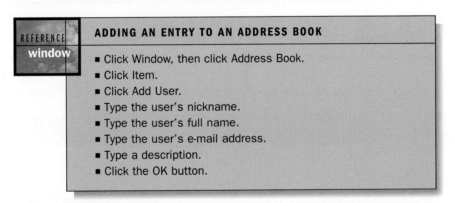

REFERENCE
window

ADDING AN ENTRY TO AN ADDRESS BOOK

- Click Window, then click Address Book.
- Click Item.
- Click Add User.
- Type the user's nickname.
- Type the user's full name.
- Type the user's e-mail address.
- Type a description.
- Click the OK button.

To add an entry to an address book:

1. In the Address Book window, click **Item** on the menu bar. The Item menu opens.

2. Click **Add User** to open the Address Book dialog box.

3. Type **Rose** in the Nick Name text box. Press the **Tab** key to move to the Name text box, and type **Rose Hensyel**. Press the **Tab** key to move to the e-mail address text box, and type **roseh@copperk.com**. Press the **Tab** key to move to the description text box, and then type **Proprietor**. The completed dialog box should match Figure 4-9.

Figure 4-9 ◀
Completed
address book
entry

click to save address ——

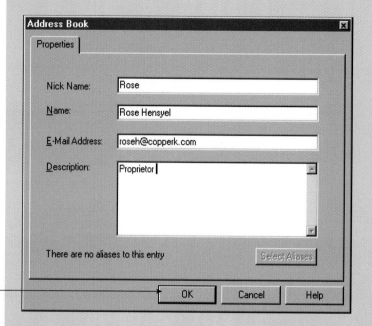

4. Click the **OK** button to save Rose's information and close the Address Book dialog box. The person icon preceding Rose's name indicates that the entry contains one person's address. Now enter the address information for Rose's husband, Richard, and other staff members.

5. Repeat Steps 1 through 4 to create an address book entry for Richard, Curtis, Amber, and Josh using the information in Figure 4-10. Netscape automatically reorders the entries alphabetically by the first letter of the entry in the Name field.

Figure 4-10 ◀
Address book
entries

Nickname	Name	E-Mail Address	Description
Dick	Richard Hensyel	dickh@copperk.com	Proprietor
Curtis	Curtis LeClair	curtisl@copperk.com	Marketing
Amber	Amber Allen	ambera@copperk.com	Advertising
Josh	Josh O'Brien	josho@copperk. com	Guide

Your completed address book should look like Figure 4-11.

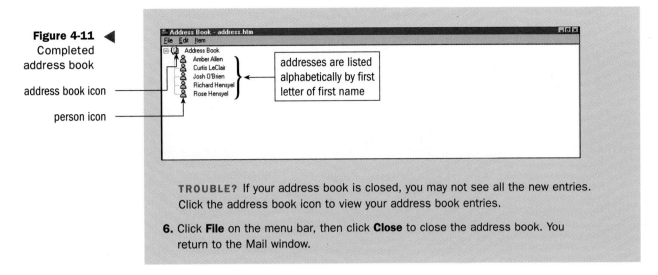

Figure 4-11 ◀
Completed
address book

address book icon ——

person icon ——

TROUBLE? If your address book is closed, you may not see all the new entries. Click the address book icon to view your address book entries.

6. Click **File** on the menu bar, then click **Close** to close the address book. You return to the Mail window.

When you are ready to send an e-mail message to one of the users in your address book, click his or her name in the address book list or simply type his or her nickname in the Mail To text box in the Message Composition window. After you provide this initial data, Netscape automatically fills in the rest of the address information. You can then compose the message text and send your e-mail.

Attaching a File to an E-mail Message

In addition to sending messages, you can use e-mail to transfer documents, or files, that are separate from your original message. This process is called sending an attachment, because you basically "attach" the document to your message, just as you would place a photograph in the same envelope to accompany a letter you send through postal mail. Attachments can include additional text items such as memos or reports, multimedia items, or even spreadsheets. Attaching files to an e-mail message is an easy and effective way to work collaboratively, as long as both the sender and recipient use compatible e-mail programs. A report attached to an e-mail message, for example, piggybacks with the message; and both reach their final destination at the same time.

You can attach an e-mail message in its original format or as an unformatted plain text file. If the recipient will open the file with the same program that you used to create the file, you should send it in its original format. This ensures that the document retains its formatting as well as its text. For example, if a document you create in Microsoft Word has embedded tables and graphics and you send the file in its original format, the recipient receives a Word file with its tables and graphics intact. If you know that the recipient doesn't have the program you used to create the file, you can send it as plain text, which strips the file of all formatting and other codes, leaving only the text.

You find a photograph of a bear taken near the lodge and feel it will be an exciting and appropriate graphic for the brochure describing the wildlife excursion. Because the picture exists in electronic format, you attach the electronic image file to an e-mail message and send it to Amber, the advertising manager, for her feedback. Once again, you send a copy of the e-mail message with the attachment to yourself for your records.

REFERENCE window	ATTACHING A FILE TO AN E-MAIL MESSAGE
	■ Click the Attachment button in the Message Composition window. ■ Click the Attach File button in the Attachments dialog box. ■ Enter or select the name of the file you want to attach, then press the Enter key. ■ Click the OK button.

To attach a file to an e-mail message:

1. Click the **To: Mail** button. The Message Composition window opens. Maximize the window.

2. Type the nickname **Amber** in the Mail To text box. Netscape automatically fills in the remainder of the address information based on Amber's address book entry.

3. Click the **Cc:** text box, and type your e-mail address.

4. Click the **Subject** text box, and type **Attached marketing material**.

5. Click the message body area, and type the introduction **Dear Amber,**. (Do *not* type the period.) Press the **Enter** key to move down one line.

6. Type the message **Please review the attached graphic for appropriateness in the wildlife excursion brochure. Let me know what you think.** Press the **Enter** key twice to insert two blank lines.

7. Type **Sincerely**, then press the **Enter** key to insert a blank line and then type your name. You now attach the electronic file of the bear photo.

8. Click the **Attach** button to open the Attachments dialog box.

   Click the **Attach File** button `Attach File...` to open the **Enter file to attach** text box.

   The default As Is radio button indicates that the file will be sent in its original format. In this case, the bear graphic is in .GIF format.

9. Make sure your Student Disk is in drive A. Click the **Look in** list arrow, and select **3 ½ Floppy (A:)**. A list of files on your Student Disk appears. Notice that bear.gif appears in the Attachment text box.

10. Click the file named **bear.gif**. The filename appears in the File name text box.

11. Click the **Open** button. The Enter file to attach dialog box closes, and the Attachments dialog box lists the image file. See Figure 4-12.

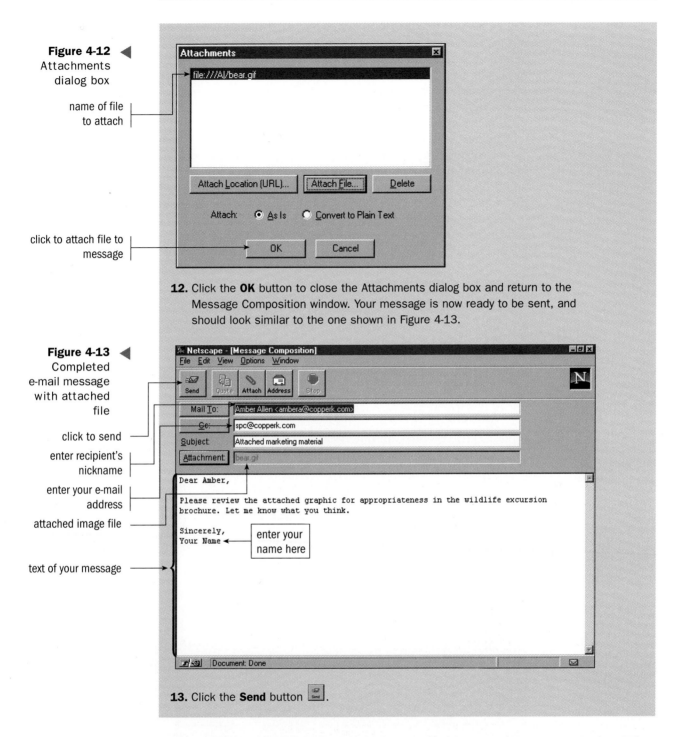

Figure 4-12
Attachments
dialog box

name of file
to attach

click to attach file to
message

12. Click the **OK** button to close the Attachments dialog box and return to the Message Composition window. Your message is now ready to be sent, and should look similar to the one shown in Figure 4-13.

Figure 4-13
Completed
e-mail message
with attached
file

click to send

enter recipient's
nickname

enter your e-mail
address

attached image file

text of your message

enter your
name here

13. Click the **Send** button.

The e-mail message and the attached image file have now been sent to Amber. When you see her later at lunch, she tells you that she thinks the photo is an excellent choice for the brochure.

Creating a Distribution List

At times, you send e-mail messages repeatedly to the same group of people, for example, to members of a specific department in your company. A **distribution list** organizes multiple e-mail addresses under a specific group heading. Instead of selecting each individual's e-mail address and sending separate messages, a distribution list lets you send the same message to every member of a group at the same time by referring to the distribution list nickname. Even though a nickname identifies the list, it does not have its own e-mail address. Instead, it uses the addresses you associate with each nickname. Each time you add an address to a distribution list, Netscape creates a shortcut telling the mailer where to find address information. This shortcut, called an **alias**, is a symbolic link assigned to an e-mail address. Whenever you want to send an e-mail message to a person or a group of people, you can select any combination from the entries listed in your address book. Placing a person's name on a distribution list doesn't prevent you from sending that person individual e-mail messages. In addition, you can place a person's name on as many distribution lists as you want.

You create distribution lists by adding an entry to the address book. Folder icons on your screen represent distribution lists. A person icon outside the list also represents each individual in a distribution list. To add an address to a distribution list, you simply drag and drop the person's icon onto the distribution list folder icon. As soon as you release the mouse button, the alias address entry appears in the distribution list.

Because you'll regularly route messages about the excursion project to Rose, Curtis, Amber, and Josh, you create a distribution list for this group rather than sending the same e-mail messages to them one at a time. You use the address book to create the list.

To create a distribution list:

1. Click **Window** on the menu bar, then click **Address book** to open the Address Book window.

2. Click **Item** and then click **Add List** to open the Address Book dialog box.

3. Type **Excursion** in the Nick Name text box, then press the **Tab** key; type **Project Team** in the Name text box, then press the **Tab** key, then type **Fall Wildlife Photography Excursion** in the Description text box. See Figure 4-14.

Figure 4-14 ◀
Completed
distribution list
entry

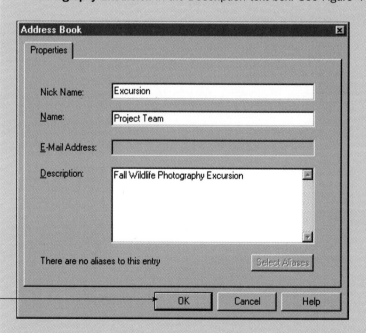

click to return to
Address Book window

4. Click the **OK** button to create the new list, and close the Address Book dialog box. Although you created the list, it doesn't yet contain any entries. You add this information by copying the entries from the address book you created earlier.

5. Click the address book entry for **Amber**, hold down the mouse button and drag the pointer down to highlight the **Project Team** list icon; then release the mouse button. After you release the mouse button, Amber's entry appears in both the main Address Book listing and in the Project Team listing as an alias.

6. Repeat Step 5 to add the entries for Curtis, Josh, and Rose. See Figure 4-15. Now that you have modified the address book, you again save the address book file on your disk.

Figure 4-15
Completed
project team
distribution list

distribution list
names

e-mail address
aliases

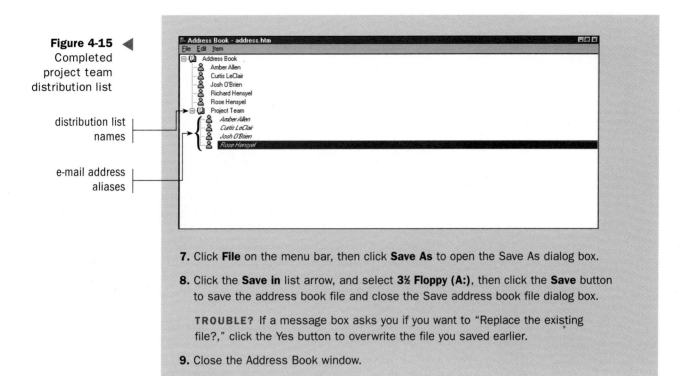

7. Click **File** on the menu bar, then click **Save As** to open the Save As dialog box.

8. Click the **Save in** list arrow, and select **3½ Floppy (A:)**, then click the **Save** button to save the address book file and close the Save address book file dialog box.

TROUBLE? If a message box asks you if you want to "Replace the existing file?," click the Yes button to overwrite the file you saved earlier.

9. Close the Address Book window.

Quick Check

1 List three tasks mail client software is used for.

2 On what type of technology is e-mail based?
a. POP mail
b. store-and-forward
c. Internet Mail Access Protocol
d. TCP/IP mail

3 An e-mail address consists of two distinct parts: the _____ and the _____.

4 The Netscape Mail window consists of three panes: the _____, _____, and _____ panes.

5 The _____ of an e-mail message contains information about the origin and destination of the message, while the _____ contains the actual message text.

6 The _____ feature can be used to store frequently used e-mail addresses.

7 You can send a graphical image with an e-mail message by including it as an _____.

8 What are three reasons a message may bounce?

You have completed Session 4.1. If you are not going to continue to Session 4.2 now, you should exit Netscape. When you are ready to begin Session 4.2, start Netscape, then open the Netscape Mail window, and continue with Session 4.2.

In this session you will learn how to retrieve, reply, edit, and save e-mail messages. You will forward an e-mail message, as well as learn how to handle e-mail attachments that you receive. You will learn ways to organize your e-mail messages and, finally, how to print and delete e-mail messages.

Retrieving an E-mail Message

Since e-mail is a store-and-forward technology, your mail server collects all your incoming e-mail messages and stores them for you until your mail client software contacts the server and requests that your mail messages be delivered to your electronic mailbox. When you check for incoming e-mail messages, Netscape sends a request to the server and returns only those messages that arrived since your last check. Depending on how much mail you receive, you may want to check for new mail messages throughout the day or a few times a week. Netscape initially checks the mail server for messages when you launch it and also periodically rechecks the server throughout your e-mail session informing you of any new messages.

Although Netscape acknowledges the arrival of new messages, it does not automatically display them. To see what messages you have received, you click the Inbox folder in the mail folder pane. If you receive more than one message, you don't necessarily need to read them in order or all at once. You can select the message you want to retrieve by simply clicking the subject of that message as listed in the message header pane. If the subject of the message is too long to fit in the Subject column, a portion of it appears, and an ellipsis (...) represents the rest. After you select the message, it appears in the message content pane and includes the header line information as well as the message body.

Because you've been away from your desk for a couple of hours, you decide to check if you've received any new e-mail. You use the Get Mail button in the Mail window to check for new messages.

To check for incoming mail:

1. Click the **Get Mail** 🖳 button on the Mail toolbar to receive all incoming mail messages. The status message area indicates how many messages you received. When all incoming messages have been transferred, the status message area displays "Document: Done."

   TROUBLE? You may be asked to provide your e-mail password. If so, type it in the Password Entry dialog box, then click the OK button to receive your mail. If you don't know your password, ask your instructor or technical support person for assistance.

   You may already have several messages in your Inbox folder. Now that you have confirmed the arrival of new messages, you need to retrieve them to review their content.

2. If necessary, click the **Inbox** folder in the mail folder pane to list all incoming messages. Recall that you had sent yourself copies of the staff meeting and the attached marketing material messages. You retrieve the staff meeting message first.

3. Click **Upcoming meeting** in the Subject column of the message header pane. The message displays the message content pane.

4. Scroll through the message content pane to view the message header lines and read the message. See Figure 4-16.

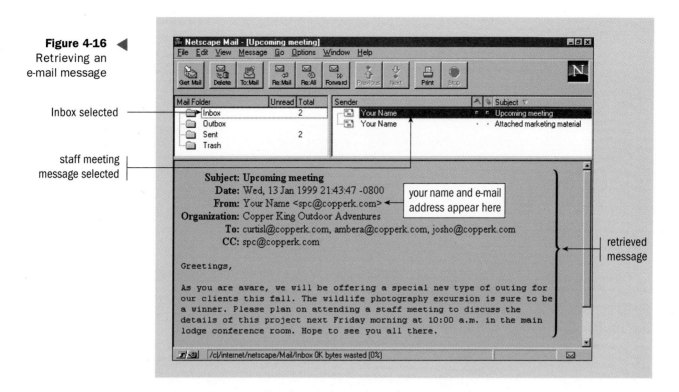

Figure 4-16
Retrieving an
e-mail message

Inbox selected

staff meeting
message selected

Replying to an E-mail Message

In addition to creating and sending e-mail messages, you may often need to respond to questions or comments posed in messages you receive. The **Re:Mail** button lets you easily reply to the original sender of the message. The Reply window works like the Message Composition window, except Netscape automatically displays the original message in the message content area. The Subject text box contains the original message subject heading, and the original sender's e-mail address is automatically placed in the To text box. The original message appears with a greater than sign (>) before each line in the message, indicating it was quoted from the original e-mail, referred to as **quoting**. When a message is sent back and forth between users several times, and layered > symbols designate which quote came from which sender. With the To text box entry automatically supplied, the reply to the message automatically goes to the last sender when you click the Send button. Replying to a message saves time if you need to respond quickly to the person who sent you the message or if you cannot easily locate the recipient's address in your address book. It is also convenient for replying to a number of people who were included in the original header lines, such as in the Cc text box. If the message was copied to another individual or group, the Re:All button routes your response to each recipient on the original distribution list.

Because the Reply To feature automatically places a copy of the original message within the new message being created, responding to different portions of the message directly is easy. Although you can place your reply anywhere in the message content area, placing your response near the original question establishes the context for the reader. Proper placement of the reply assures both sender and recipient that the narrative being responded to is indeed correct. Similar to the "trail" hyperlinking leaves for you to follow back to Web pages you visited, the reply function lets you see a conversation "trail" back and forth between sender and recipient. It is considered good netiquette to include only the portions of the message in your reply that pertain to the ongoing discussion. This helps to minimize disk storage space and Internet resources required to deliver the message.

Since CKOA uses e-mail extensively to communicate internally with staff members and externally with vendors and clients, you decide to practice replying to a message. As a test, you reply to the staff meeting message that you sent earlier and is currently displayed in your window. Because you are the original sender, your e-mail address is automatically placed in the To text box.

To reply to an e-mail message:

1. Click the **Re:Mail** button 📧 on the Mail toolbar to open the Reply window. Maximize the window. The original message text appears in the message content area. The Mail To text box and Subject text box appear already filled in. Your cursor is in the bottom line of the message content area.

2. At the bottom of the message content area, type **This is a test of the reply function within Netscape Mail.** This text is added to the end of the original message. See Figure 4-17.

Figure 4-17
Replying to an e-mail message

your e-mail address automatically appears

indicates message is a reply

reply text

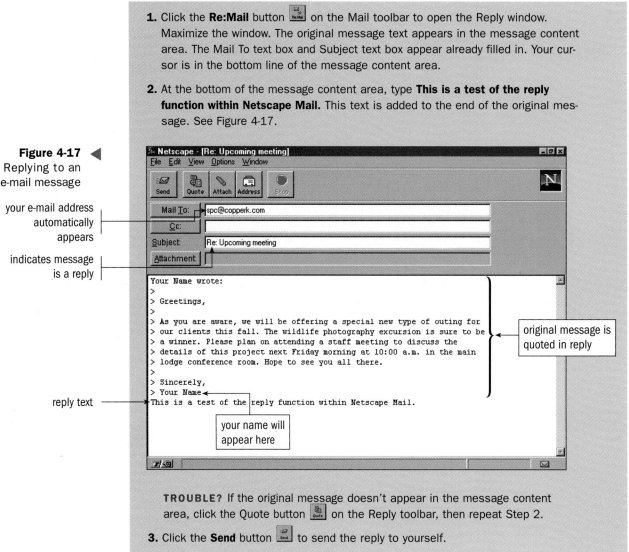

original message is quoted in reply

your name will appear here

TROUBLE? If the original message doesn't appear in the message content area, click the Quote button 📋 on the Reply toolbar, then repeat Step 2.

3. Click the **Send** button 📧 to send the reply to yourself.

Editing an E-mail Message

When composing or replying to a message, you can use many of the same editing features available in a word processing program, such as Cut, Copy, Paste, Undo, and Find. You can add to the beginning, middle, or end of a message to edit any word or phrase it contains. Text editing features let you modify or change your message easily without retyping it. These features also let you cut or copy text from another document and paste it into your current message.

Rose wants you to arrange another staff meeting to monitor the excursion project's progress. Because she needs to verify the conference room's availability, Rose gives you tentative information. Rather than creating a new message, you decide to edit the original message you sent the group, copy the relevant parts, and then replace specific items that need changing, such as day and time. You also send a copy of the message to yourself for your records.

To edit an e-mail message:

1. With the original staff meeting notice message displayed in the message content pane, click and drag to select the message body text. See Figure 4-18.

Figure 4-18 ◀
Editing an
e-mail message

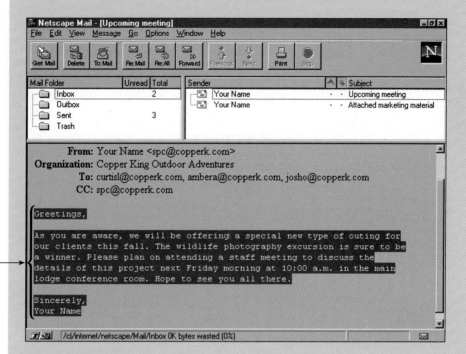

selected text to be
copied to Clipboard

2. Click **Edit** on the menu bar.

3. Click **Copy** to copy the selected message body text to the Clipboard. Rather than pasting the message contents into one of your word-processing programs, you paste it in a new message.

4. Click the **To:Mail** button. The Message Composition window opens. Maximize the window.

5. Type **excursion** in the Mail To text box. This addresses the message to all members of the project team distribution list.

6. Type your e-mail address in the Cc text box. This sends a copy of the message to you.

7. Type **Next project meeting** in the Subject text box.

8. Click in the message content pane. Click **Edit** on the menu bar, then click **Paste**. This pastes the Clipboard contents into the message content pane.

9. To update the original message, click and drag or select the entire first sentence and press the **Delete** key.

10. At the end of the new first sentence, replace the period with a semicolon and type **thanks for being a part of the project team**. You now need to update the meeting date and time.

11. Place your pointer before the word "Friday." Select **Friday** and type **Monday**. Now place your pointer between the colon and the second "0" in the time 10:00 a.m. Select the **0** and type **3** so that the time now reads 10:30 a.m. The meeting place is the same, so leave it as is.

Your completed message should look like the one in Figure 4-19.

Figure 4-19 ◀
Edited e-mail
message

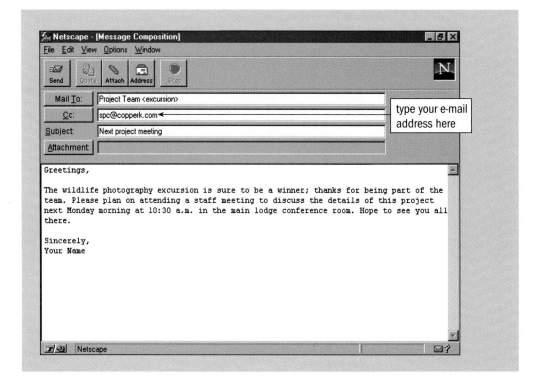

Saving an E-mail Message

At times you may want to delay sending a message because you need to verify or gather more information. Netscape lets you postpone message delivery. Deferring message delivery is also convenient for users who pay for Internet access based on how much time they spend online rather than a flat fee. You can create messages offline, store them in the Outbox mail folder, and send them all at once when you log on to the Internet, thus decreasing the time you spend online. When you are ready to send your e-mail message, you select the Send Messages in Outbox option on the File menu.

You decide to save the new e-mail message until you receive final confirmation from Rose about the conference room.

To save an e-mail message in the Outbox folder:

1. Click **Options** on the menu bar.

2. Click **Deferred Delivery**. A check mark appears, indicating the postponed delivery option is selected.

3. Click the **Send** button. Netscape saves the message in the Outbox mail folder until you are ready to send it.

   While you are saving the message, Rose pokes her head in your office to let you know that the conference room is all set for the day and time scheduled. You now send your saved message.

4. Click **File** on the menu bar, then click **Send Messages in Outbox** to deliver the staff meeting message you saved earlier.

Forwarding an E-mail Message

Forwarding an e-mail message to another person is like replying to a message, except that it sends the entire message to the recipient, not portions of it. Forwarding is helpful when you want to route a message to someone who might find the information useful, timely, or valuable. When forwarding a message, you can add new comments to the original message. You can place this new information in the message body along with the original message.

You forward a message to another user by selecting the Forward button on the Mail toolbar. Netscape automatically fills in the Subject text box, noting that the message is forwarded and, if applicable, also fills the Attachment text box with information from the original message. The Mail To text box remains blank so you can add the new recipient's address either manually or by selecting it from your address book.

Rose stopped by to inform you that Richard wants to attend the upcoming staff meeting. Although he generally does not get too involved with the marketing aspects of the resort, Richard foresees photography excursions as a natural extension of the business. He is interested in learning about the team's progress on this project. You check your mailbox for the message about the upcoming meeting that you sent to yourself in order to forward it to Richard.

REFERENCE window	**FORWARDING AN E-MAIL MESSAGE**
	■ Select the message to be forwarded.
	■ Click the Forward button on the Mail toolbar.
	■ Type the new recipient's address in the Mail To text box.
	■ Add any new text required in the message content area.
	■ Click the Send button.

To forward an e-mail message:

1. Click the **Get Mail** button to check for new e-mail messages. The new staff meeting message is in your mailbox along with the reply test message.

2. Click the **Next project meeting** message in the Subject column to select the message.

3. Click the **Forward** button on the Mail toolbar to forward the message. The partially completed Message Composition window opens. Maximize the window. The Subject text box includes the original subject title preceded by "FWD," indicating that this is a forwarded message.

4. Click the **Mail To** text box, and type **Dick**, the nickname you assigned to Richard in your address book.

5. Click in the message content area, then type **Dick, hope to see you there.** to add new text to the message. Your forwarded message should look like Figure 4-20.

Figure 4-20 ◀
Forwarded
message

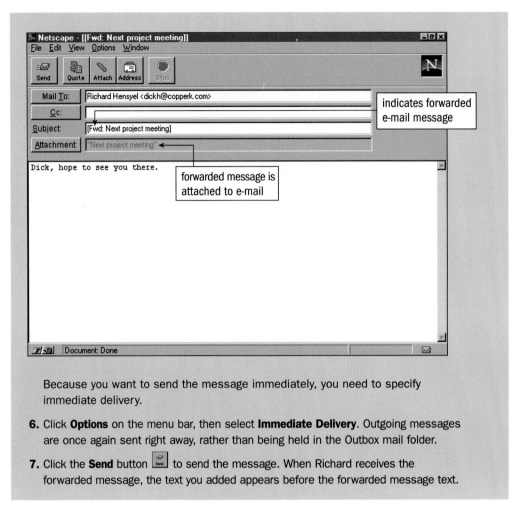

Because you want to send the message immediately, you need to specify immediate delivery.

6. Click **Options** on the menu bar, then select **Immediate Delivery**. Outgoing messages are once again sent right away, rather than being held in the Outbox mail folder.

7. Click the **Send** button 🖂 to send the message. When Richard receives the forwarded message, the text you added appears before the forwarded message text.

Printing an E-mail Message

Although you can access an e-mail message anytime electronically, at times you may still need a printout of an e-mail message. You may need to include a copy of a message with a report, keep a copy in your files, or refer to the message later when you don't have access to a computer. Netscape Mail uses the same print features as the main Netscape window. You can preview the e-mail message before you print it, make several copies, or print only portions of a message of more than one page.

You start to prepare your materials for the upcoming meeting. The first page of your packet will be a printed copy of the e-mail message you sent notifying the team of the second project meeting.

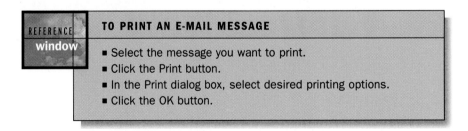

REFERENCE
window

TO PRINT AN E-MAIL MESSAGE

- Select the message you want to print.
- Click the Print button.
- In the Print dialog box, select desired printing options.
- Click the OK button.

To print an e-mail message:

1. Click the **Get Mail** button 📥 to check for incoming messages. Newly arrived messages appear in the Inbox folder.

2. Select the **Next project meeting** message that you just sent to the Project Team. The message appears in the message content pane.

3. Click the **Print** button on the Mail toolbar to open the Print dialog box. Notice that you used the same print dialog box to print Web pages in Tutorial 3. Accept the default print settings.

4. Click the **OK** button to print the e-mail message.

Handling Files Attached to E-mail Messages

If you receive an e-mail message with an attached file, you can view the file in several different ways. Netscape may not recognize the file's format and may need to treat it differently, depending on the configuration of the file itself or the Netscape program. If Netscape has the built-in capability, it automatically displays the file on your screen. Viewing attachments **inline** lets you view a message attachment as part of the message, with the formatted file appended to the message body. By default, Netscape views attachments inline if possible, as designated on the View menu. Netscape determines its ability to display an attachment by checking the filename extension, which indicates the file format and the program needed to view it. If the Attachments as Links option is selected on the View menu, the file may appear as a hyperlink in an Attachment box within the e-mail message, as shown in Figure 4-21. Clicking the Attachment box in the message is like clicking a hyperlink; you click the link and Netscape jumps to and displays the specified file. If you were to forward your address book to Rose's secretary, for example, Netscape could display the attached file because the address book is in HTML format.

Figure 4-21 ◀
Viewing attachments as hyperlinks

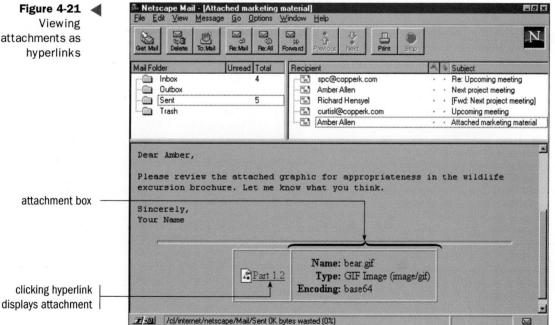

attachment box

clicking hyperlink displays attachment

If Netscape is not capable of viewing the attachment's file format but recognizes the format by the filename extension, it can launch the needed program so that the attached file automatically appears in that program. For example, if you receive a message with a Microsoft Excel spreadsheet attached, Netscape can automatically launch Excel and display the spreadsheet in your window if you have Excel. Depending on Netscape's configuration, it may prompt you for an action, such as saving the file, or entering the name of the program you want to launch. Lastly, if Netscape does not recognize the file format, it lets you save the attached file on disk so that you may open and view it separately with the appropriate program. For example, if you receive a presentation composed in Microsoft PowerPoint and Netscape does not recognize the .PPT file format, you can still save the attachment as a separate file and then open the presentation in PowerPoint on your system, totally independent of Netscape.

You decide to include a copy of the bear image that you sent to Amber as part of the materials you are preparing for the meeting. However, after Amber approved the bear image for the brochure, you gave her the original disk that contained the electronic image. You can still view the bear image by retrieving and displaying the e-mail message you sent to Amber with the image attached.

To view an attachment inline:

1. Click the **Sent** folder located in the message folder pane. In the message header pane, Netscape lists all e-mail messages you sent.

2. In the Sent folder, click the **Attached marketing material** message in the Subject column to select the message with the attached image file. The message, along with the attached .GIF file, appears in the message content pane.

3. Scroll through the message content pane until you see the attached bear image inline. You may need to adjust the message content pane to see the entire attachment. See Figure 4-22.

Figure 4-22 ◀
Viewing an
attachment
inline

attached image
appears in message

4. Position your pointer over the **bear.gif** image, then click the **right** mouse button to open a shortcut menu.

5. Click **View Image** to view the file independently of the e-mail message. The image file appears in the Netscape browser window.

Now that you have located the bear image, you can print it to use as the second page in your packet.

Organizing E-mail Messages

Throughout a normal workday, you may receive many pieces of information and documents, including e-mail messages. Some people rely quite heavily on e-mail for professional and personal communication, receiving and sending dozens of messages each day. Some people retrieve and then delete messages they no longer need; others save messages to reference them at another time or as a record of contact. Just as filing cabinets and desk drawers help organize crucial office documents, Netscape's default message folders help organize e-mail messages. In addition to the default Inbox, Outbox, Sent, and Trash folders, you can create other folders to help organize your e-mail messages.

By creating your own customized folders to help organize your e-mail messages, you can design a very efficient electronic filing system. For example, you can create individual folders to store messages related to school, work, or personal projects, or you can use various folders to store messages from specific groups of people, such as classmates, colleagues, or friends. Another organizational strategy is to create folders for each month or week and then organize messages by date. After you create a folder, you can transfer the original e-mail message into it or just place a copy of it in the folder.

Because you anticipate receiving quite a lot of e-mail in your newly acquired position, you decide to use Netscape's folders feature to create an organizational scheme that defines each special project you are working on. You create a new folder for the Wildlife Photography Excursion and place messages related to the excursion in this folder.

To organize your e-mail messages using folders:

1. Click the **Close** button ☒ on the Netscape browser window to return to the Netscape Mail window.

2. Click **File** on the Mail menu bar, and then click **New Folder**. The Netscape User Prompt dialog box appears.

3. Type the folder name **Wildlife Photography** to name the folder, then click the **OK** button. You now have a new folder with the name Wildlife Photography. Netscape automatically places this folder in your mail folder pane. See Figure 4-23.

Figure 4-23 ◀
Adding a new
folder

new folder is added
to the message
folder pane

TROUBLE? If the entire mail folder name is not visible in the mail folder pane, you can adjust the column size by dragging the Mail Folder column marker to the right.

4. Click the **Inbox** folder, then click the **Upcoming meeting** message. Holding down the mouse button, drag the message to the new Wildlife Photography folder. Notice that your pointer shape changes from an arrow ⤾ to a drag and drop pointer ⤾. See Figure 4-24. This moves the message to the new folder.

Figure 4-24 ◀
Moving an
e-mail message
to a new folder

release mouse to
place message in
folder

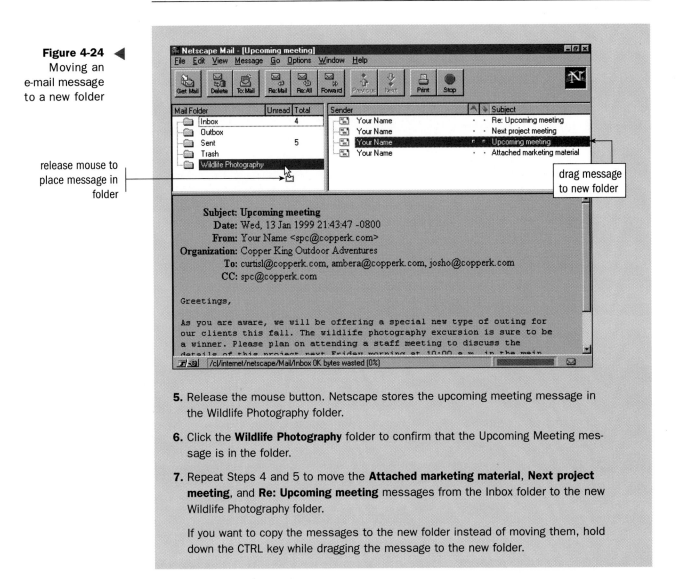

drag message
to new folder

5. Release the mouse button. Netscape stores the upcoming meeting message in the Wildlife Photography folder.

6. Click the **Wildlife Photography** folder to confirm that the Upcoming Meeting message is in the folder.

7. Repeat Steps 4 and 5 to move the **Attached marketing material, Next project meeting**, and **Re: Upcoming meeting** messages from the Inbox folder to the new Wildlife Photography folder.

   If you want to copy the messages to the new folder instead of moving them, hold down the CTRL key while dragging the message to the new folder.

Deleting an E-mail Message

After you retrieve an e-mail message and perform any related tasks such as replying, saving, or forwarding, you may want to delete the message. To delete a message, you select the message and then click the Delete button ![Delete] or press the Delete key. If you want to delete several messages at once, hold down the Shift key while selecting the group of messages with your pointer, then click the Delete button. Deleting a message moves it to the Trash folder, where it remains until you empty the folder. The Trash folder, provides a final opportunity to retrieve a message before it is completely erased. Messages in the Trash folder are permanently deleted when you empty it.

Although creating folders can help you to organize the messages you receive, you should periodically re-evaluate your messages for relevance. If you no longer need a folder that you created, you can delete it, but only after you delete the messages saved in it.

Because you already printed a copy of the e-mail message about the upcoming meeting, you delete it from the Wildlife Photography folder and then empty the Trash folder, permanently removing the message from storage.

To delete an e-mail message:

1. In the Wildlife Photography folder, click the **Next project meeting** message in the Subject column to select it. The message appears in the message content pane.

> **2.** Click the **Delete** button [icon] on the Mail toolbar to move the message to the Trash folder. Notice that the number of files in the Trash folder increases by one and the total column for the Wildlife Photography folder in the Mail Folder pane decreases by one.
>
> **3.** Click **File** on the menu bar, then click **Empty Trash Folder** to permanently remove the Trash folder's contents. The status message area shows the process of deleting the contents of the Trash folder. The number in the Trash Folder Total column should now be zero. Netscape automatically compresses the folders to a size just large enough to hold the remaining mail and recovers the storage space made available by emptying the Trash folder.

You have completed Session 4.2. If you are not going to continue to Session 4.3 now, you should exit Netscape. When you are ready to begin Session 4.3, start Netscape and continue with the tutorial.

If you would like more information on e-mail, you can find additional resources using the New Perspectives on the Internet Using Netscape Navigator Software—Introductory Student Online Companion for this tutorial by accessing the Tutorial 4 links.

Quick Check

1 To answer a question posed to you in an e-mail message, you can use the _____ button to quickly respond to the sender of the message.

2 When you respond to a message, the response automatically includes the original message. This is called _____.

3 When you defer a message for later delivery, Netscape temporarily stores the message in the _____ folder.

4 List three ways Netscape may handle a file attached to an e-mail message.

5 To systematically store messages on your computer, you may wish to create individual _____ to store them in.

6 True or False: Clicking the Delete button [icon] permanently removes e-mail messages from disk storage.

SESSION 4.3

In this session, you will learn what mailing lists are and how they work. You will also learn about how list servers function. Finally, you will complete such tasks as searching for and subscribing and unsubscribing to mailing lists.

Understanding Mailing Lists

Another popular group communications tool available on the Internet is a mailing list. A **mailing list** is a list of Internet users who share a common interest. To become part of a mailing list on a particular topic or subject, a user subscribes to a list. Requesting membership on a mailing list is called **subscribing** to the list; users who participate on a list are called **subscribers**. A subscriber automatically receives copies of any e-mail messages concerning the subject that other participants have sent to those on the mailing list. Mailing lists are used to distribute messages to a large number of people without sending individual messages to each user, and to create and maintain large distribution lists. Over

20,000 mailing lists on the Internet cover a wide variety of subjects ranging from astrophysics to zoology. Each mailing list has a unique name. Businesses often use mailing lists as a customer forum.

If you decide to participate in a mailing list, you need to send an initial e-mail message to its specific address, asking that you be added to the member list. The subscription message may go to the list **moderator**, the person responsible for maintaining a mailing list's membership roster. Some lists rely on computer automation, using specialized software programs to accomplish tasks a human moderator traditionally performs, such as adding members to or deleting them from a list. One drawback to computerized moderators is that user requests for help or additional assistance sometimes go unanswered if the program hasn't been automated to accept commands other than simple help requests.

In addition to performing maintenance tasks, a human moderator sometimes screens messages that are posted to the list. The moderator passes along only those messages that he or she feels fit the spirit of the list. The moderator may also organize submitted messages, packaging all related discussions into a few e-mail messages before distributing them. This is called a **moderated list**. These postings sometimes take longer to reach subscribers than non-moderated list messages because they must first go though the list administrator. After you subscribe to a mailing list, you receive messages automatically via e-mail. These messages are those that other subscribers have sent to the mailing list. The messages are sent to an e-mail address different from the subscription address. The messages are then redistributed, or **broadcast**, to individual members. Mailing lists are also sometimes called **mail reflectors**, because messages sent to a special e-mail address are automatically "reflected" or re-sent to everyone on the mailing list. The concept of mail distribution through a centralized server has also been called **mail explosion**, because a single piece of e-mail posted to a list can result in thousands of copies subsequently being sent from the list server to each and every list member.

Managing Mailing Lists with List Servers

Software that automatically manages many mailing list functions is called a list server. **List servers** are electronic moderators that handle many tasks associated with maintaining mailing lists such as database management and archiving. They can also handle routine chores such as adding and deleting users from the mailing list or forwarding messages. List servers have their own e-mail address, usually in the form Listserver@domain. List servers can manage more than one mailing list at a domain. They differ from moderators in that they use software programs rather than personnel to manage a mailing list. Human moderators often rely on list servers to perform some mailing list maintenance tasks so they can handle more intricate tasks themselves—those that need human intervention. Although you can often manage your own smaller distribution mailing lists using e-mail client software, many Internet mailing lists contain thousands of participants' e-mail addresses. Instead of using the same group mailing list to track users who have come or gone, mailing lists, with the help of list servers, maintain large groups of e-mail addresses. The list server maintains the central mailing list so that one change affects everyone, and each subscriber does not need to change his or her individual mailing list. This allows quick and efficient management of e-mail messages pertaining to a certain group or topic. Anyone can create and maintain a mailing list, although doing so requires time and money for hardware, software, and human resources. Throughout this session you will use Listserv, one of the most popular list servers. Other major list servers include Majordomo and Almanac. Figure 4-25 shows how a list server operates.

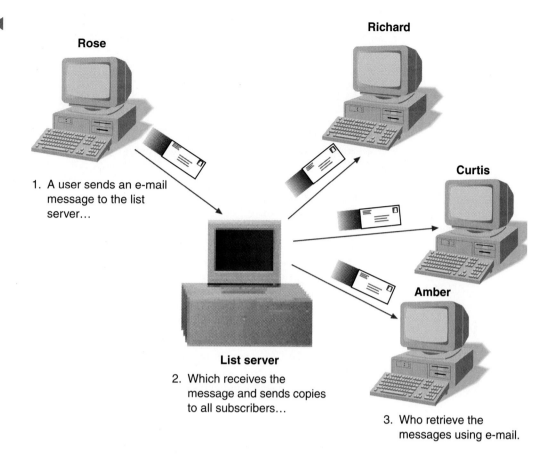

Figure 4-25
How a list
server operates

Rose

Richard

Curtis

Amber

1. A user sends an e-mail
   message to the list
   server...

List server

2. Which receives the
   message and sends copies
   to all subscribers...

3. Who retrieve the
   messages using e-mail.

Searching for a Mailing List

As with e-mail addresses, there is no central repository for mailing list addresses. You can find mailing list addresses through traditional sources such as colleagues, company Web pages, or trade magazines. One of the best resources for finding mailing lists is to use one of the many Web search tools. Refer back to Figure 3-34 for a list of popular search engines on the WWW. By accessing one of these search tools and typing a key word or words that describe the type of mailing list you are searching for, you can locate mailing lists related to your particular interest areas. The search tool returns a list of possible Internet resources to assist in your quest for an appropriate mailing list to join.

You decide to try to locate and subscribe to at least two photography mailing lists. From the messages passed back and forth, you hope to gather information that will help you find materials for the information packets you will distribute to clients at the beginning of the excursion. You use the Lycos search tool to locate the mailing lists.

To search for a mailing list:

1. Return to the main Netscape window, and click the **Home** button 🏠 to return to your home page, the New Perspectives on the Internet Using Netscape Navigator Software—Introductory Student Online Companion.

2. Click the **Tutorial 4** link. In the Session 4.3 section, click the **Lycos** link. This opens the Web site for the Lycos organization's search tool. Your screen should look like the one shown in Figure 4-26. As you recall, Web sites change occasionally, so your screen may look different.

Figure 4-26 ◀
Lycos search
tool

type search
criteria here

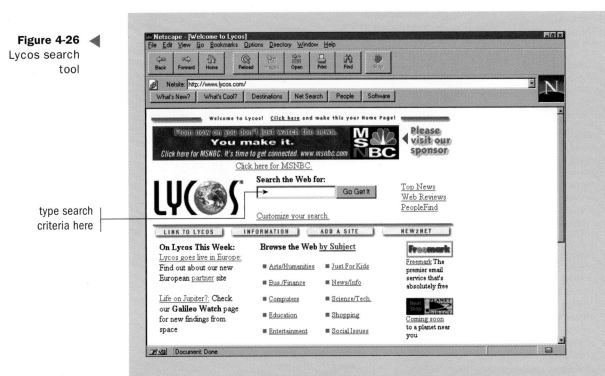

3. Type the words **mailing lists photography** in the Search the Web for text box.

4. Click the **Go Get It** button ⟨ Go Get It ⟩. Lycos returns a list of items that match your query. Only the first 10 are listed, but you can access additional sets of matches, each with 10 items. See Figure 4-27. Your screen may differ from the one in Figure 4-27 due to updates.

Figure 4-27 ◀
Photography
mailing lists

click to connect to a
photography-related
Web page

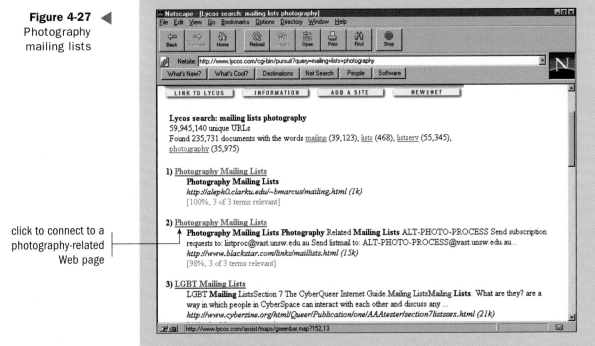

5. Click the **Photography Mailing Lists** link to connect to the Black Star Communication Specialist Photography-Related Mailing List Web page.

TROUBLE? If you cannot locate the Photography Mailing List hyperlink, select another one that relates to photography.

6. Scroll down the Web page until you find the PhotoForum and the PhotoHst mailing lists. You may need to scroll down quite far to find them. Write down the e-mail addresses for each mailing list. Hint: See the "Send subscription requests to" category to find the e-mail addresses.

   TROUBLE? If you cannot find the mailing list subscription addresses, note that the PhotoForum list server address is listserv@rit.edu and the PhotoHst list server address is listserv@asuvm.inre.asu.edu.

7. Click the **Home** button 🏠 to return to your home page.

Subscribing to a Mailing List

If you locate a mailing list that interests you, you may want to subscribe to it. Keep in mind that some mailing lists are more active than others. Because a particular mailing list may receive a few messages a week while another receives several hundred a day, starting slowly is a good idea. Subscribing to one or two mailing lists will help you gauge how much traffic each list generates and keeps things manageable.

To subscribe to a mailing list, you need to send an e-mail message to the list server e-mail address or moderator. Unlike a random request sent via e-mail, the structure and content of this message need to meet certain standards. The message itself consists of three pieces. First, the Mail To text box contains the list server e-mail address. Second, the Subject text box must be purposely left blank so that the mailing list server recognizes the message as a subscription request. Third, the message body must consist of one line that specifies whether you want to subscribe or unsubscribe to the mailing list, the name of the list that interests you, and the name you wish to be known by on the list.

For example, to subscribe to the PhotoForum mailing list, the message body phrase would read "sub PhotoForum *yourname*," where the keyword "sub" is a Listserv command that instructs the list server to subscribe you to the list specified by the keyword "PhotoForum." The keyword yourname instructs Listserv to use a name of your choosing as your mailing list name. Because the list server obtains your return e-mail address directly from the header lines within the subscription message, it is important to subscribe from the account at which you want to receive messages. For example, if you send a mailing list subscription request using Rose's computer, the mailing list messages arrive at her e-mail address unless you reset the address information to your own. After you successfully subscribe to the mailing list, you should start receiving copies of related e-mail messages within a few days. Some mailing lists take longer to process subscription requests than others, while others have more traffic to route, so it may take a few days before forwarded mail begins to flow. If you don't receive any messages from the mailing list within a week, you may want to send a message directly to the list moderator to ensure that you subscribed correctly and are on the membership roster.

Although you found two interesting mailing lists, you decide to subscribe to just one to get a feel for the content of the messages, and to see what type of traffic the mailing list attracts. You subscribe to the PhotoForum mailing list by using Netscape to send an e-mail message to the special subscription addresses you located using Lycos.

To subscribe to a mailing list:

1. Return to the Netscape Mail window, and then click the **To Mail** button 📧 to open the Message Composition window. Maximize the window.

2. Click the **Mail To** text box, and type **Listserv@rit.edu**. This is the subscription address of the Listserv software at Rochester Institute of Technology. Leave the Subject text box blank.

3. Click the message body area, and type **sub PhotoForum yourname**, replacing "yourname" with the name you want to be known by on the mailing list. Your e-mail message should look like the one shown in Figure 4-28 and is ready to be sent.

Figure 4-28 ◀
Subscribing to
a mailing list

subscription
instructions

leave subject blank

list server address

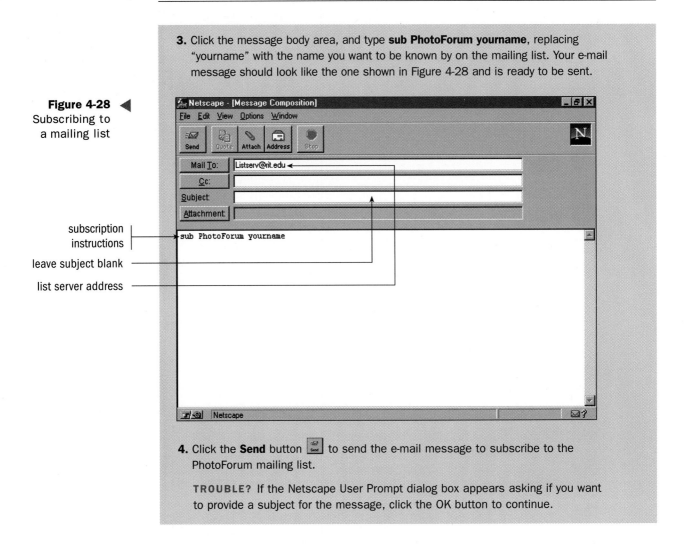

4. Click the **Send** button to send the e-mail message to subscribe to the PhotoForum mailing list.

TROUBLE? If the Netscape User Prompt dialog box appears asking if you want to provide a subject for the message, click the OK button to continue.

Sending Mail to a List Server

It is a good idea to observe mailing list activity for a couple of weeks before joining the conversation and contributing a message. That way you can learn the netiquette used, get a feel for the content of the information relayed, and make sure that the content of your message is appropriate to the topic and the group before posting it. Inappropriate messages, called **junk mail**, are considered bad netiquette. If a user posts inappropriate messages, especially repeatedly, the list moderator can choose to remove a user's name from the mailing list.

When you are confident about the material you want to contribute to the mailing list, you can "join in" the conversation by sending a message. When sending a message to the mailing list, you should address it to the mailing list address, for example, PhotoForum@ rit.edu, rather than the list server address. The list server software or list moderator then redistributes your message to all list participants. It is not unusual for a mailing list to request that you introduce yourself to the membership. At times, you may strike up a conversation with a specific list member and want to send that person an individual e-mail message. In this instance, be especially careful when using the e-mail reply function so as not to accidentally send a personal message to the entire group.

Retrieving Mail from a List Server

E-mail messages you receive from a mailing list arrive in the same way as regular e-mail messages. You retrieve the message you want to display by clicking its subject in the message header pane. The message then appears in the message content pane. The first e-mail message you receive after subscribing to a mailing list is generally a welcoming message from the moderator, or one that the list server software automatically generates. Although this message may seem insignificant, it contains important information about the mailing list itself and should be kept. This message may contain key information such as appropriate netiquette for the list, and instructions on how to unsubscribe or request additional information. Figure 4-29 shows a typical welcoming message from a mailing list.

Figure 4-29 ◀
Mailing list welcoming message

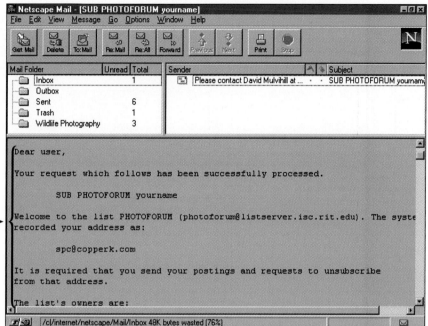

welcoming message lists pertinent subscription information

If you have a problem sending messages to or receiving them from a mailing list, or want to access additional information about the list, you can send a help request to the list server or the list moderator. Your help request should be sent to the list server as a brief e-mail message, usually consisting of one or a few words. For instance, if you want to know what other mailing lists may be available at a list server, your message to the list server address would contain a blank subject line and a single word, "List," in the message body.

Unsubscribing from a Mailing List

For the same reasons that you cancel other memberships or subscriptions, you may want to cancel your subscription to a particular mailing list. You may find that the content shared on a list isn't interesting or helpful to you, or that you don't have time to read the messages. **Unsubscribing**, or withdrawing from a mailing list, is similar to subscribing. Again, you send an e-mail message to the list server address or list moderator, leaving the subject line blank. In the message body, you type the phrase "unsubscribe listname," substituting the name of the mailing list for the term "listname." It sometimes takes a week or more for the list server to process your unsubscribe request, so don't be concerned if you continue to receive messages from the mailing list for a while. If you still receive messages two weeks after you unsubscribe, you may want to send a message to the list server or moderator.

After observing the PhotoForum mailing list for a few weeks, you find that the information isn't as helpful as you anticipated. You have so much work to do in the next couple of days, you probably won't have much time to read mailing list messages anyway. You decide to unsubscribe from the PhotoForum mailing list. When things quiet down, however, you hope to try subscribing to the PhotoHst list to see if it is more helpful.

To unsubscribe from a mailing list:

1. Click the **To Mail** button 🖳 to open the Message Composition window. Maximize the window.

2. Click the **Mail To** text box, and type **Listserv@listserver.isc.rit.edu**. This is the subscription address for the Listserv software at Rochester Institute of Technology. Leave the Subject text box blank.

3. Click the message body area, and type **unsubscribe PhotoForum**. Your e-mail message should look like the one shown in Figure 4-30 and is ready to be sent.

Figure 4-30 ◀
Unsubscribing from a mailing list

subscription instructions

leave subject blank

list server address

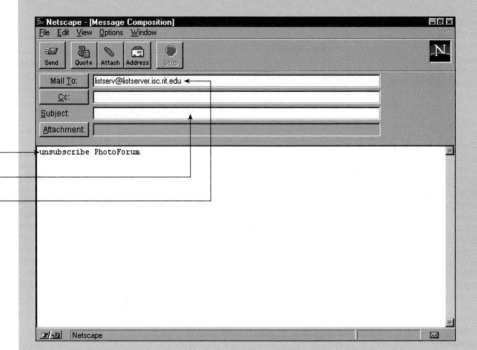

4. Click the **Send** button 🖳 to send the e-mail message to unsubscribe from the PhotoForum mailing list.

TROUBLE? If the Netscape User Prompt dialog box appears asking if you want to provide a subject for the message, click the OK button to continue.

TROUBLE? If you still receive messages from the mailing list, remember that processing your request may take a week or more processing. If you are still receiving messages from the list after two weeks, you may want to send a message directly to the list server or moderator.

5. Close the Netscape Mail window.

6. Exit Netscape.

Mailing Lists and Bitnet

Many mailing lists on the Internet first began on a network called **Bitnet**. Bitnet began in 1981 as a network separate from the Internet, with the purpose of keeping faculty members from different universities in touch with each other. Today, Bitnet reaches over 3,000 educational institutions and contains thousands of mailing lists. On many Internet hosts, you can reach Bitnet through a computer that acts as a gateway between the two networks. A user's mailing address often tells you whether a computer is on the Bitnet network. For example, the address smith@portal.bitnet means that a user named Smith has an account on the Bitnet host named "portal."

Richard and Rose are extremely pleased with your use of e-mail and list servers. You have found the tools invaluable for helping coordinate the wildlife photography excursion and have suggested that CKOA create a mailing list to keep its clients apprised of all the exciting happenings at Copper King Outdoor Adventures.

If you would like more information on mailing lists, you can find additional resouces using the New Perspectives on the Internet Using Netscape Navigator Software— Introductory Student Online Companion for this tutorial by accessing the Tutorial 4 links.

Quick Check

1. True or False: When you belong to a mailing list, you automatically receive copies of e-mail messages that other members send to the list.

2. The person or software responsible for maintaining a member list is called the _____.

3. Requesting placement on a mailing list is called _____ to the list.

4. Software programs that automatically manages many mailing list functions are called _____.

5. List three ways to locate the addresses of mailing lists.

6. The list server recognizes your e-mail address from the _____ within the message.

7. True or False: To post a message for an entire mailing list to see, you address the message to the list moderator.

8. To receive assistance on a mailing list, you usually send your request to the _____ in the form of _____.

Tutorial Assignment

After completing arrangements for the wildlife photography excursion, you turn your efforts to new projects. To add to the regular activities CKOA offers, you always keep your eyes and ears open for new and exciting ways to expand the organization's unique offerings. You find the Internet is a useful communication tool for researching outdoor enthusiasts' interests. You decide to send an e-mail message to Rose and a copy to Richard, listing some of your ideas for future activity offerings. You attach a table you created in Microsoft Word that lists some activities, along with URLs of Web pages that are good examples of how other businesses market similar offerings.

Do the following:

1. Open Netscape, then open the Netscape Mail window.
2. Click the To Mail button to open the Message Composition window.
3. Click the Mail To text box, and type the nickname for Rose's address book listing.
4. Click the Cc text box, and type the nickname for Richard's address book listing.
5. Click the Subject text box, and type the phrase: "New project ideas."
6. Click the message body area, and type a greeting and description of the attached file.
7. Click the Attachment button to open the Attachments dialog box.
8. Click the Attach File button to open the Enter file to attach text box.
9. Make sure your Student Disk is in drive A. Click the Look in list arrow, and select 3½ Floppy (A:).
10. Click the Ideas file, then click the Open button to attach the Ideas file to the e-mail message.
11. Click the OK button to close the Attachments dialog box and return to the Message Composition window.
12. Click the Send button to send the e-mail message to Richard and Rose.
13. Exit Netscape.

Case Problems

1. Creating a Signature File for Lucky Friday Ski Resort Eric Zacharia runs the marketing department at a regional ski area, the Lucky Friday Ski Resort. The ski resort caters to both young and old, and is built over the top of the Lucky Friday Gold Mine in Orem, Utah. The marketing department recently connected to the Internet and is working hard to put their Web site together. The Web site features information about accommodations at the resort, descriptions of the ski runs, and pricing information. One hyperlink Eric wants to add to the Web site is a comment form for users to complete. The form will let users request additional information concerning the resort, such as ski package availability or current skiing conditions. After the user submits the comment form, Eric wants the potential customer to automatically receive an e-mail acknowledging receipt of the message and promising an answer within 24 hours. Eric wants your assistance in creating a signature file to append to the end of the automated reply e-mail message. The signature file will be similar to a small ad. In addition, this signature file will be appended to the marketing department's general day-to-day e-mail messages sent in response to requests for information on the ski area.

The address of the resort is 364 Old Raven Road, and the telephone number is (303) 889-3090. Eric's e-mail address is ericz@ski.com. Create two signature files for Eric that are no more than four lines long and that list the resort name, address, phone number, and Eric's e-mail address. You may want to include emoticons and other keyboard symbols to help convey your message. Eric will evaluate both signature files and select the one he feels best reflects the resort's needs. You print and save the signature files on your Student Disk and then send a copy of the files as an attachment to your instructor asking for feedback.

Start Netscape. The New Perspectives on the Internet Using Netscape Navigator Software—Introductory Student Online Companion Web page appears in your window.

Do the following:

1. Click the Tutorial 4 link.
2. Click the Case Problems link.
3. Scroll down until you see the Case Problem 1 section for the Lucky Friday Ski Resort.
4. Use the links in the section to look at additional samples of .SIG files.
5. Launch a word-processing program such as Windows 95 WordPad on your computer.
6. Using the above information, create two signature files for the Lucky Friday Ski Resort that contain no more than four lines. Include just the company's vital information in the first, such as name and address; include a company slogan in the second signature file.
7. Print two copies of the signature files.
8. Save the document.
9. Open the Netscape Mail window, and create a message to your instructor explaining the use of a signature file and requesting feedback on the files you created.

10. Attach the signature files that you saved on your Student Disk to the e-mail message.
11. Send the e-mail message to your instructor, close the Mail window, and then exit Netscape.

2. Creating a Project Distribution List Dana Alia is a senior attending California State University, Long Beach. She is working toward her BA in Technology Management with a focus on computer ethics and law. Dana uses the Internet to complete much of her term paper and report research. The current assignment in her Computer Law class is to find the e-mail addresses of four prominent figures in the computer technology field, and then to create a distribution list of the addresses and save them on disk to hand in to her instructor. Dana has located the e-mail addresses using various search tools but needs your assistance in using the address book feature of Netscape Mail to create the distribution list. You develop the distribution list using the information in Figure 4-31, and then save the address book on disk.

Figure 4-31 ◀
Distribution list
information

NickName	Name	E-Mail Address	Description
Nik	Nik Runner	nikr@moft.com	Founder of Electronic Freedom
Tim	Tim Cascade	tbc@inland.net	Freedom of speech
Ann	Annie Prauchnau	aprauchnau@nri.org	Privacy and encryption
Louie	Louis Theriault	louist@qual.va.us	Computer crime

Start Netscape. The New Perspectives on the Internet Using Netscape Navigator Software—Introductory Student Online Companion Web page appears in your window. Do the following:

1. Open the Netscape Mail window.
2. Open the Address Book window, and then open the Add User Address Book dialog box.
3. Add address book entries for each person using the e-mail information listed in Figure 4-31.
4. Open the Add List Address Book dialog box.
5. Create a list using the name "Computer Ethics and Law."
6. Add members to the list by copying the entries for the users you created in Step 3 to the distribution list.
7. Save the address book file on your Student Disk.
8. Close the Address Book window.
9. Close the Mail window and then exit Netscape.

3. Finding Windows 95 Mailing Lists for Sky High Sounds Arielle Cook is a sound technician employed at Sky High Sounds, a music recording studio. Arielle uses special software to mix recorded sounds, such as vocals and instruments, before they are saved as tracks on compact discs. Arielle has been using software on a Macintosh computer for the last three years, but now the studio is converting to a sound-mixing software program that runs on the Windows 95 operating system platform.

Although Arielle is somewhat familiar with a GUI, she needs to learn more specific information about the Windows 95 operating system. She asked you to find at least two mailing lists regarding Windows 95 software. Once you have located the mailing lists, you note specific information available about subscribing to them. You e-mail this information to yourself as a reminder to pass the specifics along to Arielle, and you print a copy of the message for your files.

Start Netscape. The New Perspectives on the Internet Using Netscape Navigator Software—Introductory Student Online Companion Web page displays in your window.

Do the following:
1. Click the Tutorial 4 link.
2. Click the Case Problems link.
3. Scroll down until you see the Case Problem 3 section for Sky High Sounds.
4. Use links in the section to locate addresses and subscription information for two mailing lists that pertain to Windows 95.
5. When you find the information, note the list server addresses and moderator addresses for the mailing lists and any special instructions for subscribing to the lists.
6. Compose a message to yourself that includes the mailing lists names, their location, addresses, and corresponding subscription instructions.
7. Send the message.
8. Open the Sent folder, retrieve the message you just delivered, and print it.
9. Close the Mail window, then exit Netscape.

4. The Alberts & Alberts Accounting Firm Learns More about Listserv Commands Nadine Alberts, a partner in the Alberts and Alberts accounting firm, is actively searching for ways to keep in better contact with her clients. She recently learned about list servers and wants to try using a mailing list to distribute information to clients about tax breaks and new tax legislation. She is very busy with the upcoming tax season and doesn't have time to learn all the commands that can be used on the Listserv list server. Nadine asks you to research the **index**, **review**, **stats**, and **get** commands and let her know if they will be useful for her mailing list project. Once again, you e-mail the information to yourself for future reference but print two copies of the message; one for Nadine and one for yourself.

Start Netscape. The New Perspectives on the Internet Using Netscape Navigator Software—Introductory Student Online Companion Web page displays in your window.

Do the following:
1. Click the Tutorial 4 link.
2. Click the Case Problems link.
3. Scroll down until you see the Case Problem 4 section for Alberts & Alberts.
4. Use the links in the section to locate the Listserv commands' purposes and identify their potential benefits for Nadine's project.
5. Compose a message to yourself listing each Listserv command and its purposes. Include a sentence or two on how the accounting firm may be able to use them to create and maintain a client mailing list.
6. Send the message to yourself.
7. Open the Sent folder, retrieve the message you just delivered, and print two copies.
8. Close the Mail window, then exit Netscape.

Lab Assignment

E-mail

This Lab Assignment is designed to accompany the interactive Course Lab called E-mail. To start the Lab using Windows 95, click the Start button on the Windows 95 taskbar, point to Programs, point to Course Labs, point to New Perspectives Applications, and click E-mail. To start the Lab, double-click the Course Labs for the Internet group icon to open a window containing the Lab icons, then double-click the E-mail icon. If you do not see Course Labs on your Windows 95 Programs menu, or if you do not see the Course Labs on your Program Manager window, see your instructor or technical support person.

E-mail that originates on a local area network (LAN) with a mail gateway can travel all over the world. That's why learning how to use it is so important. In this lab you use an e-mail simulator, so even if your school computers don't have an e-mail service, you will know the basics of reading, sending, and replying to e-mail.

Do the following:

1. Click the Steps button to learn how to work with e-mail. As you proceed through the steps, answer all Quick Check questions that appear. After you complete the steps, you see a Quick Check summary report. Follow the instructions on the screen to print this report.

2. Click the Explore button. Write a message to re@films.org. The subject of the message is Picks and Pans. In the message body, describe a movie you have seen recently. Include the movie's name, briefly summarize its plot, and rate it thumbs up or thumbs down. Print the message before you send it.

3. Look in your In Basket for a message from jb@music.org. Read the message, then compose a reply indicating that you will attend. Carbon copy mcic-cone@music.org. Print your reply, including JBs original message text before you send it.

4. Look in your In Basket for a message from leo@sports.org. Reply to the message by adding your rating to the text of the original message as follows:

Equipment:	Your rating:
Rollerblades	2
Skis	3
Bicycle	1
Scuba gear	4
Snow mobile	5

5. Print your reply before you send it.

6. Go to the lab with a partner. You should each log into the E-mail Lab on different computers. Look at the Addresses list to find your partner's user ID. You should each send a short e-mail message to your partner. Then, you should check your mail message from your partner. Read the message and compose a reply. Print your reply before you send it. *Note: Unlike a full-featured mail system, the e-mail simulator does not save mail in mailboxes after you log off.*

Newsgroups and IRC

Using Newsgroups and IRC in a Mayoral Campaign

OBJECTIVES

In this tutorial you will:

- Learn what newsgroups are and how they work

- Identify components of the Netscape newsreader

- Retrieve, reply, save, and print newsgroup articles

- Subscribe and unsubscribe from a newsgroup

- Learn what IRC is and how it works

- Connect to a text-based IRC server

- Participate in an IRC session

- Explore a WWW chat site

- Learn about MUDs and MOOs

CASE

Mayoral Candidate Jack McLeod

Jack McLeod is running for public office. He wants to be mayor of Minneapolis, Minnesota. Jack has been told that Usenet newsgroups could be a beneficial communication tool in his campaign, letting him tap into the current political climate among voters in his district, as well as nationally. However, he is unfamiliar with how Usenet works and unsure how valuable this service would actually be. Jack currently uses Internet Relay Chat (IRC) to keep in touch with his daughter, who attends a university in another city. These real-time conversations help minimize long distance phone bills and are a way to communicate easily and regularly. IRC could be another beneficial way for Jack to reach the voting population. Jack asked you to join his office as the technology public relations director. In this position, you will evaluate the effectiveness of using Usenet newsgroups as a campaign tool. In addition you will recommend the best method of using IRC to discuss important political topics with local citizens.

SESSION

5.1

In this session you will learn what Usenet newsgroups are and how they work. You will also learn about the elements of the Netscape News window in order to use newsgroups. You will retrieve, reply, save, and print posted newsgroup articles using the Netscape newsreader. Finally, you will subscribe to and unsubscribe from a newsgroup.

Understanding Usenet Newsgroups

Usenet stands for Users' Network, a networking service consisting of thousands of servers hosting online discussion groups where users gather to exchange ideas on topics of shared interest. The computer discussion groups that communicate through Usenet are called **newsgroups**. Currently over 25,000 newsgroups exist, with topics ranging from business ethics to the latest entertainment reviews. Newsgroups are like mailing lists in that they function as a type of electronic bulletin board where users "post" comments or ideas, called **postings** or **articles**, for anyone who wants to read them. However, unlike mailing list messages that are automatically forwarded to subscribers via e-mail, newsgroup articles are not forwarded to users' mailboxes. Rather, subscribers periodically check newsgroup postings with special software and read them when they have time or interest. While mailing lists can be used for group discussions, newsgroups are more appropriate for a mailing list so large that sending individual messages to every subscriber's e-mailbox becomes unfeasible. No matter how many people are interested in reading a posting, the server only needs to store one copy. While mailing lists serve as a group communication tool, newsgroups function as distributed messaging services that broadcast information from your computer to other hosts around the world. These hosts may or may not be connected to the Internet.

Usenet began in the late 1970s as a type of electronic bulletin board service that universities used to share messages and news items. Today, businesses and individuals alike use newsgroups not only to distribute information, but as a resource for learning about virtually any subject and as sounding boards for new ideas.

How Newsgroups Work

Newsgroup communications are **asynchronous**: users do not need to be online at the same time for communication to occur. Rather, users post directly to the newsgroup site, and the server distributes their articles to a specific newsgroup's address. You can locate newsgroup addresses through traditional Internet searching methods such as search tools, or find them in computer magazines or journals. Postings can include the items that typical e-mail messages do, including attachments; businesses often use them to announce new products or to provide technical support.

The act of sending an article to a newsgroup is called **posting**. After you post an article, it arrives at a Usenet host system, known as a news server. The **news server** stores and manages all articles that are posted to a newsgroup in one central place. Many news servers share their newsgroups with one another. For example, each news server that receives an article stores it locally and then forwards it to other hosts that are part of the network. In this way, Usenet is a store and forward technology. When two host systems connect, they compare which postings they have in common by tracking ID numbers that accompany the articles. If one system misses a posting, the other transmits, or feeds, the information through the network to the requesting news server. Receiving articles via this type of transfer is called a **newsfeed**. One news server may feed many other news servers, thus articles can spread to other news servers very quickly. Some news servers request a newsfeed daily or hourly; others keep a constant connection between news servers for almost instantaneous sharing of postings.

No single entity controls the Usenet network. Instead, **news administrators** are employed by ISPs or individual organizations that have their own newsfeeds to perform such activities as monitoring newsgroup storage. Because some newsgroups use large amounts of disk space on a news server, news administrators often accept or reject a newsgroup based on size constraints, ensuring enough space for incoming postings from other newsgroups. News administrators may also monitor how many postings a newsgroup receives and can opt to cancel or drop a newsgroup that does not experience much traffic.

Although not part of the Internet, Usenet is like the Internet in that protocols regulate how Usenet host systems pass and maintain information. For Internet access to Usenet, an article posted to a newsgroup travels from one Usenet host system to another using one of several specific Internet protocols. The protocol most commonly used to distribute Usenet postings is the **Network News Transfer Protocol** (NNTP). NNTP, a part of the TCP/IP protocol suite, is a network standard that governs how Usenet articles are sent and routed across news servers on the Internet. News servers use the common set of rules to route all postings accurately and efficiently on the Net.

To read or reply to an article, you need to retrieve it using a client software application called a **newsreader**. There are many different types of newsreaders; you will use the built-in newsreader included with Netscape, called Netscape News, or News, to access newsgroups throughout this tutorial. Similar to using Netscape Mail to read e-mail messages, Netscape News is used to retrieve, save, and manage articles. You can compose articles to be posted to a newsgroup using newsreader software and then send them to the news server using the NNTP protocol. Postings are usually sent directly to a local news server, where other news servers may or may not opt to transfer the posting. Figure 5-1 shows Usenet's structure.

Figure 5-1 ◀
Structure of
Usenet

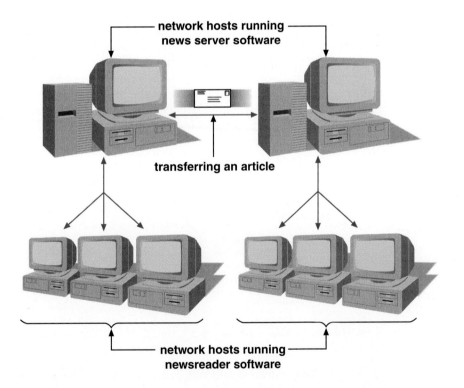

network hosts running
news server software

transferring an article

network hosts running
newsreader software

After a user retrieves a newsgroup article, he or she can choose to respond by replying to an article. There is no set time frame for replying; a user may receive 100 replies immediately after posting an article, one reply over the course of several hours or days, or none at all. Usually the number of replies depends on such factors as how many users subscribe to the newsgroup or the topic of discussion. Some postings are like an electronic discussion: users start an ongoing dialog by replying to one another's responses. For example, if someone posts an article requesting help on using a spreadsheet to perform scientific notation calculations, another user may post a reply giving specific assistance on the formula to use. Another user may reply with information on additional resources. The postings may soon lead to a general discussion on spreadsheets or on the characteristics of calculating scientific notations. Face-to-face discussions may jump from topic to topic; Usenet discussions do as well. Sometimes a newsgroup has many discussions going on at once. The sequence of postings, or responses to a particular discussion is called a **thread**.

The posted replies to threaded articles appear adjacent to the original article. Some threads are very short, with perhaps a single posting and a single reply; others are large, contain hundreds of articles, and continue for years. Although some newsgroup postings are kept on a news server longer than others, typical storage time for articles is about a week. This time frame varies based on the news administrator's discretion, the hard disk space available on a news server, or the ISP's policy. When a newsgroup "expires," its articles are deleted and replaced with newly posted articles.

Because no one person or organization has authority over Usenet as a whole, the service relies on volunteers and cooperation for regulation. Like mailing lists, some newsgroups use moderators to screen the various postings received. A moderator's tasks range from routing postings to the correct recipient and eliminating those mistakenly sent to the newsgroup, to ensuring that the postings' context does not violate netiquette standards of the organization that provides the newsgroup site. The moderator may also read and edit articles before posting them to the newsgroup.

Understanding Hierarchies

Newsgroup names are distinct and reflect the discussion topic within a particular newsgroup. Newsgroup addresses are like Internet addresses, but the most general category appears first instead of last in their names. Just as domain names are divided into categories, newsgroup names are organized hierarchically and consist of lowercase words or abbreviations separated by periods, as Figure 5-2 shows. The first level of a newsgroup name, appropriately called the **top level**, is a broad category that identifies the newsgroup's general topic. An arbitrary number of categories, called **sub-categories**, under the top level further define topics related to the top level and become more specific at each level. For example, in Figure 5-2, the top-level category comp identifies the topic of the newsgroup as being computer-related. The sub-category os, under the comp category, is more specific in relation to computer operating systems. Finally, the unix and ms-windows sub-categories are even more specifically related to these distinct operating systems.

Figure 5-2
Hierarchy of a
newsgroup
address

top-level newsgroup

sub-categories

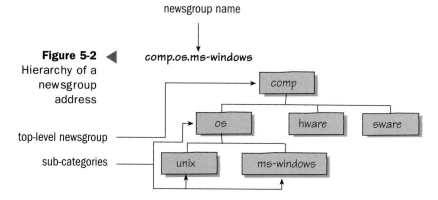

Newsgroups are divided into traditional and alternative newsgroups according to top-level categories. Traditional newsgroup categories consist of the seven original categories established at Usenet's inception. Categories additional to these seven are called "alternative" newsgroups, even though most news servers carry them. Local newsgroups, a special category of newsgroups, provide forums on topics related to a specific organization, city, or region that do not necessarily appeal nationally or internationally. For example, the alt.minneapolis newsgroup lists discussions related to that city's happenings. In addition, Clarinet is a category devoted solely to commercial news services. **Clarinet** primarily offers United Press International (UPI) service and various syndicated newspaper columns indexed for the Usenet news system. Not all ISPs carry the commercial newsgroups because they are only available on a contract basis and can be too expensive for the average user.

Figure 5-3 lists some examples of common newsgroup categories; the first seven listings are traditional newsgroups. As you become more familiar with newsgroups, you will notice that some articles fit in more than one category. For example, articles about baseball may be found in the alt.sport.baseball newsgroup, and they may also be found in the rec.baseball newsgroup.

Figure 5-3 ◄
Newsgroup
categories

Hierarchy	Description	Sample
comp	Computer related topics	comp.hware.printers
rec	Recreational topics	rec.gardening
sci	Topics related to sciences	sci.biology
soc	Topics related to social issues	soc.rights.elderly
news	Topics related to the operation and administration of network news and the software used to transmit, retrieve, and create articles	news.newusers.questions
talk	Conversational topics, oftentimes argumentative discussions	talk.philosophy.humanism
misc	Miscellaneous topics	misc.entrepreneurs
alt	Alternative discussions	alt.adoption.agency
bionet	Topics devoted to biological sciences	bionet.immunology
k12	Topics devoted to education in grades kindergarden through 12	k12.teachers.lessons
biz	Business and commercial topics	biz.products.new
fj	Japanese newsgroups	fj.rec.music
vmsnet	Discussion of VMS computer operating system	vmsnet.help
clari	Commercial news service from Clarinet	clari.living

Becoming Familiar with Netscape News

Netscape News is an easy-to-use graphical user interface (GUI) newsreader used to view and participate in Usenet newsgroups. News lets you search for newsgroups you may be interested in according to topic or view postings before you subscribe to a newsgroup. It controls how postings pass between the news server and a user's computer, letting you retrieve, compose, send, and save articles. To use News, Netscape must contain a news server host name in the Mail and News Preferences options. If you are unsure if your Netscape installation is configured for an available news server, ask your instructor or technical support person for assistance.

Launching the Netscape Newsreader

Because Jack is interested in exploring the possibility of utilizing newsgroups in his campaign, you will spend some time over the next few days exploring their use and evaluating their feasibility. Your first order of business is launching the Netscape newsreader to learn more about its function and use.

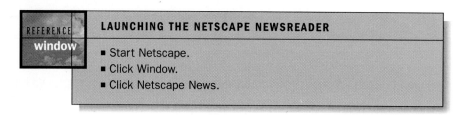

REFERENCE window

LAUNCHING THE NETSCAPE NEWSREADER

■ Start Netscape.
■ Click Window.
■ Click Netscape News.

To launch the Netscape newsreader:

1. Start Netscape. The New Perspectives on the Internet Using Netscape Navigator Software — Introductory Student Online Companion Web page appears on your screen.

2. Click **Window** on the menu bar, then click **Netscape News** to open the News window. Your screen should look like Figure 5-4. You may see additional information in your window because different news servers support different newsgroups.

Figure 5-4 ◀
Netscape News window

menu bar
news server
newsgroups
subscribe column
message pane
status bar

toolbar
status indicator
read column
flag column

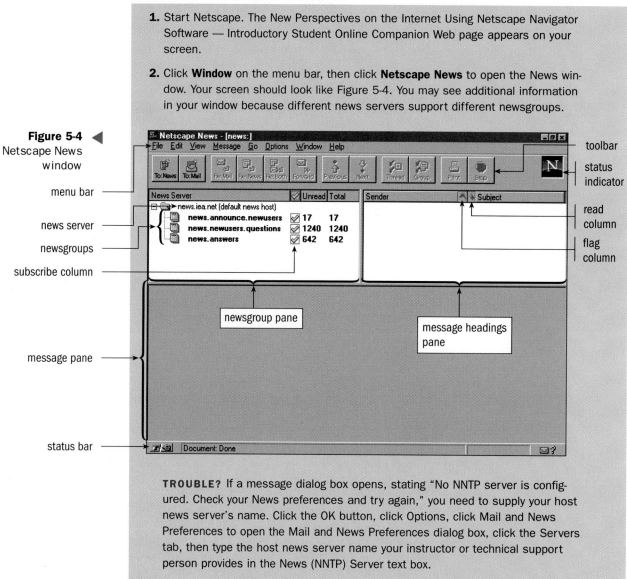

TROUBLE? If a message dialog box opens, stating "No NNTP server is configured. Check your News preferences and try again," you need to supply your host news server's name. Click the OK button, click Options, click Mail and News Preferences to open the Mail and News Preferences dialog box, click the Servers tab, then type the host news server name your instructor or technical support person provides in the News (NNTP) Server text box.

Elements of the News Window

The Netscape News window operates and looks like the Netscape Mail window discussed in Tutorial 4. The menu items, toolbar buttons, and icons in the News window let you view and compose articles much the same way as you retrieve and create e-mail messages. Figure 5-4 shows the News window's elements.

The News window contains three panes: a newsgroup pane, a message headings pane, and a message pane. When you first open the News window, the set of newsgroups you subscribe to appears in the **newsgroup pane**. The newsgroup pane consists of several columns, including the News Server column, which lists the names of news servers available through your ISP, the newsgroup categories available, and the names of newsgroups you either already subscribe to, or those available for subscription. These items appear as folders in the News Server column of the newsgroup pane in hierarchical order, with the news server name showing in the left-most position, the category listing indented below the news server name, and finally the available newsgroups indented below the category listing, shown as a document icon. When you click a check box in the Subscribe column, you subscribe to that particular newsgroup. If no check mark appears in the check box, you are not subscribed. The Unread column shows the number of unread messages in the newsgroup, and the Total column shows the total number of articles available for viewing in a newsgroup.

Clicking an item in the newsgroup pane displays a listing of associated articles in the **message headings pane**, along with several columns of information. The Sender column indicates the name of the person who sent a particular article. The next two columns are the Flag icon and Read icon columns. These columns have toggle indicators noting if you have flagged, or marked, an article as noteworthy or remarkable or if you have read the article or not. You can change the column status by clicking the respective check boxes. The Subject column displays the subject line, or message heading, of an article indicating the article's topic.

You use the **message pane** to view newsgroup articles. Clicking a specific article's message heading in the message headings pane displays its contents in the message pane along with header information. This header information includes items like the e-mail address of the user who posted the article and names of other newsgroups that the article may have been posted to.

At the bottom of the News window is the **status bar**. It shows your progress as you connect to a news server or as you retrieve newsgroup articles. The status bar changes to indicate when you are connected to a news server and how much information has been loaded into your computer's memory. Then it displays the "Document: Done" message when the requested articles are loaded.

As with the Mail window, you can resize each of the three panes to accommodate news information in them by positioning the cursor on the border lines between two panes and dragging the panes to the dimensions you want. Another method of modifying the panes' layout is to adjust the settings in the Mail and News Appearance menu, which you access from the Options menu. For example, instead of displaying the panes horizontally, Netscape can display them vertically. The News toolbar buttons and other menu items offer additional alternatives for viewing, creating, sending, and saving news articles. The Next 🔲 and Previous 🔲 buttons let you move quickly through the displayed articles. At times you may have a backlog of hundreds of articles that you have no time to read. The Thread button 🔲 automatically marks all messages in a thread as if you have read them. One display option in News displays only unread articles in a newsgroup so that you do not have to browse through a list of articles you've already retrieved.

Now that you are familiar with the News window's elements, you can use the newsreader to view posted articles. You begin by retrieving an article in one of the default newsgroups.

Retrieving an Article

Each newsgroup typically presents its articles along threads that show the original posting as well as any responses. If postings were simply listed chronologically, it would be difficult to determine if an article is a response to another message or is an original article. By grouping articles and threads, newsreaders present postings in a topical context. You can quickly gain an overview of a discussion by looking at the thread's message headings, which are listed in the message headings pane. Netscape News displays each threaded article by indenting its name below the original posting. Figure 5-5 shows an example of a news article thread.

Figure 5-5 ◄
News article
thread

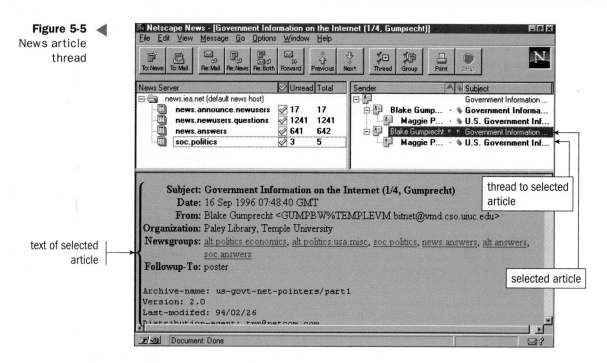

text of selected
article

You access an article by clicking the appropriate newsgroup name in the newsgroup pane. Doing so displays all postings associated with that newsgroup. To retrieve an individual article, you simply click the article's message heading in the message headings pane, and its text appears in the message pane. When you retrieve an article, several things happen. First the Stop button ![Stop] changes to red—its active state—and the status indicator becomes animated. Next, the status bar changes to show that News has contacted the news server, is transferring data, and finally, completes the transfer. In the header lines shown along with the article in the message pane, you may notice that the article has been posted to several newsgroups, in addition to the one you are accessing. Posting an article to several newsgroups at once is called **cross-posting**. Cross-posting is useful for distributing the same information to several related newsgroups. For example, an article about a new mathematics teaching method for elementary students may be posted to the k12.news newsgroup, the k12.ed.math newsgroup, as well as the sci.math.research newsgroup.

To become more familiar with using newsgroups, you can select one of the default newsgroups Netscape automatically subscribes you to, which contains general Usenet information. Netscape automatically subscribes you to three newsgroups that were designed to help newcomers understand more fully how the Usenet newsgroup service works. These groups are news.announce.newusers, news.newusers.questions, and news.answers. An article that describes some general rules of conduct in Usenet is in the news.announce.newusers newsgroup. You access this newsgroup and retrieve the article.

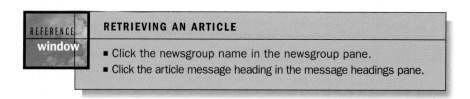

REFERENCE
window

RETRIEVING AN ARTICLE

- Click the newsgroup name in the newsgroup pane.
- Click the article message heading in the message headings pane.

To retrieve an article:

1. Double-click the **news.announce.newusers** newsgroup name in the newsgroup pane. A list of articles posted to the newsgroup and their responses appears in the message headings pane.

TROUBLE? If the news.announce.newusers newsgroup does not show in your newsgroup pane, click Options, then click Show All Newsgroups, and repeat Step 1.

2. Read through the list of articles until you locate one whose subject is similar to "Rules for posting to Usenet." Click **Rules for posting to Usenet** or a similar heading to retrieve the article. The posting appears in the message pane. See Figure 5-6. Using the scroll bar in the message heading pane, read the article.

Figure 5-6 ◄
Retrieving a newsgroup article

selected newsgroup

newsgroup articles

retrieved articles

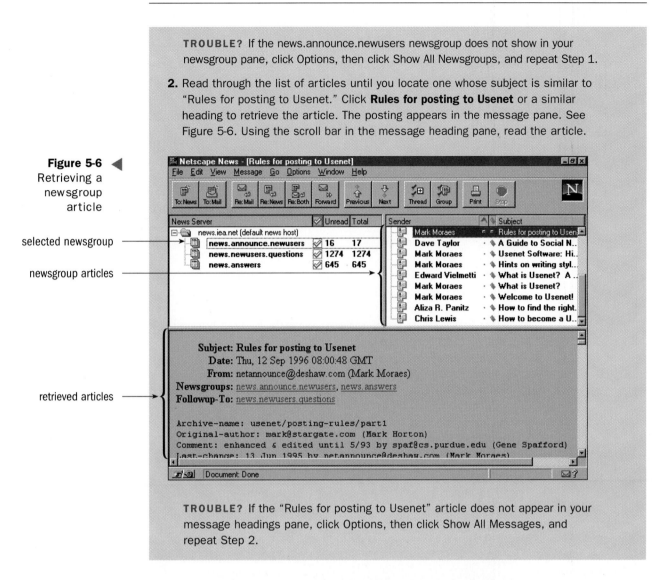

TROUBLE? If the "Rules for posting to Usenet" article does not appear in your message headings pane, click Options, then click Show All Messages, and repeat Step 2.

After retrieving and reading the article, you have a question about time intervals on receiving replies to postings. You want to post this question to the newsgroup in response to the original article.

Replying to an Article

After you retrieve an article, you may feel compelled to join the discussion and send a response. Sometimes you want to share additional information on the topic, or perhaps you want to clarify a point made in the article. A news option lets you either reply to the newsgroup, to the user who originally posted the article, or both. For example, if someone posts an article quoting information from new clinical trials for a cancer vaccine, you may reply to the posting and ask where you can find additional facts on the trials. You can post your reply to the newsgroup so that all subscribers may read it, or you may opt to send your response directly to the user who posted the original article.

Users should follow some common netiquette when replying to a posting. For example, make sure to provide the context for your response by including a portion of the original article in your reply. This helps other users who are following the discussion to understand your posting's context. Before composing a reply that asks a question, take time to read and understand the current threads and transcripts of previous newsgroup discussions. That way you won't repeat a question already addressed in the newsgroup and risk receiving a **flame**, a nasty or insulting message. Another way to become familiar with a newsgroup is to read its FAQs before posting a message. **FAQs** stands for Frequently Asked Questions (pronounced "facts"). These documents contain questions that newcomers to each individual newsgroup commonly ask about that particular newsgroup, such as those relating to netiquette, content, and subject area. You can find many FAQs for different newsgroups in the *.answers groups, but usually the FAQs document is posted periodically to the newsgroup. After reading a newsgroup's articles for a period of time and reading its FAQs, you are likely to have a feel for what topics the group commonly discusses, who sends postings regularly, and how new users are treated. If you receive an answer to a question that you think may help other newsgroup users, you may want to post a summary to the newsgroup, or notify the person who maintains the FAQ so that the information can be shared. Finally, keep in mind that an e-mail message is more appropriate than a Usenet posting if your reply is for just one newsgroup subscriber or even a few.

As you recall from the earlier discussion regarding the News window's elements, you can use the set of toolbar buttons in the News window for various functions. One is replying to newsgroup articles. To reply to a posting, you retrieve the article so that it appears in your Message Composition window with the context carried through to the threaded response. When you post a reply to a newsgroup, a header line in the Message Composition window shows the newsgroup to which the article will be automatically posted. The most common method of replying to news postings is to send an article using the Re:News button 🔲, which sends the reply to the newsgroup. The Re:Mail button 🔲 lets you reply directly to sender's original article via an e-mail message, while the Re:Both button 🔲 lets you reply with both a posting and an e-mail message.

You decide to reply to the posting, hoping to receive a response to your question. Because this is your first posting, you send your reply to yourself before submitting it to the newsgroup. It is important to understand the process since a posting has the potential to reach thousands, or even millions, of subscribers.

To reply to an article:

1. Click the **Re:Mail** button 🔲 located on the News toolbar. The Mail composition window opens. **Maximize** the window. Note that the Mail To: text box automatically contains the article author's e-mail address, the Subject text box indicates that the message is a reply, and the original posting is quoted in the message body area. See Figure 5-7.

Figure 5-7 ◀
Replying to
an article

indicates replying to
original article

subject of original
article

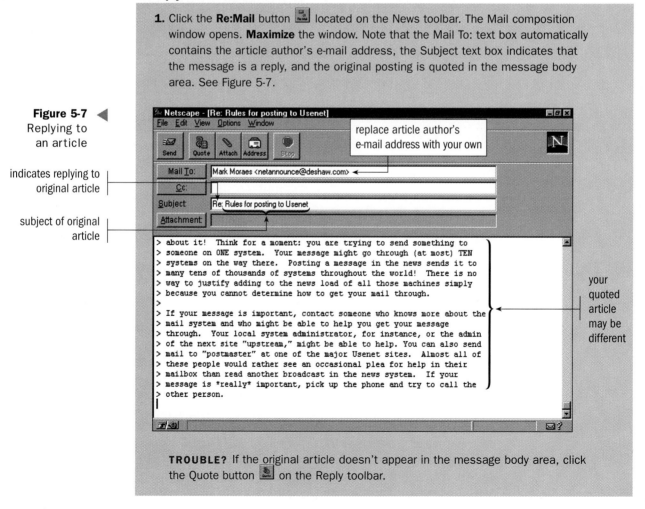

TROUBLE? If the original article doesn't appear in the message body area, click the Quote button 🔲 on the Reply toolbar.

2. Highlight the author's name and e-mail address in the Mail To: text box to select it, then press the **Delete** key.

3. Type your e-mail address in the Mail To: text box, and then press the **Tab** key three times until your cursor is in the message body area. Note that the cursor automatically appears at the end of the quoted article.

4. In the message body area, type **In your article, you state that posted questions that aren't answered within a decent interval probably won't be answered at all. What is a typical interval to determine if a posting will receive a response? Thank you.** Your completed reply should look like Figure 5-8.

Figure 5-8 ◀
Completed
reply

click to send
reply to yourself

your quoted article
may be different

completed reply
message

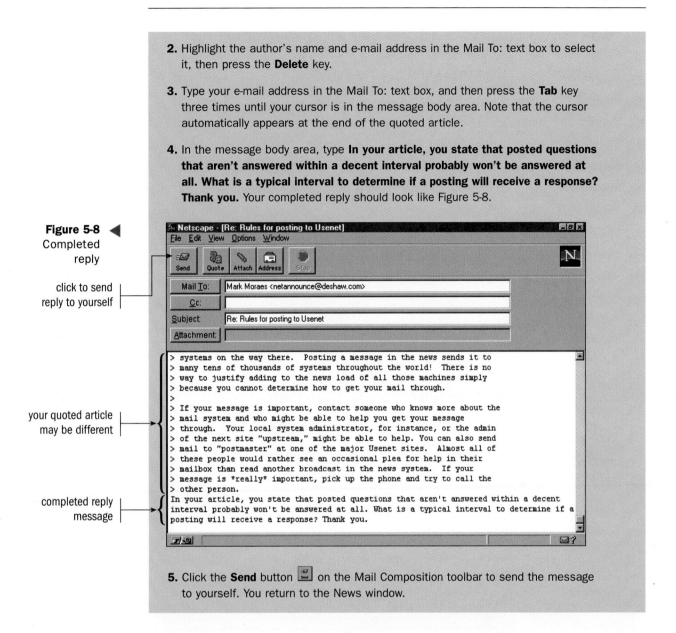

5. Click the **Send** button 🖃 on the Mail Composition toolbar to send the message to yourself. You return to the News window.

You see how easy it is to reply to an article using the same features you use to create e-mail messages. Because the rules for posting to Usenet contain a lot of valuable information about using newsgroups, you want to save the information in the article as a reference so that you don't have to retrieve it each time.

Saving an Article

Because articles generally expire within a predetermined time period, at times you may want to save a copy of an article on your local hard drive or on a floppy disk. This option is useful if you do not have time to read the article, or if you want a permanent copy of the posting. Netscape gives you the option of saving the article as either an .HTML or .TXT file.

You now save the article on your Student Disk.

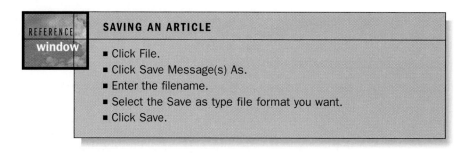

REFERENCE
window

SAVING AN ARTICLE

- Click File.
- Click Save Message(s) As.
- Enter the filename.
- Select the Save as type file format you want.
- Click Save.

To save an article:

1. Insert your Student Disk in drive A or the appropriate drive on your computer.

2. With the article still displayed in the message pane, click **File** on the menu bar, then click **Save Message(s) As** to open the Save Messages As dialog box.

3. Click the **Save in** list arrow, then select **3 ¹/₂ Floppy (A:)**.

4. Click the **Filename** text box, then type **rules** to name the file you're saving. You will save the article in the default format .HTML as indicated by the HTML files information in the Save as type text box. See Figure 5-9.

   TROUBLE? If the Filename text box already contains a filename, highlight the name in the File name text box and press the Delete key to clear the File name text box. Repeat Step 4.

Figure 5-9 ◀
Saving an
article

type filename here ——

click to save article
on your Student Disk

5. Click **Save** to save the article on your Student Disk and close the Save Messages As dialog box.

You now have a permanent copy of the article for your records. You can reference this information later if you have questions about using newsgroups.

Subscribing to a Newsgroup

Newsgroups are like mailing lists: you can subscribe to any that interest you. In the context of newsgroups, a subscription means that a newsreader keeps an ongoing account of your subscribed newsgroups and notes which postings you have read. Subscribing to a newsgroup does not automatically copy articles to your local hard drive. Rather, retrieving articles saves them in your computer's memory. When you no longer want to participate in a newsgroup, you can unsubscribe from it. While subscribing to or unsubscribing from a mailing list may take hours or days to take effect, these actions occur instantaneously with Netscape News.

The easiest way to subscribe to a newsgroup is to display all available newsgroups in the newsgroup pane, locate the newsgroup you want to subscribe to, and then click the corresponding check box in the subscribe column. When you subscribe to a newsgroup, its name is added to a list and stored in a News file (also called a News RC or newsrc file) that the Netscape software maintains. If you don't have a news file, Netscape creates one for you the first time you use the newsreader.

If a newsgroup you are interested in is not listed on your news server, you may want to send an e-mail message to the news server administrator requesting that the news server carry or include the particular newsgroup. In addition, if you are not sure if a newsgroup exists, you can use one of many Internet search tools available to enter your newsgroup search criteria.

After you subscribe to a newsgroup, the newsgroup heading appears on the opening newsgroup screen in the newsgroup pane. As a result, you don't need to scroll through the list of every newsgroup your news server offers to access the one you subscribe to. In addition, you can set up News to list only the newsgroups you subscribe to every time the News window opens. You can also choose to have just the active newsgroups appear. **Active newsgroups** are newsgroups you subscribe to that contain new postings.

Jack and you agree that accessing a political newsgroup would be a helpful way to learn about the range of ideas and topics that voters discuss. He gives you the names of several newsgroups he obtained while networking at a recent fundraising dinner. You decide to subscribe to the soc.politics newsgroup, whose members discuss politics on local, state, national, and international levels.

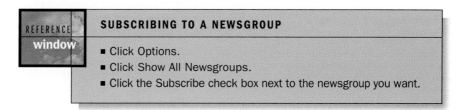

REFERENCE
window

SUBSCRIBING TO A NEWSGROUP

- Click Options.
- Click Show All Newsgroups.
- Click the Subscribe check box next to the newsgroup you want.

To subscribe to a newsgroup:

1. Click **Options** on the menu bar, then click **Show All Newsgroups**. See Figure 5-10. A list of all newsgroups available on your news server appears in the newsgroup pane. Your screen may differ from that shown in Figure 5-10.

Figure 5-10 ◀
Listing of all available newsgroups

newsgroup category

newsgroup heading

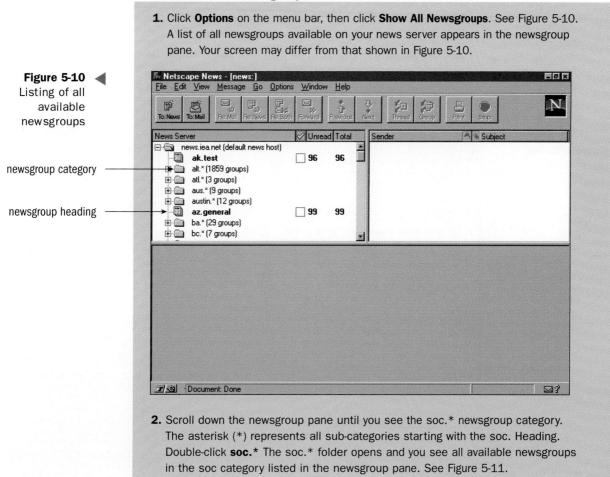

2. Scroll down the newsgroup pane until you see the soc.* newsgroup category. The asterisk (*) represents all sub-categories starting with the soc. Heading. Double-click **soc.*** The soc.* folder opens and you see all available newsgroups in the soc category listed in the newsgroup pane. See Figure 5-11.

Figure 5-11 ◀
Soc.* category
newsgroups

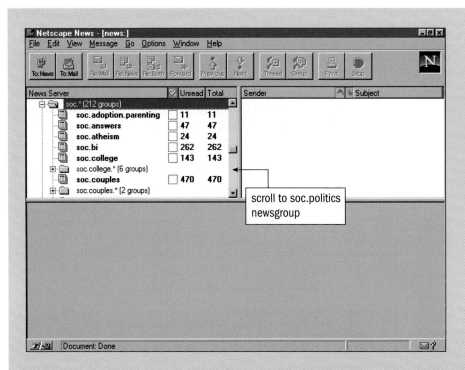

scroll to soc.politics
newsgroup

3. Scroll down the newsgroups list until you see the soc.politics newsgroup. Click the **check box** in the Subscribe status column next to the soc.politics newsgroup name so that a check mark appears in the check box. You have now subscribed to the soc.politics newsgroup.

   Now that you have subscribed to the soc.politics newsgroup, you want only the newsgroups to which you've subscribed to appear every time you open the News window. You set your newsreader to use this option.

4. Click **Options** on the menu bar, then click **Show Subscribed Newsgroups**. Only newsgroups to which you've subscribed now appear in the newsgroup pane. See Figure 5-12. Your newsgroup subscription listing may differ slightly from the one shown in Figure 5-12. Note that the soc.politics newsgroup you just subscribed to appears in the newsgroup pane.

Figure 5-12 ◀
Subscribed
newsgroup
listing

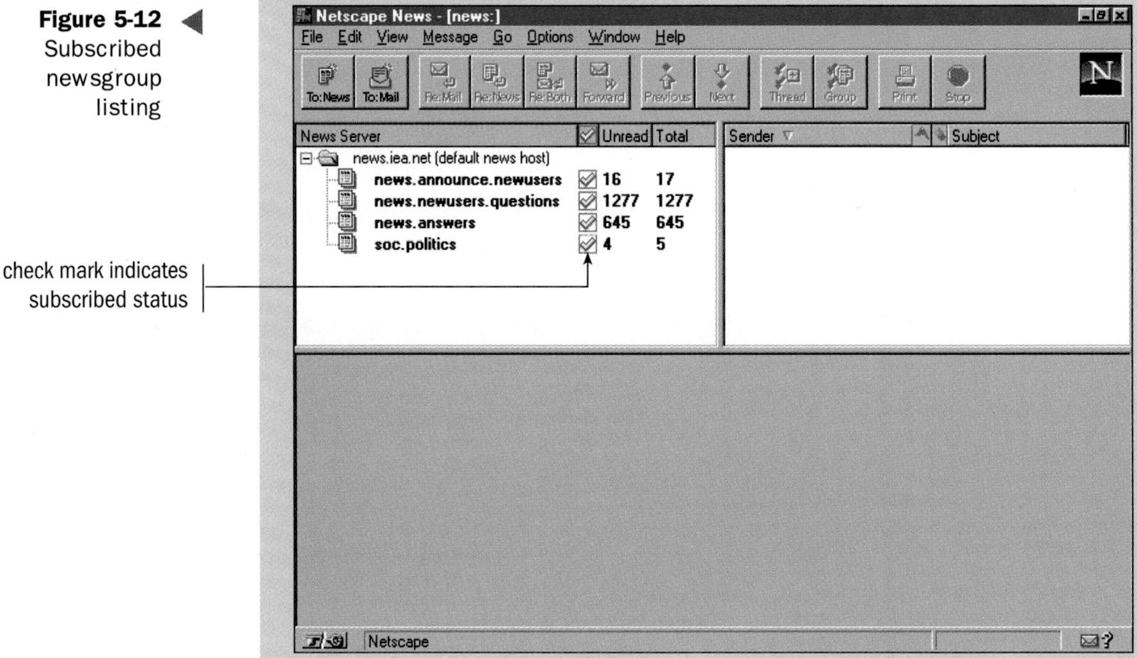

check mark indicates
subscribed status

Now that you have subscribed to the soc.politics newsgroup, you want to show Jack a sample article from this newsgroup by printing one out for him.

Printing Articles

As with e-mail messages, sometimes you may want to print newsgroup articles for future reference. Printing an article is especially useful when you want to give it to another person who doesn't have Usenet access or simply want to read it yourself later. You can preview the article before you print it, just as you preview e-mail messages and Web pages. The Print Preview option is available on the File menu.

You decide to print a copy of the first article in the soc.politics newsgroup for Jack. This information will help him determine if he is interested in subscribing to this newsgroup. Because you are sure you want to print the entire article and do not need to preview it, you are now ready to print.

To print an article:

1. Click the first article that appears in the soc.politics newsgroup in the message heading pane. The article's text that appears in the message pane in your window may look different from Figure 5-13.

click to open Print dialog box

retrieved article

Figure 5-13 ◄
Soc.politics newsgroup article

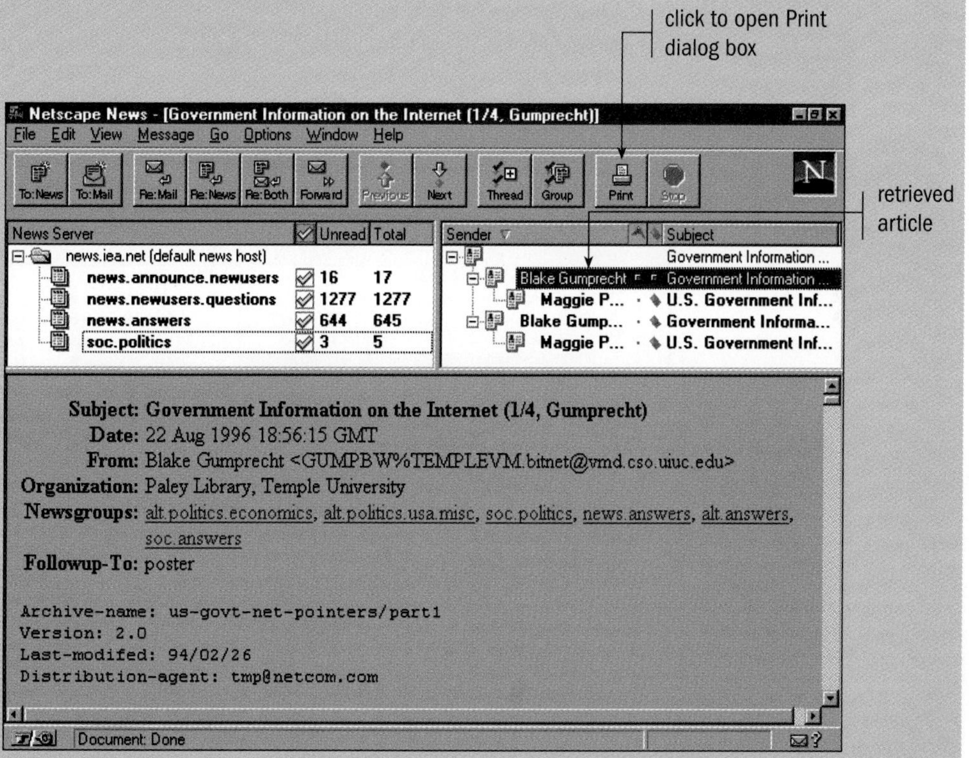

2. Click the **Print** button on the toolbar. The print dialog box opens.

3. Click the **OK** button to print the article. A Printing Status box may appear on your screen to update you on your print job's progress. The entire article is printed.

You give the printed article to Jack. He promises to let you know in a couple of days if he finds this newsgroup useful. If so, you will configure his newsreader to subscribe to the soc.politics newsgroup.

Unsubscribing from a Newsgroup

When a newsgroup no longer interests you or its information does not meet your needs, you can unsubscribe from it. Unlike the unsubcribe command used for mailing lists, the unsubscribe command for newsgroups takes effect immediately. This feature makes trying several different newsgroups convenient and finding the one you like easier.

After Jack reads the printed article that you gave to him, he decides that the soc.politics newsgroup does not provide exactly the type of information he hoped to find. You will continue to search for other politically oriented newsgroups that may help him get in touch with voters' concerns and ideas. In the meantime, you unsubscribe from the soc.politics newsgroup.

REFERENCE
window

UNSUBSCRIBING FROM A NEWSGROUP

- Click the check box in the Subscribe column next to the news-group name to delete the check mark.

To unsubscribe from a newsgroup:

1. Locate the **soc.politics** newsgroup in the newsgroup pane. Click the **check box** next to it in the Subscribe column to delete the check mark and unsubscribe from the newsgroup. See Figure 5-14.

Figure 5-14
Unsubcribing
from a
newsgroup

soc.politics
newsgroup is no
longer subscribed to

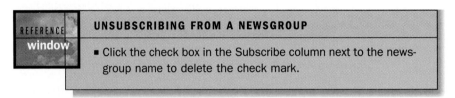

You are finished working with newsgroups for today and want to exit Netscape.

2. Click **File** on the menu bar, then click **Exit** to close the Netscape News window.

3. Click **File** on the menu bar, then click **Exit** to exit Netscape.

TROUBLE? If a Netscape Exit Confirmation box appears on your screen asking if you want to close all windows and exit Netscape, click the Yes button.

You are anxious to find other newsgroups that can assist Jack in his campaign. From what you've learned about newsgroups, you think they are a useful way for Jack to keep abreast of any changes in voter attitudes or concerns until the election. You also recommend to Jack that he host at least two newsgroups. Jack can use the first, a moderated newsgroup, to distribute general information. Among the postings in this newsgroup will be a FAQs section for answering common questions. Your second newsgroup recommendation is for a more open forum for citizens to share ideas and concerns not only with Jack, but with each other as well.

Quick Check

1 True or False: Newsgroup participants must be online when an article is sent to receive it.

2 In which Usenet category would you most likely find an appropriate newsgroup for group discussions about computers?
(a) soc
(b) rec
(c) comp
(d) news

3 True or False: All newsgroup postings are retained for at least six weeks.

4 The flow of conversation in a newsgroup listing both the original posting and its responses is called a _____.

5 The act of distributing a newsgroup posting to several different newsgroups is called _____.

6 You can reply to a news posting by sending an article to _____ , _____, or _____.

7 Many FAQs for newsgroups are found in the _____ newsgroups.

8 True or False: When you unsubscribe from a newsgroup, you may continue to receive articles for the next few days.

SESSION 5.2

In this session you will learn how Internet Relay Chat (IRC) works and become familiar with its various components. You will connect to an IRC server, participate in an IRC chat session, and connect to a WWW IRC site. Finally, you will learn about MUD and MOO chat sessions.

What Is Internet Relay Chat (IRC)?

IRC, short for **Internet Relay Chat**, is an Internet service that utilizes real-time interactive technology to let users participate in live text-based conversations with one another. During these conversations, known as **sessions**, users talk (type) and listen (read) at the same time. Like a group discussion, IRC lets many users participate in the session but from the convenience of their computers. **Channels**, also called **chat rooms**, are virtual places where users gather to participate in an IRC session. Like newsgroups, IRC offers over 25,000 channel topics. However, any person can create a channel and choose its topic. Upon entering a chat room, you may find participants discussing everything from stocks and bonds to the latest hockey league standings.

Jarkko Oikarinen originally developed the IRC software in 1988 at the University of Oulu, Finland, as a type of online bulletin board service so users could chat among themselves in real-time. During the 1990s, scientists and scholars began using IRC to conduct informal discussions with geographically distant colleagues. Today, IRC is one of the Internet's fastest growing areas. Businesses use it for a wide variety of purposes because it provides opportunities for companies, their customers, and even off-site employees to have real-time interaction. A primary business use of IRC is for virtual meetings. When remote participants meet on an IRC network at a given time, geographic and time boundaries fade. Less travel time, fewer expenses, and lower long distance charges mean cost savings. Some retail businesses put experts online to answer customers questions via IRC, providing a cost-effective way to meet customers' needs without tying up telephone lines and incurring costly long distance charges. Other popular IRC uses include live coverage of news events and political discussions. For example, IRC gained international recognition during the 1991 Persian Gulf War when news updates and eyewitness reports were relayed through the Internet via IRC.

Understanding How IRC Works

IRC utilizes the unique client-server model, shown in Figure 5-15. Typically, when studying computers, you learn that a client is a computer user and a server is generally a host computer. However, in the context of IRC, the terms "client" and "server" also refer to types of software applications that let users communicate over networks configured for IRC. A user runs a **client** program to connect to the IRC network via another program called a server. Clients connect to **server** programs, which transfer messages from user to user over the IRC network. A server can handle many different types of clients, ranging from GUIs to text-based interfaces. Servers also provide a site for other servers to connect to, forming an **IRC network**. A typical chat session involves the user launching an IRC client program, connecting to an IRC server. The IRC server then connects to additional IRC servers. The user **joins** or connects to a channel, and as she types her message, it is transferred quickly to all interconnected servers, so sessions can include users from any number of servers.

Figure 5-15 ◀
How IRC works

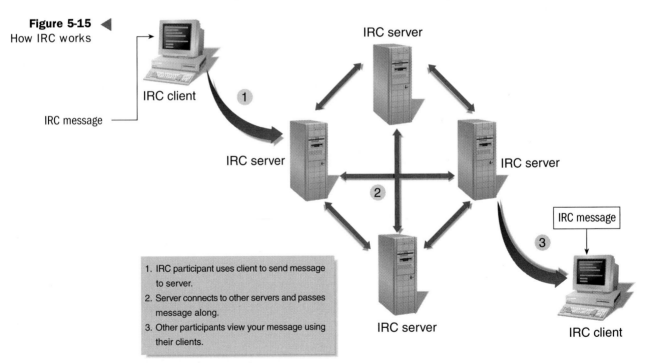

1. IRC participant uses client to send message to server.
2. Server connects to other servers and passes message along.
3. Other participants view your message using their clients.

IRC uses the IRC protocol, a part of the TCP/IP protocol suite. Although hundreds of IRC networks exist, the three most popular public ones are EFnet, Undernet, and DALnet. In addition, some Web sites have built-in client programs. You use the WebChat Web site later in this tutorial to view a graphical-based chat session.

From what you learned about how IRC works, you already thought of ways that Jack could use IRC to benefit his campaign. Perhaps he could hold a press conference over the IRC service or host a "call in" program so citizens could meet online to ask about his position on community issues. Before you jump too far ahead with these ideas, you need to learn how to use IRC to participate in a session.

Getting Familiar with an IRC Session

To understand the various components involved in an IRC session, understanding what happens during a typical session may be helpful. Later in the tutorial you will set up and participate in your own chat session.

Almost all IRC servers have a channel named #newbie that is popular among users who are new to the IRC service. It is a practical starting point for users to try IRC and master its various commands. Figure 5-16 shows a sample IRC session on the #newbie channel.

Figure 5-16 ◀
Sample IRC
chat session

asterisks denote
action of user "beck"
leaving the #newbies
channel

nicknames of
participants

command line

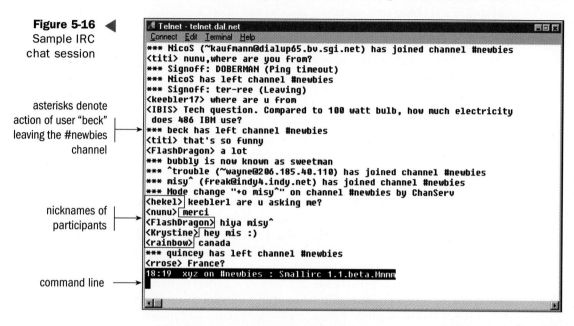

During a session, messages other participants send appear on the top of the screen; IRC commands and messages that you type appear on the last line of the screen, called the **command line** or **message line**. When participating in an IRC session, you simply type your message in the message line and then press the Enter key. Your name (displayed within brackets < >) and your message text simultaneously appear on computers of all other users who join the channel and participate in that particular chat session. Any messages you type appear on your computer screen as well, but without your name. Messages other participants send appear on your screen with their names in brackets < >, followed by their messages' text. Conversations tend to move very quickly on IRC. Many people may be participating on a channel, conducting several conversations at once. As more messages come over the channel, the conversation scrolls off the top of the screen; only the most current messages show.

Understanding Channels

Channel subjects range from the broadest of topics, such as discussions about the Windows 95 computer operating system on the #Win95 channel, to the very narrowest, such as Great Lakes economic development discussion issues on the #GLED channel. In IRC, the number symbol (#) refers to the channel heading, or topic. A **channel heading**, or channel name, is a character string, usually a single word, that describes the topic discussed on the channel. Users refer to the channel by its heading. When users join a channel, they receive messages addressed to the channel. The IRC protocol lets users participate on several channels at once, although it is recommended that new users begin by participating on a single channel. Channels on IRC are dynamic because anyone can create a new channel. The channel is created simply when the first participant joins, and it ceases to exist when the last participant leaves. If no channel exists for the topic you would like to discuss, you can simply create one. Individuals and businesses alike create channels to distribute information, express ideas, or to gather feedback on any topic imaginable.

Each channel on an IRC server has a least one **channel operator**, who is responsible for managing the channel. By default, the person who first created the channel is the channel operator, or its **chop**, and "owns" the channel. The channel operator has certain rights that other participants don't, such as the capability to change the channel heading and discussion topic. One of the channel operator's main responsibilities is to determine which users may participate on the channel he or she is administering. Channel operators are also responsible for maintaining the channel by monitoring its various settings, for example, settings for private or public access, and keeping the channel running as smoothly as possible. Users who experience a problem on a particular channel can direct a message to the operator for assistance. Channel operators have the authority to ban, or kick off, users who do not follow general netiquette rules. A channel operator can also pass along operator status to another user. This sometimes becomes necessary if the operator needs to be absent for awhile, or simply no longer wants to monitor the channel.

The channel operator also has authority to change the channel mode. The **channel mode** is a setting that alters the channel's characteristics. Although there are several possible channel modes, the three most commonly used in IRC are public, private, and secret. **Public mode** is the default mode for a channel when it is created. If a channel is public, any user can participate in its conversation. Channel headings that include a number between 1 and 999, or a plus sign (+), typically denote public channels. A user must know a **private mode** channel's name to join. Most users can only participate in a private channel if the channel operator invites them. Private channels' headings often have a number above 1,000. Private channels are commonly used for internal communications within a company. A user must also know the heading of a **secret mode** channel to join. However, a secret mode's channel heading is never made available to the general public. Like the private mode, participants must be invited to join the channel. A secret mode channel is highly secure and nearly impossible to detect.

Other channel modes determine if a user or a group of users moderates the channel, limits the channel topic and/or number of people who can participate, or even bans certain users from the channel. Figure 5-17 shows some examples of mode commands that channel operators can initiate and their effects on channel usage for the #politics channel.

Figure 5-17 ◀
Mode
commands

Mode Commands	Description
mode#politics p	Makes channel private
mode#politics s	Makes channel secret
mode#politics l 20	Maximum number or participants on channel is set to 20
mode#politics m	Channel is moderated
mode#politics i	Participation on channel is by invitation only

Using IRC Commands

IRC commands send directions to the server to perform specific tasks, such as letting users join or leave a channel. You type commands in the command line on your screen, the same area where you type your messages when you participate in a session. Before you type a command, precede it with the slash symbol (/). This symbol tells the IRC server that the information that follows is an operation to be performed, rather than a message to appear on the channel. If you type a command without the preceding slash, the IRC server displays the command on all participants' screen as if it were a message.

A user who wants to join an existing IRC conversation first joins the channel, such as the #newbie channel, by issuing the command: /join #newbie. If you want to know what other users are participating on the channel you joined, such as the #newbie channel, the command: =who #newbie lists their names and e-mail addresses. You can obtain additional detail by adding an argument to certain commands. **Arguments** are words or numbers following a command that modify or expand its results. For example, if you add the argument min-20 to the command /list, the server returns only the headings of channels that have a minimum of 20 people currently connected. Without the argument, the /list command returns a listing of all channel headings on the server you are connected to, which can be extremely long, usually in the thousands! Figure 5-18 lists common IRC commands, with and without arguments, and their uses.

Figure 5-18 ◀
Common IRC commands

Commands	Result
/admin	Displays administrative details about the IRC server
/away	Lets others know you are still connected to the channel, but have left your computer
/date	Shows the current time and date
/help	Brings up a list of commands for which there is a Help file
/ignore	Ignores messages sent by another user
/invite nickname#channelname	Sends a message to the user asking him/her to join you on the channel specified by the #channelname. The channel name is optional
/join	Used to join, switch to, or create a channel
/leave#channelname	Exits you from a channel specified by #channelname
/msg nickname	Sends a private message to the specified user
/mode	Determines who can join a channel you've created
/mode#channelname +s	Creates a secret channel
/mode#channelname +p	Makes a channel private
/nick	Change your nickname
/query nickname	Sets up a private conversation between you and another IRC user, specified by his/her nickname
/quit	Exits IRC
/signoff	Exits IRC
/who	Shows the e-mail address of participants on a particular channel
/whois nickname	Lists specific information about an IRC user

Using Nicknames

Unique **nicknames**, or aliases, identify all IRC users on channels. The same nickname cannot be used by more than one user on the same IRC server. In addition, on most IRC servers, a nickname is limited to nine characters, although a few servers now allow longer names. By default, a user's nickname is generally his or her login name, although a user can change it after logging on to the IRC server. Some users prefer to keep their login names as their nicknames, while others prefer the anonymity of a nickname. Some users change their nickname to reflect their occupation, interests, or hobbies. To change your nickname after you join a channel, issue the command /nick alias, replacing the word "alias" with the nickname you would like to be identified as while using IRC.

Understanding Bots

A **bot**, short for robot, is an automated program that runs on IRC and lets some functions be performed without human intervention. Some bots maintain databases of messages, some log server traffic, and some provide more tangible services, such as metric-to-English conversions. A bot generally appears in one of two forms: either as a collection of commands loaded from a script (text) file into the IRC client or as an actual computer program.

Script bots are part of a group of /on IRC commands that specific incidents trigger, such as when a particular person joins a channel or when the number of participants on a channel reaches a set amount. For example, a script bot could let users know when a new person joins a channel, sending an automatic message welcoming the newcomer. The computer program bots, often written in the C or Perl programming languages, monitor and react in a specific manner to certain events, such as a banned user trying to access a specific channel or a /help command a user issues. For example, a program bot could take over channel operation when the channel operator is away. The bot may watch for malicious behavior on the channel and automatically kick a participant off the channel, banning him or her from further use.

Connecting to an IRC Server

After you use your client software to connect to an IRC server, you're prompted to log on. After you log on, you're automatically at the 0 channel, or the null channel. The **null channel** is the main entrance channel on an IRC server. It's the starting point to join other channels. The null channel also is a place to receive help immediately. Typing the /help command while you're in the null channel gives you a listing of all commands available on the server.

The null channel is also where the message of the day, called the motd, appears on your screen. The **motd** lists basic information about the server, including any recent notices or changes. Additional information can include the name of the IRC server you are connected to, the number of other users connected to the server, the number of channel operators, or any other significant announcements. The motd changes often, sometimes daily or weekly, depending on the specific server. It is the user's responsibility to read the current motd information. Individual channels sometimes have motd listings as well. Channel motds often include information about the channel topic or channel netiquette.

You want to evaluate two methods of accessing IRC and then recommend to Jack which will work best for his campaign needs. The first method is participating in a text-based IRC session. You now connect and log on to a DALnet IRC server using a text-based client.

To connect to an IRC server:

    1. Start Netscape. The New Perspectives on the Internet Using Netscape Navigator Software — Introductory Student Online Companion Web page appears in your window.

2. Click the **Tutorial 5** link, then click the **Session 5-2** link on the Web page. See Figure 5-19.

Figure 5-19 ◄
Tutorial 5 Web
page

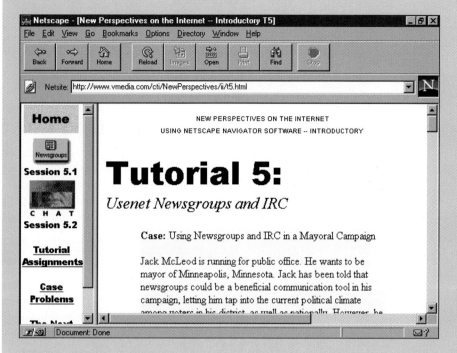

3. Click the **DALnet IRC server** link to connect to the DALnet IRC network. Netscape launches the Telnet client and connects you to the network.

   TROUBLE? If your copy of Netscape is not configured for Telnet, ask your instructor or technical support person for assistance.

4. Type **dalnet** after the login prompt.

   TROUBLE? If the server does not accept the login, repeat Step 4, making sure that you type dalnet using all lowercase letters with no punctuation or spaces.

5. Type your first, middle, and last initials at the prompt: "What would you like your nickname on DALnet to be?" Press the **Enter** key to log on to the DALnet IRC server. You are now at the null channel and receive a welcoming message and a motd like the one shown in Figure 5-20.

Figure 5-20 ◄
DALnet IRC
server

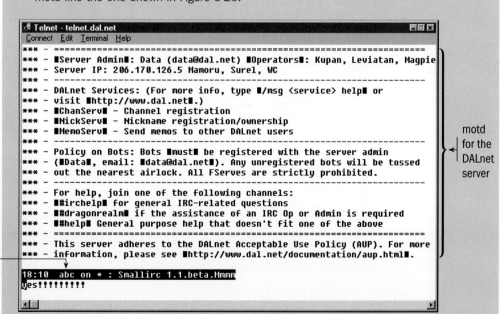

motd
for the
DALnet
server

user with initials abc
is logged on to server

TROUBLE? If your connection request does not go through, the DALnet server may be busy. Try Steps 3 through 5 again.

TROUBLE? If you receive a prompt requesting that you use a different nickname, another user is already using the same nickname. Type /nick xyz where "xyz" is the nickname you want to use, then press the Enter key.

You are now connected and logged on to the DALnet network.

Participating in a Text-Based IRC Session

When you log on to a text-based IRC server, you see information strictly as characters and numbers. You cannot view graphics or other multimedia items without first downloading them to your computer. Even without these items, you quickly become involved with conversations flowing on your screen. Text-based clients are generally fast since you don't need to wait for graphics or other multimedia items to load onto your screen.

Joining a Channel

Although observing the format of a text-based session is important, unlike Jack, you have no experience participating in an IRC session. You decide to join one of the more popular introductory channels so that you may view how a session unfolds without feeling intimidated. You join the #newbie channel.

To join a channel:

1. Type **/join #newbie** in the command line, then press **Enter** to join the newbie channel. See Figure 5-21. If other participants are on the channel, you will probably see an ongoing conversation immediately. Your screen differs from Figure 5-21, depending on the session's participants and topic.

Figure 5-21 ◀
Joining a channel

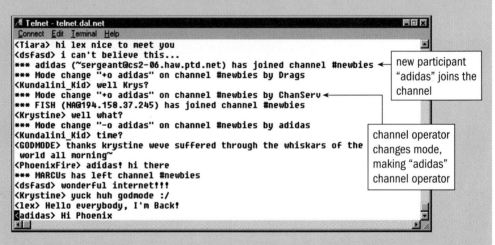

TROUBLE? If you do not see conversation flowing, no other participants may be on the channel, or you may have typed the join command incorrectly. Repeat Step 1.

As you observe messages sent from other channel participants, you'd like to know the identities of all users on the channel.

2. Type **/names #newbies** in the command line, and then press the Enter key. See Figure 5-22. A list of current channel users appears.

Figure 5-22 ◀
Viewing
channel
participation

channel participants'
nicknames are listed

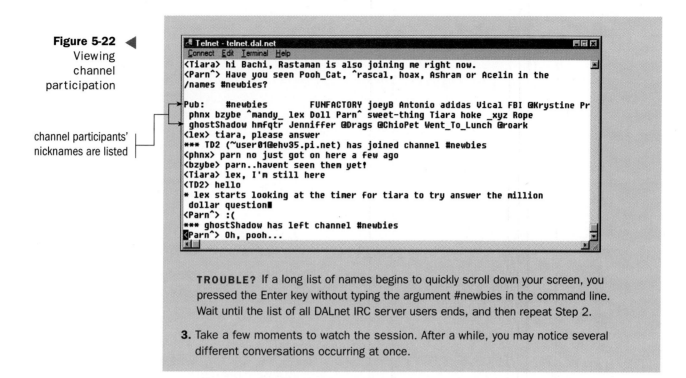

```
Telnet - telnet.dal.net
Connect  Edit  Terminal  Help
<Tiara> hi Bachi, Rastaman is also joining me right now.
<Parn^> Have you seen Pooh_Cat, ^rascal, hoax, Ashram or Acelin in the
/names #newbies?

Pub:    #newbies        FUNFACTORY joeyB Antonio adidas Vical FBI @Krystine Pr
 phnx bzybe ^mandy_ lex Doll Parn^ sweet-thing Tiara hoke _xyz Rope
 ghostShadow hmfqtr Jenniffer @Drags @ChioPet Went_To_Lunch @roark
<lex> tiara, please answer
*** TD2 (~user01@ehv35.pi.net) has joined channel #newbies
<phnx> parn no just got on here a few ago
<bzybe> parn..havent seen them yet!
<Tiara> lex, I'm still here
<TD2> hello
* lex starts looking at the timer for tiara to try answer the million
  dollar question█
<Parn^> :(
*** ghostShadow has left channel #newbies
<Parn^> Oh, pooh...
```

> **TROUBLE?** If a long list of names begins to quickly scroll down your screen, you
> pressed the Enter key without typing the argument #newbies in the command line.
> Wait until the list of all DALnet IRC server users ends, and then repeat Step 2.

3. Take a few moments to watch the session. After a while, you may notice several
different conversations occurring at once.

Now that you have a general feel for the #newbie channel, you join the conversation
by sending a message.

Sending a Message

Because IRC is a very spontaneous way to communicate, participants are encouraged to
think about what they are going to say before sending a message. **Lurking** is when a user
enters a chat room and does not immediately participate in the discussion but just
observes. Lurking helps a user get an impression of the discussion and decide whether to
participate. Before joining a discussion, make sure your comment or thought fits the topic
of the discussion and matches the netiquette currently being used. Just as you may
encounter a flame in newsgroup postings, you may experience harsh words or bad netiquette on IRC channels. Sending disturbing or malicious messages during a session is for-
bidden and considered harassment. Users who send this type of message are promptly
kicked off a channel. Some servers ban an entire organization if a single member of that
organization acts maliciously on a channel. If you encounter an individual who sends
unpleasant messages, you can block receipt of this user's messages by issuing the /ignore
nickname command, where "nickname" is the individual's nickname.

You do not need to wait for a break in conversation to send a message. You enter no
special codes, characters, or commands to send a message; you simply type the message
in the message line and then press the Enter key. Also, it is unnecessary to greet everyone
on a channel personally. Usually one greeting message addressed to the entire channel suf-
fices. If 20 participants on a channel said "hello" and "goodbye" to everyone coming or
going, greetings would clog the channel.

You now participate in the #newbie session by sending a message to the channel.
Rather than responding to another participant's message or expressing an opinion, you
simply send a general greeting to the channel and see what happens.

To send a message:

1. Type **hello** in the command line, and press **Enter**. You may receive a welcome
greeting from other participants on the channel who read your message.

> **TROUBLE?** If at any point you feel another user is harassing you, use the /ignore nickname command to suppress messages from that user or send a message to the channel operator for assistance.
>
> **2.** If you want, you can continue to send messages and participate in the session. Simply type your message in the message line, and then press Enter.

The #newbie channel has good participation. By viewing and participating in a session, you see how easy using IRC is. You want to check out one more channel before you exit the server.

Switching Channels

When you finish participating on a particular channel, you can either switch to another, commonly called **channel surfing**, or you can exit IRC. Connecting to another channel is easily accomplished by issuing the /join command followed by the name of the new channel.

Now that you have some experience on a general IRC channel, you want to switch to a more politically oriented one. You decide to switch to the #politics channel.

To switch channels:

> **1.** Type **/join #politics** in the command line, and then press the **Enter** key.
>
> **TROUBLE?** If you do not see conversation flowing on the channel, you may be the only participant. You can wait to see if any other users join the channel, or you can ask a classmate to join you on the channel.
>
> **2.** If you want, you can continue to send messages and participate in this session. Simply type your message in the message line, and then press the **Enter** key.

Leaving a Channel and Logging off from IRC

When you finish participating on a channel you can exit, or leave the channel. Keep in mind that you can leave a channel at any time by typing the command /quit. You can issue the /quit command either while you are connected to a channel or while you are at the null channel. When you leave a channel, other participants receive a message on their screen noting that you left. When you finish using the IRC service, you must log off the IRC server. You do not need to save files or documents before you log off an IRC session.

Now that you've spent some time observing and experiencing a text-based IRC session, you are ready to move on to your next evaluation. You leave the #politics channel.

To leave a channel and log off an IRC server:

> **1.** Type **/leave #politics** in the command line, and then press the **Enter** key. See Figure 5-23. You exit from the #politics channel and return to the null channel.

Figure 5-23 ◀
Leaving a
channel

indicates you have
left the channel

At this point you can join another channel. Because you don't want to join any other channels and completed testing the text-based chat session, you log off the IRC server.

2. Type **/quit** in the command line, and then press the **Enter** key. You are logged off the IRC server and returned to the Netscape program.

The next time you connect to a server, you automatically see the motd and are again in the null channel.

TROUBLE? If you cannot automatically exit from the Telnet client, close the program by clicking File and then clicking Exit to return to the Netscape program. If you still are unable to exit, check with your instructor or technical support person for assistance.

Now knowing how easy participating in a text-based IRC session is, you are eager to evaluate a Web-based chatting session.

Chatting through the WWW (WebChat)

Unlike text-based IRC, some chatting services are available through the WWW using a GUI. **WebChat** is a popular multimedia chatting program that includes the capability to incorporate images, video and audio clips, and hyperlinks in a chat session. While WebChat does not use the IRC protocol, a Web-based chatting session works similarly to a text-based IRC session except that multimedia aspects are also incorporated. For example, on a Web-based server you can type messages in the message text box, send a multimedia item, or communicate using both methods. A participant's nickname will appear as a hyperlink to that user's e-mail address instead of appearing on the screen enclosed in brackets. Businesses currently use Web-based IRC sessions to conduct virtual conferences and remote communications. For example, a realtor can attach a graphical image of a piece of property while participating in a Web-based session with a client. Figure 5-24 shows a sample of a WebChat session that includes messages, multimedia items, and links to the participants' e-mail addresses.

Figure 5-24
WebChat
session

link to participant's
e-mail address

multimedia item sent
with participant's
message

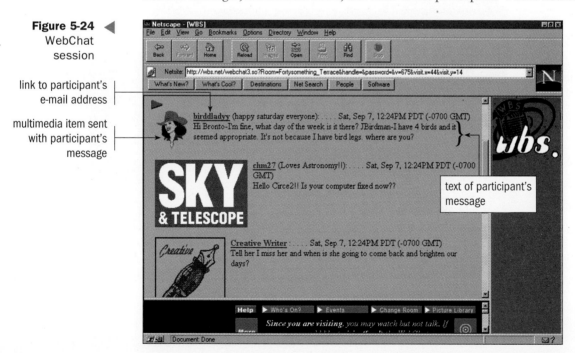

Besides being graphically oriented and having the capability to display multimedia items with messages, the major difference between text-based IRC and Web-based chatting sessions is that Web-based chatting sessions are **asynchronous**. While text-based IRC sessions are synchronous—almost instantaneously displaying the messages that users send—the Web-based counterparts must be refreshed continually. Remember that when a Web page is loaded, the browser connects to a server, retrieves the Web page information, posts it on your screen, and then terminates the connection. With WebChat you need to continually update the screen in order to show new messages by clicking the more messages button. Netscape then connects to the WebChat server, retrieves the new information, and posts it to your screen.

To evaluate the appropriateness of a Web-based chat session, you connect to a WebChat site and observe a current session.

Connecting to a WebChat Site

Connecting to a WebChat site is like connecting to a text-based IRC server, except that access and participation methods are graphically oriented, not textually oriented. As in text-based IRC sessions, after you connect to a Web-based chatting site you can join a channel, assign yourself a nickname, and send messages to other channel participants. After you connect to a chatting server through the WWW, you use Netscape to navigate the WebChat site.

Figure 5-25 shows an example of a typical online form used to send a message during a Web-based chat session. The message input form lets you add a graphic or other multimedia item to your message, send a private message to another participant, or attach a Web page URL to the message. A user completes the form and then simply clicks the Send button to transfer the message to the chat room for other participants to see.

Figure 5-25
Sending a message in WebChat

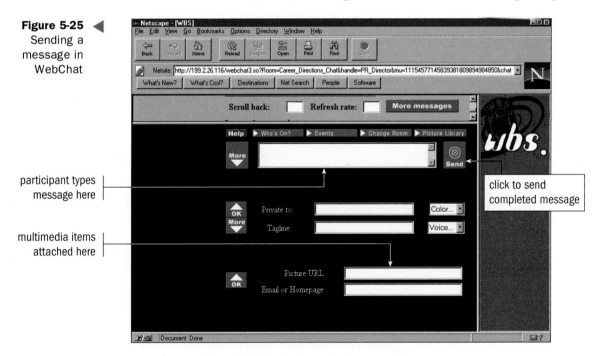

While surfing the Web looking for Web-based chatting sites, you come across the WebChat Broadcasting System (WBS) Web site. Because the WBS chatting service requires you to register to participate in chat sessions, you view a session as a visitor, not as an active participant. This gives you a good idea about how Web-based sessions function. If you decide that the Web-based session is useful for Jack's campaign needs, you can register later.

To connect to a WebChat site:

1. Make sure the Tutorial 5 Web page for the New Perspectives on the Internet Using Netscape Navigator Software — Introductory Student Online Companion Web page appears in your window. Click the **Session 5-2** link, and then click the **Webchat Broadcasting System** link. This brings you to the WBS Web page, where you can access the Career_Directions_Chat chat room. Your screen may differ from Figure 5-26 because Web pages are continually modified.

Figure 5-26
WBS chatting
Web site

chat categories

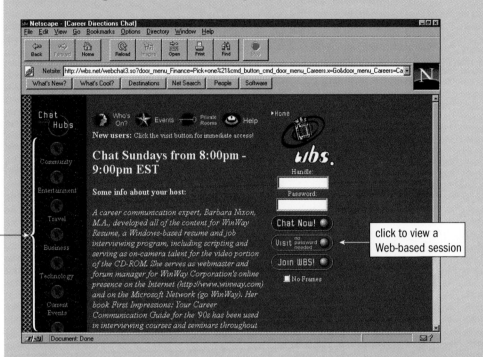

TROUBLE? If the chat room no longer exists, enter the URL http://wbs.net in the Location text box, press the Enter key, and select another category and chat room.

2. Click the **Visit** button to enter the Career_Directions_Chat chat room. The Web page loads. You may immediately see conversation flowing in the session.

TROUBLE? If the Visit button is not visible on your screen, click the Business link, then click the list arrow in the Careers and Business category. Select Career_Directions_Chat and click the Go button to enter this chat room, and then repeat Step 2.

3. Scroll down the page and then click the **More messages** button. See Figure 5-27. If any new messages have been sent to the chat room, they appear on your screen.

Figure 5-27 ◄
Retrieving
messages

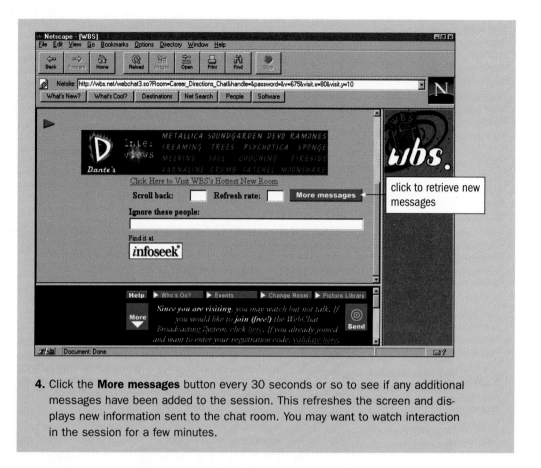

click to retrieve new
messages

4. Click the **More messages** button every 30 seconds or so to see if any additional messages have been added to the session. This refreshes the screen and displays new information sent to the chat room. You may want to watch interaction in the session for a few minutes.

Printing a WebChat Message

You may wish to keep a record of valuable conversations that occur in Web-based chat sessions. For example, if you chat with someone about a specific marketing strategy that you would like to try, saving the conversation is beneficial: you can read and reference it later. One way to save the conversation is to print the messages before you refresh your screen. When you find a section of a chat session you want to print, you simply click the Print button on the toolbar. The Print dialog box opens, and you can set specific print options, such as printing multiple copies. You now print a portion of the Web-based chat session you observed to give to Jack.

To print the text of a WebChat session:

1. With the session still showing on your screen, click the **Print** button 🖨 on the toolbar. The Print dialog box opens.

2. Click the **OK** button to print the article. A Printing Status box may appear on your screen to update you on your print job's progress. The text of the session is printed.

Now that you have finished evaluating a Web-based chatting session, you leave the WebChat site and exit Netscape.

3. Click **File** on the menu bar, then click **Exit** to close Netscape.

On the Career_Directions_Chat channel, you have found that many people take advantage of the real-time communications that Web chatting sessions offer. Your recommendation to Jack notes that although the text-based IRC session is quicker than the Web-based session, you feel that the capability to attach multimedia items to messages may be a great campaign tool. You suggest possible multimedia items to attach—sound clips of a campaign speech or a picture of the candidate may work well.

Using MUDs and MOOs

Another popular use of chat sessions is through **MUD**, which is short for **Multiple User Dimension**. MUD is a synchronous, computer-generated environment for user communication. The process of using MUDs to communicate is called **MUDing**. MUDs are sometimes described as text-based virtual realities because the computer provides all detailed text narrative descriptions of the environment. Roy Trubshaw and Richard Bartle created MUDs when they were students at Essex University in England in 1979-1980, so that users playing the game Dungeons and Dragons® could role play in real-time with other players.

Users log on to a MUD much as they log on to an IRC session. Users can use their own names or assume the identity of a fictitious computerized character, known as an **avator**. A welcoming message and a narrative description of the MUD environment follow. When users enter a MUD environment or virtual room, they see exits that they can move through to enter another room by reading the text description and replying appropriately. The description is based on a directional scheme (east, west, north, south) that helps orient users in the virtual space. After users read the written narrative, they then decide how to proceed through the text-based environment. For instance, the text may suggest that users enter the "law library" directly to the east to learn more about corporate law, or that they enter the "courtroom," due south, to observe a legal proceeding in action. Users respond to the MUD by typing instructions, such as "proceed east and enter law library," or by sending messages to other participants in the session.

A **MOO** environment, which stands for **Multi-user Object Oriented,** is like a MUD except that it lets the participants create and manipulate objects in the virtual environment. MOOs sometimes include graphics and, when specifically interfacing on the WWW, are called **WOOs**, which stands for **Web Object Oriented**. MUDs, MOOs, and WOOs all let many users participate in the same "virtual environment," interacting with one another. Although MUDs and MOOs let the participant type directions, the WOO environment also includes hyperlinking capability. For example, if you participate in the previous scenario and have the same two choices, you may click either the graphic of a library or a courtroom. If you click the library link, you see a detailed narrative describing the room, as well as a graphic of the library complete with a librarian, who actually may be another participant in the environment. Figure 5-28 shows an example of a WOO.

Figure 5-28 ◀
A WOO environment

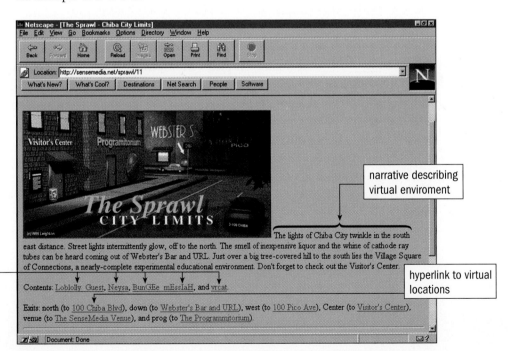

narrative describing virtual enviroment

participants' nicknames

hyperlink to virtual locations

Most MUD and MOO commands differ from IRC commands, but many of their basic functions are identical. Most MUDs, MOOs, and WOOs also have an extensive help menu system. In addition to common IRC commands such as join and quit, commands like whisper let you speak to only a specific user, rather than everyone in the room, while the command page lets you talk to someone who is in another virtual room. Commands may vary from one MUD, MOO, or WOO to another.

Originally created for entertainment, both MUDs and MOOs have quickly been adopted for educational and business uses. Educational institutions use them as interactive virtual classrooms; the most common business use is training. For example, businesses and schools alike access the MOO called schMOOze University. Established in 1994, schMOOze University is a place where people studying English as a second or foreign language can practice using the language and share ideas and experiences. Students have one-on-one or group conversations, as well as access to language games and an online dictionary. Some organizations use MUDs and MOOs to create virtual environments where customers can browse an entire community or store. Others use them for specific applications, such as training grounds for hazardous or dangerous environments. MUD and MOO simulations let users see outcomes without making potentially dangerous mistakes in a real life situation. For example, a scientist may use a MUD to see the outcomes of experiments involving certain chemical combinations without experiencing potentially hazardous results.

Based on your recommendations, Jack now routinely depends on newsgroups to keep a pulse on voters' reactions to events that affect their locality as well as the world in general. In addition, Jack routinely participates on a local text-based IRC channel throughout his campaign.

Quick Check

1. _____ are virtual chat rooms on the IRC service where people gather to have group topic discussions.

2. In IRC, the _____ are programs that connect a user to a server. A _____ is a program that transports messages from one user to another.

3. True or False: You can set up your own chat room.

4. _____ are additional pieces of information added to a command to modify or expand its results.

5. When first entering an IRC server, you see general information about the server. This announcement is called the _____.

6. Observing an IRC conversation before joining is called _____.

7. When participating in a Web-based chat session, you must _____ your screen to display new messages.

Tutorial Assignments

Jack won the election and the city of Minneapolis has grown tremendously since he took office. Newsgroups have proven to be a successful way for Jack to communicate with citizens and employees alike. Jack wants to post a job opening in the biz newsgroups category. He asks you to search for an appropriate newsgroup for the posting. The position opening is for Director of the Water Works Department. You use Netscape's newsreader to search for a newsgroup.

If necessary, start Netscape. The New Perspectives on the Internet Using Netscape Navigator Software — Introductory Student Online Companion Web page displays in your window. Do the following:

1. Launch Netscape News.
2. Show all newsgroups.
3. List the biz.* newsgroups.

4. Locate a biz newsgroup that would be appropriate for posting a job opening. Are there more than one?
5. Subscribe to the newsgroup(s).
6. Read and print two sample articles that have been posted to the newsgroup(s).
7. Unsubscribe from the newsgroup(s).
8. Exit the newsreader.
9. Exit Netscape.

Jack is also interested in knowing if any other cities use IRC channels to communicate with citizens. He asks you to log onto the DALnet IRC network for the following cities: Los_Angeles, LA; Chicago; Austin; New_York, NY; and London to see if any of these channels exist.

If necessary, start Netscape. The New Perspectives on the Internet Using Netscape Navigator Software — Introductory Student Online Companion Web page displays in your window. Do the following:

1. Click the Tutorial 5 link.
2. Click the Tutorial Assignments link.
3. Locate the Telnet to DALnet link in the Tutorial Assignments section.
4. Click the DALnet link to connect to the DALnet IRC server.
5. Enter dalnet as your login name.
6. Enter your initials for your nickname.
7. Join the #Los_Angeles channel.
8. Write the number of participants on the channel, if any. *Hint*: You enter the /names #channelname command to determine channel participation.

9. Leave the #Los_Angeles channel.
10. Repeat Steps 8 and 9 for the channels #LA; #Chicago; #Austin; #New_York; #NY; and #London.
11. Exit the DALnet server.
12. Exit Netscape.

Case Problems

1. StarChat Nicole Katt is the technology director of a company called StarChat that contracts with show biz celebrities and popular athletes to appear on IRC channels. StarChat uses a different celebrity each week. On Friday nights, the celebrity logs on to the IRC server from whatever location is convenient and chats with fans from all over the world for approximately two hours. Because attendance for StarChat's IRC sessions have risen 50% in the last six months, one of Nicole's responsibilities is to contract with at least two new celebrities a month. Nicole does not think her present IRC server is the most productive one for her job: response time is slow and users often experience problems logging on to the server. She asks you to evaluate the WebChat server and to determine how many users are on the network and how many channels have an entertainment topic.

If necessary, start Netscape. The New Perspectives on the Internet Using Netscape Navigator Software — Introductory Student Online Companion Web page displays in your window. Do the following:

1. Click the Tutorial 5 link.
2. Click the Case Problems link.
3. Click the WebChat link in the Case Problem 1 section.

4. How many users are currently online on the server?

5. Navigate through the Web site to determine how many chat rooms have an entertainment topic. Write the name of each chat room.

6. Join one entertainment chat room as a visitor and view a conversation. Is there much traffic in the chat room? Is the server response fast or slow? What is the chat room's general atmosphere?
7. Print a section of an entertainment topic chat session that you think represents the service.
8. Write a two-paragraph summary evaluating WebChat's features. Include the pros and cons to using this service.
9. E-mail your summary report to your instructor, and send yourself a copy.
10. Exit Netscape.

2. Far North Journey Ben Johnston is a computer programmer at Ironwood, Inc., a company that creates computer action adventure games. Ironwood has always distributed its games on CD-ROMs but has recently begun researching ways to distribute them over the Internet. Ben is creating a new interactive adventure game called Far North Journey that features the player as a contestant in the Iditarod dog sled race. Each player faces many different choices along the race course. Ben has heard of MUDs and MOOs and is considering writing the program for the WOO technology to distribute on the Internet using the WWW. He wants you to evaluate a portion of a WOO on the Internet called The Sprawl. The Sprawl uses two Internet technologies, Telnet and the WWW. Rather than participate in the Telnet portion of the game, you explore the online WOO environment using your Web browser. After you explore the virtual environment, you write a summary report for Ben.

If necessary, launch Netscape. The New Perspectives on the Internet Using Netscape Navigator Software — Introductory Student Online Companion Web page displays in your window. Do the following:

1. Click the Tutorial 5 link.
2. Click the Case Problems link.
3. Click The Sprawl link in the Case Problem 2 section.
4. Navigate the WOO, taking notes on the virtual places you visit and the objects you encounter. Is the narrative descriptive? Does the graphical environment lend itself to an interactive game?
5. Determine how many players are participating in the game. Find the link that lists information about the game's participants, and print the Web page(s).

6. Determine the name of the city featured in The Sprawl. Describe three objects and three rooms or locations you find while exploring The Sprawl.
7. Name and describe three objects and three locations you would use if you were writing the text for a WOO for the Far North Journey game.
8. Write a two-paragraph summary report for Ben describing your overall reaction to the WWW portion of the WOO. Include impressions such as whether you found navigating easy, and your likes and dislikes.
9. E-mail your summary report to your instructor and send a copy to yourself.
10. Exit Netscape.

3. Sterling Skiware Dave Sterling is the owner of a chain of retail stores called Sterling Skiware, which carries ski and snowboard equipment and accessories. Recently, Dave learned the basics of accessing Usenet. He tries to take at least a half hour each day to access various outdoor recreation topic newsgroups. The postings help keep him abreast of the public's interests in ski and snowboard equipment and new trends. Dave also subscribes to a few business-related newsgroups. Because Dave is still fairly new to the Internet, as well as to the Usenet technology, he has some general and specific questions about its capabilities. Research Dave's questions and send an e-mail message with your findings.

If necessary, start Netscape and then do the following:
1. Launch Netscape News.
2. Show all newsgroups.
3. Locate postings in the news.newusers.questions newsgroup that would be appropriate for locating general Usenet information.

4. Explore the postings to help research the following questions for Dave.
   (a) Can I post a newsgroup article to sell a product? If so, what is the name of the newsgroup?
   (b) What does the "rc" at the end of the newsrc file mean?
   (c) Can I post to more than one newsgroup at a time? If so, how?
   (d) Does any newsgroup deal specifically with skiing or snowboarding? If so, what is the name of the newsgroup?
5. Write a two-paragraph summary report with the answers to Dave's questions.
6. E-mail your summary report to your instructor and send yourself a copy.
7. Exit Netscape.

4. Earth Essentials Cheri McNealy is sole owner of a jewelry design company called Earth Essentials. She lives in a remote area of New Mexico and works with Mankayto Productions (MP), a company in Los Angeles that produces the jewelry she designs. Often MP needs to modify Cheri's designs in order to accommodate manufacturing specifications. This requires Cheri and MP to exchange overnight mail packages sometimes daily over the course of several days to agree on necessary changes. Cheri wants to eliminate this mailing process to save both time and money. Because she uses the Internet for personal communication with friends and family, she is open to using online technology as a solution to this challenge. She recalls a discussion between her husband and a friend in the high tech field about electronic whiteboards. Over dinner that night, her husband tells her what he knows: the electronic whiteboard in Netscape's CoolTalk feature functions like a virtual location where two participants can change the same document, or graphic, while online at the same time. Cheri wants you to research the CoolTalk electronic whiteboard and report to her on its potential for replacing costly and time-consuming mailings.

If necessary, start Netscape and then do the following:
1. From Windows Explorer, click Start, then click Programs.
2. Click the Netscape Navigator 3 icon, then click the CoolTalk program icon. *Hint*: If you don't see the CoolTalk program icon, it may not be part of your Netscape installation. You cannot complete this case problem without CoolTalk. Ask your instructor or technical support person for assistance.

3. Click Help in the CoolTalk menu bar, then Help Topics to learn more about the White Board program's features and functions. When done, close the Help window.
4. Click the White Board icon to launch the White Board program.
5. Explore various tools on the White Board screen, and then close the White Board program.
6. Click the Conference button and then click Address Book.
7. Type the address of one of your classmates to conduct a live electronic White Board experiment. Your classmate must also be online and have the CoolTalk program running. If you are not sure what address to type, ask your instructor. If you have no classmate to work with, you may find a participant at the URL http://live.netscape.com.
8. After you contact another user, launch the White Board program. Use the White Board's features to collaborate on a graphic with the other participant. Write down the answers to these questions: Is the program hard to use? What program features do you like? Could you immediately see the other participant's changes, additions, and deletions?
9. After experimenting with the electronic White Board, write a two-paragraph summary report, including the answers to the above questions. Include your recommendation about whether this capability would work well for Cheri's needs.
10. E-mail your summary to your instructor and send yourself a copy.
11. Exit the White Board program, and then exit the CoolTalk program.
12. Exit Netscape.

Telnet, Gopher, and FTP Services

Providing Research and Assistance at Clark University

Clark University

CASE

Grace Andrews is professor and chairperson of the Physics and Astronomy department at Clark University. The department works with the Dominion Astrophysical Observatory and the Pacific Geoscience Center to provide real-life exposure to the sciences within the classroom. You are currently working on your Ph.D. degree under Grace's tutelage. As a part of your graduate program, you need to complete 50 hours of research in either a university or business environment related to your doctoral program. Grace selects you to work as her research assistant and aide for the semester.

In addition to gathering research materials to help Grace prepare lectures, you will assist her in three other areas. You will be responsible for overseeing the university's astronomy club, which the department sponsors. The club meets twice a month to share information and conduct experiments. You will also help Grace update the computer lab handbook she distributes to students at the beginning of the semester. Finally, Grace wants you to locate appropriate software on the Internet to use in the physics computer lab, as well as make sure that the lab is ready for the upcoming semester. Throughout the semester, you use the Telnet, Gopher, and FTP Internet services to locate information and resources for Grace, as well as assist you with the astronomy club, class handbook, and computer lab projects.

In this session you will learn what Telnet is and how it works. You will connect to a Telnet host, connect to and browse a Telnet site, and disconnect from a Telnet session. You will also search for Telnet sites using the Hytelnet program.

What Is Telnet?

Telnet, short for telephone network, is an Internet service that lets you access a remote host computer on the Internet. The remote host can be across the hall or across the globe. Telnet is one of the Internet's most powerful services; it lets you utilize the processing strength of more complex and usually more expensive hardware and software without the associated costs. Telnet, part of the TCP/IP protocol suite, is known as the remote login protocol.

Utilizing the Telnet service is like borrowing a computer and its programs. Common Telnet uses include accessing large databases of information, searching library card catalogs, and running programs on large computers. For example, you can use Telnet to access a remote host and run software that is not capable of running on your computer's operating system. Telnet is also useful if you want to use software that is too complex to run on your computer, or if copyright restrictions prevent you from downloading the software to your own computer. Telnet lets remote users participate in day-to-day business tasks that the host makes available, such as online transaction processing. An example of this is a university's registration process. Clerks in the registrar's office can access the school's host computer and register students for classes through a LAN, while clerks in small outlying towns can register students remotely using the Telnet service to access the same host computer.

How a Telnet Session Works

Telnet operates using two compatible software programs located at different sites. The first software program, called the **client**, initiates the communication to the remote computer by sending a request to establish communication through the login process. After you log on to the remote host, your computer essentially becomes part of the host's network, and your session begins. The time you spend accessing the remote host's services is called a **Telnet session**. A user who needs to locate information may complete a Telnet session in a few minutes, while a user who wants to accomplish specific processing tasks may spend several hours connected to the host. For most of this tutorial you will use the Windows 95 Telnet client program.

The second software program, called the server, runs on the host computer. The **server** program accepts or rejects the client's request for service based on the user's login information. If the user's account name and password are valid, the server accepts the request and the user can access programs available on the host based on access rights associated with the user's account. For example, university registration clerks may have access to programs that let them register students for classes but have no access to the employee payroll program that also resides on the host. The server also helps negotiate how information is sent between computers. Tasks included in this process range from the server recognizing how much data your computer screen can display to determining exactly how information is processed as it travels between systems. If the remote host is not running the server software, the host is unavailable. Figure 6-1 illustrates how a typical Telnet session works.

Figure 6-1 ◀
How Telnet
works

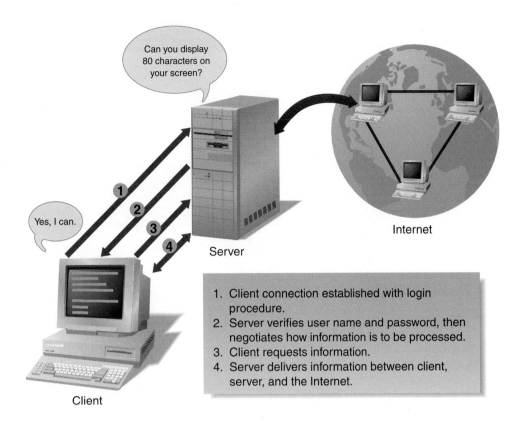

1. Client connection established with login procedure.
2. Server verifies user name and password, then negotiates how information is to be processed.
3. Client requests information.
4. Server delivers information between client, server, and the Internet.

Although you use your own computer when you connect to a host, you feel you are directly connected to the host, because your computer display and keyboard respond to commands accessed through the host system. The illusion of direct connection to the remote host is called **terminal emulation**. Terminals are computers that generally have no central processing power. Instead, they are restricted to interacting with a multi-user computer. During terminal emulation, you do not use your own computer's central processing power but rather that of the remote host. Some hosts prompt you for a terminal type to use for emulation when you Telnet to them. The terminal type tells the remote host how to interpret your keystrokes and what characteristics and capabilities your client offers, for example, the capability to display special text formatting attributes like boldface and underlined when displaying text on your computer's screen.

To access a remote system, you must have an access privilege account on the remote host or use a host that has public or guest accounts. Public and guest accounts let any user gain access to at least part of its information and files. In contrast, Telnet privilege accounts are generally given only to users who have a specific need to access portions of a host system not available to the public. For example, only faculty, students, and staff members can access the Washington University Services Telnet service, located at library.wsustl.edu, due to licensing restrictions on the information stored on its host .

When you Telnet to a remote host, you must know the name and location of the remote host system that you want to access. Addresses are usually organized as hostname.-domainname. For example, a common Telnet host that Grace uses in class is the Weather Underground report service offered by the Department of Atmospheric, Oceanic, and Space Sciences at the University of Michigan. This service offers up-to-date weather reports for locations around the world. The Telnet address for the Weather Underground is um-weather.sprl.umich.edu; um-weather is the name of the host system. Figure 6-2 lists other popular Telnet sites. You can find Telnet addresses using traditional Internet searching methods and through publications such as trade journals. You can also access Telnet hosts by their IP addresses, which reflect the names of Internet hosts. For example, the IP address for um-weather is 141.213.23.244.

Figure 6-2
Popular Telnet
sites

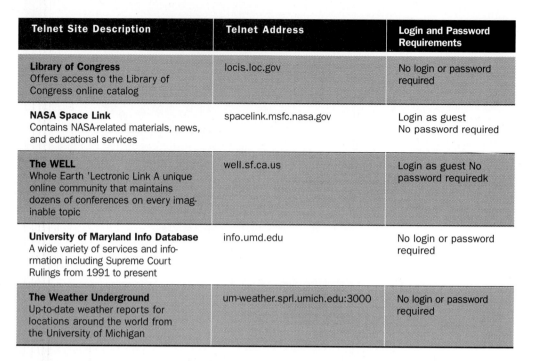

Telnet Site Description	Telnet Address	Login and Password Requirements
Library of Congress Offers access to the Library of Congress online catalog	locis.loc.gov	No login or password required
NASA Space Link Contains NASA-related materials, news, and educational services	spacelink.msfc.nasa.gov	Login as guest No password required
The WELL Whole Earth 'Lectronic Link A unique online community that maintains dozens of conferences on every imaginable topic	well.sf.ca.us	Login as guest No password requiredk
University of Maryland Info Database A wide variety of services and information including Supreme Court Rulings from 1991 to present	info.umd.edu	No login or password required
The Weather Underground Up-to-date weather reports for locations around the world from the University of Michigan	um-weather.sprl.umich.edu:3000	No login or password required

Some Telnet hosts that you log on to offer several types of services. One way users indicate to the remote host which service they want to access is by using a port number appended to the host address. A **port number** designates a specific service on a remote host. The standard port on hosts for the Telnet service is 23. Unless you specify a different port, this port number is assumed by the remote host and is the starting place to access other services available on the host. Figure 6-3 shows some common port numbers found on a host, as well as the services available at each port. To access a particular service on a host that offers more than one service, you can include the service's port number in your Telnet login command. For example, to specify the weather report service at The Weather Underground Telnet site, you add the port number 3000 to the end of the address: um-weather.sprl.umich.edu 3000. The port number 3000 tells the host to specifically initiate the weather report service. All Internet hosts use this standard numbering scheme, so if another Telnet host offers a weather service, you can also access it by adding 3000 to the host's address.

Figure 6-3
Telnet ports

Port Number	Service Description
119	NNTP
161	SMTP
37	Time
21	FTP

You can also access Telnet sites by using specific URLs. To access a Telnet site using a URL, you specify the Telnet protocol, the Telnet host's name, and, if you want to access a specific service, the port number. As mentioned previously, if no port number is specified, Telnet automatically defaults to port 23 on the host. You can enter URLs for the host and service in the Location text box or in the Open Location dialog box, such as the URL address telnet://um-weather.sprl.umich.edu:3000. Notice that the Telnet service is listed after the host name and is separated by a colon. After you press the Enter key, Netscape launches the Telnet client configured in its General Preferences menu. Hyperlinks on Web pages that link to a Telnet host are common. Whether you type the Telnet host information in the Open Location text box or access the service using a hyperlink, the Telnet client starts the Telnet session and attempts to connect to the remote host.

Sometimes you may encounter difficulties when trying to connect to a Telnet host. For example, a host may only grant a certain number of users access to a specific service at one time. Thus, if you try to access a service and the allotted number of participants are using it, you may receive an error message or message that the service is not available at this time. Figure 6-4 lists some common error messages you may receive when connecting to a Telnet site.

Figure 6-4 ◀
Common
problems when
connecting to
a Telnet site

Error Message	Problem	Solution
Unknown host	Typed host name incorrectly	Re-type information
Unknown host	Domain name has changed or no longer exists	Try accessing through another method such as the WWW
Foreign host not responding	Site is busy	Try connecting at a later time, preferably during non-peak hours
Maximum number of users exceeded	Allotted number of users are already accessing the site	Try connecting at a later time, preferably during non-peak hours

After you successfully Telnet to a host, an interface used to navigate the host opens in your window. This interface usually appears in one of two formats: a text-based menu or a command prompt. The text-based interface leads you through the Telnet host site using menu items you select by typing a letter or number. Figure 6-5 shows an example of the text-based interface menu that appears on the opening screen of the Weather Underground Telnet site.

Figure 6-5 ◀
Text-based
menu interface

Telnet site name ─┐

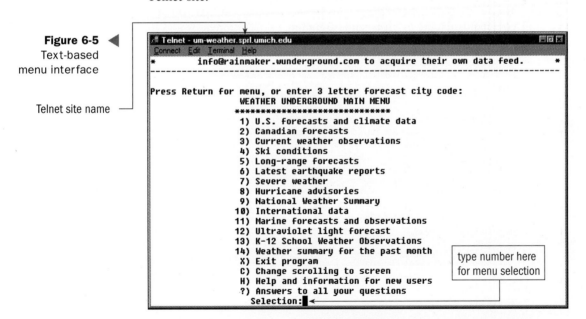

In a command-prompt interface, users navigate a Telnet site by typing specific Telnet commands. These commands instruct the remote host to perform certain tasks, such as listing the names of the files on the host or accessing an available service. For example, typing the ls command after the command prompt lists the file and folder names in the current directory, while the Pine command launches a text-based e-mail program of the same name. Figure 6-6 shows a sample opening screen for a Telnet session using a command-prompt interface.

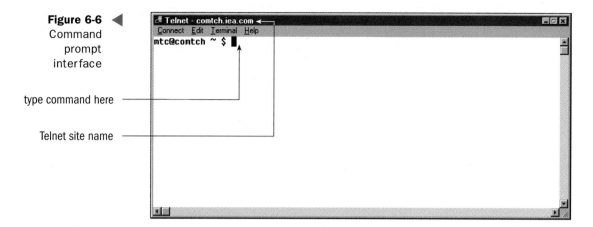

Figure 6-6
Command
prompt
interface

type command here ———

Telnet site name ———

Regardless of which interface type you use to navigate a Telnet site, reading the information on the opening screen is important. It provides key information, such as specific instructions for navigating the site, details on accessing available help resources, and the site's AUP. Keep in mind that the information on the opening screen differs for each Telnet site.

Common Telnet Commands

Because Telnet allows you to log on to many different computer types, no standard set of Telnet commands work universally. Instead, commands may vary from system to system. However, most Telnet hosts use the question mark (?) command. Typing ? after a command prompt instructs the remote host to list the host's available commands. In addition, most hosts recognize the help command, which offers an easy way to learn more about a specific command's use. To access help, type help commandname after the command prompt, replacing commandname with the name of the command you want to learn about. Most Telnet systems provide a menu driven, text-based interface so that you don't need to know specific commands. Figure 6-7 lists some common Telnet commands and their functions.

Figure 6-7
Telnet
commands

Command	Description
?	Returns a list of possible Telnet commands
Enter key	Returns you to the remote host to which you are connected
close	Closes the current connection and disconnects you from the remote machine
display	Shows the current operating parameters for your Telnet session
open	Connects you to a remote host from within Telnet
quit	Exits you from the Telnet program
z	Suspends your Telnet session

Connecting to a Telnet Site

As mentioned previously, the same host computers that allow general Telnet access are also often used for specific day-to-day business tasks. Common Telnet netiquette is to access a host during non-peak business hours, usually early in the morning or late in the evening, and to stay connected only as long as necessary. This is especially true of Telnet hosts that allow guest logins. When you Telnet to these hosts, you are a guest, borrowing the resources available on the host.

REFERENCE window

CONNECTING TO A TELNET SITE USING NETSCAPE

- Click the Open button.
- Enter the Telnet URL, including the Telnet protocol and the host address.
- Press Enter the Key.
- Select terminal emulation mode if required.

Jeffery Howard, president of the student astronomy club, is interested in the Telescopes in Education (TIE) project. He recently read that educational groups can use special software to gain remote access to a giant space telescope located at the Mt. Wilson Observatory. To find a contact name at TIE to determine if the astronomy club qualifies for the project, you Telnet to the University of Maryland in College Park, Maryland, which hosts a large database of information, including astronomy.

To connect to a Telnet site:

1. Start Netscape. The New Perspectives on the Internet Using Netscape Navigator Software—Introductory Student Online Companion Web page displays in your window.

2. Click the **Tutorial 6** link, then click the **Session 6.1** link.

3. Click the **University of Maryland** link. The Telnet client on your computer accesses the Telnet host at the University of Maryland. An opening screen, similar to Figure 6-8, appears in your window, containing general site information.

Figure 6-8 ◄
University of Maryland Telnet host

press the Enter key to access the main menu

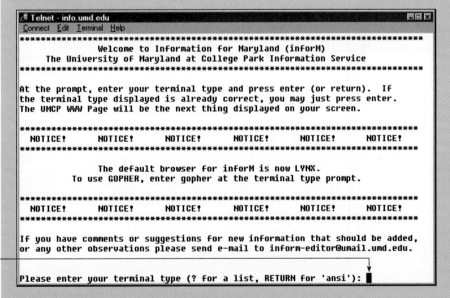

TROUBLE? If you receive a Time Out error while trying to access the server, the host may be too busy to accept new requests. Wait a few minutes, then repeat Steps 2 and 3.

4. Press the **Enter** key after the **Please enter your terminal type** prompt to access the University of Maryland Telnet site. Your screen should look like Figure 6-9. Note the text-based menu that the university's Telnet site uses.

You navigate the site by hyperlinking with a text-based browser interface called **Lynx**. To move through the Telnet site, type the number associated with the link you want to access, then press Enter, or use the ↑ and ↓ arrow keys to highlight the link, then press Enter. The ← and → arrow keys move you backward and forward one screen at a time.

Figure 6-9
Hyperlinking at
a Telnet site

select a menu item,
then press the
Enter key

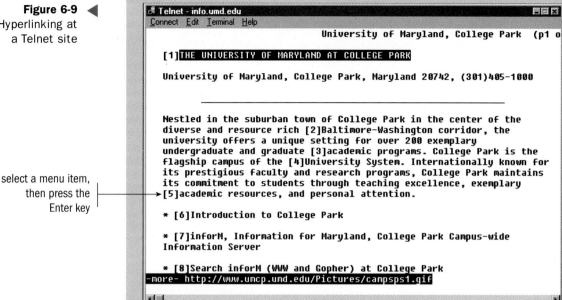

5. Press **5** to access the academic resources link, then press the **Enter** key. The academic resources menu appears on your screen. See Figure 6-10.

Figure 6-10
Academic
resources link

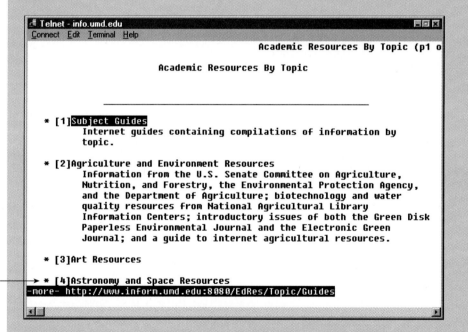

select to link to the
Astronomy and Space
Resources page

TROUBLE? Your screen may differ from Figure 6-10 because host menus change often. If the academic resources link is no longer number 5, press ↓ or ↑ until you locate the academic resource link. Press the Enter key and continue to Step 6.

6. Using your arrow keys, locate the **Astronomy and Space Resources** link, then press the **Enter** key.

7. Locate the **Mount Wilson Observatory** link, then press the **Enter** key.

8. Locate the **Education** link, then press the **Enter** key.

9. Locate the **Telescopes in Education** link, then press the **Enter** key.

10. Locate the **The main WWW page for the TIE Project** link, then press the **Enter** key.

11. Locate the **Information on How You or Your School can use the TIE** link using the ↓ key. Your screen should look like Figure 6-11, which shows the contact information for the TIE project.

> **TROUBLE?** If you cannot find the appropriate link, press the ← key to return to the previous screen. Repeat Steps 10 and 11.

Figure 6-11
TIE contact information via Telnet site

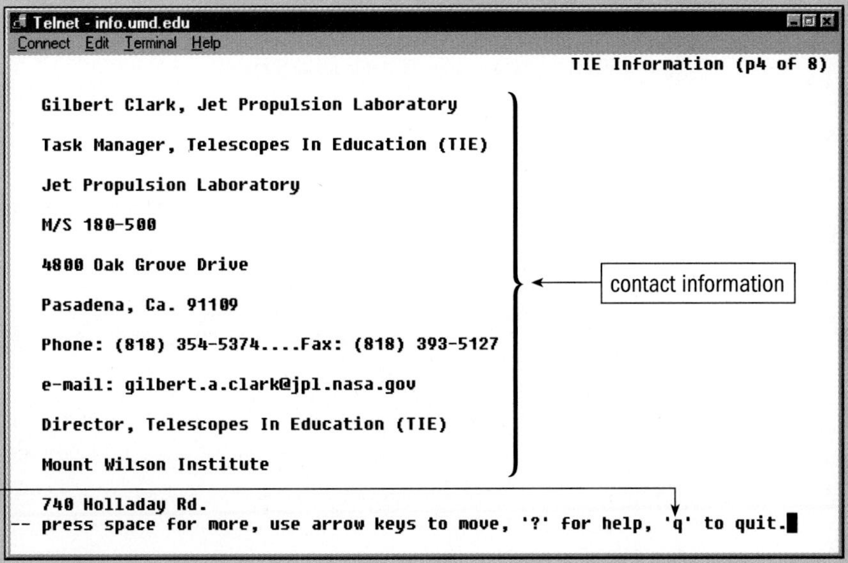

You copy the contact information for Jeffrey and make a note to tell the astronomy club that they may find the University of Maryland Telnet site a useful resource for astronomy research.

Disconnecting from a Telnet Session

Most Telnet sites have a specific method for logging off a Telnet session. Although systems differ, the opening screen usually specifies log off information. The most common log off commands are logout, logoff, exit, quit, or bye, or an abbreviation of one of these commands. Issuing one of these commands disconnects your computer from the remote host and ends the session. If you terminate the session incorrectly, your computer may remain connected to the Telnet host. If you pay for Internet access by the minute or hour, this error could be costly.

Now that you have recorded the TIE contact information, you are ready to log off from the Telnet host.

To disconnect from a Telnet host:

1. Press **Q** to disconnect from the University of Maryland's Telnet host. A prompt appears which asks if you are sure you want to quit. See Figure 6-12.

Figure 6-12 ◀
Disconnecting
from a
Telnet site

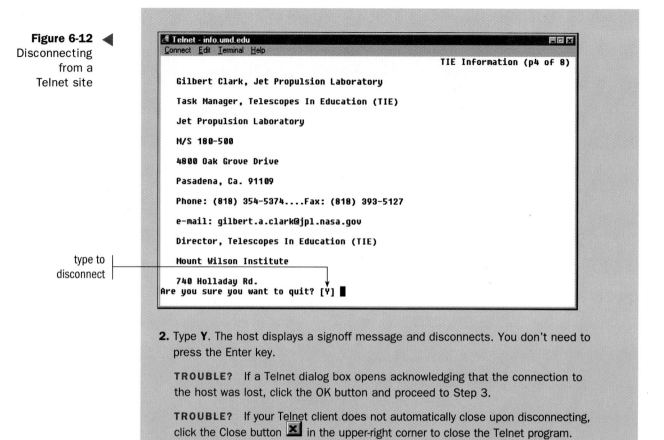

type to
disconnect

2. Type **Y**. The host displays a signoff message and disconnects. You don't need to press the Enter key.

    TROUBLE?   If a Telnet dialog box opens acknowledging that the connection to the host was lost, click the OK button and proceed to Step 3.

    TROUBLE?   If your Telnet client does not automatically close upon disconnecting, click the Close button ☒ in the upper-right corner to close the Telnet program.

3. If necessary, click the **Netscape** button on the Windows 95 taskbar to return to Netscape.

Escape Character Command

If you encounter any problems when browsing a Telnet site or logging off your Telnet session, such as garbled text appearing on your screen or your screen freezing, you may want to try the escape character command. This is *not* the Escape key on your keyboard. Rather, it is a keystroke combination that signals the Telnet host to temporarily cease interaction between the two systems. The escape code varies from system to system, but the most common one uses the Control and Right Bracket keys. To issue the escape command, press the Control and the Right Bracket keys at the same time. This returns you to a Telnet prompt, where you can follow one of the log off procedures. The escape character command may be listed on the opening screen, in subsequent Telnet menus, or in the text as the caret command (^).

Using Hytelnet

In addition to finding Telnet host addresses using standard WWW search tools, you can also use a program called Hytelnet. Installed on many Telnet hosts, **Hytelnet** provides a database of information about Telnet sites. It offers address, login, and descriptive information about thousands of hosts in a hypertext format. Figure 6-13 lists some common Hytelnet sites.

Figure 6-13 ◀
Common
Hytelnet sites

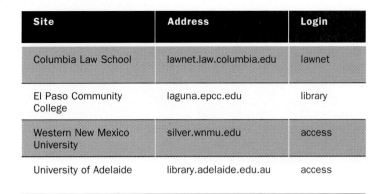

Site	Address	Login
Columbia Law School	lawnet.law.columbia.edu	lawnet
El Paso Community College	laguna.epcc.edu	library
Western New Mexico University	silver.wnmu.edu	access
University of Adelaide	library.adelaide.edu.au	access

When you first log on to a Telnet host, you may see a menu option to access the Hytelnet program. If you access a Telnet host with a command-prompt interface, you can run Hytelnet by simply typing hytelnet and then pressing the Enter key. When you locate an interesting menu item, you access it by using the arrow keys to move the cursor to highlight the link and then press the Enter key, which will lead you to another hyperlinked document. In addition to using arrow keys to navigate the site, you can use specific one-letter commands to browse the information. Figure 6-14 lists some common Hytelnet commands.

Figure 6-14 ◀
Common
Hytelnet
commands

Command	Description
m	Returns you to the introductory screen
+	Moves you forward a page at a time
–	Moves you back a page at a time
?	Displays help information
q	Exits the Hytelnet program
/	Initiates a search for information

At the beginning of each semester, Grace gives her students a computer lab handbook containing information about general computer lab usage and the university's AUP. One handbook section also contains Internet addresses of interesting physics and astronomy sites. To prepare for the upcoming semester, Grace asks you to add a Telnet site to this section relating to the National Aeronautics and Space Administration (NASA). You Telnet to the Columbia Law Library to access the Hytelnet program to find the names of some NASA databases to which the students can Telnet.

To access the Hytelnet program:

1. Make sure that the New Perspectives on the Internet Using Netscape Navigator Software—Introductory Student Online Companion Web page is displayed in your Netscape window.

2. Click the **Tutorial 6** link, then click the **Session 6.1** link.

3. Click the **Columbia Law School** link to access the university's Telnet host.

4. Type **lawnet** when prompted for your login name, then press the **Enter** key twice. The CU-Lawnet InfoSystems opening screen, which uses a text-based interface, appears.

5. Type **7**, then press the **Enter** key to access the Advanced Worldwide library access (HytelNet) menu item. This links you to the Hytelnet program. See Figure 6-15.

Figure 6-15 ◀
Hytelnet
program

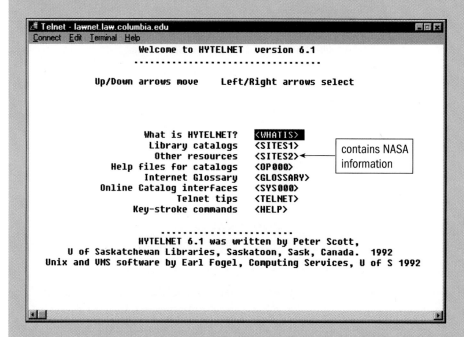

6. Press ↓ until the **<SITES2>** hyperlink for the Other resources category is highlighted. Press the **Enter** key to connect to a menu of other Telnet resources.

7. Use ↓ to highlight the NASA databases link, then press the **Enter** key.

You notice links to many NASA databases and write down their titles. You are now ready to exit the Hytelnet program and disconnect from the Telnet session.

8. Press **Q** to quit Hytelnet and return to the Columbia Law School main menu.

9. Type **q**, then press the **Enter** key to quit the Telnet session. A prompt asks you to verify that you indeed want to exit the site and disconnect from the host.

10. Press **Q** and then press the **Enter** key. The Telnet session ends.

TROUBLE? If a Telnet dialog box opens acknowledging that the connection to the host was lost, click the OK button.

TROUBLE? If your Telnet client does not automatically close upon disconnecting, click the Close button ⊠.

11. If necessary, click the **Netscape** button on the Windows 95 taskbar to return to Netscape.

Quick Check

1. Software on a user's computer that lets the host and remote computers communicate is called a _____.

2. True or False: You can access a remote Telnet server by using either its domain name or its IP address.

3 You can use a _____ to indicate to the remote Telnet host which service you want to access.

4 The _____ command displays a list of commands available on most Telnet hosts.

5 The correct URL to access a Telnet host at the University of Saskatchewan with the domain name access.usask.ca would be in the form: _____ .

6 The _____ command assists you in exiting from your Telnet session if you experience trouble.

You add information about the NASA database sites to the current handbook and prepare to help Grace with her next project.

You have completed Session 6.1. If you are not going to continue to Session 6.2 now, you should exit Netscape. When you are ready to begin Session 6.2, start Netscape, make sure that the toolbar, directory buttons, and Location text box are visible, then continue to Session 6.2.

SESSION 6.2

In this session you will learn about the Gopher Internet service. You will connect to a Gopher server using both Netscape and a Telnet client, browse Gopher sites for information, and use Veronica to perform a Gopher search.

What Is Gopher?

Gopher is a menu-driven Internet service that helps you easily locate information and network services from servers around the world. Internet host computers that offer Gopher services are called **Gopher servers**; the worldwide network of linked Gopher servers is called **Gopherspace**. Gophers present, organize, and distribute various Internet services, including text and multimedia documents, FTP services, Telnet resources, Usenet archives, and database searches. Gopher is not the document or file itself but rather the menu that offers you the resource. The Gopher protocol, part of the TCP/IP protocol suite, was developed to provide document searching and retrieval capabilities.

Both Gopher and the WWW help you locate information by proceeding from one Internet site to another. However, unlike Web pages, Gopher organizes its links in simple text-based menus rather than graphical links. Gopher menus list selections that let you link to other **submenus** to find information. These nested, hierarchical submenus work like file directories or folders; many items can be placed within a folder, or in this case, listed on the menu. Menu selections may include a link to a specific document or multimedia item stored on that particular Gopher server, or a link to another Gopher server.

How Gopher Works

Like other Internet services such as IRC, Gopher is based on the client-server method of providing services over a network. Your computer uses Gopher client software to interpret the Gopher protocol and access information by communicating with a Gopher server program. The server presents information in the nested menus described previously or in documents on the Gopher server.

To access a Gopher server, you use the URL format: gopher://gophername, where gophername is the name of the Gopher server you want to access. For example, to access a Gopher server named Spacelink at NASA, you type the URL gopher://spacelink.msfc.nasa.gov in the Netscape Location text box. Figure 6-16 lists some common Gopher servers and their addresses. You can find additional Gopher server addresses using one of the WWW search tools.

Figure 6-16 ◀
Sample Gopher
servers

Destination	Gopher Address
World Health Organization	gopher://gopher.who.ch
United Nations	gopher://gopher.undp.org
House of Representatives	gopher://gopher.house.gov
U.S. Senate	gopher://gopher.senate.gov
Library of Congress	gopher://marvel.loc.gov
Internic Domain Registry	gopher://internic.net
Internet Wiretap	gopher://wiretap.spies.com
Educational Resources Information Center	gopher://ericir.syr.edu
National Public Radio	gopher://gopher.npr.org
University of Minnesota	gopher://gopher.tc.umn.edu

After you connect to a Gopher server, a menu appears from which you can choose files, other Internet services, or other menus. Items you can select on a Gopher menu appear as icons that indicate what type of information that particular menu offers. Figure 6-17 lists some Gopher menu icons and their specific functions. For example, the folder icon before a menu selection indicates that the selection links to a submenu. When you click a menu selection, Gopher returns one of a few different results. First, it may either display the item indicated in the selection description, such as a text document, or initiate the Internet service you choose, such as Telnet. For selections not directly associated with a specific file or service, Gopher displays a submenu or links you directly to another Gopher server. To open a submenu, you click the selection indicating another menu from the top-level menu. Again, the submenu either contains links to specific files about the particular topic or offers you additional submenus. You continue clicking various menu selections until you locate the file or resource you want.

Figure 6-17 ◀
Gopher icons

Icon	Description
	Submenu
	Document
	Telnet site
	Graphic image
	Search tool

Two frequently offered Gopher menu selections are All the Gopher Servers in the World and Gopher Jewels. These menu selections display a comprehensive list of Gopher servers. In addition, most Gopher servers offer a Help or Information About Gopher menu selection to help you learn more about a particular Gopher server or about the Gopher protocol itself. Although you may begin browsing from a particular Gopher, you may find quickly that the menu selections hyperlinks have taken you to a completely different Gopher server.

Connecting to a Gopher Server

To connect to a Gopher server, you simply type its URL in the Location text box and click the Open button. Netscape displays the Gopher menu in your window. You can then navigate the menu by using your pointer to click menu selections.

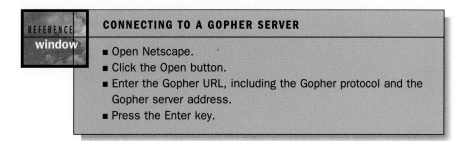

REFERENCE
window

CONNECTING TO A GOPHER SERVER

- Open Netscape.
- Click the Open button.
- Enter the Gopher URL, including the Gopher protocol and the Gopher server address.
- Press the Enter key.

Grace needs your help in researching information for her upcoming lecture about the Hubble telescope. She knows that the telescope is named after the famous astronomer Dr. Edwin P. Hubble but needs some background information on how long he worked at the Mount Wilson Observatory. Grace suggests starting at the NASA Gopher server. You browse through the NASA Gopher, find the information, and print it for Grace.

To connect to a Gopher server:

1. Start Netscape if necessary. Make sure that the New Perspectives on the Internet Using Netscape Navigator Software—Introductory Student Online Companion Web page is displayed in your window.

2. Click the **Tutorial 6** link, then click the **Session 6.2** link.

3. Click the **NASA Gopher** link to open the NASA Spacelink Gopher server. A Gopher opening menu, like the one shown in Figure 6-18, appears in your window.

Figure 6-18
NASA's
Spacelink
Gopher server
opening menu

folder icons indicate
additional submenus

click to access
submenu

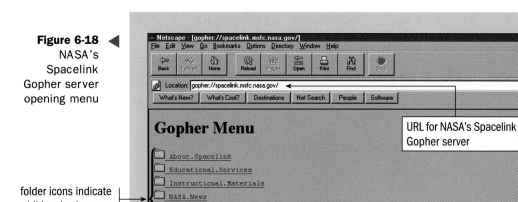

TROUBLE? If you receive a Time Out error message while trying to access the server, the host may be too busy to accept new requests. Wait a few minutes and repeat Steps 2 and 3.

4. Click the **Spacelinks.Hot.Topics** link to access a submenu containing "hot topics" relating to the Gopher server.

5. Click the **Hubble.Space.Telescope** link to access a submenu containing additional information and links related to the Hubble Space Telescope.

6. Click the **Edwin.Hubble** link to access a submenu containing information about the astronomer.

7. Click the **Edwin.P.Hubble.Biography** link. A text document with biography information displays in your window. See Figure 6-19. Scroll down to find the information Grace wants on Dr. Hubbell's tenure at Mount Wilson Observatory.

Figure 6-19
Result of
Hubble search

scroll through page
using arrow keys or
scroll bar

biographical
information on
Edwin Hubble

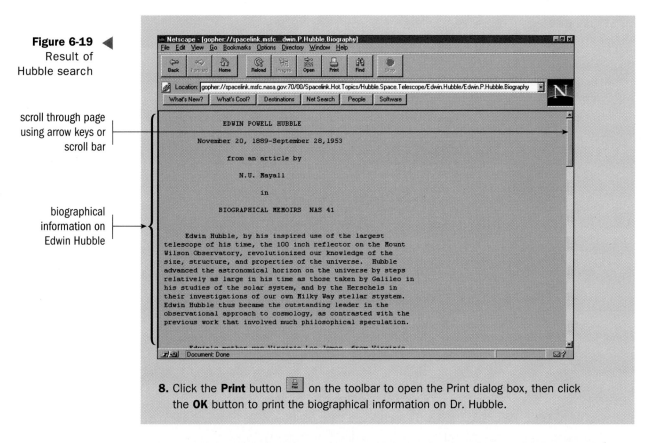

8. Click the **Print** button on the toolbar to open the Print dialog box, then click the **OK** button to print the biographical information on Dr. Hubble.

Before giving the information to Grace, you make a copy to take to the upcoming astronomy club meeting, because its members have shown such interest in telescopes lately.

Ending a Gopher Session

Because no separate program exists for accessing Gopher servers when using Netscape as your client, you need not exit from a Gopher site or end a Gopher session. If you want to return to a Gopher server later, you can create a bookmark in Netscape for that site, following the steps in Tutorial 3 in the section "Using Bookmarks."

Accessing Gopher Using Telnet

In addition to using Netscape to access Gopher through the WWW, you can also access Gopher through a Telnet session. Accessing Gopher through Telnet is especially helpful to users who use text-based shell accounts rather than GUI browsers to access the Internet, because Gopher's menuing system is text-based. Instead of using Netscape's toolbar buttons and menus to navigate the Gopher site, you use numbers that relate to the menu selections or the arrow keys on your keyboard. Instead of using the Gopher URL to instruct Netscape to access a Gopher server, you use the Telnet URL to Telnet to a Gopher server, specifying the Gopher service address or port number. Figure 6-20 shows some commands commonly used to navigate a Gopher menu accessed via Telnet.

Figure 6-20
Commands
used to
navigate
Gopher menus
via Telnet

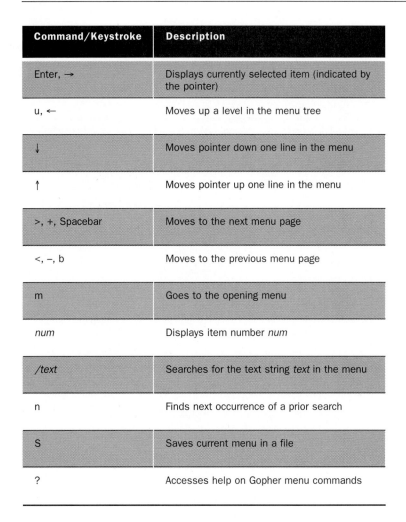

Command/Keystroke	Description
Enter, →	Displays currently selected item (indicated by the pointer)
u, ←	Moves up a level in the menu tree
↓	Moves pointer down one line in the menu
↑	Moves pointer up one line in the menu
>, +, Spacebar	Moves to the next menu page
<, −, b	Moves to the previous menu page
m	Goes to the opening menu
num	Displays item number *num*
/*text*	Searches for the text string *text* in the menu
n	Finds next occurrence of a prior search
S	Saves current menu in a file
?	Accesses help on Gopher menu commands

Browsing through the handbook's Telnet section, you are surprised to read that navigating a Gopher server is equally easy from either a browser or a Telnet session. You decide to test this by accessing the same Gopher server you used to retrieve information on Dr. Hubble, this time using Telnet.

To access Gopher using Telnet:

1. Make sure that the New Perspectives on the Internet Using Netscape Navigator Software—Introductory Student Online Companion Web page is displayed in your window. Click the **Tutorial 6** link, then click the **Session 6.2** link.

2. Click the **NASA Telnet** link. The Telnet client on your computer accesses the Telnet host and initiates the Gopher service.

   TROUBLE? If a dialog box opens stating the Telnet client cannot be found, one may not be installed on your computer or Netscape may need to be reconfigured. Ask your instructor or technical support person for assistance.

3. Type **guest** when prompted for your login name, then press the **Enter** key twice. A text-based opening menu, like the one shown in Figure 6-21, appears in your window. Notice that the menu selections are the same as those offered when you accessed the Gopher via Netscape.

Figure 6-21 ◀
NASA's
Spacelink
Gopher server
via Telnet

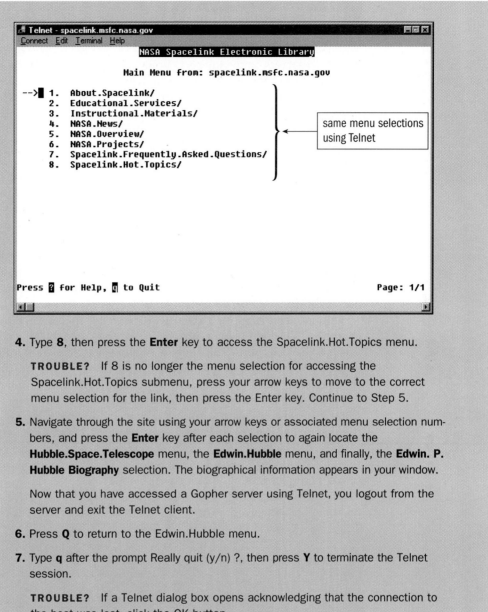

4. Type **8**, then press the **Enter** key to access the Spacelink.Hot.Topics menu.

   TROUBLE? If 8 is no longer the menu selection for accessing the Spacelink.Hot.Topics submenu, press your arrow keys to move to the correct menu selection for the link, then press the Enter key. Continue to Step 5.

5. Navigate through the site using your arrow keys or associated menu selection numbers, and press the **Enter** key after each selection to again locate the **Hubble.Space.Telescope** menu, the **Edwin.Hubble** menu, and finally, the **Edwin. P. Hubble Biography** selection. The biographical information appears in your window.

   Now that you have accessed a Gopher server using Telnet, you logout from the server and exit the Telnet client.

6. Press **Q** to return to the Edwin.Hubble menu.

7. Type **q** after the prompt Really quit (y/n) ?, then press **Y** to terminate the Telnet session.

   TROUBLE? If a Telnet dialog box opens acknowledging that the connection to the host was lost, click the OK button.

   TROUBLE? If your Telnet client does not automatically close upon disconnecting, click the Close button ⊠ .

8. If necessary, click the **Netscape** button on the Windows 95 taskbar to return to Netscape.

You found exactly the same information on Dr. Hubble using a different navigation method.

Gopher Search Tools

As mentioned earlier, using one of the numerous WWW search tools and Gopher can make it easy to find information using Gopher. In addition to the various WWW search tools you learned about in earlier tutorials, there are specific Gopher search tools. The most commonly used Gopher search tool is Veronica. **Veronica** provides an index of thousands of Gopher menu selections, along with keyword searches of those selections so that a user can easily locate information. **Jugheads** are similar to Veronica, except they limit their searches to the specific Gopher systems on which they reside. Finally, Wide Area Information Systems, or **WAIS**, are programs that search both documents and databases indexed by keywords. Unlike Veronica and Jughead, WAIS servers index an entire document.

Searching with Veronica

Veronica was developed at the University of Nevada to help users navigate the thousands of Gopher servers on the Internet. Veronica obtains information much like the spider programs discussed in Tutorial 3, continually visiting Gopher servers around the world to locate information listed in menu titles. Veronica then indexes the words in the titles and stores them in large databases. Publicly available through one of the many Veronica servers, these databases are continually updated as Veronica obtains new information.

The Gopher server directly handles access to Veronica. Some Gopher servers only search locally on the particular server you are visiting, while others search worldwide. Veronica most commonly appears on most Gopher servers as a menu item titled "Search in Gopherspace," "Search in all Gophers," or "Keyword-Search." After you access a Veronica server from a Gopher menu selection, an online search form displays in your window. You enter your search criteria in the search text box provided.

You can type search criteria using mixed-case letters. For example, Veronica returns the same results when you enter the search word "asteroid," "ASTEROID," or "Asteroid." Also, Veronica treats a space between the words of your search as the AND Boolean operator. Thus, if your search words are "Asteroid Comets," Veronica finds titles that include both words.

Veronica also supports partial word searches that use the asterisk (*) as a wildcard character. When searching with a wildcard, the asterisk cannot be the first or only character in a search word, and Veronica ignores all characters following the wildcard. For example, "*steroid" is not a valid search because Veronica ignores any characters after the asterisk; "aster*" returns all menu titles that include the character string "aster."

By default, Veronica servers deliver only the first 200 items that match your query. You can request any number of items by including the -mX argument in your query, with X specifying how many items you want returned. Omitting X sets no limit on the number of titles delivered. For instance, the search "Asteroid Comets -m1000" returns 1,000 titles, if 1,000 items are actually available. When Veronica finishes searching, it returns results in the form of another Gopher menu.

During her upcoming lecture, Grace wants to distribute a disk containing software that relates to telescopes. She asks you to locate software specific to the Hubble Space Telescope. You use Veronica to complete this search.

To search a Gopher server using Veronica:

1. Make sure that the New Perspectives on the Internet Using Netscape Navigator Software—Introductory Student Online Companion Web page is displayed in your window. Click the **Tutorial 6** link, then click the **Session 6.2** link.

2. Click the **University of Minnesota Gopher** link to connect to this Gopher server.

3. Click the **Other Gopher and Information Servers** link to access the next menu. A menu of search tools and general Gopher server categories appears.

4. Click the **Search titles in Gopherspace using veronica** link to access the next menu. This menu includes several Veronica search servers and additional help information on using Veronica's search capabilities.

5. Click the **Find GOPHER DIRECTORIES by Title word(s) (via NYSERNet)** link to access a Veronica search server. See Figure 6-22.

   TROUBLE? If the NYSERNet link is not available, select another Veronica server link from the menu.

Figure 6-22 ◀
Veronica
search

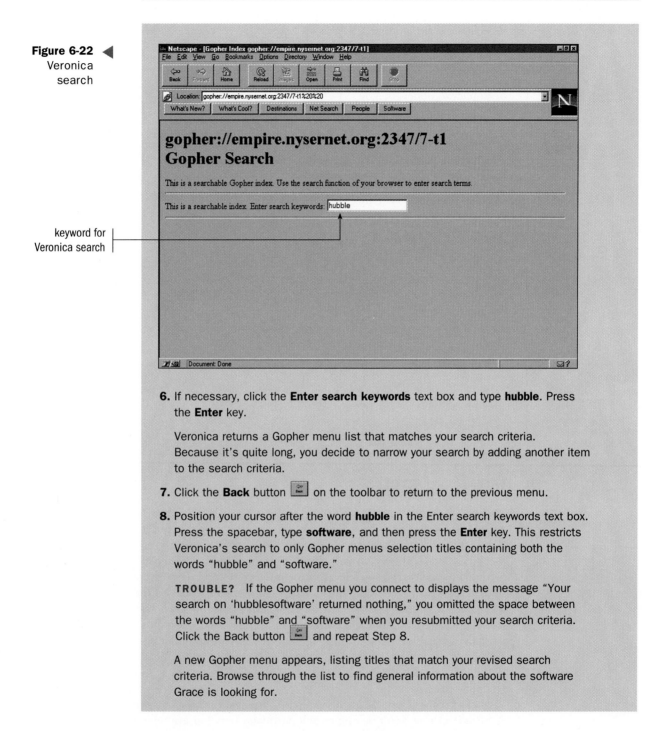

keyword for
Veronica search

6. If necessary, click the **Enter search keywords** text box and type **hubble**. Press the **Enter** key.

Veronica returns a Gopher menu list that matches your search criteria. Because it's quite long, you decide to narrow your search by adding another item to the search criteria.

7. Click the **Back** button 📇 on the toolbar to return to the previous menu.

8. Position your cursor after the word **hubble** in the Enter search keywords text box. Press the spacebar, type **software**, and then press the **Enter** key. This restricts Veronica's search to only Gopher menus selection titles containing both the words "hubble" and "software."

TROUBLE? If the Gopher menu you connect to displays the message "Your search on 'hubblesoftware' returned nothing," you omitted the space between the words "hubble" and "software" when you resubmitted your search criteria. Click the Back button 📇 and repeat Step 8.

A new Gopher menu appears, listing titles that match your revised search criteria. Browse through the list to find general information about the software Grace is looking for.

You give Grace the software information. She will use it to evaluate each software program's relevance to her lecture. She will also check on any copyright restrictions regarding the software's distribution.

Quick Check

1 True or False: Menus on a Gopher server can link you to different Internet services.

2 The linked network of Gopher servers is sometimes called _____.

3 Which is a valid Gopher URL?
a. gopher.loc.gov
b. http://gopher.loc.giv
c. gopher\gopher.loc.gov
d. gopher://gopher.loc.gov

4 When accessing a Gopher server through Telnet, you can choose menu selections by either using the _____ key(s) or by referencing their associated _____.

5 When navigating a Gopher site using Telnet, you can return to the main menu by issuing the _____ command.

6 Veronica conducts searches on Gopher menu _____.

7 You can perform partial word searches with Veronica by using an_____ to represent a wildcard character.

You have completed Session 6.2. If you are not going to continue to Session 6.3 now, you should exit Netscape. When you are ready to begin Session 6.3, start Netscape, make sure that the toolbar, directory buttons, and Location text box are visible, then continue to Session 6.3.

SESSION 6.3

In this session you will learn what FTP is and how it works. You will search an FTP server using the Archie search tool, download a file to your computer, and then uncompress the downloaded file.

What Is FTP?

FTP, which stands for File Transfer Protocol and is part of the TCP/IP protocol suite, is an Internet service that allows for file transfer from one computer to another. FTP's function is to efficiently transfer any type of file—software, text, graphics, sound, animation, or even video clips—by downloading or uploading. To **download** is to transfer a copy of a file from another computer to your own computer. For instance, to upgrade to the newest version of Netscape Navigator, you download a copy of the software to your hard drive from a server at Netscape Communications. To **upload** is to transfer a copy of a file from your own computer to another computer over the Internet. For example, if you need to share a blueprint with a building contractor, you upload a copy of the graphic file to a server. The contractor then downloads the copy to his or her own computer. FTP lets you quickly and efficiently share data with others without spending time or money on shipping and postage.

Some ISPs and organizations maintain a **public directory** as part of their FTP servers. Public directories don't belong to any particular user but are open for the general public's use to FTP files. The **system administrator** who owns or runs each server decides whether to establish a public directory that lets anyone FTP a file to or from the directory, or both. For example, the Netscape FTP site allows users to access certain public directories in order for them to download copies of Netscape software. However, users cannot upload their own files to Netscape's directories, so the system administrator retains control over the types and number of files stored on its server. Figure 6-23 lists some popular FTP sites.

Figure 6-23 ◀
Popular
FTP sites

FTP Site	URL	Description
Netscape	ftp://ftp.netscape.com	Netscape products and support files
U.S. Supreme Court	ftp://ftp.cwru.edu	Full text of court decision
Microsoft	ftp://ftp.microsoft.com	Device drivers and technical support files for Microsoft products
Center for Innovative Computer Applications at Indiana University	ftp://ftp.cica.indiana.edu	Software archives for Unix machines and pcs
Jumbo	http://www.jumbo.com	Over 60,000 shareware and freeware programs
Consummate Winsock Applications	http://www.cwsapps.com	Software for attaching to the Internet, helper applications
Yahoo!	http://www.yahoo.com/Computers/Software/Shareware/	Yahoo directory listing for Computers and Internet Software
The Shareware Link	http://www.sdinter.net:80/~rbeck	Shareware resources

How FTP Works

The FTP protocol lets you connect to a remote server, view its directories, and then transfer the files you want to and from your computer. To use the Internet's FTP service, you must connect to a server running the FTP server software, called an **FTP server**. You upload or download files using **FTP software**. After you connect to the FTP server using FTP software, you essentially become part of the FTP server's network. You can connect to an FTP server through a Telnet session or directly from Netscape, because FTP is a protocol that Netscape recognizes. An FTP site is distinguishable by its URL, which begins with "ftp://" instead of "http://" or any other protocol Netscape supports. When accessing FTP sites through Netscape, you use the URL format: ftp://domain/subdirectory/filename, where domain is the name of the host you want to access, subdirectory is where the file is stored, and filename is the name of the file you want to download. In this tutorial, you will use Netscape to FTP a file.

To upload or download files to and from a non-public directory on a remote server using FTP, users need to supply **login ID** and **password** codes that identify them to the server. These codes verify that the person logging into the server indeed has the correct access rights to FTP files. Only users with the correct login ID and password can transfer files to and from a specified directory. When using Telnet to access an FTP site, the user is prompted for the login ID and password during the login process. When accessing a restricted FTP site or directory using Netscape, the URL includes the login ID. For example, if you type ftp://loginID@domain in the Open Location text box, and then click OK, Netscape displays a dialog box prompting you for your password. The correct login ID and password tell the FTP server that you have access rights to FTP files to or from that particular server.

Sites that have files available to the public use **anonymous FTP**. Users can access the server without a login account, by using the login ID "anonymous." When you access an anonymous FTP site, you generally use your e-mail address as the password, or sometimes use a generic word like "guest." Although users can download files from an anonymous FTP site, FTP site administrators usually restrict uploading so they can control the files added to their servers. When you connect to an anonymous FTP site using Netscape, the browser automatically supplies the login ID "anonymous" and the password needed to access the remote computer, as specified in the Mail and News Preferences dialog box. By default, Netscape uses your e-mail address as the password.

After your computer is connected to a remote server, you can browse its files. Netscape displays an FTP site as a list of links. An icon preceding each link indicates if the link is a file or a directory, also know as a folder. When available, Netscape lists as much information as possible about the files stored on the server, such as filename, date and time of creation, and file size. When you click a folder's link, Netscape jumps to a file list and/or other folders in the directory. When you locate the file you want, simply click its filename to download a copy to your computer. Netscape then prompts you to indicate where you want the file saved and what name to assign to the file. Netscape then downloads, or FTPs, a copy of the file to the location you specify, such as your computer's hard drive or floppy disk. Figure 6-24 shows an example of an FTP server accessed using Netscape.

Figure 6-24 ◀
FTP server
accessed using
Netscape

folders indicate
additional folders
or files

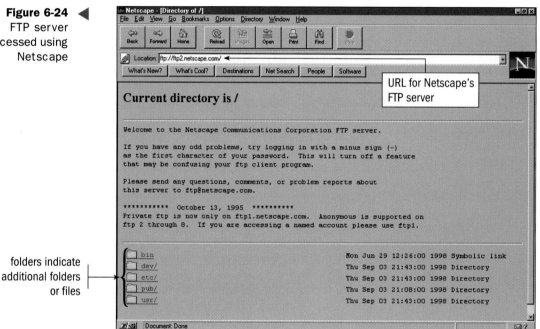

Often, files uploaded to an FTP server are compressed first and then copied to the server. **Compression** is the process of compacting data to a smaller size by scanning a file, eliminating duplicate words or phrases, and replacing them with reference codes. During the compression process, a small internal chart accompanies the compressed file and tracks information designating where a code was assigned wherever a repeated word appeared. For example, if the compression process was used on this tutorial, every time the word "Netscape" appeared, it might be replaced by the code #"1." This significantly reduces the amount of disk space the tutorial would occupy. Compression is generally used to make files smaller so that they transfer more quickly, in order to save room on a FTP server, or to efficiently send more information in one file. Compression is especially useful if a file is larger than the space available on a floppy disk. If you pay for Internet access by the minute, compressing a file before uploading it saves time and money because the file transfers more quickly.

The extension .ZIP at the end of a filename identifies most compressed files. Before you can use a compressed file, you must **uncompress**, or expand, the file, restoring its original structure and size. An **uncompression program** is a general-purpose program that restores the compressed file to its original size. One popular compression/uncompression program, PKZip, creates compressed files that appear with the extension .ZIP and also uncompresses, or extracts, files so that you can use them. Other files whose names end with the file extension .EXE may be compressed. These are called **executable files** and require no expansion with an uncompression utility. They have a built-in uncompression feature and automatically uncompress when launched. A file downloaded from an FTP server may or may not need to be uncompressed. If it does, after the file is extracted, you can use it on your computer.

The general rules of etiquette for FTP are similar to Telnet's. Sometimes archive sites of FTP servers used for crucial business tasks have time restrictions on their sites. If so, abide by the rules listed, which usually appear when you access the FTP server. Also, when downloading programs, it is your responsibility to check for copyright and licensing restrictions.

Searching with Archie

There are millions of useful files accessible for downloading from the Internet. Keeping track of all the available files is nearly impossible. **Archie** is a service used to locate files stored at anonymous FTP sites. Internet host computers offering Archie service are called **Archie servers**. Archie servers maintain databases of information that Archie references when you instruct it to search for a particular file. The database located on the server is updated routinely, usually about once a week, so that it includes newly available file information. Archie servers continually scan anonymous FTP sites for new information. An Archie server typically checks only selected FTP sites, so that your query result does not necessarily include files added to an FTP site after its last update. Unlike WWW search engines that often reference filenames and content when indexing information, Archie servers reference only the filenames when searching for files that have been added to an anonymous FTP site. The servers then add new filenames to the index of available files.

Archie servers work only when you know the exact name of the file you want to locate. Although every Archie query form can look different, they all work similarly. You enter a keyword query using the filename you want to find and then press the Enter key or click the Start Search button to begin the search. You usually receive a response within a few seconds or a few minutes. The resulting reference list includes only those FTP sites that have a copy of the file you are interested in.

If you don't find the file you're looking for using one Archie server, you should try another because hundreds of such servers are available for your use. You can locate Archie servers by using one of the many WWW search tools. Gopher menus often list Archie servers; many Web sites have links to Archie servers as well.

If you do not know the exact filename you are looking for or want to browse through the available file types, you can search for the file type that interests you using a WWW search tool. Using a WWW search tool, you enter your search criteria along with the file type you are looking for. In addition, if you know the URL of the FTP site you want to browse, you can use the folder and document icons representing hyperlinks to move through the site until you locate the file that interests you.

Many files you want to download for the computer lab are compressed. You currently do not have a program to uncompress the files, so you need to locate an uncompression utility program. Grace suggests that you download a shareware program called PKZip that you can use to compress or uncompress files. First, you use Archie to find an anonymous FTP site to download the file from.

To search for a file using Archie:

1. If necessary, start Netscape. Make sure that the New Perspectives on the Internet Using Netscape Navigator Software—Introductory Student Online Companion Web page displays in your window.

2. Click the **Tutorial 6** link, then click the **Session 6.3** link. You use the links on this page to locate an available Archie server.

3. Click one of the **Archie server** links and, if necessary, click the **query form** link to access an Archie query form. Your screen should look similar to the one shown in Figure 6-25.

Figure 6-25 ◄
Searching for
files with
Archie

enter search
criteria here

click to begin search

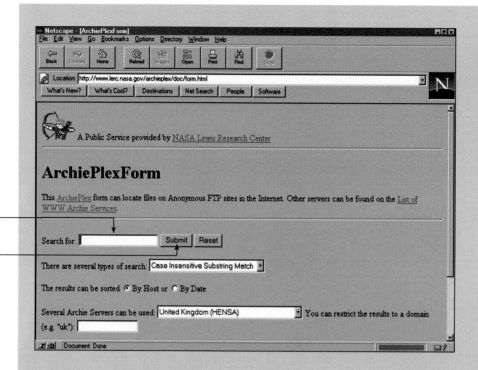

TROUBLE?   If the Archie server link you select does not return an Archie query form, the server may be too busy to accept new requests. Repeat Step 3 using one of the other Archie servers listed.

The name of the file Grace suggested you download is Pkzws201.exe.

4. If necessary, scroll down until you see the Search for query text box. In the Query text box, type **pkzws201.exe** to indicate the name of the file you are searching for.

5. Press the **Enter** key, or click the **Submit** button or **Search** button, depending on the Archie server you are using, to initiate the search. The Archie server searches its database and returns a list of sites where the pkzws201.exe file is available. See Figure 6-26.

You notice that some FTP sites have newer file dates than others. By selecting one of the newer sites, you are more likely to get a version of the program with recent updates.

Figure 6-26 ◀
Archie search
results

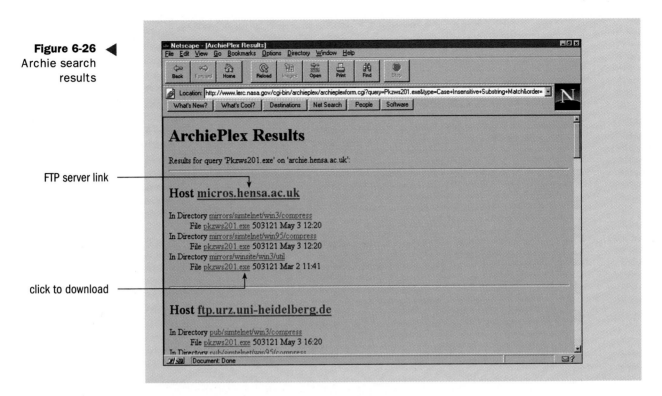

FTP server link ——

click to download ——

Now that you have found several locations where you can download the PKZip file, you use FTP to download a copy.

Downloading a File Using FTP

When you find a file you want to copy to your computer, you instruct your FTP software to download the file. After you click the name of the file, Netscape connects to the requested FTP server. If you have access rights to copy the file, Netscape prompts you to specify where you want the file copied, and the name with which you want to save the file. The FTP software then downloads a copy of the file to the designated location. The download processing time varies depending on the file's size, how busy the FTP server is, and the proximity of the FTP server. When the transfer process begins, Netscape displays a dialog box in your window indicating the download's progress, including the file's size and the time estimated for file transfer. Because Windows 95 is a multitasking operating system, you need not wait for the file to download before performing other tasks on your computer. **Multitasking** is the capability to execute more than one program at once on a computer. For example, if you download a large file that takes several minutes to transfer, you can return to the Netscape browser and continue to surf the Internet while you wait.

Some FTP servers let only a certain number of users access their files at once. If you try to download a file and receive a "server busy" message, try again in a few minutes, or try to locate another server where the file resides. Some FTP sites are busier than others. For example, when a new version of a popular software program such as Netscape Navigator becomes available, you may need to make several attempts to access the FTP server because many people are trying to download the same file.

You may need to use the uncompression utility on many computers in the lab, so you copy it to a disk that you can easily take from one machine to another. The Pkzws201.exe file needs to be uncompressed after you download it. To ensure that all files associated with the program are kept in an organized manner, you first create a folder on your disk to store the compressed program. Because you used Archie to locate the file you want to download, you need not browse through the FTP's site directory structure. Archie displays a direct link to the requested file.

To download a file using FTP:

1. While still on the Archie search results page, insert your Student Disk in the appropriate drive.

2. Click the **Start** button [Start] on the Windows 95 taskbar with the right mouse button, then click **Explore** to open the Windows Exploring window.

3. Scroll to the top of the All Folders panel, then click **3½ Floppy (A:)**. Click **File** on the menu bar, point to **New**, and then click **Folder**.

4. Type **Pkzip** to name the folder, then press the **Enter** key. A new folder with the title Pkzip appears in the content area of your 3½ Floppy (A:) window.

5. Click the **Close** button [X] to exit the Windows Exploring window and return to the Archie search results list.

6. Position your pointer over one of the Pkzws201.exe links that has a current date. The URL in the status message area displays the FTP site information, including the server and directory where the file resides, along with the filename.

7. Click the **Pkzws201.exe** link to download the file. A Save As dialog box opens.

   TROUBLE?   If the Save As dialog box does not open and strange characters appear in the window, click the Stop button [Stop] on the toolbar to abort the link, then click Options, click General Preferences, click the Helpers tab, scroll down to and click the exe, bin line in the extensions column, click the Save to Disk radio button, click the OK button, then repeat Step 7.

   TROUBLE?   If the Unknown File type dialog box opens, click the Save to Disk button to open the Save As dialog box. Continue to Step 9.

   TROUBLE?   If you recieve an error message stating, "FTP Error Could not login to FTP server," the site you linked to is busy. Click the Back button [Back] on the toolbar to return to the Archie search results page and try a different site. If no other sites are listed, click [Back] until you return to the Session 6.3 page, and repeat the query with another Archie server.

8. Click the **Save in** list arrow, then select **3½ Floppy (A:)**. Your Student Disk contents appear in the window.

9. Double-click the **pkzip** folder to open it.

10. If necessary, click the **Filename** text box and type **Pkzws201.exe** to name and save the file you are transferring to your Student Disk.

11. Press the **Enter** key to download the Pkzws201.exe file to your Student Disk. The Saving Location box, shown in Figure 6-27, shows your download's progress.

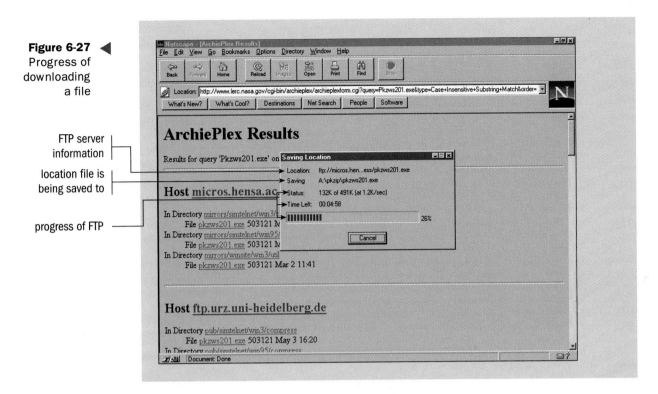

Figure 6-27
Progress of
downloading
a file

FTP server
information

location file is
being saved to

progress of FTP

With the file downloaded to your disk, you now uncompress it so that you can use the PKZip program.

Uncompressing a Downloaded File

Although some files you download from the Internet are ready to be used immediately, some need to be uncompressed before you can use them. Because uncompressing a file sometimes creates several new files, common practice is to place a compressed file in its own subdirectory before uncompressing it. This way, all related files are in one organized location. After you extract the files, you can view, run, or edit them using your programs. Because Pkzws201.exe is a self-extracting executable file, you simply run the program using the Windows 95 Run command.

To uncompress the Pkzws201.exe file on drive A:

1. Make sure your Student Disk is in drive A or the appropriate disk drive.

2. Click the **Start** button on the Windows 95 taskbar, then click **Run** to open the Run dialog box.

3. Click the **Browse** button in the Run dialog box to open the Browse dialog box.

4. Click the **Look in** list arrow, then click **3½ Floppy (A:)**. The contents of your Student Disk are displayed.

5. Double-click the **pkzip** folder to open it.

6. Double-click the **Pkzws201.exe** filename to return to the Run dialog box. Click the **OK** button to open a PKZip© for Windows - Shareware Version - Installation dialog box and begin the self-extraction process.

7. Click the **Drives** list arrow, then click **A:**. The PKZip program uncompresses and is stored in the Pkzip folder on your Student Disk. See Figure 6-28.

Figure 6-28 ◀
Uncompressing
the
Pkzws201.exe
file

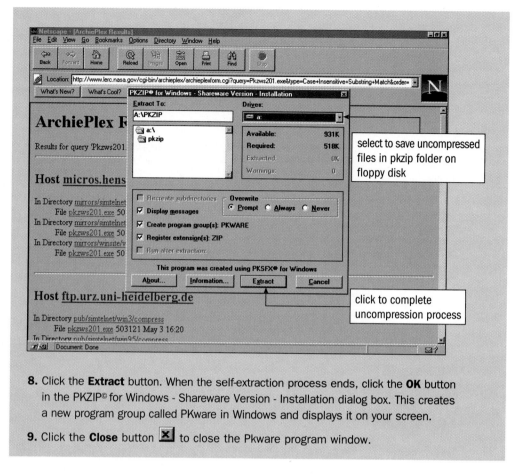

8. Click the **Extract** button. When the self-extraction process ends, click the **OK** button in the PKZIP© for Windows - Shareware Version - Installation dialog box. This creates a new program group called PKware in Windows and displays it on your screen.

9. Click the **Close** button ▣ to close the Pkware program window.

The PKZip program is installed and ready to use. You can use it to uncompress files that you download from the Internet, or you can compress files that you want to upload. After you uncompress a downloaded file, you no longer need the original. To save room on your disk, you delete the compressed Pkzws201.exe file.

To delete a file:

1. Click the right mouse button on the **Start** button 🏁Start in the Windows 95 taskbar to open a shortcut menu. Click **Explore** to open the Windows Explorer program.

2. Scroll up to the All Folders panel, then click **3½ Floppy (A:)** to display the Pkzip folder.

3. Double-click the **Pkzip** folder to open it and list the files in it.

4. Click **Pkzws201** to select the Pkzws201.exe compressed file.

5. Click **File** on the menu bar, then click **Delete**. The Confirm Delete dialog box opens so you can confirm that you want to delete the file. Click the **Yes** button to delete the file.

6. Click the **Close** button ▣ to close the Exploring window and return to Netscape.

Any file transferred from one computer to another is subject to viruses. A **virus** is a destructive program code embedded, or hidden, in an executable file. When you run an infected program, the virus can affect your computer's performance, display garbled messages or images on your screen, or even erase information on your hard drive.

You use the Microsoft Anti-Virus program that comes with Windows 95 to scan your Student Disk for viruses.

To scan for viruses:

1. Make sure your Student Disk is in drive A or the appropriate disk drive.

2. Click the **Start** button ![Start] on the Windows 95 taskbar, then click **Run** to open the Run dialog box.

3. Type **c:\dos\mwav.exe** in the Run text box, then click the **OK** button to launch the Microsoft Windows Anti-Virus program. See Figure 6-29.

Figure 6-29 ◀
Microsoft Anti-Virus program

click to select floppy disk for virus scan

click to scan disk for viruses

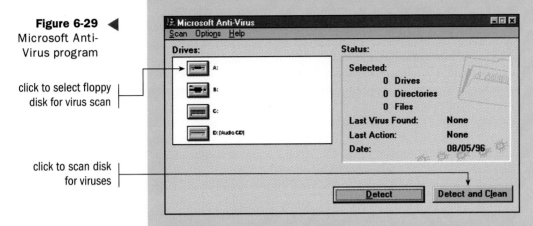

TROUBLE?   If you receive an error message stating that the mwav.exe file cannot be found, you may have typed the program name incorrectly; repeat Step 2. If the same message appears, then the mwav.exe file might not be installed on your computer. Ask your instructor or technical support person to help you find another anti-virus program installed on your computer.

4. Click the **drive A** icon, then click the **Detect and Clean** button to start the anti-virus program. When all files on your Student Disk are scanned, a statistics dialog box opens, like the one shown in Figure 6-30, indicating the scan's results. If the anti-virus program found a virus on your Student Disk, the statistics box indicates that the infected file has been cleaned.

Figure 6-30 ◀
Virus scan statistics

categories break down number and types of disks

indicates no viruses were detected

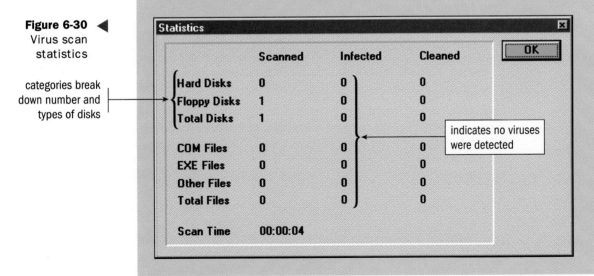

After you check a file or program for viruses, it is probably safe to use on your computer.

Using Shareware

One common use of FTP is downloading shareware and freeware from the Internet. **Shareware** are programs that you can try and evaluate before purchasing, whereas **freeware** are programs that you can download and use free. Literally millions of files are available to the public on the Internet, from software that displays a simulated meteor shower, to graphic images you can use in an upcoming marketing campaign. Using FTP, you can easily access these files for your own use. After you download the files to your computer, you can view, run, or edit them using the appropriate program.

If you decide to keep a shareware program, you must send its creator a fee. A text file attached to the program or on the program Help menu usually outlines payment terms. To ensure that users send payment after the free trial period expires, many authors distribute a demonstration version of the software with some features disabled. When you register and purchase a shareware program, you receive a full working version and information about program **updates**, or revisions. While shareware is supported software, distributed with documentation and continuous updates, freeware is distributed as is. Many shareware and freeware authors are hobbyists and college students interested in computer programming who want to test their program ideas. The Internet provides a convenient and inexpensive way for marketing or testing programs and receiving feedback. Registering for shareware encourages authors to continue developing new versions and to work on program improvements.

Quick Check

1. _____ is the protocol used to transfer a copy of a file from your own computer to another computer over the Internet.

2. The FTP URL format is _____.

3. True or False: You can FTP files to your computer using a Telnet session.

4. An FTP site open to the public for downloading without a login ID and password is called an _____.

5. An _____ is a general-purpose program that expands compressed files to their original component size.

6. True or False: When using Microsoft Windows 95, Microsoft you must wait for a file to download before you can access other programs on your computer.

7. Programs available for downloading and evaluating for a period of time are called _____.

You have now completed Session 6.3. If you want more information about Telnet, Gopher, and FTP, you can find additional resources using the New Perspectives on the Internet Using Netscape Navigator Software—Introductory Student Online Companion for this tutorial by accessing the Tutorial 6 and Session 6.1, 6.2, 6.3, and the Next level section links.

Tutorial Assignments

Grace has recently read about an astronomy simulation program named Astronomy Lab 2. This shareware program uses Windows 95 to animate astronomical events such as eclipses and meteor showers. She feels that it may be a good program for the computer lab and wants you to evaluate it. Grace forwards the compressed simulation program filename, Alw203.zip, and asks you to use Archie to locate an FTP site so that you can download the program. Although Grace wants you to evaluate the program, she would also like to evaluate the program herself, so she asks you to save it on disk for her. Grace also wants you to send along any registration information you can find on the shareware program. After you locate the file, you use Netscape's built-in FTP capabilities to download the file to your disk. You then use the PKZip program to uncompress the file and then run the Astronomy Lab 2 program. You locate registration information and print it to give to Grace with the disk.

If necessary, start Netscape. Make sure that the New Perspectives on the Internet Using Netscape Navigator Software—Introductory Student Online Companion Web page displays in your window. Do the following:

1. Insert your Student Disk in drive A.
2. Create a folder on your disk called "Astrolab."
3. Click the Tutorial 6 link on The New Perspectives on the Internet Using Netscape Navigator Software—Introductory Student Online Companion Web page, then click the Tutorial Assignments link.
4. Locate the Archie Server links in the Tutorial Assignments section, and then connect to a server by clicking one of the links.
5. Type "Alw203.zip" in the Query text box, then press the Enter key to initiate the search.
6. Click one of the file links to initiate the FTP process, and save the file in the Astrolab folder with the name "Alw203.zip."

7. Open the Run dialog box, type "a:\pkunzip\pkunzip.exe a:\astrolab\alw203.zip a:\astrolab," then press the Enter key.
8. If necessary, close the DOS window when uncompression is finished.
9. Delete the Alw203.zip file from your disk. *Hint:* Use Windows Explorer to locate the file, and then delete it.

10. Reopen the Run dialog box, type "a:\astrolab\alw.exe" in the Open text box, then press the Enter key.
11. Click Movies, then click Jupiter Moons Top.
12. Select the current Year, Month, Day, and Time, then click OK. Watch the simulation for a few minutes, and then stop the movie.
13. Click Help, then click How to Register. Print the registration information.
14. Exit the Astronomy Lab 2 program by clicking the Close button in the upper-right of the program window.
15. Exit Netscape.

Both Grace and you feel that the Astronomy simulations program will be a good addition to the computer lab's software. The shareware program is an inexpensive teaching tool. Grace asks that you access the NASA Spacelink Gopher to see if it offers any freeware or shareware for Macintosh computers. As she studied the information on software for telescopes that you gave her, Grace did not see much software available for Macintosh computers. Because many elementary schools have Macintosh computers, she wants to know what specific software is available for this computing platform. You Telnet to the NASA Gopher and browse the site to find suitable software programs. You write down the name, size, and general description of at least four programs you feel might meet Grace's needs.

If necessary, start Netscape. Make sure that The New Perspectives on the Internet Using Netscape Navigator Software—Introductory Student Online Companion Web page displays in your window. Do the following:

1. Click the Tutorial 6 link.
2. Click the Tutorial Assignments link.
3. Locate the Telnet to NASA Spacelink Gopher Server link in the Tutorial Assignments section, then click this link.
4. Enter the login name "guest" to log on to the Gopher server.
5. Select the Instructional.Materials link.
6. Browse the site to find software for Macintosh computers.
7. Locate descriptive information about the software available.
8. Write a summary of the information Grace requested.
9. Exit Gopher.
10. Close the Telnet program, if necessary.
11. Exit Netscape.

Case Problems

1. Retrieving a Graphics Utility Program for Performance Marketing Resources Nancy C. Thomson, an associate at Performance Marketing Resources, develops Web pages for clients. Nancy is responsible for converting photographs and graphics into formats suitable for Web page creation. By reading trade journals and accessing Internet marketing newsgroups, she has learned about a shareware program that easily converts graphic files and manipulates text files for placement on a Web page. Several graphic utility programs are available on the Internet, but Nancy is interested in one called Lviewpro that has received rave reviews. Nancy is unsure of the file's location and asks you to use an Archie server to find it. After you locate the file, Nancy wants you to download it to a disk for her.

If necessary, start Netscape. Make sure that the New Perspectives on the Internet Using Netscape Navigator Software—Introductory Student Online Companion Web page displays in your window. Do the following:

1. Insert your Student Disk in drive A.
2. Create a folder on your disk called "Lview."
3. Click the Tutorial 6 link on The New Perspectives on the Internet Using Netscape Navigator Software—Introductory Student Online Companion Web page.
4. Click the Case Problems link.
5. Click the link for Retrieving a Graphics Utility Program for Performance Marketing Resources in the Case Problem 1 section.
6. Type "Lviewpro.zip" in the Query text box.
7. Press the Enter key to initiate the search.
8. Click one of the file links to initiate the FTP process.
9. Save the file in the Lview folder with the name "Lviewpro.zip."
10. Exit Netscape.

2. Robyn Lake Learns New Terminology Using a Gopher Server Robyn Lake's company, Inland Forestry Management, is downsizing. Due to restructuring, Robyn's job and another person's job have been consolidated into one position. Each employee has the option to leave the company with generous severance pay. Robyn has been with the company for a long time and has decided to take a break to explore new career opportunities. Over the last year or so, Robyn has participated in many services the Internet offers. She is intrigued by the amount of information available and the ways companies take advantage of the technology. Before she updates her resume, she decides to take time to learn as much as possible about the Internet. She knows the knowledge will be useful in her job hunting. One area she wants to concentrate on is simply understanding Internet terminology. You help Robyn learn the definitions of some key terms and phrases used to describe the technology by accessing a well-known work by Brendan P. Kehoe called *Zen and the Art of the Internet*. The document gives an overview of available Internet services and has a glossary and a bibliography listing additional references. The electronic version of this document is stored on a Gopher server at the University of Minnesota. You Telnet to the Gopher site, browse the site to locate the electronic document, and then scan the glossary to learn specific definitions.

If necessary, start Netscape. Make sure that the New Perspectives on the Internet Using Netscape Navigator Software—Introductory Student Online Companion Web page displays in your window. Do the following:

1. Click the Tutorial 6 link.
2. Click the Case Problems link.
3. Click the link for Robyn Lake Learns New Terminology Using a Gopher Server in the Case Problem 2 section.
4. Type "gopher" when prompted for a login ID, then press the Enter key twice.
5. Select Libraries.
6. Select Electronic Books.
7. Locate the book *Zen and the Art of the Internet*.

8. Browse through the book's glossary to find definitions of the following terms: fully qualified domain name, node, polling, medium, and interoperate. Rewrite the definitions in your own words.
9. Exit the glossary.
10. Quit the Gopher session and exit the Telnet program, if necessary.
11. Exit Netscape.

3. Finding Information for a New Business Leroy Landgraf has recently been laid off and wants to start a new business, Landgraf Machine and Engineering. His company will produce the small metal parts needed to construct goods used by governmental agencies. Leroy wants to learn as much as possible about starting a new business, including tax regulations, potential loans, start-up capital, and so on. You access the Small Business Administration's Gopher to search for helpful information for Leroy.

If necessary, start Netscape. Make sure that the New Perspectives on the Internet Using Netscape Navigator Software—Introductory Student Online Companion Web page displays in your window. Do the following:

1. Click the Tutorial 6 link.
2. Click the Case Problems link.

3. Click the Small Business Administration Gopher site link in the Case Problem 3 section. Browse the site to find the following information:
   a. Where is the closest SBA office? What is the address and the telephone number?
   b. What is SCORE? Is there a local chapter in your area?
   c. What type of loans are available to startup business?
   d. What other types of services are available? Are there any upcoming events in your area that Leroy might find useful?
4. Compile the information you found in a report format and e-mail to your instructor.
5. Exit Netscape.

4. Scavenger Hunt for FTP, Telnet and Gopher Sites While reading the latest issue of Clark University's school paper, the *Clark Cardinal Review*, Scott Forsell notices information about a school-sponsored contest. Students can participate in a scavenger hunt to find information through the Internet. The Computer Science Department is sponsoring the contest to encourage students to discover the myriad of information and files available on the Internet. After students find the information, they turn their entry in to the school paper. The Computer Science Department will review all entries and then draw a winner from all correct entries. Three contest winners will receive a free full year of home Internet access. The department encourages students to work in teams. Scott asks you to help him find the information listed on the entry form. You must use at least two methods to search FTP, Telnet, and Gopher sites, including Veronica and Archie, to find information on the Internet. Keep track of all information you find so that you can include it on the entry form.

If necessary, start Netscape. Make sure that the New Perspectives on the Internet Using Netscape Navigator Software—Introductory Student Online Companion Web page appears in your window. Do the following:

1. Find these Telnet sites and identify their URLs: the Air Force Institute of Technology, the Library of Congress, the National Technical Information Service, and the Federal Information Exchange. Do you need a login ID and/or password to connect to these sites? List three types of information found at each site.

2. Find a Telnet or Gopher server that displays the current time anywhere in the world. What is its URL? Find a Telnet or Gopher server that displays the current weather anywhere in the world. What is its URL?

3. Locate at least four different screen-saver shareware programs for Microsoft Windows 95. What are their filenames? Where can they be downloaded from? How much disk space do they require to run? What do they do?

4. Locate at least three different Gopher servers that offer maps. What kind of maps are they? What is the Gopher URL to locate them?

5. Write a summary of all information you found.

6. Exit Netscape.

Accessing Internet Services with Unix

Finding Online Resources for the Libby Civic Theater

OBJECTIVES

In this tutorial you will:

- Learn what Unix is and how to use it to access the Internet

- Access a Unix host on the Internet using Telnet

- Use Unix commands during a Telnet Internet session

- Use the Unix Pine e-mail program to compose, edit, and send an e-mail message

- Use the Unix Pine e-mail program to retrieve, reply, save, print, and delete e-mail messages

- Log on to an anonymous FTP server on a Unix host

- Navigate an FTP server on a Unix host

- Download a file to your Student Disk using FTP

- Telnet to a Unix host computer to access a freenet

CASE

Libby Civic Theater

The Libby Civic theater, a newly formed not-for-profit public community theater, opened approximately one year ago. Box office ticket sales and membership gifts from individuals, corporations, and foundations make its productions possible. Much of the theater's costuming inventory comes from donations, and volunteers create stage sets. As the theater's director, Michael Mukai is responsible for marketing and overall operations. He faces constant challenges: the budget is minimal, and the costs of purchasing play scripts, printing services, and supplies continually rise. Michael reports directly to the Performing Arts Council, which is run by a volunteer board of directors.

Recently a board member donated a used computer to help Michael manage the theater's affairs. Michael uses the Internet at home and was pleased to learn that the donated equipment included a modem. Although the modem is not fast enough to support a GUI browser, and the theater cannot currently afford a PPP dial-up Internet account, Michael plans to connect to the Internet via the local freenet. A **freenet** is a nonprofit organization offering free access to networking services, and sometimes to the Internet, to individuals within a geographical region. Michael hopes to find free or low-cost play scripts and other performing arts resources on the Internet to help build the Libby Civic Theater's inventory and repertoire. As Michael's new assistant, your main responsibility is to use the Internet to find new and inexpensive resources for the theater. In addition, you will use the donated computer to assist with general office correspondence. To access the Internet, you need to learn to use the Unix operating system, as well as the Unix Pine e-mail program for general communications.

In this session you will learn what Unix is and how to use it to access various Internet services. You will use Telnet to connect to a remote Unix host computer. You will learn to use Unix commands and to access Unix Help.

What Is Unix?

Unix is a multi-user and multitasking computer operating system. An **operating system** is the program that controls the computer's internal functions and, in turn, lets the user control the computer's operations, including its software and hardware. Unix is used on a wide variety of computers, from mainframes to personal computers. It was one of the first computer operating systems to take advantage of a distributed programming environment. Instead of existing as one single program, the Unix operating system consists of many software tools that work together. The programs can rely on their own features and the specific operating system tools necessary for performing individual functions.

Unix was first developed at the AT & T Bell Laboratories in the early 1970s. Educational institutions were some of the earliest Internet users to utilize this operating system for Internet access. In 1979 the operating system was modified and enhanced at the University of California at Berkeley. The Berkeley Unix version was used extensively to develop the IP protocols and served as the model for many of today's popular Internet tools such as e-mail, FTP, and remote login capabilities.

Using Unix to Access the Internet

Before the development of GUIs to access the Internet, most Internet services were only available through computers using the Unix operating system. Throughout the previous tutorials you have used the Netscape GUI to access Internet services. However not every computer system you work with will have a GUI browser. Although GUIs are popular on the Internet, many educational institutions and local ISPs continue to offer Internet access through a computer, or host, using Unix.

The powerful and flexible Unix operating system allows individual configurations for each user. Although your Unix Internet connection at school may look entirely different from the one you use at home, they both function in the same way. You begin your Internet session by logging on to a remote host using your specified login ID and password. Most Unix hosts require you to have an established account on the system to access its services, although some let you log on anonymously, using the word "anonymous" or "guest" as your login ID and your e-mail address as your password. Often your login ID is the same as the user ID portion of your e-mail address. If a LAN already links your computer to the Internet, the login process is usually accomplished by using a Telnet, FTP, or Gopher client. For example, to access an Internet service using a computer already connected to the Internet, you select a menu item or icon. If your computer is not already connected to the Internet, you reach the host via a dial-up communication program. The communication program uses configuration settings you provide, such as the phone number to reach the host and the host's Internet address, to access the system. You are prompted to enter your login ID and password to connect to the host, like you do in a network session. After you connect to the Unix host, you use the programs or services available to you according to your access rights.

You will use Telnet to access Unix hosts on the Internet throughout this tutorial. Telnet is the cornerstone protocol that Unix systems use to handle the remote login capability to another Internet host. After it negotiates opening a session on another host, you can issue commands to the Telnet server on the remote computer for execution.

When you log on to an Internet host using Unix, you are usually placed in a program called the shell. The **shell** is a utility program that provides a text-based menu to interface with the operating system. As with Telnet, you may also encounter a host with a command-line interface, or **command prompt**, where you enter commands to accomplish tasks. **Commands** are special words or character strings that are part of the operating system's language used to invoke specific operations. You can either type commands after the command prompt and press the Enter key to execute them, or the shell can act as a command interpreter, taking each command you issue and passing it to the operating system for execution. Commands you may commonly invoke with either a shell or command prompt interface include the rm command, used to remove or delete a file, and the passwd command, used to change your account password. The upcoming section discusses commands in more detail.

Often the command prompt displays a character at the start of the command line that indicates that the operating system is ready to receive your commands. This is usually a percent sign (%) or a dollar sign ($), but it may vary on different hosts. Sometimes the command prompt also displays the user's login ID, the date and time, or the default sub-directory name. Although some Unix hosts bypass the command prompt and place the user directly in a shell, others use a Gopher menu system, Lynx, or Hytelnet for access. You will use the Unix command prompt throughout this session to access the Internet.

After completing a Unix session, a user logs off the Unix host by issuing the command logout, bye, exit, or quit, or an abbreviation of these. He or she then exits the program used to access the remote host, such as a Telnet client.

Accessing the Internet Using Unix

To access the Internet using a Unix host, you connect to the host, enter your login ID, and then enter your password. Unix hosts are case-sensitive, so you must type the login ID and password exactly as they appear. A Unix host interprets a capital Z differently than a lowercase z.

Michael gave you the login information for the theater's Unix account, obtained through the local freenet, along with some general Unix command information to help you navigate the Unix host. You connect to the Unix host and access the Internet using the Telnet client that comes with Windows 95, known as Microsoft Telnet.

REFERENCE window	**ACCESSING THE INTERNET FROM A UNIX HOST**
	■ Connect to the Unix host using a client program or dial-up communications program.
	■ Enter your login ID, then press the Enter key.
	■ Enter your password, then press the Enter key.
	■ Initiate an Internet service by issuing a Unix command or by selecting a menu item from the shell program.

To access the Internet from a Unix host:

1. Click the **Start** button on the Windows 95 taskbar, then click **Run** to open the Run dialog box.

2. Type **Telnet** in the Run dialog box, then click the **OK** button. This launches the Windows 95 Telnet client on your computer.

   TROUBLE? If an error message states the file cannot be found, you might have typed the program name incorrectly, or the installed Telnet client on your computer might have a different name. Ask your instructor or technical support person for assistance.

   TROUBLE? Your school may not have a Unix host or may not allow student access to its Unix host. Ask your instructor or technical support person for assistance.

3. Click **Connect** on the Telnet menu bar, then click **Remote System**. The Connect dialog box opens. See Figure 7-1.

Figure 7-1 ◀
Using Telnet to
connect to a
Unix host

type your school's
Unix host address
here

click to connect to the
Unix host

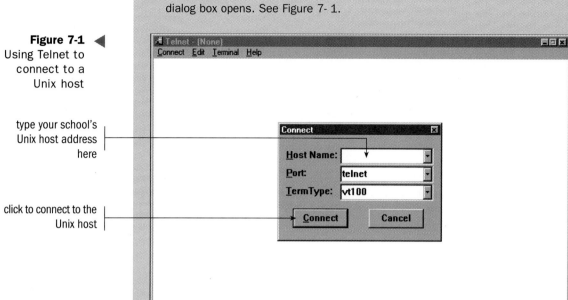

TROUBLE? If your screen looks different than the one in Figure 7-1, you may be using a Telnet client other than Microsoft's Telnet. If necessary, ask your instructor or technical support person for assistance.

4. Type the **host name** (the domain name or IP address associated with your school's Unix host) in the Connect dialog box. Click the **Connect** button to connect your computer to the remote host computer. You are now prompted for your login ID and password.

TROUBLE? If you do not know your Unix host's name, ask your instructor or technical support person for assistance.

5. Type your **login ID** after the user name prompt, and press the **Enter** key. A password prompt appears.

6. Type your **password** after the password prompt. For security, your password may not appear on the screen, or it may appear as a series of asterisks. Press the **Enter** key to log on to the Unix host.

You are now logged on. Your cursor appears after the Unix command prompt, and you may see a welcoming screen or a motd (message of the day).

TROUBLE? If you receive the message "user unknown" or "incorrect password" when you try to log on, you may have typed your login ID or password incorrectly. Repeat Steps 5 and 6, making sure to use uppercase and lowercase letters correctly.

TROUBLE? If you are placed directly in a shell program, choose the menu selection Unix command prompt, Unix prompt, Unix commands, or a similarly worded menu selection to place your cursor after the Unix command prompt. If a menu selection for reaching the command prompt does not exist, your Internet account may not allow you this level of access. Ask your instructor or technical support person for assistance.

Now that you have successfully logged on to the Unix host, you are ready to learn some common Unix commands, including the one you need to begin your Telnet session.

Using Unix Commands

Many Unix commands perform tasks similar to those in other operating systems, such as listing all of the files in a particular directory. Michael has given you a list of common Unix commands and their functions, shown in Figure 7-2. Not all hosts utilize the same Unix commands, because there are different versions of the Unix operating system. To instruct the operating system how to perform a command, some commands require additional information. This additional information is called an **argument**. Unix arguments are words or numbers added to a command to modify or expand its results. An argument is typed on the same line as the Unix command. Figure 7-3 shows an example of an argument added to the Unix print command to instruct Unix to print a document called "donations.ltr".

Figure 7-2 ◀
Common Unix commands

File Manipulation	Description	Process Control	Description
cat F	Display contents of file F on screen.	^Z	Suspends current process.
chmod	Changes access protection modes.	bg	Puts suspended process into background.
cp F1F2	Copies file F1 into F2.	^S	Stops output.
mv F1F2	Renames file F1 as F2.	^Q	Resumes output.
rm F	Removes file F.	fg	Puts suspended process in the foreground

Environment Status	Description	Environment Control	Description
ls	Lists files in current working directory.	cd D	Changes to directory D.
who	Lists users logged in.	mkdir D	Creates new directory D.
pwd	Displays working directory.	rmdir D	Removes directory D (D must be empty).
date	Displays date and time.	mv F D	Moves file F to directory D.
help	Displays list of help topics.	passwd	Changes password.
man C	Displays UNIX help for command C.	login L	Logs onto account with login name L.
uptime	Displays how long UNIX system has been functioning and number of users logged on.	logout	Ends current login session.
		^D	Same as logout.

Figure 7-3 ◀
Unix print command with argument

command prompt

command prints specified file

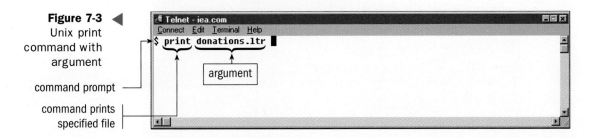

You can modify the actions of many Unix commands by using switches. **Switches** are options that can be added to a command to change its output or action. You can identify a switch by typing a preceding hyphen (-). For example, the ls command displays a listing of files in a directory, but by adding a -l switch (ls - l), Unix lists not only the contents of a directory, but additional information such as the size of each file and the time and date the file was last changed. Similar to arguments, switches are typed on the same line as a command. When you press the Enter key, the operating system invokes the command while performing the specifications noted by the switch.

The Unix account set up for you at the theater has disk space available for downloading files. You begin your Telnet session by issuing the list command to see what files already exist in the theater's allotted disk space on the Unix host.

To issue the Unix list command:

1. After the Unix command prompt, type **ls**. See Figure 7-4. Your command prompt may differ depending on your account type or the Unix version installed on your Unix host.

Figure 7-4 ◀
Unix list
command

command prompt ──────

press the Enter key
to display a list of
files in the current
directory

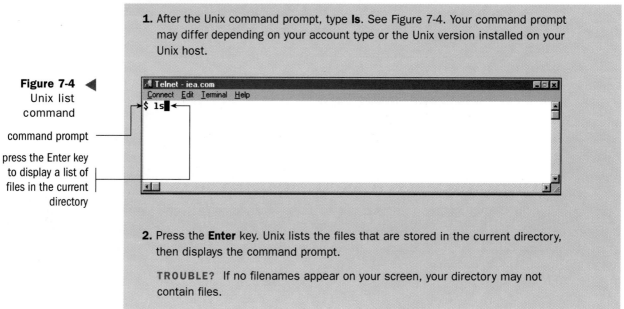

2. Press the **Enter** key. Unix lists the files that are stored in the current directory, then displays the command prompt.

TROUBLE? If no filenames appear on your screen, your directory may not contain files.

The result of the ls command is similar to the results of the DOS dir command and to the Windows 95 Explorer that displays directory file listings. You can use one of Unix's help facilities to locate additional arguments or switches used with the ls command.

Getting Help in Unix

The three most common methods of locating help are using the man (short for manual) command, accessing command-line help, or using the apropos command. Figure 7-5 explains each method. The main help facility for the Unix operating system is in the online reference manual, located in a directory with other operating system files on the Unix host. To access reference information about a specific command in this manual, type man *command* where *command* is the Unix command's name, and then press Enter. The help information that appears in your window lists the command and describes its use and format(s), including arguments and switches. The manual page sometimes references software release and update information and also directs you to information on related topics.

You now use the man help command to locate additional information about the ls command.

Figure 7-5 ◀
Unix help
methods

Method	Description	Example
man	Online Unix manual includes command names, usage, and description.	"man print" displays detailed information about the Unix print command.
apropos	Helps find a command name based on the command you are looking for.	"apropos print" displays a listing of Unix commands that have the word "print" in their description, such as the Unix Print or Printmail commands.
command line	Typing a Unix command without arguments after the command prompt shows reminders of options needed and sample usage.	"mkdir" displays a reminder that a directory name must be specified.

To use the manual help facility:

1. After the command prompt, type **man ls**, then press the **Enter** key. See Figure 7-6. Unix returns detailed information on the list command, including examples of arguments and switches that you can issue with the command. Your screen may differ from the one shown Figure 7-6, depending on the version of Unix your host is running.

Figure 7-6 ◀
Using the Unix
man help
command

command name ⟶

synopsis shows brief
summary of
command usage

description shows
how command
functions

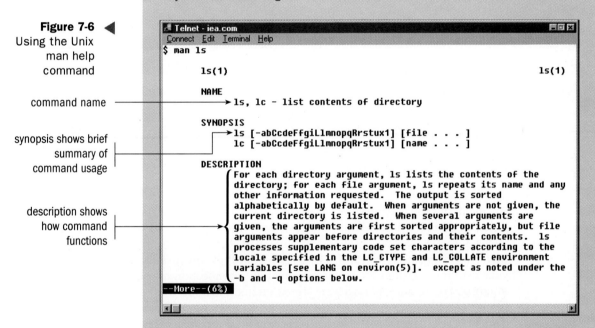

2. Continue reading and pressing the **Spacebar** until you reach the end of the help text and the Unix command prompt reappears.

Now that you know how to access a Unix host on the Internet and are familiar with some Unix commands, you can begin accessing some Internet services available from the theater's Unix account.

You have completed Session 7.1. If you are not going to work through Session 7.2 right now, log out of your Telnet session and close your Telnet client. When you are ready to begin Session 7.2, start your Telnet client, log on to your Unix host, access the Unix command prompt, and then continue with the session. If you want more information on Unix, you can select the Tutorial 7 link on your New Perspectives on the Internet Using Netscape Navigator—Introductory Student Online Companion Web page to find additional resources.

Quick Check

1 Unix takes advantage of a _____ environment that consists of many software tools working together.

2 The Unix operating system was used to help develop the _____ protocols.

3 Before the creation of a _____, command prompts and shells on Unix hosts were the primary methods of accessing Internet services.

4 When logging on to a Unix host anonymously, you use your _____ as your account password.

5 The _____, _____, or _____ commands are generally used to log off a Unix host.

6 True or False: The Unix operating system is case-sensitive.

7 _____ are options that you can add to a Unix command to change the command's output or action.

8 The _____ help command returns a description of the command's use, and format(s), including arguments and switches.

SESSION 7.2

In this session you will learn to send e-mail using the Unix Pine e-mail program. You will use Pine to compose, edit, send, retrieve, reply, save, print, and delete e-mail messages.

Using Unix Pine

The Computing and Communications group at the University of Washington created and still maintains the Unix **Pine** e-mail system. The Pine mail client supports several protocols including SMTP, which allows e-mail delivery between mail servers, and NNTP, which allows a user to read newsgroups within the mail client. Pine also uses **IMAP**, the Interactive Mail Access Protocol, which is part of the TCP/IP protocol suite. IMAP lets you retrieve your mail from various locations by providing a connection to a Unix host where Pine is installed. Your e-mail messages are stored on and retrieved from the Unix host instead of being transferred to your local hard drive. Because your e-mail messages reside on the host computer, you can access them wherever you are logged on. This feature is handy if you need to access e-mail from work, home, or school, or while traveling. A powerful e-mail program, Pine has many features that Netscape Mail supports, including file attachments, distribution lists, and folders. However, to complete your current communications at the theater you only need to perform the basic e-mail tasks, such as composing, sending, and retrieving e-mail messages.

The Pine opening screen contains three primary elements: the status bar, the main menu, and the command list. See Figure 7-7. The **status bar** located at the top of the opening screen indicates the status of the Pine program. The status bar changes depending on what Pine feature you are using; it may display the name of the folder you are currently viewing and how many messages are in the folder. The status bar always includes the version number of the Pine program you are using. The **main menu** below the status bar lists general Pine commands. To select from a menu, you may either highlight the menu selection using your arrow keys and then press the Enter key, or type the first letter of the command, for example, A to access Pine's Address Book feature. Unlike Unix commands, Pine is not case-sensitive. For example, you can access the Address Book feature by typing either A or a, or return to the main menu by typing either M or m after completing any Pine task. Finally, Pine commands are listed in a **command list** located on the bottom two lines of each screen, so you do not need to memorize commands. To select a command from the command list, simply type the highlighted letter or character associated with the command. For example, to access online help from the main menu, type a ? (question mark).

Figure 7-7 ◀
Pine opening
screen

status bar ——

main menu ——▶

command list ——▶

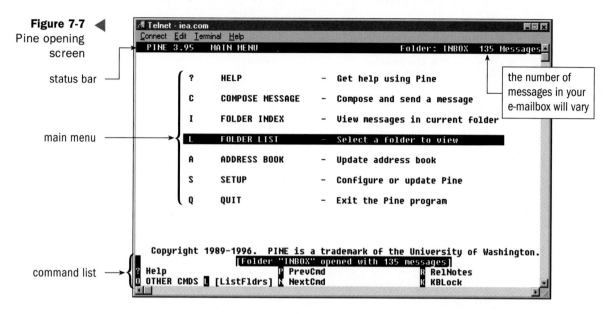

Some command lists include an option for accessing other commands, which appears as "OTHER CMDS." If this option is available, you press the highlighted letter O to view other commands available for that screen. In addition, the caret symbol (^) precedes some commands. The caret symbol indicates that you activate a command by holding down the Control key on your keyboard while pressing a particular key. For example, to send an e-mail message you compose, you use the ^X command.

You now access the Pine program from the Telnet connection you established earlier.

To access Pine:

1. After the Unix command prompt, type **Pine**, then press the **Enter** key. The Pine e-mail program starts, and the Pine opening screen appears. See Figure 7-7. Your screen may differ if your Unix host has a different version of Pine installed.

   TROUBLE? If you cannot access Pine through a Unix command prompt, you may be able to access it using the shell program installed on your Unix host. Select Pine from the shell menu. If you can't find a Pine menu selection, ask your instructor or technical support person for assistance.

   TROUBLE? If you cannot access Pine from the command prompt or shell program, your school may not have installed Pine on your host and you will have to skip this session. Continue to Session 7.3.

   You now use the Help command from the main menu to learn what type of online assistance the Pine program offers.

2. Type **?** at the main menu in Pine. General information about the Pine program appears on your screen along with a table of contents for online help. See Figure 7-8.

Figure 7-8 ◀
Pine Help

your Unix host name
is listed here (yours
will differ)

Pine version number
appears in status bar

command list
displays navigational
information and
commands for Pine
features

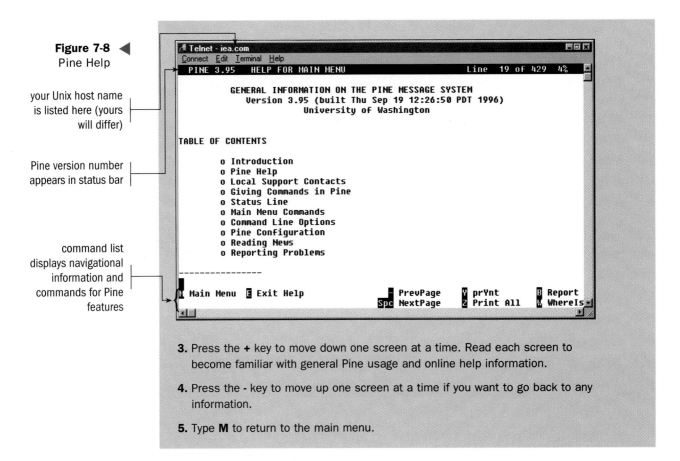

3. Press the **+** key to move down one screen at a time. Read each screen to become familiar with general Pine usage and online help information.

4. Press the **-** key to move up one screen at a time if you want to go back to any information.

5. Type **M** to return to the main menu.

You are now ready to use the Pine e-mail program to compose an e-mail message.

Composing an E-mail Message Using Pine

Pine is a character-based program with easy-to-use menus for message creation and handling. Many Pine features make composing and sending e-mail messages easy. To compose a message, you simply choose Compose Message from the main menu. This opens the Compose Message window where you type your e-mail message and supply the appropriate header line information. This window is similar to Netscape Mail: you type the recipient's e-mail addresses in the To: header line; you can send carbon copies by typing other users' addresses in the Cc: header line; and you describe the message topic in the Subject header line. If you want to attach a file to the e-mail message, specify the filename in the Attchmnt: header line. The file being attached needs to reside on the Unix host. When the Compose Message window appears, the command list at the bottom of the screen changes. Instead of displaying general Pine commands, it displays commands related to composing e-mail messages. Figure 7-9 lists and describes some of these commands. In Figure 7-9, the caret symbol precedes some command keys, indicating that you invoke these commands by holding down the Control key while pressing the highlighted letter.

Figure 7-9 ◀

Pine Compose
Message
window
commands

Command	Keystrokes	Description
Cancel	^C	Cancels message composition and returns you to the main menu.
Cut Line	^K	Cuts marked text or deletes current line.
Get Help	^G	Obtains help on command used for composing an e-mail message.
NxtP/End	^V	Moves you to the next page or the end of a message.
PrvPg/Top	^Y	Moves you to the previous page or the beginning of a message.
Send	^X	Sends the current message.
To AddBk	^T	Launches Pine's built-in Address Book.
UnDel Line	^U	Restores previously cut text.
Del Char	^D	Deletes the current character.
Rich Hdr	^R	Displays detailed header line information.
Attach	^J	Attaches a file to a message.
Postpone	^O	Postpones composing or sending a message.

Because scripts are expensive and the theater has a tight budget, Michael wants you to locate public domain plays. He is particularly interested in the Shakespearean comedies. Resources, such as plays, musical scores, and other literary works available through the **public domain** are not copyrighted. Authors make their works available through the public domain so that users do not need to incur redistribution costs and modification fees, or acquire permissions to use the resources. Michael knows that many Shakespearean plays are in the public domain, but he is not sure of their location. However, Michael's former associate, Cheryl Leonetti, may be able to help you locate them. Cheryl is presently coordinator for the annual Oregon Shakespeare Festival in Ashland, Oregon. You now compose a message to Cheryl, asking if she has information about the public domain Shakespearean play scripts. You also route a copy to Michael for his reference.

REFERENCE **window**

COMPOSING AN E-MAIL MESSAGE USING PINE

- In the opening Pine screen, press C.
- Type header line information.
- Type a message in the Message Text area.

To compose an e-mail message using Pine:

1. At the Pine main menu, press **C** to open the Compose Message screen. Your cursor automatically appears in the To: header line and the screen's name appears in the status bar. You are now ready to enter Cheryl's e-mail address.

2. Type **cheryll@vmedia.com** in the To field, then press the **Enter** key. Your cursor automatically moves to the Cc field.

3. Type **michaelm@libby.org** in the Cc field, then press the **Enter** key. Michael's e-mail address appears in the Cc field. Your cursor automatically moves to the Attchmnt field.

4. Press the **Enter** key to leave the Attchmnt field blank. If you wanted to attach a file to your message, you would enter its name here and Pine would send it with your message. Your cursor moves down to the Subject field.

5. Type **Shakespeare Play Scripts** in the Subject field, and then press the **Enter** key. The cursor moves down to the Message Text area.

   TROUBLE? Be sure to type the subject exactly as shown with initial capitalization.

6. Type the message shown in the Message Text area in Figure 7-10 exactly as it appears. Your completed message should look like Figure 7-10.

Figure 7-10 ◀
Composed
message

header lines ────▶

type your name here ────▶

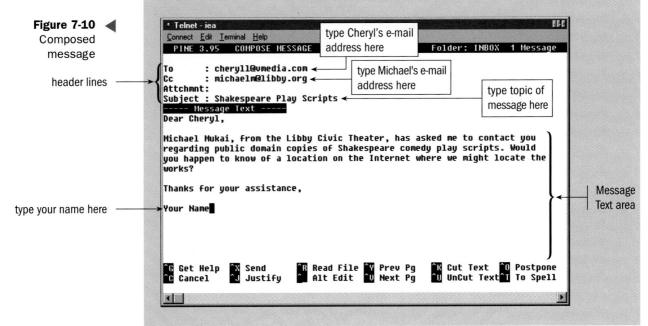

Because you are using Pine for the first time, you want to review the message you just composed and, if necessary, edit it before sending to Cheryl.

Editing an E-mail Message Using Pine

Pine's text-editing features let you modify your e-mail message easily without re-typing its entire contents. When editing an e-mail message you have many of the same text-formatting features available as in a word-processing program, but Pine's keystrokes for editing differ. Pine offers the Cut and Paste functions, as well as keystroke combinations for moving quickly through an e-mail message. You can add to the beginning, middle, or end of a message or edit any word or phrase it contains just as in your word-processing programs.

After reviewing your message, you decide to edit it to indicate that you are interested in Shakespeare's comedy plays.

To edit an e-mail message:

1. Press ↓ and → until your cursor is between the words "Shakespeare" and "play" in the Message Text area.

2. Press the **Spacebar** and then type the word **comedy**. See Figure 7-11.

Figure 7-11 ◀
Editing a
message

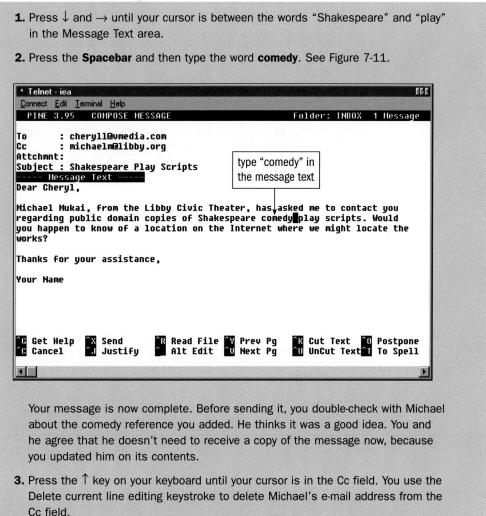

Your message is now complete. Before sending it, you double-check with Michael about the comedy reference you added. He thinks it was a good idea. You and he agree that he doesn't need to receive a copy of the message now, because you updated him on its contents.

3. Press the ↑ key on your keyboard until your cursor is in the Cc field. You use the Delete current line editing keystroke to delete Michael's e-mail address from the Cc field.

4. Press **Ctrl + k** to delete the entire line in the Cc field.

With Michael's approval, the completed e-mail message is ready to send.

Sending an E-mail Message Using Pine

After composing and editing a message and filling in additional header information, such as supplying e-mail addresses to send copies to other recipients or specifying file attachments, you are ready to send the message to the intended recipient(s). To send a Pine e-mail message, you press Ctrl + X. The same method you learned about in Tutorial 4 delivers the e-mail message. Other e-mail clients can retrieve a message created in Pine, and vice versa.

You now send the completed message to Cheryl.

To send an e-mail message using Pine:

1. With the e-mail message still displayed in your window, press **Ctrl + X**. A confirmation message appears asking you to confirm that you want to send the current message. See Figure 7-12.

Figure 7-12
Sending a
message

type "y" to send
e-mail to Cheryl

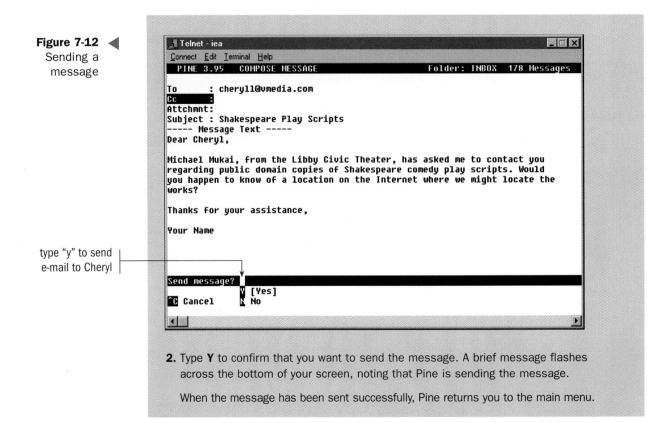

2. Type **Y** to confirm that you want to send the message. A brief message flashes across the bottom of your screen, noting that Pine is sending the message.

When the message has been sent successfully, Pine returns you to the main menu.

Your inquiry to Cheryl is finally on its way. Michael will be unavailable for most of the afternoon and asks you to go to the local building supply center to pick up materials for a new set. You hope Cheryl's reply will be waiting for you when you check your e-mail messages upon returning.

Retrieving an E-mail Message Using Pine

Pine organizes e-mail messages in three main folders, or storage areas, for related messages. When you first start Pine, it automatically assigns you three folders: Inbox, Sent-mail, and Saved-messages. Like Netscape Mail, Pine lets you create additional folders for organizational purposes; for example, folders for work-related and personal messages. Pine automatically places incoming e-mail messages in the Inbox folder. They remain there until you decide to delete the messages, or save them in another folder. To retrieve an e-mail message, you use the Folder Index screen to view a folder's contents. You can then access the Folder Index screen for the Inbox folder when starting Pine by typing an I at the main menu. Figure 7-13 list some commands available in the Folder Index screen that help organize e-mail messages. For example, to mark a message for deletion, you highlight the message you want to delete, then select the Delete command by pressing the D key on your keyboard.

Figure 7-13
Folder Index
screen
commands

Command	Keystroke	Description
Delete	D	Marks highlighted message for deletion.
Forward	F	Forwards highlighted message to another user.
Help	?	Obtains help on commands used to maintain a message list.
Main Menu	M	Returns to Pine main menu.
NextMsg	N	Highlights the next message in the folder.
PrevMsg	P	Highlights the previous message in the folder.
Other Cmds	O	Displays another command list.
ViewMsg	V	Displays highlighted message.
Spc	Spacebar	Displays next screen of messages.
Undelete	U	Undeletes a message marked for deletion.

The Folder Index screen presents a detailed summary of incoming or outgoing messages in the current folder. For instance, the Folder Index for the Inbox folder lists new messages with the N prefix, messages that you replied to with the A prefix, and messages that you marked for deletion with the D prefix. The Folder Index screen also lists the numbers that are automatically assigned to messages, the dates the messages were sent, the senders' names, the length (or size) of the messages in bytes, and the subjects of the messages. The status bar indicates the name of the folder you are viewing and the total number of messages in the folder.

After you view the contents of the Incoming folder, you can retrieve a message by using the arrow keys to highlight it, and then pressing the Enter key. The message's contents appear on your screen with the message's header line information. If the message takes more space than one screen, you can quickly view the next screen by pressing the Spacebar. To move to a previous screen, press the hyphen key (-).

Having returned from your errand, you check your Inbox folder to see if Cheryl replied to your e-mail message.

REFERENCE window

RETRIEVING AN E-MAIL MESSAGE USING PINE

- Highlight the message you want to retrieve.
- Press the Enter key.

To retrieve an e-mail message using Pine:

1. At the Pine main menu, type **I** to view the Folder Index for the Inbox folder. The Folder Index window displays your message list. See Figure 7-14. There is a new message, as the N prefix indicates. The message's date and length as well as its sender are also noted. The message is from Cheryl.

Figure 7-14 ◀
Folder Index
window

message arrives in
the Inbox folder (your
folder may differ)

"N" indicates a new,
unretrieved message

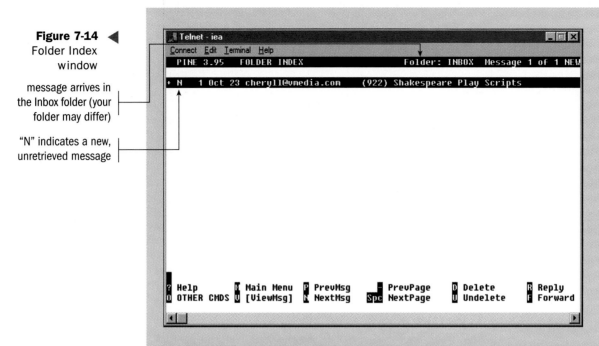

TROUBLE? Your Folder Index window may list other messages in addition to
Cheryl's. Continue to Step 2.

2. If necessary, press ↑ or ↓ to highlight Cheryl's message, then press the **Enter**
key. Figure 7-15 shows the text of Cheryl's message as it appears in the
Message Text window.

Figure 7-15 ◀
Retrieved
message

text of Cheryl's
message

command menu

TROUBLE? If you did not receive Cheryl's message, type M to return to the
main menu, wait a few minutes, and then repeat Steps 1 and 2. If you still do not
receive her message, repeat the Steps "To compose an e-mail message using
Pine." Be sure to type the subject line exactly as shown in Step 5 of those steps.

As you view the command menu on the Message Text window, you notice
commands to perform actions such as forwarding and replying to a message. To
perform any of these tasks, simply type the corresponding highlighted command
letter while the message is on your screen.

Cheryl provided the information that Michael wants. Grateful for her prompt response, you reply to her e-mail message.

Replying to an E-mail Message

You often need to reply to a received message. To reply to an e-mail message using Pine, you press the R key on your keyboard while the sender's message is in your Message Text window. You then answer a series of prompts concerning your reply. For example, the first prompt asks you if you want to include a copy of the original message in the reply. If you respond Yes, Pine places the original message in the e-mail reply and a greater than sign (>) before each line of text in the message indicating that it is quoted from the original e-mail. If more than one person received the original message, you need to indicate whether you want your reply routed to all original recipients. If you respond Yes, Pine automatically fills in the header line information for all recipients. The Message Text area then appears for you to type your reply. After composing the reply, you send the message using the Send command.

You compose a reply to Cheryl's message to thank her for the information.

To reply to an e-mail message using Pine:

1. With Cheryl's message still in the Message Text area, press the **R** key to invoke the Reply command.

2. When prompted "Include original message in Reply?", type **Y**. Pine automatically quotes the original message in the Message Text area.

3. Type the message reply shown in the Message Text area in Figure 7-16 exactly as it appears. When completed, your reply message should look like Figure 7-16.

Figure 7-16 ◀
Composed
reply

indicates message
is a reply

your reply

type your name here

quoted original
message

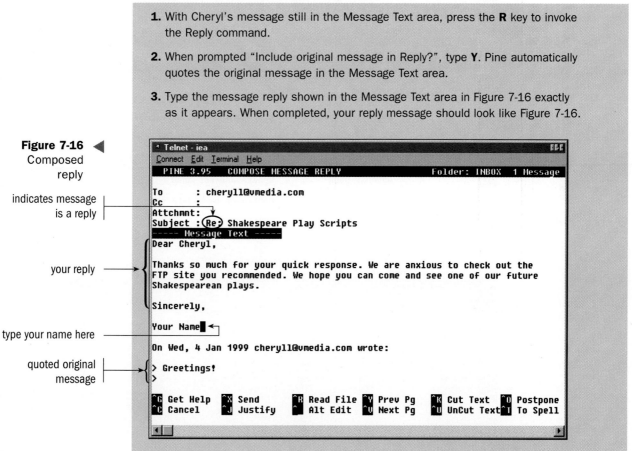

Before you have a chance to send your message to Cheryl, volunteers arrive to work on an upcoming production stage set. You need to help with this task. You haven't reviewed your reply message, so you are hesitant to send the message just yet.

Postponing an E-mail Message Using Pine

At times you may not have time to finish composing a message or you may need to gather more information before replying to e-mail you receive. Pine's **postpone** feature lets you save your e-mail message for future editing or delivery. By postponing a message, you can continue writing where you left off without starting from scratch. To postpone sending an e-mail message in Pine, you type CTRL + O while the message is still displayed in the Message Text area. When you are ready to access the message again, you redisplay it on your screen by typing C at the main menu or any message folder. Pine prompts you to confirm if you want to continue composing the postponed message. If you type Y, the incomplete message appears; if you type N, Pine opens a new message composition screen, and the postponed message remains inactive.

You decide to postpone sending your message to Cheryl until you can review your reply.

To postpone an e-mail message using Pine:

1. With the reply message still in the Message Text area, press **Ctrl + O** to postpone sending the current message.

Michael arrives back at the theater and stops to say hello. You mention the e-mail message you received from Cheryl and the reply you composed. Although pleased with your progress, Michael asks you not to send the reply to Cheryl; he wants to send her a handwritten note instead. You cancel the reply that you composed.

2. Type **C** at the Pine main menu. You are prompted to continue composing your message. See Figure 7-17.

Figure 7-17
Postponing an
e-mail message
using Pine

type "y" to continue
composing message

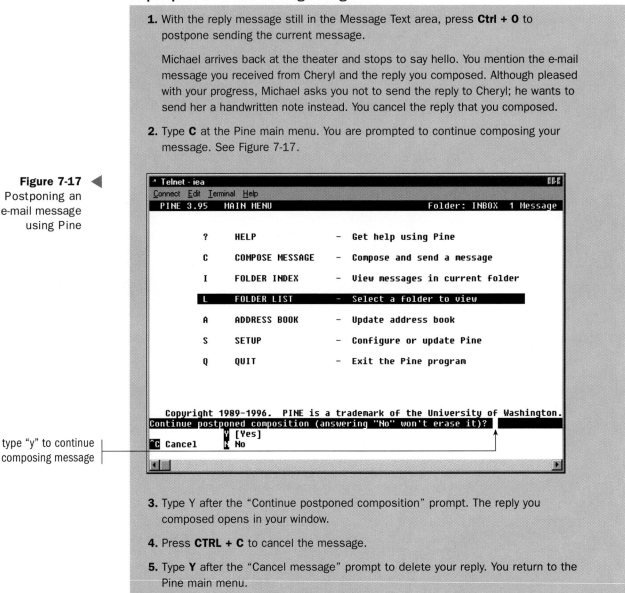

3. Type Y after the "Continue postponed composition" prompt. The reply you composed opens in your window.

4. Press **CTRL + C** to cancel the message.

5. Type **Y** after the "Cancel message" prompt to delete your reply. You return to the Pine main menu.

With your reply canceled, you want to print a copy of Cheryl's message for Michael, in case he wants to reference it when he composes his note.

Printing an E-mail Message Using Pine

When you want to keep a hard copy of an e-mail message, you can use Pine's print command. To print a message's contents, you can either highlight the message while viewing the Folder Index and type Y, or type Y when your retrieved message is in the Message Text window. Pine prompts you to confirm the print process with either method. Typing Y confirms the print action and subsequently prints the message.

You now print Cheryl's message for Michael and leave the printed copy on his desk.

To print an e-mail message using Pine:

1. With the Folder Index window for the Inbox folder still displayed on your screen, highlight Cheryl's message using the arrow keys, if necessary.

2. Type **Y**. A prompt asks you to confirm the print command. See Figure 7-18.

Figure 7-18 ◀
Printing an
e-mail message
using Pine

type "y" to print
message

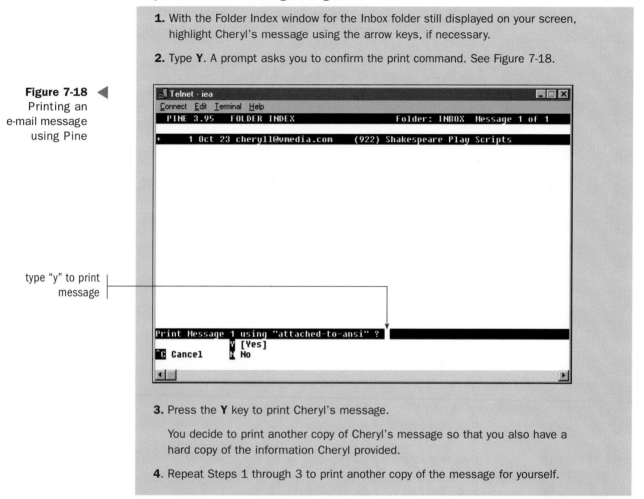

3. Press the **Y** key to print Cheryl's message.

You decide to print another copy of Cheryl's message so that you also have a hard copy of the information Cheryl provided.

4. Repeat Steps 1 through 3 to print another copy of the message for yourself.

Now that you have a hard copy of the FTP information Cheryl provided, you clean up your e-mail Inbox by deleting her message.

Deleting an E-mail Message Using Pine

You can delete an e-mail message you no longer need. Pine does not permanently delete a message until you **expunge**, or permanently remove, it from its folder. Like the Empty Trash Folder command in Netscape Mail, expunging a message erases it from the host's hard drive. If you do not expunge a message, you can always un-delete it and work with it again. When you quit Pine, a prompt asks if you want to expunge messages you marked for deletion during your Unix session. Deleting and expunging messages regularly keeps your folders manageable and saves disk space on the host server.

Because you have the FTP address for the Shakespearean works, you delete Cheryl's message.

To delete an e-mail message in Pine:

1. With Cheryl's message still highlighted on the Message Text window, press the **D** key to mark the message for deletion. Notice that a D now appears next to Cheryl's message. Because you are done for the day and the work crew is wrapping up, you expunge the deleted message and exit Pine.

2. Press the **X** key to expunge the message that you marked for deletion. Cheryl's original message disappears.

> **3.** Press the **Q** key to quit Pine, then press the **Y** key to confirm the quit. The Pine program closes and a command prompt appears.
>
> **4.** Type **Exit** to end your Telnet session, then close your Telnet client, if necessary, by clicking **File**, then clicking **Exit**.

Tomorrow you will follow Cheryl's lead to see if the Shakespearean site is available and what types of public domain works can be downloaded from it.

You have completed Session 7.2. If you would like more information on Pine, you can select the Tutorial 7 link on your New Perspectives on the Internet Using Netscape Navigator—Introductory Student Online Companion Web page to find additional resources.

Quick Check

1. Pine uses the _____ protocol that lets you retrieve your e-mail from different computers and have it reside on the mail server.

2. True or False: The Pine program is case-sensitive.

3. The _____ symbol shown on the Pine command list indicates that you press and hold down the Control key while pressing the highlighted letter to initiate a command or feature.

4. Pine automatically places incoming e-mail messages in the _____ folder.

5. The _____ window displays the contents of a Pine folder.

6. Pine does not permanently delete messages until you _____ them from the folder.

SESSION 7.3

In this session you will learn to browse an FTP site on a Unix host, FTP a file to your Student Disk, and connect to a freenet on a Unix host to locate information for the theater.

Accessing an FTP Site on a Unix Host

In Tutorial 6 you learned to use FTP to transfer files from one computer to another. Using FTP you can upload virtually any type of file to a remote computer, or download a file to your own computer. When connecting to a Unix host to download a file, you need to indicate the exact FTP server address to connect to, the directory where the file resides, and the file you want to retrieve. You can locate this information in many ways, including using search tools, reading newsgroup postings, or accessing the readme or index files found at most FTP sites. The readme and index files generally contain information about and descriptions of the files available at that site. Like Telnet, FTP has some use restrictions. You must either have an account on the remote computer you are trying to access, or the remote host must allow guest accounts. Recall from Tutorial 6 that sites allowing open access are called anonymous FTP servers. Most anonymous FTP servers contain the name ftp in their Internet address, but often the only way to tell if an FTP server offers guest logins is to try to access it. If using an anonymous or guest login, and your e-mail address as your password does not connect you to the server, the server most likely does not offer its files to the general public. The FTP server Cheryl suggested, ftd.std.com, does allow anonymous guest logins.

After you locate an FTP server to download files from, you must either have FTP client software installed on your computer, or the Unix host you are accessing the FTP server from must have the FTP server software installed. If you are not sure if your Unix host offers FTP, type FTP after the command prompt and then press the Enter key. If FTP is installed, the FTP prompt (ftp>) displays. To return to the command prompt from the FTP prompt, you type quit and press the Enter key. Later in this tutorial you will use the Windows 95 built-in FTP client to download a file.

It is important to remember that FTP servers on Unix hosts are case-sensitive. For example, a file directory named /PUBLIC differs from a directory named /public. FTP commands are case-sensitive as well. Figure 7-19 shows some commands used to navigate FTP servers. For example, if you want to list FTP commands available on an FTP server, you type the ? command at the FTP prompt.

Figure 7-19 ◀
Common
FTP commands

Command	Description
?	Displays a list of FTP commands.
bye or quit	Terminates the FTP session and quits the FTP client.
cd *directory*	Changes to the subdirectory named "directory."
lcd *directory*	Changes the current local directory to "directory."
ls or dir	Lists the contents of the current directory.
open	Connects to another remote FTP server.
pwd	Displays the current directory name.

When using an FTP client on your computer to download a file from a Unix host, you launch the FTP software client, specifying the domain name or IP address of the FTP server you are trying to access, and press the Enter key. For example, the command ftp cwru.edu connects you to the Case Western Reserve University FTP server, which contains the full text of U.S. Supreme Court decisions. The server then prompts you for a login ID or account name. If you have an account on the remote server, you enter your login ID; if the FTP server is anonymous, you type "anonymous" as your login ID and press the Enter key. After the password prompt, you type your account password; or if the FTP server is anonymous, you type your complete e-mail address. At this point, you can browse the site or search for files that you want to download. You use the cd command to change to the directory where the file you want resides.

As you look over the FTP information that Cheryl sent you, you analyze the address: ftp.std.com/obi/Shakespeare/Comedies/Shakespeare.comedies. The Shakespearean plays are stored on the FTP server named ftp.std.com. This stands for the anonymous FTP server at World Software Tool and Die, one of the world's oldest ISPs. The slash characters (/) denote subdirectories. The address tells you that a file named Shakespeare.comedies resides in a subdirectory named Comedies within a subdirectory named Shakespeare that is in a directory named obi, which stands for Online Book Initiatives.

You now access the FTP service to download a file from the Unix host to your Student Disk.

To FTP a file from a Unix host:

1. Click the **Start** button on the Windows 95 taskbar, then click **Run** to open the Run dialog box.

2. Type **FTP ftp.std.com** in the Run dialog box, then click the **OK** button. This launches the FTP client program on your computer and connects you to the anonymous FTP server at World Software Tool and Die. The FTP server prompts you for your login ID as shown in Figure 7-20.

Figure 7-20 ◀
Accessing an
FTP server on a
Unix host

type "anonymous"
as your login ID

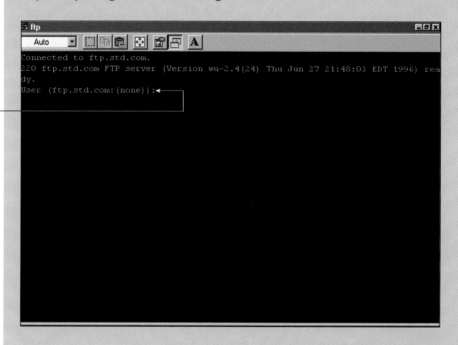

TROUBLE? If an error message displays stating that Windows 95 "Cannot find the file," you may have typed the FTP client program name incorrectly, or the installed FTP program on your computer may have a different name. Ask your instructor or technical support person for assistance.

TROUBLE? If you cannot connect to the FTP site, you may have typed its name incorrectly. The site may also be busy. Repeat Steps 1 and 2. If you continue to have trouble, ask your instructor or technical support person for assistance.

3. Type **anonymous** at the user name prompt as your login ID. Press the **Enter** key.

4. Type your **e-mail address** at the password prompt. Notice that your e-mail address does not appear as you type it. Press the **Enter** key.

You are now connected to the World Software Tool and Die anonymous FTP server. A welcoming message appears in your window, similar to the one shown in Figure 7-21. Once you've accessed an FTP server, you usually have to move around the directory to find the file you want. You navigate the World FTP site to see what files are available.

Figure 7-21 ◀
Connecting to
an FTP server

welcoming message
lists account
application
information for
std.com

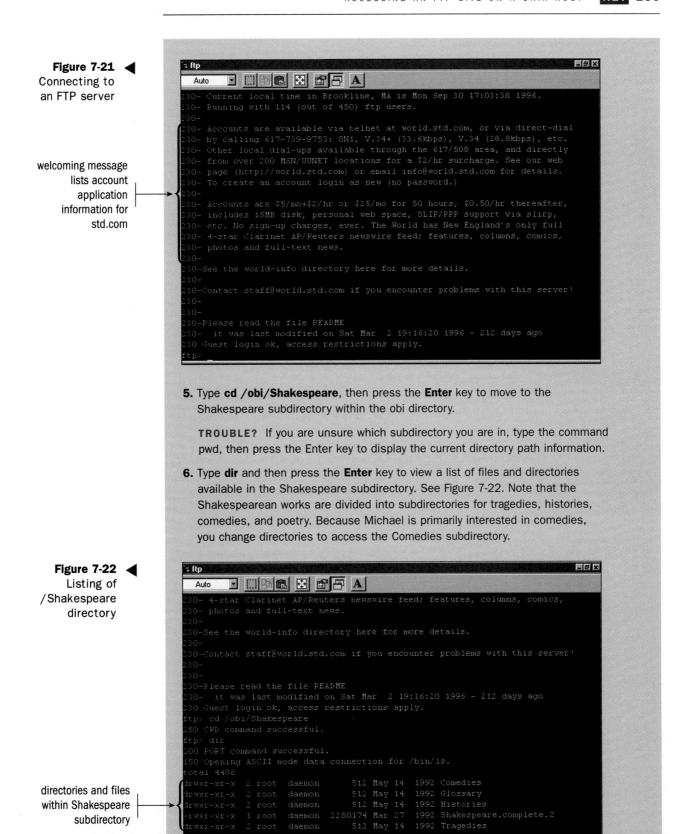

5. Type **cd /obi/Shakespeare**, then press the **Enter** key to move to the Shakespeare subdirectory within the obi directory.

TROUBLE? If you are unsure which subdirectory you are in, type the command pwd, then press the Enter key to display the current directory path information.

6. Type **dir** and then press the **Enter** key to view a list of files and directories available in the Shakespeare subdirectory. See Figure 7-22. Note that the Shakespearean works are divided into subdirectories for tragedies, histories, comedies, and poetry. Because Michael is primarily interested in comedies, you change directories to access the Comedies subdirectory.

Figure 7-22 ◀
Listing of
/Shakespeare
directory

directories and files
within Shakespeare
subdirectory

ftp prompt

7. Type **cd Comedies** at the ftp prompt, then press the **Enter** key to access the Comedies subdirectory.

8. Type **dir** at the ftp prompt, then press the **Enter** key to list files available in the Comedies subdirectory. You locate the file you want: Shakespeare.comedies. The Shakespeare comedies file is a large one. Before downloading it, you check with Michael to make sure he is aware of the file's size.

Downloading a File

When you find the directory where a file resides, you can download the file. To begin the downloading process, you issue the get *filename* command, where *filename* is the name of the file you want to download, and then press the Enter key. Use extra caution when downloading a file, as the get command overwrites existing files with the same name without warning. The FTP server reports the download's progress and indicates the size of the file to be transferred. The speed of file transfers depends on the size of the file you are downloading, the proximity of the FTP server, and the number of other users who are accessing the server. Common netiquette is to try to access FTP servers during non-peak hours if you need to download several files. After you finish accessing the FTP server, you type "quit" and the FTP program closes.

At times you may want to specify where to save a downloaded file, such as a directory on a host computer where you have your Internet account, your local hard drive, or your floppy disk drive. The **remote directory** is the directory on the FTP server that stores the files available for downloading, while the **local directory** is the directory on your computer or the host computer where you have an Internet account that is used to store the downloaded file. By default, the local directory is the directory where you initiate the FTP session. For example, using the Windows 95 FTP client located in the C:\Windows directory, the C:\Windows directory is the default local directory where a downloaded file would be copied. To save a file in a new location, you can use the lcd command.

Since the Shakespeare comedies file is a large file to download, Michael wants to view downloading policies first to make sure that there are no copyright restrictions and that the works are in the public domain. Since an FTP site's README file often contains rules governing downloading of files from a site, you return to the /obi directory and download the README file. Because Michael may want to view the README file on his home computer, you decide to save the file on a disk.

To download a file using the get command:

1. Make sure your Student Disk is in drive A or the appropriate drive.

2. After the ftp> prompt in the Comedies directory, type **lcd a:** to specify a default drive location for the downloaded files. Press the **Enter** key to save the downloaded file on your Student Disk.

The ftp> prompt reappears. You return to the /obi directory to search for the file.

TROUBLE? If you receive an "invalid command" message, you may have typed the lcd command incorrectly. Repeat Step 2.

3. Type **cd/obi**, then press the **Enter** key to connect to the obi directory. You can now download the README file.

4. Type **get README**, then press the **Enter** key to download the file. Figure 7-23 shows the FTP server's report on the size of the file to be transferred and the time it takes to transfer the file.

When the FTP server indicates the file has been transferred you receive a confirmation message. You now end the FTP session and close the FTP client software.

Figure 7-23 ◀
Transferring a
file with FTP

information regarding
the file transfer

```
ftp                                                            _ 8 X

Auto

drwxrwxr-x  40 obi    src      1024 Nov  1  1995 Zines
drwxr-xr-x   3 obi    obi       512 Aug 22 02:16 alt.quotations
drwxrwxr-x   2 obi    src       512 Sep 19  1991 crucible .
drwxrwxr-x   2 root   src       512 Jan 30  1995 customers
-rw-rw-r--   1 obi    src         0 Jan 23  1991 desert-storm.irc.5
drwxrwxr-x   2 obi    src       512 Sep 19  1991 hakmem.order
drwxr-xr-x   4 obi    src       512 Apr  7 22:55 incoming
drwxr-xr-x   2 obi    src       512 Mar 25  1996 lost+found
-rw-r--r--   1 src    src    837975 Sep 30 09:02 ls-lR
-rw-r--r--   1 src    src    213895 Sep 30 09:02 ls-lR.Z
-rw-r--r--   1 obi    src      3002 Feb  1  1993 marshall.islands
lrwxrwxr-x   1 root   0           3 Sep 11 05:37 obi -> obi
drwxrwxr-x   2 obi    src     17408 Dec  6  1993 opinions.supreme-court
drwxrwxr-x   2 obi    src      1024 Feb 10  1996 pr
-rw-r--r--   1 obi    src      3506 Feb  1  1993 tahiti
drwx------   4 root   0         512 Apr 17  1994 tmp
-rw-r--r--   1 obi    obi    216373 Sep 19  1995 unabomber
226 Transfer complete.
15606 bytes received in 13.57 seconds (1.15 Kbytes/sec)
ftp> get README
200 PORT command successful.
150 Opening ASCII mode data connection for README (4396 bytes).
226 Transfer complete.
4487 bytes received in 2.42 seconds (1.85 Kbytes/sec)
ftp>
```

5. Type **quit** after the FTP command prompt, and then press the **Enter** key to exit the FTP session and close the connection to the FTP server. Type **Exit** to close your FTP program.

You can download more than one file at a time by using the mget command and explicitly naming the file you want to retrieve. You can also download multiple files by using wildcards. Recall from Tutorial 6 that wildcards act as a match for a character or a group of characters or symbols. Although wildcards differ on individual servers, on Unix hosts, wildcards stand for any character, symbol, or set of symbols, such as numbers or letters. The most common Unix wildcard is the asterisk (*). For example, if you want to download all files that end with the file extension .TXT, you issue the mget *.txt command to retrieve them. Another common wildcard, the question mark symbol (?), stands for any single character. For example, by issuing the mget ca? command, you can download files named "cat," "can" and "cap," where the ? wildcard replaces the last letter of each filename when searching for files to transfer.

Based on the list of Shakespearean comedies available at the FTP site and the downloaded README file you gave him, Michael will decide which plays the theater will perform next season. Michael asks you to monitor other areas of the Internet for resources that may meet the theater's needs.

Accessing a Freenet

As you learned earlier in this tutorial, freenets are nonprofit organizations that provide networking services and sometimes free Internet access to individuals within a geographical region. Freenets have been compared to community bulletin boards where you can find community information. Users can post messages on a freenet for other users to read without paying membership dues or access fees. Public libraries often run freenets as a community service and rely heavily on volunteers for assistance in maintaining them. While freenets offer any individual guest access, some services such as e-mail are only available to registered users who set up an account. Account information usually appears in the opening window that displays once a user logs on to the freenet. Using menu-driven interfaces, you navigate a freenet by typing letters or numbers to make menu choices, which is common practice with many Unix shells.

Many freenets use the metaphor of a city to organize their services and files. Figure 7-24 shows the main menu for the Cleveland freenet, the oldest freenet in existence. The Cleveland freenet is divided into sections that offer specific types of information. To select a category you type its corresponding number. For instance, to select the Post Office section where you send and receive e-mail, you type the number 2 after the Your Choice prompt. Command information is listed at the bottom of the screen. For example, typing "h" accesses a Help menu, while typing "x" exits you from a freenet.

Figure 7-24 ◀
Cleveland
freenet main
menu

freenet address ──────

type a menu number
to access various
information and
services

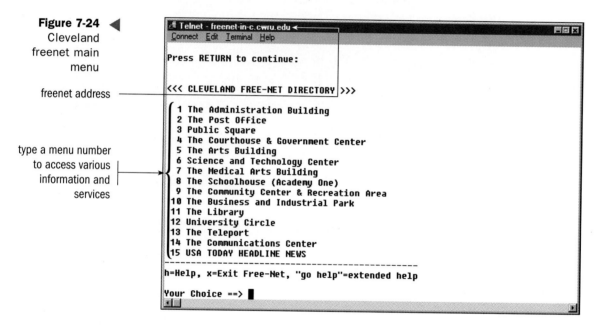

While browsing other Internet services to find pertinent resources for the theater, you find a reference to a Community Arts section on the freenet in the nearby city of Cleveland. You decide to Telnet to this freenet site to see if any information is available that may benefit the theater.

To connect to the Cleveland freenet:

1. Click the **Start** button on the Windows 95 taskbar, then click **Run** to open the Run dialog box.

2. Type **Telnet freenet-in-c.cwru.edu** in the Run dialog box, then click the **OK** button to start the Telnet client on your computer and connect to the remote Unix host that offers the Cleveland freenet service.

   TROUBLE? If the site is busy, try another address to reach the site, such as freenet-in-a.cwru.edu or freenet-in-b.cwru.edu.

3. Type **2**, then press the **Enter** key to enter the freenet site as a visitor. A menu similar to the one shown in Figure 7-25 appears.

Figure 7-25 ◀
Entering the
Cleveland
freenet

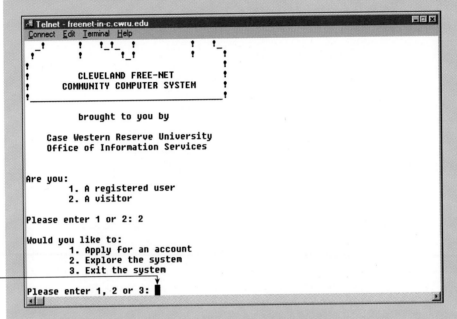

type "2," then press
the Enter key to
explore the
Cleveland freenet

4. Type **2**, then press the **Enter** key to explore the freenet. You may be presented with several windows of information. Read the navigation information listed at the bottom of the screen, and continue pressing the **Spacebar** or the **Enter** key until you reach the main Cleveland freenet directory.

5. Type **5**, then press the **Enter key** to Enter the Arts Building, type **2**, and then press the **Enter** key to enter the Literary, Theatre and Cultural Arts section.

6. Type **2**, then press the **Enter** key to enter the Theatre Arts section. See Figure 7-26. Scanning the list of available subjects, you notice that several may be relevant to the theater's needs, including a reciprocal script swap and a place to post current productions.

If you had more time you could browse this section further by selecting individual menu items, but for now you jot down the subjects to discuss with Michael later.

Figure 7-26 ◀
Theatre Arts
section of
Cleveland
freenet

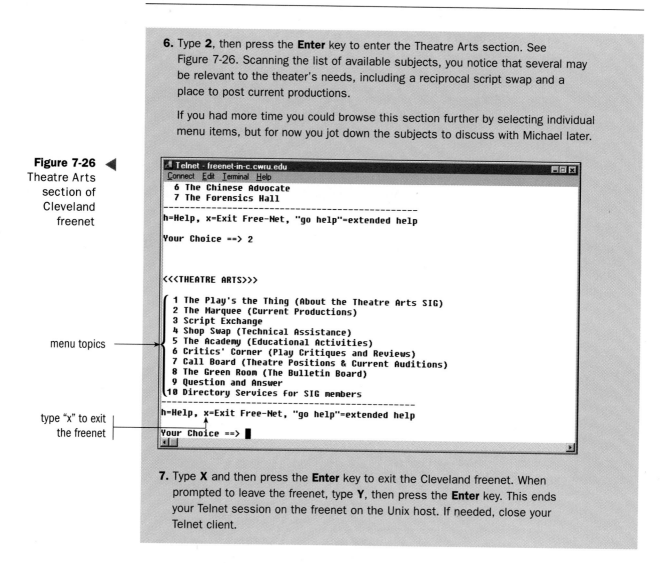

menu topics

type "x" to exit
the freenet

```
Telnet - freenet-in-c.cwru.edu
Connect  Edit  Terminal  Help
   6 The Chinese Advocate
   7 The Forensics Hall
----------------------------------------------------------
h=Help, x=Exit Free-Net, "go help"=extended help

Your Choice ==> 2




<<<THEATRE ARTS>>>

    1 The Play's the Thing (About the Theatre Arts SIG)
    2 The Marquee (Current Productions)
    3 Script Exchange
    4 Shop Swap (Technical Assistance)
    5 The Academy (Educational Activities)
    6 Critics' Corner (Play Critiques and Reviews)
    7 Call Board (Theatre Positions & Current Auditions)
    8 The Green Room (The Bulletin Board)
    9 Question and Answer
   10 Directory Services for SIG members
----------------------------------------------------------
h=Help, x=Exit Free-Net, "go help"=extended help

Your Choice ==> █
```

7. Type **X** and then press the **Enter** key to exit the Cleveland freenet. When prompted to leave the freenet, type **Y**, then press the **Enter** key. This ends your Telnet session on the freenet on the Unix host. If needed, close your Telnet client.

Later in the day you let Michael know about the value of the Cleveland freenet and some of the topics you found relating to theaters. It appears that the Cleveland freenet will be a viable place to network with other performing arts enthusiasts as well as a way to distribute information about the Libby Civic theater's productions. Based in part on your efforts, the theater is planning to sponsor two Shakespeare comedies, *The Taming of the Shrew* and *Much Ado About Nothing*, in the coming year.

You have completed Session 7.3. If you want more information on using FTP from a Unix host or freenets, you can select the Tutorial 7 link on your New Perspectives on the Internet Using Netscape Navigator—Introductory Student Online Companion Web page to find additional resources.

Quick Check

1. Which two files generally contain information and descriptions about files available at an FTP site?
   a. info.txt
   b. index
   c. descriptions.doc
   d. readme
   e. file_names

2. True or False: The FTP get command overwrites existing files with the same name without warning.

3. List three things that affect the transfer speed of a file being downloaded from an FTP server.

4. Using the FTP _____ command, you can specify the _____ to save the downloaded file to.

5. Which command FTP's a single file from a Unix host?
   a. ftp
   b. transfer
   c. get
   d. download

6. A wildcard stands for any _____, _____, or _____.

7. Write a two-sentence definition of a freenet in your own words.

Tutorial Assignment

The Libby Civic Theater has experienced great success and growth over the last year. You received a promotion to operations manager and you work full-time. Next week Michael is purchasing a new computer to assist you with your new responsibilities. He has hired Pat Aumundson, a part-time office assistant, to fill your old job. Pat's primary responsibility is box office activities, and she is using your old computer. To make the transition easier, Michael has asked you to spend the next week helping to train Pat and creating an office procedures manual that references key office tasks, including computer use. As you begin compiling material for the manual, you come across a reference that you think comprehensively explains the FTP process. However, you think the language may be too technical. You FTP the FAQ file from the Massachusetts Institute of Technology site and print it later for possible inclusion in the new manual. Also, as part of your training curriculum, you decide to create an e-mail message that will be used to demonstrate Pine's features. You create the e-mail and send it to your own e-mail address because Pat doesn't have a freenet account yet. During the training session, Pat uses your account and retrieves your message to learn how to compose and send e-mail messages.

Do the following:

1. Make sure your Student Disk is in drive A.
2. Start the FTP client on your computer.
3. Open the rtfm.mit.edu anonymous FTP site.
4. Log on to the server as "anonymous."
5. Use your full e-mail address as your password.
6. Change to the /pub/usenet/news.answers/ftp-list directory, the FAQ file's location.
7. Type "lcd a:\" to change the local drive and directory to your Student Disk in drive A.

8. Make sure you are in the /pub/usenet/new/answers/ftp-list subdirectory.
9. Type "get faq" to download the file to your Student Disk.
10. Type "quit" to exit the FTP session and close the FTP program.
11. Start the Pine e-mail program.
12. Compose an e-mail message welcoming Pat to the theater.
13. Send the message to your own e-mail address.
14. Exit Pine.

Case Problems

1. Exploring the Victoria Freenet Nikki Louis is president of the student council of the University of Victoria in Victoria, British Columbia, in Canada. She uses the local freenet to do research on the Internet for school work, to communicate with her parents and friends, and to track local events and regional topics. The university has a sister college in Fairbanks, Alaska; the University of Alaska. As sister colleges, the two institutions exchange ideas and promote one another through goodwill. Soon, several students from the student council of the University of Alaska will visit the University of Victoria to help foster the relationship between the two schools. As president of the council, Nikki is making arrangements for the student's arrival and looking for different types of entertainment for the visiting students while they are in Victoria. She wants you to help by exploring the Victoria freenet to search for upcoming community events. Nikki will use this information to help plan some outings for the visiting colleagues.

Start Netscape. The New Perspectives on the Internet Using Netscape Navigator—Introductory Student Online Companion Web page appears. Do the following:

1. Click the Tutorial 7 link.
2. Click the Case Problems link.
3. Click the link for Exploring the Victoria Freenet for Nikki Louis in the Case Problem 1 section.
4. Log on to the freenet as a guest, and enter your e-mail address if you are prompted for a password.
5. Browse the site to find the following information. Make sure to compile the information, and write a report summarizing your findings.
6. Find three events listed in the Greater Victoria Community Bulletin Board Local Events section. What are the events? Where are they being held? What are the dates and times of the events?
7. Find three events listed in the Arts and Entertainment section. What are the events? Where are they being held? What are the dates and times of the events?
8. Are there any Special Interest Group (SIG) meetings that the students may be interested in attending? List three SIGs described on the freenet. For each SIG, are there any upcoming events or workshops? If so, where are they being held? What are the dates and times of the events?
9. Exit the freenet.
10. Close the Telnet client, if necessary.
11. Exit Netscape.

2. Baseball Statistics for Elliot Elliot Benjamin is a baseball scout for the New York Giants. He travels around the country to baseball games of the American and National Baseball Leagues and does much of his work on the road. Elliot often needs quick access to detailed information, such as player profiles; batting, fielding, and hitting statistics for individuals; game recaps; and current injury lists. He accesses the Internet by dialing his Internet Service Provider's 800 number, then uses a Telnet client and Lynx to access many sports-related Web sites. He recently became aware of a subscription service that ESPN offers on the World Wide Web (WWW). The service is called ESP-NET SportZone. Elliot wants you to research the ESPN site and locate information about the service, including the types of information offered and the costs associated with subscribing.

You Telnet to the Unix host at the University of New Jersey Institute of Technology and use their Lynx program to access the Web site. You then report the information to Elliot so that he may decide whether this service is valuable.

Start Netscape. The New Perspectives on the Internet Using Netscape Navigator Software—Introductory Student Online Companion Web page appears. Do the following:

1. Click the Tutorial 7 link.
2. Click the Case Problems link.
3. Click the link for Baseball statistics for Elliot in the Case Problem 2 section.
4. Enter your login name as "www."
5. Select VT100 terminal emulation.
6. Type g, then enter the URL for ESPN: http://espnet.SportsZone.com.
7. Highlight the Subscriber Features topic hyperlink using your arrow keys, then select the link by pressing the Enter key.
8. Browse the site to find resources available from the service as well as subscription information.
9. Write a summary for Elliot, outlining the types of information available at the site and subscription information, including costs.
10. Exit the Lynx program and log off the Sunsite server.
11. Exit the Telnet client, if necessary.
12. Exit Netscape.

3. Monitoring Weather for Holland Farms Helen and Joe Fisher own and operate a family business, the Holland Farm, which has been in their family for years. Joe's great-grandfather originally bought the land and homesteaded on it in the late 1800s. Since then, it has passed from generation to generation. The farm primarily grows wheat; the warm, sunny climate of the Rathdrum Prairie region in central Kansas makes it the ideal location for wheat production.

Helen manages the farm's bookkeeping records. She markets and sells the wheat and tracks all records associated with the business. To help anticipate the next season's harvest and to keep an eye on world markets, Helen uses the Internet to monitor worldwide weather and trade markets. She gathers much of her information from the agricultural market database, called PEN pages, that the Pennsylvania State University maintains. The Telnet server on the Unix host at the school keeps recent updates on national agricultural markets; grain, meat, fruit, and vegetable futures; auctions; and worldwide weather information. Nancy wants you to find current weather conditions in two competitive grain market areas, Australia and South America.

Start Netscape. The New Perspectives on the Internet Using Netscape Navigator Software—Introductory Student Online Companion Web page displays. Do the following:

1. Click the Tutorial 7 link.
2. Click the Case Problems link.
3. Click the link for Monitoring Weather for Holland Farms in the Case Problem 3 section.
4. Enter your state's abbreviation as your login ID.
5. Enter the PEN pages section, then enter the Market News section.
6. Browse the site until you locate the weather information.
7. Select the Weather database.
8. Browse until you locate weather information for Australia and South America.
9. Write a brief summary report of your findings, making sure to include the date of the weather report.
10. Log off the Pennsylvania State Agricultural PEN pages server.
11. Close the Telnet client, if necessary.
12. Exit Netscape.

4. Underwater World E-mail Address Book Underwater World proprietor Rylee Wright uses information from the Internet for her monthly newsletter on scuba diving. On the Internet, she locates information such as reviews of the best scuba diving locations in the world, diving conditions reports, and diving tips. Although the main goal of her business is to sell scuba diving equipment, Rylee views the newsletter as a means of keeping in touch with customers. While researching information for the newsletter, Rylee has corresponded with many Internet users. She uses Pine to e-mail these users and others with whom she communicates regularly because e-mail is a quick, efficient method of corresponding. She repeatedly sends e-mail messages to many of the same people and asks you to help locate a more pragmatic method for addressing messages without remembering individual e-mail addresses. You use Pine's Address Book feature to create an entry for Steve and Susan Selway, a couple with whom Rylee frequently corresponds using e-mail.

Do the following:

1. Click the Start button on the Windows 95 taskbar, then click Run.
2. In the Run dialog box, type "Telnet," then click OK.
3. Click Connect, then click Remote System. Type your educational institution's host name in the Connect dialog box, then click Connect.
4. When prompted, enter your login ID and password.
5. After the Unix command prompt, type Pine, then press the Enter key, or select Pine from the Unix shell.
6. At the Pine main menu, type A to access the Address Book.
7. Type A to add a new entry to the Address Book.
8. Type "Selway" in the Nickname field, "Steve and Susan Selway" in the Fullname field, and "selway@uu.net" in the Addresses field. *Hint:* Press CTRL + G to access Pine's online help for the Address Book feature.
9. Press CTRL + X to exit the Address Book and save your new entry.
10. Press Q to quit the Pine program.
11. Close the Telnet client, if necessary.
12. Exit Netscape.

Answers to Quick Check Questions

SESSION 1.1

1 False

2 Defense

3 protocols

4 networks, protocols

5 names, numbers

6 World Wide Web

SESSION 1.2

1 Tim Berners-Lee

2 Browsers

3 highlighted, underlined or in a different color

4 hypertext linking

5 Web site

6 The first Web page to appear on your screen when you start a browser such as Netscape, or connect to a Web site.

7 an intranet

SESSION 1.3

1 True

2 newsgroup

3 subscribe

4 File Transfer Protocol (FTP)

5 gopher

6 Acceptable Use Policies (AUPs)

7 netiquette

SESSION 2.1

1 486

2 digital, analog

3 digital, analog

4 graphical

5 gateway

6 full-time or dedicated

7 firewall

SESSION 2.2

1 origination/destination addresses, size of datagram, sequential number

2 True

3 A router is responsible for physically moving datagrams of information from one Internet location to another.

4 to break up and sequentially number information into datagrams, to re-sequence out of order datagrams at their destination, and to perform error-checking activities to ensure reliable and accurate transmission

5 to provide addressing information to move datagrams across Internet networks, can break a datagram into smaller datagrams if needed, and to perform error-checking activities to ensure reliable and accurate transmission.

6 False

7 True

8 Domain Name Services (DNS)

SESSION 3.1

1 False

2 Yes. A home page is the first Web page to appear on your screen when you start a browser such as Netscape, or connect to a Web site.

3 scroll bars

4 frames

5 Universal Resource Locator (URL)

6 status bar, status indicator

7 Hyperlinking

8 handbook

SESSION 3.2

1 Hypertext Markup Language (HTML)

2 True

3 c

4 Universal Resource Locators (URLs)

5 True

6 True

7 .GIF, .JPG

8 False

SESSION 3.3

1 search tools

2 proximity of keywords within a document, frequency the keywords appear in a document

3 A boolean operator

4 What's Cool, What's New

5 navigational guide

6 Bookmarks

7 viewers or helpers

8 True

SESSION 4.1

1 retrieve, compose, send, save or delete e-mail messages

2 b

3 user ID, host address

4 mail folder, message header, message content

5 header lines, message body

6 address book

7 attachment

8 mistyped address, unknown host, unknown user, faulty hardware or software, malfunctioning transmission lines

SESSION 4.2

1 Re:Mail

2 quoting

3 Outbox

4 displays the file in your window, displays the file as a hyperlink, launches the necessary program, prompts you to save the file in a separate file

5 folders

6 False

SESSION 4.3

1 True

2 moderator

3 subscribing

4 list servers

5 colleagues, company Web pages, trade magazines, Web search tools

6 header lines

7 False

8 list server, an e-mail message

SESSION 5.1

1 False

2 c

3 False

4 thread

5 cross-posting

6 the newsgroup, the user who originally posted the article, both

7 *.answers

8 False

SESSION 5.2

1 Channels

2 clients, server

3 True

4 Arguments

5 motd (message of the day)

6 lurking

7 refresh

SESSION 6.1

1 client

2 True

3 port number

4 question mark

5 telnet://access.usask.ca

6 escape character

SESSION 6.2

1 True

2 Gopherspace

3 d

4 arrow, numbers

5 m

6 selections

7 asterisk

SESSION 6.3

1 File Transfer Protocol (FTP)

2 ftp://domain/subdirectory/filename

3 True

4 anonymous FTP site

5 uncompression utility

6 False

7 shareware

SESSION 7.1

1 distributed programming

2 IP (Internet Protocol)

3 Graphical User Interface (GUI) browser

4 e-mail address

5 logout, bye, exit

6 True

7 Switches

8 man or manual

SESSION 7.2

1 IMAP (Interactive Mail Access Protocol)

2 False

3 caret

4 Inbox

5 Folder Index

6 expunge

SESSION 7.3

1 b and d

2 True

3 size of the file, proximity of the FTP server, the number of other users accessing the server

4 lcd, default local directory

5 c

6 character, symbol, set of symbols

7 Freenets are non-profit organizations that provide networking services and sometimes free Internet access to individuals within a geographical region.

Index

Task Reference

TASK	PAGE #	RECOMMENDED METHOD	NOTES
Address Book, save	NET 112	From Address Book window, click File, Save As	Ctrl + S
Address Book, add entry	NET 113	From Address Book window, click Item, Add User, fill-in properties, click OK	Enter your Nick Name using all lowercase letters
Address Book window, open	NET 113	Click Window, Address book	
Address Book, use	NET 115	From Message Composition window, click Window, Address Book, double-click desired entry	
Archie, search	NET 205	Access from Gopher menu or Web sites, enter file name, press Enter	Must know exact name of file you are searching for
Attachment, include file with e-mail	NET 116	From Message Composition window, click [Attach], click [Attach File...]	
Attachment, include inline	NET 128	From Message Composition window, click View, Attachments as Links to toggle off (if necessary)	Attached files included in message body
Bookmark, add	NET 95	Click Bookmarks, Add Bookmark	Saves bookmark for current page, Ctrl + D
Bookmark file, create	NET 93	Click Bookmarks, Go to Bookmarks, File, Save As	Stores bookmark in separate file
Bookmark file, open	NET 94	Click Bookmarks, Go to Bookmarks, File, Open	To use an alternate Bookmark file
Bookmark, access	NET 95	Click Bookmarks, click desired Web page title	Ctrl + B
Bookmark, delete	NET 97	From Bookmarks window, click unwanted bookmark, press the Delete key	

Task Reference

TASK	PAGE #	RECOMMENDED METHOD	NOTES
Clipboard, copy to	NET 123	Select text, click Edit, Copy	Ctrl + C
Directory Buttons, show	NET 60	Click Options, Show Directory Buttons	
Distribution list, create	NET 118	From Address Book window, click Item, Add List	
Distribution list, add item	NET 118	Click Address Book entry, drag to list icon	Creates an alias to Address Book entry
File, download to disk	NET 208	Click hypertext link for file, click Save in list arrow, select 3½ Floppy (A:), click File name text box, type *filename*, press Enter	*filename* is the name of the downloaded file
File, open	NET 76	Click File, Open File	Ctrl + O
File, uncompress with PKUNZIP program	NET 209	Click Start, Run, type a:\pkzip\pkunzip.exe *filename*	*filename* is the name of compressed file
FTP, connect to a Unix FTP server	NET 238	Telnet to server, log on	To access server by domain name or IP address, use Telnet URL or Telnet client
Gopher, connect to a server with Netscape	NET 195	Click Open, type Gopher://*host.address*, press Enter	*host.address* is domain name or IP address of the Gopher site
Gopher, connect to a server with Telnet	NET 198	Click Open, type Telnet://*host.address*, press Enter	*host.address* is the domain name or IP address of the Gopher site
Gopher, navigate with Telnet	NET 197	Type number associated with link, or use arrow keys to highlight link, press Enter	Left and right arrow keys (←,→) move backward and forward one screen at a time

Task Reference

TASK	PAGE #	RECOMMENDED METHOD	NOTES
Gopher, navigate with Netscape	NET 195	Position mouse over hypertext link(s), click	Links can connect to multimedia items, documents, or other Internet services
Help, Netscape	NET 62	Click Help, Handbook	
History log, use	NET 73	Click Go, click page to return to	Ctrl + H
Hyperlink, abort	NET 69	Click [Stop]	
Hyperlink, initiate	NET 67	Position mouse over hypertext or hypermedia, click	
Hytelnet, access	NET 191	Telnet to a server offering Hytelnet, log on, select Hytelnet from menu	Using a server offering Hytelnet, type hytelnet at Unix command prompt
Hytelnet, navigate	NET 191	Type number associated with link, or use arrow keys to highlight link, press Enter	
Image, open	NET 78	Click File, Open File	
Image, save	NET 78	Click right mouse button on image to save, click Save this Image as	Saves image to a new file
IRC, connect to Unix IRC server	NET 166	Telnet to server, log on	To access server by domain name or IP address, use Telnet URL or a Telnet client
IRC, join or switch to a channel	NET 168	Type /join #*channelname*, press Enter	*channelname* is the name of channel to join or switch to
IRC, leave a channel	NET 170	Type /leave #*channelname*, press Enter	*channelname* is the name of channel to exit

Task Reference

TASK	PAGE #	RECOMMENDED METHOD	NOTES
IRC, log off a server	NET 170	Type /quit, press Enter, close Telnet client (if necessary)	
IRC, send a message	NET 169	Type *message*, press Enter	*message* is the text being sent
Location box, show	NET 60	Click Options, Show Location to toggle on (if necessary)	
Location, open	NET 72	Click 📖, type URL, press Enter	Ctrl + L
Lynx, access	NET 187	Telnet to a server running Lynx, log on	Using a server offering Lynx, type lynx at Unix command prompt
Lynx, navigate	NET 187	Type number associated with link, or use arrow keys to highlight link, press Enter	Left and right arrow keys (←,→) move backward and forward one screen at a time
Mail folder, create	NET 129	Click File, New Folder	
Mail Preferences, set identity	NET 110	Click Options, Mail and News Preferences, Identity, type user ID and name	
Mail Preferences, set servers	NET 106	Click Options, Mail and News Preferences, Servers, type SMTP and POP servers	
Mail, compose	NET 110	From Mailbox window, click 📧	
Mail, delete	NET 130	From Mailbox window, select mail, click 🗑	Must empty trash to erase messages from hard drive
Mail, empty trash	NET 131	From Mailbox window, click File, Empty Trash Folder	

Task Reference

TASK	PAGE #	RECOMMENDED METHOD	NOTES
Mail, forward	NET 125	From Mailbox window, select mail, click [icon]	Ctrl + L
Mail, get	NET 120	From Mailbox window, click [icon]	Ctrl + T
Mail, move messages to folders	NET 129	From Mailbox window, click message, drag to desired folder	
Mail, print message	NET 126	From Mailbox window, retrieve message, click [icon]	
Mail, reply	NET 122	From Mailbox window, select mail, click [icon]	Ctrl + R
Mail, retrieve	NET 120	From Mailbox window, click folder, click subject of message	
Mail, save message	NET 124	From Message Composition window, select mail, click File, Save As	Ctrl + S
Mail, send	NET 111	From Mailbox window, click [icon]	
Mail window, open	NET 106	Click Window, Netscape Mail	
Mailing list, subscribe	NET 135		See Reference Window "To subscribe to a mailing list"
Mailing list, unsubscribe	NET 138		See Reference Window "To unsubscribe from a mailing list"
Netscape, exit	NET 82	Click File, Exit	Ctrl + W
Netscape, launch	NET 54	Click Start, Programs, Netscape, click Netscape Navigator	
News window, open	NET 150	Click Window, Netscape News	

Task Reference

TASK	PAGE #	RECOMMENDED METHOD	NOTES
News, save article	NET 156	From News window, select article, click File, Save As	
News, print article	NET 159	From News window, select article, click [Print icon]	
News, reply to article with e-mail	NET 154	Click [Re: Mail icon]	
News, reply to article with posting	NET 154	Click [Re: News icon]	
News, retrieve article	NET 153	From News window, double-click newsgroup name, click article heading	
News, show newsgroup availability	NET 158	From News window, click Options, Show All Newsgroups	
News, subscribe to newsgroups	NET 158	From News window, click Subscribe status column to toggle on	
News, unsubscribe from newsgroups	NET 160	From News window, click Subscribe status column to toggle off	
Page, print	NET 82	Click [Print icon]	
Page, print preview	NET 80	Click File, Print Preview	
Pine, compose message	NET 228	From the Pine main menu, type C	
Pine, expunge deleted messages	NET 235	From Folder Index screen, type X	
Pine, mark message for deletion	NET 235	From the Folder Index screen, type D deletion	E-mailbox must be expunged to erase message
Pine, postpone sending a message	NET 234	From the Pine Compose message screen, press Ctrl + O	

Task Reference

TASK	PAGE #	RECOMMENDED METHOD	NOTES
Pine, print message	NET 235	From the Folder Index screen, type Y, Y	
Pine, reply to message	NET 233	From the Folder Index screen, select message, type R	
Pine, retrieve message	NET 230	From the Folder Index screen, select message, press Enter	
Pine, send message	NET 229	From the Pine Compose Message screen, type Ctrl + X, Y	
SMTP, set	NET 111	Click Options, Mail and News Preferences, set servers	
Source, view	NET 64	Click View, Document Source	
Telnet, connect to a server	NET 187	Click Open, type Telnet://*host.address*, press Enter	*host.address* is domain name or IP address of the Telnet site
Telnet, disconnect from a session	NET 189	Type logout, log off, exit, quit, bye, or q, press Enter	Individual Telnet sites differ
Telnet, issue escape character	NET 190	Press Ctrl +]	
Toolbar, show	NET 60	Click Options, Show Toolbar to toggle on	
Unix, listing of files	NET 222	At a Unix command prompt, type ls	
Unix, online manual help	NET 223	At a Unix command prompt, type man *commandname*	*commandname* is the name of command referencing help for
UserID, set	NET 110	Click Options, Mail and News Preferences, Identity	

Task Reference

TASK	PAGE #	RECOMMENDED METHOD	NOTES
Veronica, search	NET 200	Access from Gopher menu, enter search criteria, press Enter	Entering more than one word in search criteria is similar to using AND Boolean operator
Viruses, scan disk for	NET 211	Click Start, run, type c:\dos\mwav.exe, click OK, drive A, Detect and Clean	Check downloaded files
Web page, navigate to end	NET 59	Press Ctrl + End	
Web page, navigate to next	NET 73	Click [Forward]	Alt + >
Web page, navigate to previous	NET 73	Click [Back]	Alt + <>
Web page, navigate to start	NET 59	Press Ctrl + Home	
Web page, save as text	NET 75	Click File, Save As, select Plain text in Save as type list, enter *filename*, press Enter	*filename* is selected name to save the Web page text as
WebChat, print a message	NET 174	With message displayed in window, click [Print]	